GEORGE T. FELKENES

Chairman, Department of Criminal Justice
University of Alabama in Birmingham

THE CRIMINAL JUSTICE SYSTEM

ITS FUNCTIONS AND PERSONNEL

PRENTICE-HALL, INC., Englewood Cliffs, New Jersey

Library of Congress Cataloging in Publication Data

FELKENES, GEORGE T
The criminal justice system.

    Includes bibliographical references.
    1. Criminal justice, Administration of—United
States. 2. Law enforcement—United States.
I. Title.
HV8138.F44   364'973   73–13734
ISBN 0–13–193052–4

TO SANDRA

10 9 8 7 6 5 4 3

Printed in the United States of America

Prentice-Hall International, Inc. *London*
Prentice-Hall of Australia, Pty. Ltd., *Sydney*
Prentice-Hall of Canada, Ltd., *Toronto*
Prentice-Hall of India Private Limited, *New Delhi*
Prentice-Hall of Japan, Inc. *Tokyo*

CONTENTS

Preface, ix

Acknowledgments, xi

PART I
INTRODUCTION, 1

1
The Criminal Justice System and Its Processes, 3

The Police, 5   Prosecution, 6   The Courts, 7   Corrections, 8   A Complex of Issues, 9   Summary, 11   Questions, 12

PART II
LAW ENFORCEMENT, 13

2
Municipal Police Agencies, 15

The Problem of the Police Role in Municipal Agencies, 16   Functions and Purposes of a Municipal Police Department, 18   Municipal Police Organization, 19   The Future of Municipal Policing, 33   Summary, 36   Questions, 36

3
State Police, 38

Introduction, 38   Historical Development, 41   Organization and Administration, 42   Operational Functions, 46   Training, 46   State Law Enforcement Services, 48   Looking to the Future, 49   Summary, 50 Questions, 50

4
The Sheriff, 52

Historical Development, 52   Police Power and the Sheriff, 54   Powers and Duties of a Sheriff, 55   Terms of Office and Vacancies, 57   Deputy Sheriffs and Department Organization, 60   Constraints on Activities and Powers of the Sheriff, 64   The Sheriff and County Government, 66   The Sheriff in the State Picture, 68   Political Aspects of the Sheriff's Office, 68   Summary, 70   Questions, 71

5
The Criminalist and Criminalistics, 72

Introduction, 72   Training and Education for a Criminalist, 75   The Criminalistics Laboratory, 77   Specific Functions of the Criminalistics Laboratory, 79   The Criminalist's Job Description, 81   The Criminalist as Expert Witness, 83   Prevalance of Crime Laboratories, 84   Summary, 85   Questions, 85   Bibliography, 86

6
Police and Legal Advisors, 87

Historical Perspective, 87   Manpower, 89   Goals of a Police Legal Advisor Program, 90   Nature and Purpose of Specific Functions, 92   Organization Considerations, 95   Federal-Level Legal Advisors, 97   Summary, 99   Questions, 99

7
Federal Law Enforcement Agencies, 100

General Requirements, 100   Department of Justice, 102   Department of the Treasury, 113   Department of Transportation, 120   Department of Agriculture, 121   Department of the Interior, 122   Department of State, 124   Department of Health, Education and Welfare, 126   Department of Defense, 127   Department of Commerce, 130   United States Civil

Service Commission, 130   United States Capitol Police, 131   Tennessee Valley Authority, 131   United States Postal Service, 132   United States Courts, 133   Federal Trade Commission, 135   Federal Maritime Commission, 136   General Services Administration, 137   Central Intelligence Agency, 138   Drug Enforcement Administration, 138   Summary and Questions, 139

PART III
PROSECUTION, 141

8
The Prosecutor, 143

The Office, 143   Powers and Duties, 145   Some Major Conceptions and Criticisms of the Prosecutor, 149   Summary, 160   Questions, 160

9
The Attorney General, 162

Historical Development of the Attorney General, 162   United States Attorney General, 163   Attorney General in State Government, 169   Summary, 181   Questions, 183

10
Defense Attorney, 183

Solicitors and Barristers in England, 184   Development of the U.S. Legal Profession, 185   Counsel for the Defendant, 186   The Role and Duties of the Defense Counsel, 187   Presentation of Evidence at the Trial, 189   Court-Appointed Counsel, 191   Public Defender, 194   Summary, 197   Questions, 198

PART IV
COURTS, 199

11
Judges, 201

General Considerations, 201   Duties and Powers of Judges, 202   Appointment and Removal of Court Officers, Remuneration, 202   Rights and Privileges of Judges, 203   Training for Judges, 204   The Role of the Judge, 205   Selection of Judges: Processes and Considerations, 208   Discipline and Removal, 211   Summary, 214   Questions, 214

12
Jury and Jurors, 216

History, 216   The Jury Functions, 218   Trial Jurors, 219   The Jury as a Constitutional Issue, 221   Value of the Jury, 222   The Juror's Service, 224   Specific Qualifications, 224   The Juror as a Decision Maker, 225   Summary, 227   Questions, 227

13
The Grand Jury, 229

Origins, 229   Development in the United States, 230   Functions, Qualifications, Statutory Authority, 233   The Grand Juror—Some General Characteristics, 236   The Work of the Grand Jury and Its Organization, 238   Some Current Observations on the Grand Jury, 241   Summary, 243   Questions, 243

14
Miscellaneous Court Officers, 245

Bailiffs, 245   Court Clerks, 251   Court Reporter, 253   Summary, 255   Questions, 256

PART V
CORRECTIONS, 257

15
Custodial and Institutional Persons and Places, 259

Historical Setting, 259   U.S. Jails Today, 263   State Correctional Institutions, 265   Federal Correctional System, 266   Correctional Officers' Jobs, 267   Profile of Correctional Officers, 271   Training, 272   Summary, 273   Questions, 275

16
Juvenile, Probation, and Parole Officers, 276

Historical Context of Probation and Parole, 276   Organization of the Probation and Parole Offices, 280   Presentence Investigations, 281   Training and Education, 285   Criticism of Probation and Parole, 288   Juvenile Officers, 288   Summary, 290   Questions, 290

17
Innovations in Corrections, 292

Training—Key to Change, 292   Community Correctional Programs, 295
Diagnostic Parole, 300   New Vistas—Alternative Programs, 301   Mental Health Care Enters the Prisons, 302   Summary, 303   Questions, 303

PREFACE

Ever since the detailed analysis by the Presidential Crime Commission on Law Enforcement and Administration of Justice in 1967, the criminal justice complex has been the subject of many books. Every month new works are published on critical issues in law enforcement, prosecution, corrections, and the courts. However, they seem to address themselves primarily to an analysis of problems encountered in these areas. Relatively little attention has been devoted to the actual functions and people who operate within the agencies in the whole system. This book is an effort to put into concise and practical form the general functions of the individual agencies and the duties and responsibilities of the individuals who perform these functions. Upon them depends the ultimate success of the criminal justice system as a whole.

The author believes that this basic work of limited scope will fulfill a valuable function in presenting to the layman and beginning student some of the intricacies of the complex of criminal justice agencies. It has been the author's experience that students and teachers in disciplines outside of criminal justice have commented on the need for a short book on the functions and personnel in the criminal justice system. Throughout this work expression of personal opinions has been avoided, except where it seemed that such opinions would aid in explaining the system as it is and in indicating possible trends.

The entire criminal justice complex is charged basically with enforcing the law and maintaining order. But each component within this complex has an individual responsibility. Since our contemporary society is involved in combatting increasing crime and in understanding social unrest, it is imperative for the public to become more aware of the basic functions and responsibilities of those involved in this complicated criminal justice apparatus. The police are confronted with a broad spectrum of problems and issues unique to this social control agency such as lateral transfers, minimum standards, and organizational structures. Corrections personnel are concerned about recidivism rates, reform, unionization, and the professionalization within their own ranks. The courts are involved in civil disobedience, charges of police brutality, and with such problems as plea negotiation. The prosecutor is deeply concerned about the rising crime rate, the so-called laxness of the courts in sentencing, and the difficulties the prosecutor faces in merely employing enough deputy prosecutors to handle the cases on the ever-expanding dockets.

This book offers no solutions. Its intention is to describe comprehensively what the system is about and what individuals make the individual agencies work.

ACKNOWLEDGMENTS

The author acknowledges his indebtedness to many persons who performed valuable services in the preparation of this book. Much of their work is evident in the finished product.

I should like to express my appreciation to Professor Stephen A. Schiller of the Department of Criminal Justice, University of Illinois, Chicago Circle Campus, for suggesting agencies and personnel with information on the various subjects in the book. Mr. Ronald Sostkowski, a Consultant with the International Association of Chiefs of Police, provided much information on the state police and municipal police agencies. Mr. Sostkowski, along with Mr. David B. Kelly of the I.A.C.P., Division of State and Provisional Police, deserve special thanks for their assistance. Miss Sue Giehler, School of Criminology, University of California, Berkeley, was very helpful in searching several areas, and I am indebted to her.

Professor James Osterburg of the Department of Criminal Justice, University of Illinois, Chicago Circle Campus, was helpful in the author's search for information on the criminalist and criminalistics. Mr. Ronald Rogers, Virginia Commonwealth University, Richmond, Virginia, and Mr. Don Feliz, Criminal Justice Specialist, California Council on Criminal Justice, were also helpful in this area.

I wish to express my appreciation to two former colleagues for their understanding and encouragement in this project: Professors Harold K. Becker and Paul W. Whisenand, California State University, Long Beach. Because both of them cheerfully and conscientiously complied with my requests for information, I owe them a very great debt of gratitude. In addition, Dr. Calvin Swank, Department of Criminal Justice, University of Alabama in Birmingham, assisted me by critically reviewing several chapters. Chief Thomas C. Seals, Campus Police, and Dr. John Dunbar, Vice-President, University of Alabama in Birmingham, both offered important critical comments. Professor Gordon Misner, Department of Criminal Justice, University of Missouri at St. Louis, as usual offered very relevant and timely suggestions. He is not only a friend but a valuable critic as well. A special word of appreciation is due a fine supervisor, Dr. George E. Passey, Dean, School of Social and Behavioral Sciences, University of Alabama in Birmingham.

As with any work of this type, the clerical matters are monumental. I have been fortunate in having the services of an excellent typist, Mrs. Gloria Kelley, who cheerfully and without complaint endured the frequent revisions and changes that such a work demands. In this same light I would also like to thank Mrs. Connie Melanson and Mrs. Patricia Riley.

One other person deserves to be mentioned. Anyone who has prepared a manuscript is aware of the difficult experience of editing from hand-written or rough-typed copy. My wife Sandra did this. As my critical reader her remarks were invaluable. Without her it is difficult for me to say that this book would have reached fruition. To her I dedicate this work.

I

INTRODUCTION

THE CRIMINAL
JUSTICE SYSTEM
AND ITS PROCESSES

Much has been communicated about the system of criminal justice in the United States. Some say it is interlocking and systematic; a development of a series of processes that churn into action when an accused is apprehended by the police, to be taken through succeeding, carefully planned steps until he is reintegrated into society. Others say that the concept of a system is a complete fallacy; that each step in the criminal process is dealt with by a completely independent agency owing no allegiance to anyone but itself. It cares little how its activities affect other offices that also were organized to assist in coping with illegal activities by prosecuting or rehabilitating those individuals through the *system.*

In a descriptive introductory work such as this book, there will be no attempt made to analyze these views critically. Rather, we will look at what exists, tracing the process step by step from initial arrest to the final release of an offender. The agencies and personnel will be described in detail throughout succeeding chapters.

The dictionary defines a system as "a coordinated body of methods, or a complex scheme or plan of procedure: *a system of government, a penal system.*" The criminal justice system encompasses those social agencies concerning themselves with enforcement of the laws that society has enacted for its self-protection and preservation. Theoretically, it is an integrated apparatus that is concerned with the apprehension, prosecution, conviction, sentencing, and correcting of malefactors.

From these activities, we can see that the system is designed to remove a violator from his normal social setting, and, if possible at a later time, reintroduce him into society as a person who now understands his obligation as a law-abiding citizen. One other result is supposed to flow from the system of criminal justice—deterrence of others from committing criminal acts. A serious doubt arises whether any of these goals are accomplished when statistics indicate that only a small percentage of criminal acts end up with apprehension of the culprit; recidivism rates, (a repeated relapse into delinquent or criminal habits) after so-called rehabilitation in the corrections component of the system, are high; and deterrence from criminal behavior has never been measured accurately.

The criminal justice system, in the main, is a conglomerate of functions and agencies brought over from England (such as trial courts and jury trials) as they were embodied in the common law. Still other segments are peculiarly products of the United States, such as probation, parole, and juvenile procedures. The U.S. system is further fragmented by the very nature of the federal arrangement. One might characterize the design as composed of three subsystems: state, local, and federal criminal justice agencies. Each one overlaps and there is a great amount of duplication of effort. Still more dramatic is the fact that these three subsystems seldom view the criminal problem from a total perspective. Rather, each agency is concerned solely with the milieu in which it operates.

Nevertheless, regardless of the level or lack of cohesiveness with which the system of criminal justice operates, a single philosophical ideal permeates the entire complex: protection of the offender from arbitrary state actions in the determination of guilt. A comprehensive series of measures in both the state and federal constitutions and statutes increase the goverments' burdens of proving guilt. A conscious determination was made early in our history that in the area of criminal activities, efficient law enforcement and easy prosecution must be sacrificed for the preservation of human liberty.

This philosophy has been challenged on numerous occasions by those who say that the constitution was written during a different age and in relation to conditions that have vastly changed. These individual protections hamper our society in dealing with such criminal problems of today as organized crime with its vast network of intelligence, secrecy, and corruption. The detractors postulate that ease of communication, rapid transportation, and the complexity of society demand that the hands of criminal justice agencies not be tied by hypertechnical legal rules.

In outlining our criminal justice processes, one must oversimplify in order to present to the interested student what takes place, why, and where. The system is composed of three components: *police, courts, corrections.* In spite of operating independently, whatever one agency does affects the others. For example, if corrections does not correct, a recidivist may be created. The police will stand a good chance of having to rearrest, the courts will have to retry, and corrections once again will have the task of rehabilitation. Likewise, if there is an attempt to modify the functions or activities of one agency, the others will feel the change. Should the police, by the addition of more man-power and better scientific investigational aids, be able to apprehend 25 percent more suspects, the effect of this increase on the casework of the prosecutor and courts could very well be staggering. Assume also that out of an extra 20 percent who go to trial, 80 percent are convicted. How will the corrections components be able to assimilate the additional workload in terms of proba-tion, institutionalization, and parole? Because the criminal justice system is not funded and supported as an entity, each component will stagger through until the next budget hoping then for additional funds to cope with its increasing responsibilities.

THE POLICE

A suspected offender is introduced into the system through apprehension by the police. Often, the decision must be made in haste, under pressure, and supported by little background information. The alleged offense may have been reported to the police by a third person, or the crime may actually have been observed before arrest. Frequently, where the arrest is not made as the result of observing a law violation, an investigation is conducted to determine whether or not a crime was committed. If it is determined there was none, the investigation is dropped. If an arrest is made as a result of the investigation, that investigation nevertheless may be continued until the trial starts in order to supplement the existing evidence.

Should the police, during the investigatory stage, uncover evidence in-volving a juvenile, the police juvenile unit is immediately notified. If the delinquent is arrested, he may be released after counseling or turned over to the juvenile probation office for an informal hearing. Here it is determined whether the juvenile should be held for a juvenile court adjudication hearing or referred to a welfare agency, social service office, or psychiatric counselor in lieu of court action. If the delinquent is held for the adjudicatory hearing, he may be released after the hearing or, if adjudged to be a delinquent, placed on probation or committed to an institution until he reaches a prescribed age or otherwise is released from the criminal justice system.

Arrest of a suspect occurs when there is a warrant, when an offense takes place in the presence of the officer, or when there is probable or reasonable cause to believe that an offense that may be a felony or misdemeanor, depend-ing on the jurisdiction, has been committed. (A felony is a serious offense punishable by death or imprisonment in a state prison. A misdemeanor is a less serious offense punishable by a fine or up to one year in jail, or both.) Even after an arrest is accomplished, the suspect may be subsequently released without prosecution for a variety of reasons: mistaken identity, lack of proper evidence, or a decision that prosecution would not be in the best interest of society.

After the arrest takes place, the suspect is *booked;* this basically is the first place where there is an administrative record of the arrest. It is here that the accused is photographed, fingerprinted, and temporarily released on bail, if available. Also, during the booking procedure, some suspects are released without prosecution. On important cases, the prosecutor may be present at the booking, but usually he will enter the scene during the arraignment or initial appearance of the suspect before a magistrate or other judicial officer. Before turning to the prosecution of the suspect, it must be borne in mind that the investigative work of the police may continue even though the accused now is involved with the prosecution, court, and correction phases of the criminal justice system.

PROSECUTION

Normally, the prosecutor becomes significantly involved in the case at *arraignment.* He previously may have given advice to police on securing an arrest or search warrant, but in most instances his involvement is at the arraignment stage.

At arraignment, summary trials can be held for petty offenses without further processing. The processing of these petty offenses will be discussed later.

During the initial appearance before a magistrate, commissioner, judge, or justice of the peace, the accused is called upon to answer the charges contained in the complaint, information, or indictment against him. He is required to enter a plea to the allegations after they have been read to him by the judge. If he does not, the court will enter a *not guilty* plea for him. During the arraignment procedure, the charge may be dismissed by the court for a legal reason or the prosecutor may request to have the charges dropped.

As previously mentioned, the initial appearance may also serve as the trial setting for minor offenses that have payment of a fine or a relatively short time in jail as punishment. Once the judge finds a verdict of guilt, the accused is sentenced to jail or payment of a fine. Rather than incarceration, the defendant may be placed on probation for a specified length of time. If sentenced to jail, he may be granted parole. After successful completion of the probationary or parole period, the defendant is released from the system.

The prosecutor is deeply involved in a case by the time it reaches the *preliminary examination* phase of the criminal justice system. This procedure is sometimes described as a *mini-trial.* It is an investigation by a magistrate of the facts and circumstances surrounding a suspect who has been charged with a crime (felony) and arrested, in order to determine whether there are sufficient grounds to hold him for trial. It is here that a preliminary testing of the evidence takes place. After hearing the evidence, the magistrate may find no basis for the charges and dismiss them, or he and the prosecutor may agree that the charges either are too serious or unsubstantiated by the evidence and agree to a reduction of the charges to some lesser offense. It should be noted that in some jurisdictions there is no separate preliminary hearing for misdemeanors.

If there is a reasonable belief, in the opinion of the magistrate, that a crime has been committed and that the accused was involved, the case is certified to the trial court and the prosecutor is given a statutorily defined number of days to file formal charges against the defendant. The charge is filed on the basis of information from citizen complaints and police investigations. At this point in the flow of the system of criminal justice, the courts are substantively involved. Also, the prosecutor has several avenues open to him in order formally to prosecute the accused.

For the misdemeanor, the original complaint by the police or private citizen may become the *accusatory pleading* against the defendant. In some jurisdictions, an *information* is filed. An information is a written accusation by the prosecutor in the name of the people of the state, charging the defendant with a crime. It differs from the grand jury indictment in that it is preferred by the prosecutor in those states using this procedure. For misdemeanors, the grand jury indictment is very seldom used whereas the complaint or information is very common.

THE COURTS

After the prosecutor files the accusatory pleading, another arraignment is held to determine the defendant's plea on the charges in the accusatory pleading. If the defendant pleads guilty, a date for him to be sentenced is set by the judge. If the defendant enters a not guilty plea, he may request to have a jury trial or be tried by the court without a jury. On occasion, the court also may dismiss the charges against the defendant at the arraignment thereby eliminating him from the criminal justice system. At the trial, if the defendant is convicted, a date for sentencing is set at which time he may be fined, sentenced to jail, or placed on probation. It is at this point that the corrections component of the criminal justice system begins to function. If sentenced to jail, the convicted person subsequently may be granted parole. When he pays the fine or successfully completes probation or parole, he is discharged from the system.

The procedure of prosecution for a felony is similar to that described for a misdemeanor. After a preliminary examination in which probable cause to charge the defendant with a felony is established, the prosecutor may file an information charging the defendant with the felony. Rather than utilizing the information, the prosecutor has the option to ask the *grand jury* to *indict* the defendant. In those states that use the grand jury, that body merely reviews the evidence that the state holds in order to determine if it is sufficient to justify a trial. If it is, an indictment is returned. If not, the accused is removed from the system by this method.

The next step in the felony prosecution is to have an *arraignment* on the indictment or information. The arraignment is the same as in the misdemeanor procedure. A peculiarity in the felony arraignment, however, permits the judge who is not satisfied that the evidence warrants prosecution for a felony to reduce the crime to a misdemeanor offense. Once this occurs, the defendant is tried as a misdemeanant in the procedure described above. It is also noteworthy that at the felony arraignment, a negotiation frequently occurs between the defense attorney and the prosecutor. As a result, the defendant may be persuaded to enter a guilty plea on the assurance of the prosecutor to request that the judge permit the felony charge to be reduced to a misdemeanor. This same type of negotiation occurs at any time prior to the trial and is commonly known as *plea negotiation.*

Again, at the felony arraignment, the case may be dismissed and the defendant discharged from the system. He may plead guilty, at which time a date for sentencing is set. If he decides to have a jury or nonjury trial, the date is determined and the trial held. If the defendant is convicted, a date for sentencing is set.

CORRECTIONS

Before the actual sentence is imposed, at the court's request, an investigation by the probation office takes place to assist the judge in deciding on a penalty. It is also during this period that the defendant can give notice of his intent to appeal his conviction. As a general rule, the appeal stays the execution of the sentence. If the appeal is unsuccessful or the defendant decides not to appeal in the first place, he may be placed on probation or sent to the penitentiary.

In numerous cases, the defendant believes that he is in prison for no reason. He may file a *writ of habeas corpus,* which is a challenge based on constitutional grounds. It tests the legality of the basis for his detention in prison. Although the writ often is filed during the corrections phase, it may be filed at any point in the criminal justice process.

In any event, the defendant is now involved in the corrections segment of the criminal justice system. This segment is physically isolated. Its institutions are segregated from the community either by walls or distance. It is here that rehabilitation of offenders is supposed to occur. This is the purpose of corrections. However, the custodial aspects are much more salient. Subsequent chapters describe in detail the functions of the major corrections agencies and the people who are primarily responsible for this aspect of the total system. Once the defendant has served his sentence or successfully completed probation or parole, he is discharged from the system.

The major functions and components of the criminal justice system have been described briefly in an effort to introduce and clarify the remaining analysis of the system and its agencies. However, before turning to those topics, a concise evaluation of the administration of criminal justice in the United States is in order.

A COMPLEX OF ISSUES

The presidential campaign in 1964 was the first time in our history that crime and its impact on our society was a national issue. People were worried about personal safety. Although the concern was primarily by those in the large metropolitan areas, an attitude of fear was creeping into our society. As a consequence, a presidential commission composed of experts, scholars, and distinguished citizens was established to look into the criminal justice system. The final report, *The Challenge of Crime in a Free Society,* was completed in 1967 and listed over two hundred recommendations for improving the total system.

Throughout our history, it has been difficult to convict even those who are plainly guilty. During the past forty years, our country has witnessed great changes in handling persons who enter the system. Some of the changes have come from court decisions. Still others have emerged by state and federal legislation. In the private sector, numerous groups have encouraged new laws aimed at protecting the rights of the individual.

In our system of justice, we try to strike a fair balance between individual rights and the needs of the total society; that is, liberty versus order. The system of criminal justice is pervaded by the fear of a police state induced by too much political control over the rights of the citizenry. The criminal justice apparatus functions to protect society against this eventuality in much the same manner as the workings of the federal government with its intrinsic checks and balances. To reduce the risk of conviction of an innocent person, there are checks and reviews at all stages of the criminal justice process: the prosecutor checks the police for a probable cause to search and seize property before the search warrant is presented to the magistrate; the magistrate independently determines the same facts before he signs the warrant; a judicial officer at the arraignment, preliminary examination, trial, and appeal reviews the same materials for errors. The entire system is built on the premise that individual rights must be protected.

The system also seeks to respect the dignity of the individual regardless of the severity of the offense of which he is charged. He is not supposed to be humiliated, dehumanized, or unfairly treated. He may have assistance of counsel and be tried by a body of his peers if he so desires. He may be admitted to bail before he is tried, and he may appeal his case to the highest tribunals.

The system of criminal justice often is criticized because of the delay between the arrest and the criminal trial. These delays are caused by poor administration; lack of sufficient judges; small, inadequate courtrooms; and badly trained personnel. It has also been postulated that defense attorneys actively seek delays hoping that witnesses will move away, forget, or become discouraged, and not testify. It is sometimes the impression of the citizen that the system of criminal justice, rather than working for the betterment of society, is working to its detriment. Various legal associations, state and federal study groups, and associations of judges are addressing their thinking to this nagging problem.

Also criticized are the long periods that cases are on appeal. Cases that take ten to fifteen years to complete are no longer rare. Caryl Chessmann became a household personality during the years it took to litigate his case. Repeated trials because of technical errors or procedural defects diminish public respect for the criminal justice system just as much as the cry of *police brutality.* If there is any merit in the postulate that punishment deters crime, the punishment should be swift and positive to be effective.

Japan, for one, has virtually eliminated heroin use by harsh and rapid handling of both pushers and addicts. A life sentence is imposed for selling heroin and *cold turkey* treatment of users is begun immediately upon apprehension.[1] F. Lee Bailey, during informal public discussion, has been known to voice the strong opinion that crime and recidivism rates could be considerably reduced by stronger penalties imposed quickly after apprehension. This, of course, would not apply to those in need of psychiatric or similar treatment. The point is that, in many cases, the potential offender must be made to fear a penalty that is not delayed interminably. This is hardly the situation now. As a result of all these inefficiencies, legitimate questions are being raised as to whether the criminal justice system deserves the confidence of the public.

A critical voice is often raised about the number of days over which a criminal trial extends. It is probably longer than in any other legal system

---

[1]"Sayonara Heroin," *Time,* June 19, 1972, p. 61.

because of the technicalities of pretrial and trial motions, continuances, and special hearings on the admissibility of evidence. During a trial, jurors are frequently excused temporarily due to technical arguments and, as a result, spend a great deal of time outside of the courtroom, idly, while the attorneys are in court arguing points of law.

In many instances, the public does not understand why there are so many appeals and retrials of the same defendant with what appears to be the same evidence. Extensive news coverage is given to reversals or retrials ordered for sensational cases. Quite often, press coverage gives the reason for a reversal as the improper admission of a confession or illegal seizure of evidence. The citizen wants to know why the criminal justice official does not know his job because "if he did, we would not be wasting tax money on incompetents and retrials of obviously guilty people."

The paradox is that all these apparent inefficiencies are actually encouraged by the structure of a system developed to protect the individual and render justice. Vast segments of our society have concluded, however, that our system of criminal justice does not work, that the lawyer, police, courts, and bureaucracy have constructed a cumbersome, archaic process in which they, as its functionaries, have a vested interest. Many have decided that the criminal justice system is not responsive to societal needs. As such, the emphasis is on change. New tools must be constructed to assure fairness to the offender and society without, at the same time, compromising the guarantees of the constitution as they were originally intended.

SUMMARY

The system of criminal justice, if indeed it can be called a system, is composed of the police, courts, and corrections components. The prosecution is normally included in the adjudication component. Each operates largely independently, although the activities of each have a direct effect on the other components.

The system starts to operate with the introduction of a suspect, either by a citizen complaint or police investigation and apprehension. When the suspect is formally accused of a crime, he is afforded many procedural safeguards to ensure a fair determination of his guilt or innocence. The prosecutor takes over from the police to prepare the charges against him in the adjudicatory component, the courts. Once the issue has been decided, the accused is discharged from the system if found innocent. If guilty, he is sentenced and turned over to the corrections subsystem for rehabilitation and subsequent discharge.

The process appears to be orderly but in reality is extremely complex. Succeeding chapters will present an insight into the system and people who cause it to function.

QUESTIONS

1. What is meant by the statement that the criminal justice system is not a system but a loosely linked complex of agencies of government?
2. What agencies, organizations, units, and institutions are involved in the total criminal justice system?
3. What is meant by the statement that police investigation begins before the suspect is apprehended and does not close until conviction?
4. Describe briefly the total criminal justice system.
5. What is meant by?
   Indictment
   Preliminary examination
   Information
   Arraignment
   Detention
6. Define the various legal classifications of crimes.
7. Describe the processes through which a person moves once he enters the criminal justice system.
8. At which points in the criminal justice system may a person who enters the system be discharged?
9. What is the procedure for handling juveniles who enter the criminal justice system?
10. Once a person is convicted, he must be sentenced. What factors do you consider to be important in making a sentence decision?

LAW ENFORCEMENT

MUNICIPAL
POLICE AGENCIES

"Man—What does the word really mean? To me it suggests no
mere primeval ape-like creature that walked erect and had hands.
To be truly human, he must have had the power to reason and the
ability to fashion crude tools to do his work. This is the key, the
ability to make tools, as distinct from merely using the pointed sticks or sharp
stones that lay readily at hand. Such a being, who set about shaping the raw
materials of nature in a regular pattern to suit his needs, was the one worthy
to be considered the earliest human."[1]

This earliest human, with the ability to fashion crude tools to do his
work, lived approximately 600,000 years ago according to anthropologist
Louis Leakey. Out of this 600,000-year history of man, the concept of law
enforcement has emerged from the crude tool age into a quasi science only
during the past 150 years. The innovation of Sir Robert Peel's London Police
in 1829 is generally regarded as the beginning of modern law enforcement. To
further emphasize how short a time the quasi science of law enforcement has
been practiced, it is only during the present century that most of the important
advancements actually have taken place. One finds, however, that despite the
swiftness of these advancements, the demands upon police have grown at an
even more rapid rate.

[1]L. S. B. Leakey. "Finding the World's Earliest Man," *National Geographic Magazine*
(1966), pp. 118, 420, 435.

The President's Crime Commission, in describing the problems created by these demands plus the new patterns and growth of police work, noted:

> The face of America has changed since colonial days from a collection of predominantly rural and independent jurisdictions to an industralized urban nation. Yet in several respects law enforcement has not kept pace with this change. As America has grown and policing has become more correspondingly complex, the existing law enforcement system has not always been altered to meet the needs of a mechanized and metropolitan society.
>
> Over the years the proliferation of independent, and, for the most part, local policing, units has led to an overlapping of responsibilities and a duplication of effort, causing problems in police administration and the coordination efforts to apprehend criminals. America is a nation of small decentralized police forces.[2]

As previously mentioned, the problems of the municipal police commenced in 1829, when Peel introduced a bill in Parliament that did away with the use of military force to keep the peace in London. The bill set up a professional police organization that subsequently became known as Scotland Yard. Uniforms made their appearance during the same year. After some initial opposition to the innovation, the idea and success of the professional police force, trained in the skills of their jobs, received worldwide attention. The organizational design of the London police ultimately was adopted in United States police agencies.[3]

Up to and including the first quarter of the twentieth century, the police system, especially in the metropolitan areas, trailed behind developments in science and technology in adapting itself to the needs of modern society. For years, the municipal police departments were the weakest component in the governmental complex. Health, public works, recreation, schools, and welfare moved forward rapidly, but the police, although making some gains, lagged behind. The result was corruption, poor management, and a failure to achieve objectives in the areas of crime control and prevention. The trend of the 1900–1925 period continues today as the figures from the Uniform Crime Reports so pointedly indicate. The social and economic loss from vice activities, organized crime, and poor reporting of crimes can not be calculated.

THE PROBLEM OF THE POLICE ROLE
IN MUNICIPAL AGENCIES

What is the role of the municipal police in our democratic society? Is the function of defining this role the responsibility of the police themselves, or is it the responsibility of the society they police? Perhaps it is a little of each.

---

[2]The President's Commission on Law Enforcement and Administration of Justice, *Task Force Report: The Police* (Washington, D.C.: Government Printing Office, 1967), p. 3.

[3]Charles Reith, *The Police Idea* (London: Oxford University Press, 1939), p. 240.

When Chief William Parker of the Los Angeles Police Department died in the mid-1960s, so did the idea that the only function of the municipal police was to enforce the law, for Chief Parker represented one of the last nationally known police leaders to hold this concept. The fact that police agencies tend to overemphasize the military aspect of the police function, both in structuring the department and in their perceived role with the public they serve, thwarts a meaningful relationship with the public. This authoritative relationship must be tempered with social empathy to develop a sense of partnership between the public and the police. In some police organizations, administrators envision their role as being to the extreme right of the scale in Figure 2–1.

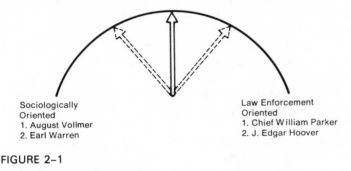

Sociologically
Oriented
1. August Vollmer
2. Earl Warren

Law Enforcement
Oriented
1. Chief William Parker
2. J. Edgar Hoover

FIGURE 2–1
Police Orientation Barometer.

That is, they believe that the police function should relate only to enforcing the law. Some other quarters, especially outside of law enforcement, define their responsibilities more liberally, emphasizing the sociological approach. This seemingly unreconcilable difference is founded on a lack of understanding of each position.

The police are aware of their grave responsibility for enforcement. Beginning in the early 1950s, the United States Supreme Court, interpreting the federal Constitution in a manner that appeared to oppose its earlier, fairly conservative orientation, set into motion the continuous reevaluation of accepted police practices. At the same time, these interpretations advanced changes in society's mores and behavior patterns. Prior to this period, the world image of the United States, and, to a great extent, its self-image, was that of an integrated people sharing common bonds. At the time of this writing, the country is fragmented, with various factions and ideologies dividing the citizenry. The decisions have created a huge social upheaval as the country tries to relocate and reestablish its values. In the middle of this schismatical chaos, to expect the police to know exactly where society's values lie is unrealistic. However, it is to this very problem, society's changing values, that the police must address themselves and stand ready to make adjustments.

Certainly, society will always need patrolmen and detectives. However, the police administrator's concept of his purpose and functions will have to change; in fact, it already is slowly taking place. Obviously, the role of the municipal police agency encompasses much more than mere enforcement of the law.

The police perform one of the most important roles in today's society. They have made great strides toward professionalization, through both education and training of the individual officer and continuous reevaluation and upgrading of police functions. One example of this is the changed attitude toward the juvenile officer. As a result of a reevaluation of the position, police no longer look down on that task.

Each day, law enforcement becomes more complex and important because of the great influence police in general have on the future of America. How the police meet ethical demands and handle community relations is instrumental in helping to maintain the United States' balance and spirit of unity. Their activity influences the social, economic, and political aspects of life. The police role, although not yet completely spelled out, is indeed crucial.

The municipal police, especially, are destined to play an important part in the social and physical planning of urban cities and thus have a legitimate role in the social process. By the nature of their responsibilities, they are applied sociologists and psychologists. The trained police officer is discovering that he cannot ignore the influence of his actions on society. It must be made clear that the way in which a police officer handles a situation not only determines the course of that particular circumstance but sets into motion undulating waves that spread far beyond the immediate condition. Perhaps no other governmental agency or group of men has as many or as varied face-to-face confrontations with society as police officers. Their opportunity for social influence is boundless.

FUNCTIONS AND PURPOSES OF A MUNICIPAL POLICE DEPARTMENT

According to the most commonly accepted standards, the primary functions of the municipal police department are the preservation of peace and order, the prevention and detection of crime, the apprehension of offenders, the protection of persons and property under the laws of the state and ordinances of the city, and the performance of a multitude of tasks relating to the public welfare and safety. For these purposes, the municipal police are endowed with legal authority. In the exercise of this power, justice should always be the actuating motive.

To achieve success, the department must win and retain the confidence and respect of the public that it serves. This can be accomplished only by constant and earnest endeavor on the part of all members and employees in the department to perform their duties in an efficient, honest, and professional manner; and, by exemplary conduct, to cultivate the fullest realization in the public mind that the department is a vital requisite to public well-being.

A police officer should remember that in the execution of his duties he acts not for himself but for the public and that his appointment is in no sense for his personal advantage. The law upon which his function is based is founded on this principle. The police officer must be able to control his feelings. Ideally, he should never allow passion to urge him to brutality; nor fear, favoritism, or sympathy to induce him to leniency or neglect of duty. The officer must bear in mind that he represents the dignity and authority of the state and is a representative of the law to whose valid demands all must submit. If the need arises, submission may be compelled. The officer must not use force unnecessarily, but he should not hesitate to use that force when the circumstances require.

In most municipal police agencies, the chief of police compiles and publishes a set of rules and regulations that serve as the instruments for information, guidance, government, discipline, and administration of the department. The individual officer, from patrolman to the chief, is expected to adhere to them in the performance of his duties.

MUNICIPAL POLICE ORGANIZATION

According to the President's Crime Commission, the organization of police departments leaves much to be desired.

> Although some forces have long been recognized as being well-organized and progressively managed, far too many of America's city . . . forces have serious organizational deficiencies. In fact, many police forces appear to have evolved over the years without conscious plan. These forces are characterized by diffusion of authority, confused responsibility, lack of strong lines of direction and control, and improper grouping of functions. An example of one such department is seen in [Figure 2-2] . . . —With virtually no exceptions the other [Commission] consultant reports found a serious weakness in forces that were surveyed.

This force of over 300 men was reputed by a consultant as having

> . . . serious deficiencies of internal communications, coordination, supervision, and direction of effort and control.

> The general dissipation of personnel resounds—the scattering of specialized work units about the Department without the essential bond of control and direction to hold each such unit to the main objectives of the organization—has reduced the ability of the department to function as an organized group. The ultimate result is a reduction in the efficiency of the total effort.[4]

[4] *Task Force Report: The Police*, pp. 45–46.

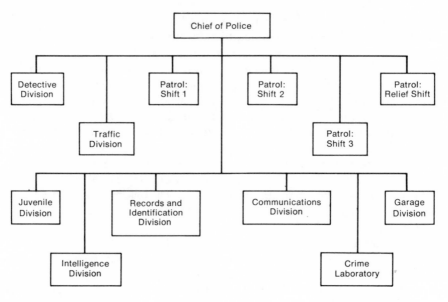

FIGURE 2–2

An Example of a Poorly Organized Municipal Police Department.

As a principle of organization, the municipal police department is under the general direction and administration of a chief of police who is appointed by the mayor, city council, or city manager, according to prevailing local government. The chief is responsible for the efficient conduct and operation of the department in conformity with the law and the policies of the appointing authority. Although the organization of no two police departments is exactly alike, we will discuss, on the next few pages, a model organization and briefly note the specific jobs found in each organizational group. In this way, the student will have a background on the typical, well-organized police department and be able to fit the functions and personnel into the proper police setting.

A police department is organized in the shape of a pyramid. The order of rank (chain of command) normally is:

> Chief of police
> Deputy chiefs of police
> Captains of police
> Lieutenants of police
> Sergeants of police
> Patrolmen-policewomen
> Civilian employees
> Special officers—includes jailers, custodial officers, matrons, vehicle inspectors, identification officers, and so forth

Depending on the specific department, staff officers are those at the deputy chief level but may include the heads of special offices reporting directly to the chief.

A deputy chief is in command of each of the major components: administration, operations, and service divisions. As such, he is responsible for the efficient operation of his division. The deputy chief usually is appointed to his rank from among the regular members of the department, and, in most instances, holds the permanent rank of captain. The chief appoints him, frequently with the approval of the mayor or chief administrator in the city.

The captain in a police department is in command of and supervises a particular component in the department and is responsible to his superior officer. For example, the captain responsible for vice or records and identification (see Figure 2–3) would be responsible to the deputy chief, services division. In large departments having a wide geographical area to cover, the police department may organize precincts or district offices throughout the city. The captain usually is in command of a district or precinct. The lieutenant is in command of a specific police unit, detail, relief, or shift. For example, the captain of patrol would have a lieutenant in command of each shift; the captain in charge of intelligence and organized crime would have a lieutenant in charge of the detail on loansharking, organized crime, and so on; and the captain in charge of vice might have a lieutenant in charge of the gambling, prostitution, and illegal whiskey details.

The sergeant is the first level supervisor and has immediate charge of subordinate members assigned to him. He supervises activities at the operational level and often is assigned to the tasks of an investigation officer. In most police departments, the activity of this individual is the most crucial because of his supervision of personnel performing activities at the operational level.

Patrolmen and policewomen make up the basic rank in the police organization. Within the rank of patrolman there are several steps from the probationary patrolman to senior patrolman. The efficiency, image, and rapport of the police department in the community rests with the patrolman who initially performs the entire range of police activities. He not only has the responsibility of responding to criminal behavior, but also performs almost every duty imaginable that serves the public. On usual duty tour, the patrolman may arrest a burglary suspect, take a lost child home, help a stalled motorist, assist a citizen attempting to navigate his way across a busy thoroughfare, transport an injured person to a hospital, stop a person for suspicious conduct, become involved in a family dispute, or arrest a drunk, to name merely a few of the patrolman's encounters.

Because of the multiplicity of often conflicting demands on the patrolman, he is taxed almost beyond the point where he can devote proper attention to criminal matters. He spends a great deal of his time coping with work of a noncriminal nature. A study conducted in California in 1970 revealed that only about 5 percent of an officer's time was involved with Part I and Part II

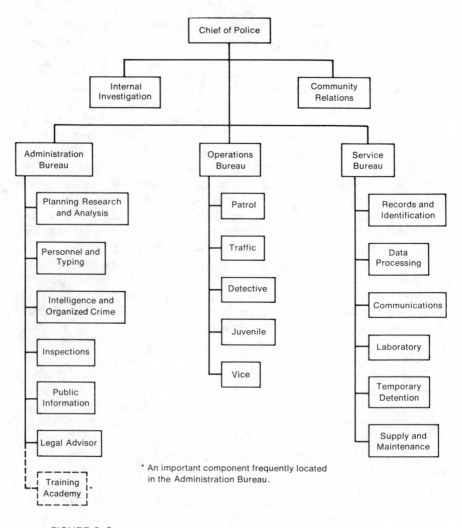

FIGURE 2-3

A Well-Organized Municipal Police Department.*

*Source: The President's Commission on Law Enforcement and Administration of Justice, *Task Force Report: The Police,* p. 47.

offenses as defined by the FBI reporting system: murder, forcible rape, robbery, aggravated assault, burglary, larceny over fifty dollars, and auto theft. The remaining 95 percent was devoted to such secondary police activities as routine patrol, administrative duties, general services to the public, traffic, gathering information, juvenile matters, and disturbances of the peace.[5] Indeed, in the municipal police agency, the patrol task does not involve active *crook catching* to any significant degree.

The patrolman normally conducts an initial investigation of a crime and then turns the case over to the detectives for any follow-up investigation. However, because of large case loads, the detectives devote most of their efforts to major incidents.

The President's Crime Commission, commenting on the patrolman's work and the skills and education necessary for him to perform adequately, notes:

> The existing wide range of patrol responsibility hampers efforts to attract more highly qualified personnel into police service. Present police departments are monolithic in structure. All sworn police personnel, regardless of individual qualifications or experience normally begin their careers as patrolmen; assigned to patrol or traffic duties. Normally personnel must remain in this category from 1 to 5 years before being eligible for promotion or transfer. Since a police officer serving in this capacity must respond to all demands upon police, whether they involve removing a cat from a roof or arresting a robbery suspect, his status is adversely affected both within and outside the police agency. Police work, therefore, tends to attract persons who are willing to perform its mechanical aspects and to accept its status and compensation. For example, in a survey conducted on the Metropolitan Police Department of Washington, D.C., in 1966, it was revealed that over 60 percent of the applicants for positions in the department were holding clerical, sales, manufacturing, or transportation jobs at the time of application and that the majority of the remaining applicants were in the military service.[6]

Because of the vast responsibilities of the patrolman, it was recommended by the Crime Commission that this one job classification be broken down into three job classifications: police agent, police officer, and service officer. Qualifications for filling of these positions would also differ according to the demands of the job. The police agent would perform the traditional duties associated with the patrolman and law enforcement. He would be assigned to the most complicated, demanding, and sensitive police tasks, such as:

1. Serving as a patrol officer in high crime and tension areas
2. Making difficult arrests
3. Enforcing gambling, vice, and narcotics laws
4. Coordinating and handling crimes involving juvenile offenders
5. Investigating major crimes while acting in a plainclothes capacity
6. Assisting in solving community relations problems while learning to understand them

[5]Michael E. O'Neill and Carlton J. Bloom, "The Field Officer: Is He Really Fighting Crime," *The Police Chief* (February 1972), pp. 31–32.

[6] *Task Force Report: The Police,* p. 121.

The police agent should be highly educated, preferably possessing the baccalaureate degree in the social sciences, behavioral sciences, or liberal arts.

The police officer would perform those police duties of enforcing the laws and investigating those crimes which can be solved by immediate follow-up investigations or are most likely to have suspects close to the crime scene. He would have the responsibility of responding to selected calls for services, perform routine patrol, render emergency services, and investigate traffic accidents. He would work in concert with the police agent and the community service officer in solving crimes and meeting other police problems. The ratio of officers to agents would be low, and officers would be encouraged to qualify for the position of police agent.

The community service officer was recommended by the President's Crime Commission to (1) improve police service in high crime rate areas, (2) enable police to hire persons who can provide greater understanding of minority group problems, (3) relieve police agents and officers of lesser police duties, (4) increase minority group opportunities in law enforcement, and (5) tap a new source of manpower by helping talented young men who have not completed educational requirements to qualify for police work.

The community service officer would assist officers and agents in their work and would improve communication between police departments and the neighborhood as a uniformed member of the working police. He would render carefully selected police services to the neighborhood. He would investigate certain minor thefts and loss of property, and provide continuing family assistance regarding domestic problems. An important part of his work would be with specialized police units such as a community relations unit.

Community service officers would not have to meet conventional education requirements; rather, selection would be on an individual basis with priority given to applicants having an interest in the community and a desire to become a police officer. While they are community service officers, they would be encouraged to continue their education for entrance into other capacities within the police department.

As was mentioned earlier, and as seen in Figure 2–3, a municipal police department has specific organizational components. What do the officers do in each of these?

Community Relations

This unit is responsible for developing and carrying out programs designed to improve relations between the citizens and the police department, with special emphasis given to relations with minority groups. This office has the responsibility for establishing working relations with public and private agencies and organizations through which it can disseminate information on the role of the police and enlist support for and cooperation with the police. The ultimate goal of community relations hopefully is to reduce crime.

The philosophy behind community relations is that crime is largely a social problem caused by society itself, and society must be enlisted to cure it. If good police-community relations can motivate the public as well as the police to participate as a cooperative community in the *war against crime,* then the objectives, efforts, and intent of the community relations bureau will be achieved.

Most departments emphasize that, although the community relations office itself is small in number, each person throughout the department is a community relation specialist, and that every person employed in the entire municipal police department can increase or hinder the objectives of the community relations efforts

Some common objectives of a community relations program are:

> To refer to the police department all questions requiring clarification of department policy
>
> To consult with police department personnel on police problems
>
> To assist in crime prevention through distributing information on crime deterrence
>
> To promote increased cooperation between the police department and other agencies
>
> To acquaint citizens with the professional operations of police activities
>
> To acquaint police officers with the citizens they protect and to consider the ideas of these citizens in police matters
>
> To provide opportunities for citizens to suggest improvements in police service
>
> To create understanding and cooperation between the citizens and the police through better communications.

Internal Investigations

This unit is responsible for ensuring that all complaints against members of the department are thoroughly and impartially investigated to determine whether the complaint is justified and whether any disciplinary action should be taken. Such complaints are first referred to the proper line commander who then turns them over to the appropriate supervisory personnel for examination. At his request, internal investigations officers also may be called in to assist. The line commander reviews the findings and conclusions of these officers. If he believes that the results are ill-founded, he will pursue the investigation further. On the other hand, if he decides that the complaints are justified, he reviews the recommendations of the line officers on disciplinary action and either endorses them or makes different recommendations.

Internal investigators maintain surveillance over the operations of the department and investigate indications of abuse of police powers, collusion with law violators, laxity of law enforcement, and other matters inimical to the proper performance of public functions and then recommend to appropriate commanders the actions needed to correct such conditions.

Personnel

The personnel unit serves the department in the handling of all matters of personnel and administration. It processes all personnel actions, maintains departmental personnel records, provides for character investigations of candidates certified by the personnel board, ensures that efficiency ratings are made, and maintains close relationships with the local civil service commission and personnel board. It develops and maintains an inventory of the special skills and training experience of police officers. Besides police skills, the inventory includes other abilities that may from time to time be useful in some police investigation or otherwise in furtherance of the work of the department. Personnel is responsible for establishing procedures for employee grievances. It also receives complaints against departmental personnel and takes necessary action for nonpayment of bills and other offenses not connected with their actions as police officers.

Planning, Research, and Analysis

This unit, as the name implies, conducts research of general policies and department operations, recommends improvements, prepares directives, updates rules and regulations, and prepares plans to carry out the objectives of the department. It takes an active part in the implementation of its recommendations and, when necessary, aids in the fulfillment of duties by officers in command of different divisions in the department.

This office serves as the staff agency that aids the chief and each of the deputy chiefs in achieving the goals of the department. Rather than being located in administration (see Figure 2–3), many departments have the planning, research, and analysis unit report directly to the chief, as do the internal investigations and community relations units.

Examples of the kinds of studies prepared by this division are research projects on the effectiveness of equipment, utilization of manpower, policing methods and techniques, training requirements, and general operating methods and procedures. Another important function is preparation of contingency plans for emergency or specialized occurrences, and for projecting the direction of the department.

Inspections

The duties of this unit are to conduct inspections of personnel, equipment, and procedures; evaluate the results of police operations; and formulate and present recommendations in regard to ways of improving police operations. It has the responsibility for developing inspection schedules and for initiating an inspection program. The inspection function concentrates upon proper performance by line supervisors from sergeants on up. Emphasis is laid upon the overall performance of the police department units rather than upon the details of equipment, uniforms, appearance, and procedural perfection.

Legal Advisor

The duties of the legal advisor, whether a single individual or several, are as wide as the range of legal services an attorney can perform. The legal advisor is often called upon to make decisions and give orders for, and in the name of, the chief of police. The need for continuing legal advice within a municipal police department long has been recognized. This lawyer furnishes advice to staff and field personnel and surveys departmental orders and practices in regard to their legality. He also helps in training and continuing education, planning, community relations, legislative drafting and lobbying, and in various departmental legal problems. He is especially valuable when advising on problems arising out of specific cases because few prosecutors' offices endeavor systematically to provide legal counsel to the police. His advice may also protect the department from civil suits arising out of hasty actions or decisions by officers who are unaware of the legal implications of their activities.

Intelligence and Organized Crime

Intelligence is the backbone of successful operations against organized crime and any other groups that may be detrimental to the peace of the community. Because its purpose is to keep the chief informed about such important matters, this activity cannot be relegated to an isolated, inferior position within the organization. Intelligence, like planning, permeates the operations of the entire department. It is needed by all command and staff personnel. The intelligence office primarily is concerned with the nature of the criminal syndicate rather than with individual criminal acts. Intelligence gathering on organized crime means placing the pieces of a jigsaw puzzle together in order to develop a picture of the ramifications of organized crime operations.

Public Information and Relations

The public relations function is aimed primarily at gaining public support for police policies and winning citizen cooperation in department programs and procedures in order to facilitate the accomplishment of police tasks. The overall function is frequently divided into four general categories:

1. Furnishing information for staff offices that may affect public support of the police department
2. Advising the chief concerning public relations aspects of new programs, policies, and practices that affect the public
3. Evaluating public opinion and attitudes with respect to the policies, methods, and personnel of the department
4. Planning and implementing policies, procedures, and programs to keep the public informed of the police function

The public information office must maintain a constant liaison between the public and the department. In its endeavors to evaluate, plan, and implement public information and relations programs, particular attention is devoted to informing the individual officer as well as the public.

Patrol

The patrol unit is responsible for preventing violations of state laws and city ordinances and for preserving law and order. Accordingly, it maintains patrols covering the entire city at all hours. This unit responds promptly to citizen calls for assistance involving actual or potential law violations, suspicious circumstances, or vehicle accidents. It makes proper initial investigations of crimes and vehicle accidents, including apprehension of any offenders. If a crime has been committed and the initial investigation does not disclose the identity or whereabouts of the offender, the patrol officer calls upon the detective division for assistance. Detective assistance is also requested in instances where a major crime has been committed.

The commander of this unit has various patrol shifts responsible to him. During the hours a patrol shift is on duty, it is responsible for the general patrol functions in the city. The shift commander has the direct responsibility for assigning his personnel and equipment in such a way as to most effectively prevent crime, preserve order, and answer complaints promptly. He is responsible for ensuring that the men under his command are instructed in the policies of the city and department, in proper police methods and procedures, and in their responsibilities as police officers. When necessary, he initiates disciplinary action to enforce compliance with instructions, rules, and regulations of the department. He delegates authority to his subordinates to assist in carrying out his responsibilities. The patrol division normally is the largest functional unit in the department in terms of manpower and equipment.

Traffic

The traffic unit usually supplements the traffic enforcement efforts of patrol at those times and in those places where more intensive police effort is required than can be provided by general patrol activity. It investigates and reports generally upon all major vehicle accidents. Officers in the traffic division respond and assist officers in general patrol as needed in the investigation of nontraffic complaints and in the preservation of law and order. They routinely observe and take action in any circumstances that call for police attention. Frequently, in municipal police agencies, officers in the traffic bureau operate as part of the tactical (emergency or specialized enforcement) squad.

The captain who normally commands the traffic bureau keeps informed of the problems of traffic movement, congestion, and parking. The incidence of traffic accidents determines the patterns of police activity that will be most effective in reducing traffic violations and accidents while expediting the safe and orderly flow of traffic. He serves as a staff officer to the deputy chief of the operations division in an advisory capacity. The commander also establishes and maintains a close working relationship with the city traffic engineering department in developing solutions to traffic problems.

Detective

The detective unit is responsible for furnishing specialized service in the investigation of crimes not solved in the preliminary investigation by the patrol division. It provides follow-up investigations and collects evidence of major crimes, apprehends persons committing crimes, recovers stolen property, and prepares and presents evidence in criminal cases. The division is responsible for continuously gathering information and evidence about the activities of known criminals and on criminal activity generally, independent of any citizen complaints, making arrests when the evidence so justifies. The division maintains surveillance over pawn shops, junk yards, and other establishments dealing in merchandise in order to recover stolen property.

In many municipal police departments, the detectives observe the activities of juveniles to forestall juvenile crimes and delinquency and to make special provision for handling cases involving juveniles. The detectives also assist merchants in preventing shoplifting, collecting bad checks, and other related business losses. The captain in command of the detective division establishes and maintains liaison with other law enforcement agencies in the area for the purpose of developing mutual assistance in the control of criminal activity and solution of crimes.

Also found in the detective division are sections specializing in crimes against the person and property, and the business services section. The crimes against the persons section investigates murder, manslaughter, rape, robbery, aggravated assault, and such other cases as it may be assigned. The crimes against property section investigates burglary, breaking and entering, larceny, auto theft, and any similar cases that may be assigned. Aiding merchants and other business establishments in preventing losses through shoplifting, fraud, forgery, bad checks, and pilfering is the job of the business services section. It may also investigate reported losses, assist in collection of bad checks, and develop evidence for prosecution of offenders.

Juvenile

The juvenile unit emphasizes crime prevention and patrols places where juveniles congregate to forestall acts of delinquency and to assist juveniles who may be in difficulty. The unit interrogates juveniles arrested for, or suspected of, acts of delinquency or crimes. The officers in the unit advise parents on the control of juvenile behavior in such cases and prepare and present cases to the juvenile court for appropriate action. The juvenile office also receives and acts upon complaints of missing persons and investigates cases of bicycle theft and other offenses that normally involve juveniles. In some police departments, this office is known as the youth or youth aid bureau.

Vice

The vice unit is responsible for suppressing prostitution, traffic in narcotics and other illegal drugs, sales of untaxed alcoholic beverages and other illegal sales of alcoholic beverages, gambling, and similar crimes. The division maintains surveillance over establishments suspected of illegal operations, develops evidence for the prosecution of violators of vice laws, and investigates complaints of vice operations. It establishes and maintains effective working relationships with federal and state agencies concerned with similar operations and with local police agencies who require its assistance. Personnel in this division also investigate applicants and the premises of those who apply for liquor licenses, pool tables, shuffleboard permits, and similar authorizations.

Records and Identification

This unit is responsible for maintenance of a complete system of police records, appropriately classified and indexed, including fingerprint and identification records. It prepares periodic summary reports of crime, arrests, accidents, and other police activity. It develops statistics and analysis of data pertaining to policing needs and police activity for the use of those charged with the administration of the department.

The division processes all financial transactions and documents relating to the budget, procurement, payrolls, and disbursements in accordance with city regulations. Accordingly, it establishes and maintains working relations with the city fiscal offices. Furthermore, it maintains a record of all the fiscal transactions of the department. According to municipal ordinance, the police chief may be responsible for investigations and inspections as a prerequisite to the issuance of permits. The records division keeps a record of permits, licenses issued for the registration of bicycles, and inspections performed on public service vehicles.

The maintenance of criminal identification records goes beyond fingerprint cards. This records-keeping function includes photographs, physical description of known criminals, methods of operation, as well as descriptions of crimes and their *modus operandi* where the perpetrators are unknown. Central maintenance of these records permits a comprehensive study of the data, an advantage that is lost when the records are located in several different offices in the department. Information that one unit possesses and that might aid in the solution of a crime may never reach another unit that is responsible for investigating the case. A central records repository greatly reduces this confusion.

Data Processing

The data processing unit is concerned with the collection of facts used in police reports. For example, distribution of patrol manpower may be based on retrieved data indicating that certain crimes occur in identifiable areas during specified days and times. This office provides electronic computing and key punch equipment to ease the task of data storage and retrieval of information used in the myriad reports generated by a police department. Data processing capability facilitates the preparation of daily attendance rosters for patrol shifts, districts, and precincts. The data processing division provides tabulated lists of crimes, accidents, arrests, traffic citations, and similar summaries for frequent distribution to command and management personnel. This type of information, produced rapidly and accurately, significantly aids in planning and analysis of departmental activities.

The data processing and records and identification divisions work closely together because the sources of statistical reports and tabulations are police records. For this reason, in many municipal police departments the two divisions are combined.

Communications

The communications unit installs and maintains the radio communications equipment of the department. It is responsible for manning the central police radio dispatching system, receiving calls for police assistance, dispatching the appropriate police response to such calls, and reporting all such calls and dispatches to the records bureau. The communications unit also operates the information center, including the National Crime Information Center (NCIC) installation, which connects the department with major law enforcement agencies in the state and nation. The division receives investigative reports and prepares a daily resume of significant crimes and other occurrences and a list of car license numbers and persons wanted by the police.

Laboratory

The crime laboratory is found in forms ranging from rudimentary to sophisticated, depending on the size of the police department. In the larger, it has highly skilled criminalists on its staff. In the small department, the laboratory technician may be a police officer with an interest in the scientific aspects of investigation. The nucleus of his laboratory is the photographic darkroom. He assists in scientific detection of crime by such activities as conducting searches, developing and photographing latent fingerprints, and making foot and tire castings.

In larger police departments, a formal crime laboratory may be established. The criminalist takes over the duties of the laboratory technician, and his duties are greatly expanded to cover all aspects of criminal investigation. (See the chapter on Criminalistics.)

Temporary Detention (Jail)

The jail in a municipal police department is responsible for the care, custody, and feeding of prisoners committed to it by the courts or arrested and delivered to it pending trial. The jail also transports prisoners to and from local courts at the times specified. It supervises prisoners committed to custody whether the tasks be on the jail farm operated by this department, in the institution, or other specified locations. Jail personnel fingerprint those persons committed to them, and the prints are then delivered to the records division for classification. A function of the jail is to determine, prior to release, whether the person is on the list of persons sought by the department for other reasons. The jail maintains proper records of all inmates and of the possessions taken from them upon their admission to the jail. It releases prisoners upon completion of their sentence, upon the payment of fines imposed, or if directed to do so by the parole board. It also accepts bail as specified by the courts and releases prisoners awaiting trial when so ordered. In addition, the jail accounts for all monies received as fines or bail and prepares applicable reports specified by city fiscal officers or the police department.

Supply and Maintenance

The materiel required in a police department and the satisfactory maintenance of it is a huge undertaking. Storage of property, its accountability, and physical location are the responsibility of the supply and maintenance division. Satisfactory maintenance and repair of property and equipment promote efficiency, prestige, and morale. The head of the supply and maintenance unit is responsible for the proper care and cleaning of the buildings in which the department is housed. A sound system of supply and maintenance will ensure many economies within the department. In addition, department-owned vehicles must be serviced, washed, and repaired. Preventive maintenance must be performed, and in many police departments this is performed daily by the individual officer as well as the maintenance staff. In a large department, vehicle maintenance can, theoretically, be most economically performed in a central garage. Whatever the case, the supply and maintenance activity must serve the department in the most efficient and effective manner. Whether the department contracts for services rather than having an in-house capability is a decision for the chief of police, but in any event, the supply and maintenance unit is invaluable to proper departmental operations.

Police Academy

The training unit is not listed in Figure 2–3 although it is one of the most important functions of the municipal police agency. Training is the direct responsibility of the chief no matter where the training responsibilities are within the organizational setting. Frequently, the training academy is found in the administration division. The academy is responsible for developing and conducting a comprehensive training program to meet the needs of the department and for conducting a program of public education in public safety. In addition, the academy arranges for attendance of members of the department at institutes and training courses in other areas. The training program includes basic recruit training, advanced and specialized in-service training, refresher courses, and courses on firearms, supervision, and subject areas designed to broaden the knowledge and capabilities of the police.

THE FUTURE OF MUNICIPAL POLICING

In view of the rapid acceleration of societal demands, changing police concepts, and new technologies, it is not surprising that radical changes are occurring in police departments. The President's Crime Commission, in describing the problems created by this rapid growth, states:

> The face of America has changed since local days from a collection of predominantly rural and independent jurisdictions to an industralized urban nation. Yet in several respects law enforcement has not kept pace with this change. As America has grown, the existing law enforcement system has not always been altered to meet the needs of a mechanized and metropolitan society.
>
> Over the years the proliferation of independent and, for the most part, local policing units has led to an overlapping of responsibilities and a duplication of effort; causing problems in police administration and in the coordination of efforts to apprehend criminals. America is a nation of small decentralized police forces.[7]

In regard to the critical problems facing the police, the President's Crime Commission continued:

> Widespread improvement in the strength and caliber of police manpower, supported by radical revision of personnel practices, are the basic essentials for achieving more effective and fairer law enforcement. Educational requirements should be raised to college levels and training programs improved. Recruitment and promotions should be modernized to reflect education, personality, and assessment of performance. The traditional, monolithic personnel structure must be broken up into three entry levels of varying responsibility and with different personnel requirements, and lateral entry into advanced positions encouraged.
>
> The need is urgent for the police to improve relations with the poor, minority groups, and juveniles. The establishment of strong community relations, recruitment of more minority group members and the strengthening of community confidence in supervision and discipline, all aim at making the police more effective in high crime areas. Increased effectiveness also requires that law enforcement improve its facilities and techniques of management—particularly that it utilize manpower more efficiently, modernize communications and records, and formulate more explicit policy guidelines governing areas of police discretion. The pooling of services and functions by police forces in each metropolitan area can improve efficiency and effectiveness.[8]

Most of the experts see a greatly increased emphasis on the role of police in preventing crime. There will be massive programs to educate citizens on the dangers of drug abuse, on how to protect themselves and their property, and on consumer fraud. These programs will be for everybody, not just the poor. There will be an increase of programs for merchants, instructing them on self-protection. Automobile manufacturers will be urged to become more ingenious in their devices to frustrate automobile theft. These functions, handled

---

[7]The President's Commission on Law Enforcement and Administration of Justice, *The Challenge of Crime in a Free Society*, (Washington, D.C.: Government Printing Office, 1967), p. 3.

[8]*The Challenge of Crime in a Free Society*, pp. 294–95.

by a special community education and crime prevention division, are a legiti-mate police service that also furthers good public relations.

In order to improve relationships with minority communities, the police will decentralize to the extent of setting up small substations or *storefronts* in these areas. Besides providing some of the basic police services on a more limited scale, the officers of the units will participate in community functions, join clubs, attend meetings, and help bring about a better understanding. These community-relating units must have officers from the minority group itself.

A further possibility is the use of a state ombudsman to keep an eye on state and local officials. Among his functions would be reviewing complaints against the police.[9]

In the field of personnel, there is a clear trend toward widespread im-provement in the strength and caliber of police manpower, but a radical revision in personnel practices suggested by the Crime Commission does not appear to be forthcoming. Nevertheless, there will be an increased use made of civilians to handle routine jobs such as directing traffic. To help handle the large numbers of police phone calls, pools of civilians will be used. Rather than send radio cars in response to all calls, certain calls, such as those relating to lost articles, suspicious occurrences, and lost license plates can be handled by civilians by phone.

More police will be employed to keep pace with society. Professionalism will increase through greater stress on training. The trend toward more highly educated officers is inevitable. In order to accomplish this, higher pay scales will develop in a highly competitive job market. The criteria for selection will be modified to take advantage of evolving techniques that will measure more accurately the potential of candidates for law enforcement work and that will not arbitrarily exclude large numbers of minority applicants through tests based on middle-class life styles and values or through application of arbitrary and over-restrictive physical standards (height, vision, age). Many depart-ments are already recognizing the inadequacy of long-used selection criteria.

In the field of organization and operations, there is a clear trend toward better training programs for the police. Some of the larger departments main-tain elaborate in-house training academies, and smaller departments receive help from other sources. For information on law and recent court decisions, some prosecutors' offices publish pamphlets primarily for police usage. An-other source of instruction comes from closed circuit TV programs, the use of which is on the rise. In an effort to encourage professionalism, some munici-pal police agencies are establishing career development offices.

In the area of management services, faster indentification using a com-puterized system should simplify many arrest procedures by permitting, in-

[9]Paul M. Whisenand and George T. Felkenes, "An Ombudsman for Police," *The Police Chief* (November 1967), pp. 17–18.

stead, release by the use of citations. More electronic equipment will be utilized, such as closed circuit TV for police surveillance. New technology also will aid in solution of problems of police deployment.

Many police experts see a trend toward the merging of police activities among agencies. Whether this might lead to one huge metropolitan police force is problematical, but in any case there will certainly be more sharing of such personnel as burglary, arson, and homicide specialists. Training, communications, records, criminal laboratories, and correctional institutions will be increasingly specialized and merged to create greater overall efficiency with little increase in cost. In some areas, cities will contract for police services of larger municipal police departments to provide more efficient protection than could be provided by a small department.

SUMMARY

New technology, more skilled manpower, and improved coordination and integration of police agencies are likely to increase the efficiency and effectiveness of police services. This efficiency will probably result in an initial increase in the number of qualified persons entering the criminal justice system, further deterring crime and delinquency.

Most of the trends envisioned assume that there will be increased government spending for law enforcement. The federal government has clearly stated its intention to improve law enforcement. This long has been overdue.

QUESTIONS

1. Describe and discuss the development of the police before and after the generally accepted birth of modern policing in 1829.
2. What social, economic, and political factors have caused a searching examination of modern law enforcement to be made during the past decade?
3. Discuss and compare the views toward law enforcement of the sociological and law enforcement schools of thought.
4. Have United States Supreme Court decisions regarding the rights of criminal defendants affected the operations of police agencies? Have they made police work more difficult?
5. According to commonly accepted standards, what are the primary functions of a municipal police department? Do these functions correspond to the actual tasks performed? Discuss.
6. The President's Crime Commission in 1967 stated that municipal police organization left much to be desired. What did the commission have in mind? Discuss some of the problems created by current police organization.

7. Describe and discuss the chain of command normally found in a municipal police department.
8. What in your opinion should be the tasks of a municipal police community relations unit? How does your opinion compare with the tasks actually performed by such a unit?
9. Define and discuss the distinction between public relations and police community relations.
10. Communications has been described as the "life blood" of a municipal police agency. What does this mean? Discuss and compare the desirable with the actual communications systems found in police departments in your area.
11. Describe some future innovations which will assist in the training of police officers.

STATE POLICE

3

INTRODUCTION

This chapter will investigate the primary systems of state law enforcement agencies found in the United States: the state police, the highway patrol, and the department of public safety. In those states that do not have a highway patrol, the state police performs this function.

Although not within the purview of this chapter, there are numerous enforcement agencies at the state level in addition to the three mentioned above. For lack of a better heading, these are categorized as *secondary police agencies* and can be divided into seven basic types of specialized law enforcement. The first type is comprised of the various bureaus involved in criminal investigation, such as the Georgia, North Carolina, and Oklahoma Bureaus of Investigation. A second type includes state narcotic bureaus. These agencies operate primarily on an independent basis within their area of specialization. Examples are found in California (Bureau of Narcotics Enforcement, Department of Justice), Florida (Bureau of Narcotics, State Board of Health), Illinois (Division of Narcotics Control, Department of Public Safety), and New York (Bureau of Narcotics Control, New York Department of Health).

The third type is broadly defined as *other traffic police* and includes departments charged with the responsibility of enforcing special kinds of vehicle laws, such as state port authorities or rivers and harbors agencies. This type also includes agencies enforcing trucking or licensing laws. The fourth and fifth kinds are fish and game and conservation departments. The functions of these two departments tend to overlap: some conservation departments are concerned with fish and game enforcement, and fish and game agencies are

intimately involved in conservation. In some states, these functions are separated into three separate agencies, as in Maryland, which set up the Departments of Game and Inland Fish, Chesapeake Bay Affairs, and Forests and
Parks. The trend, however, is to group the functions into one department, as
was done in Rhode Island in 1965 where the Department of Natural Resources
brought together the state divisions of fish, game, forests, harbors, rivers,
parks, and recreation.

Alcoholic beverage control enforcement comprises the sixth secondary
kind of state-level law enforcement. Agencies of this type are found in practically every state. The seventh type is really just a group of agencies that do
not fit into the first six types. Included therein are such diverse agencies as the
Gaming Control Board in Nevada, the California State Security Police, fire
marshal departments, racing commissions, and lottery commissions.

Although these types of state agencies are important, this chapter is
primarily concerned with the state police and highway patrols. It should be
noted at the outset that, in some states, the state police are subunits of highway
or motor vehicle departments, although the trend seems to be away from this
organizational setting. The following list indicates those state departments in
which the primary statewide law enforcement agencies are so administered.

California—Business and Transportation Agency
Colorado—Department of Highways
Florida—Department of Highway Safety and Motor Vehicles
Minnesota—Department of Highways
Nebraska—Department of Roads
Nevada—Department of Motor Vehicles
North Carolina—Department of Motor Vehicles
Ohio—Department of Highway Safety
Oklahoma—Department of Highways
South Carolina—Department of Highways
Wisconsin—Division of Motor Vehicles[1]

Twenty-six states have highway patrols[2] and twenty-three have state police.[3]
Hawaii has neither. In seven states, one or the other is located in the state

[1] International Association of Chiefs of Police, *Comparative Data Report—1970.* Prepared
by Division of State and Provincial Police (Washington, D.C., 1970), p. 12. Project was sponsored
by a grant from the National Criminal Justice Statistical Research Center, Law Enforcement
Assistance Administration, U.S. Department of Justice.

[2] Alabama, Arizona, California, Colorado, Florida, Georgia, Iowa, Kansas, Minnesota,
Mississippi, Missouri, Montana, Nebraska, Nevada, North Carolina, North Dakota, Ohio, Oklahoma, South Carolina, South Dakota, Tennessee, Texas, Utah, Washington, Wisconsin, Wyoming.

[3] Alaska, Arkansas, Connecticut, Delaware, Idaho, Illinois, Indiana, Kentucky, Louisiana,
Maine, Maryland, Massachusetts, Michigan, New Hampshire, New Jersey, New Mexico, New
York, Oregon, Pennsylvania, Rhode Island, Vermont, Virginia, West Virginia.

Department of Public Safety: Alabama, Arizona, Georgia, Oklahoma, Texas, Vermont, West Virginia.

There is a noticeable trend toward the expansion of police authority of the various highway patrols with the result that, in the future, some highway patrols that are now confined to enforcing state traffic laws on highways within their jurisdiction may be expanded into true state police agencies. From an economical and pragmatic viewpoint, this movement appears to be sound because there is a need within the state law enforcement to consolidate functions, eliminate duplication, reduce expenses, and improve the quality and quantity of the services rendered.

Coordination between local and state law enforcement agencies is also of concern. There is a definite need to identify, with greater specificity, problems within the state, to establish the relative importance of the problems, and then launch cooperative and coordinated efforts to solve the problem. The assumption of a more meaningful role of state police agencies within the law enforcement community would be an effective way to modernize the criminal justice system and a worthwhile step toward professionalism within the police service.

The state police system is a fine example of a blending of general law enforcement and specialized traffic enforcement. Where so oriented in some states, the Department of Public Safety has been the formal result. The state police, in their broadest context, conduct numerous kinds of activities ranging from multifaceted criminal investigations involving criminalistics personnel to specialized activities for traffic supervision and control. State police are changing; efforts are being directed toward a reevaluation of their position within the governmental structure. These changes are not only a result of social pressures and unrest but also of an expansion of state police services and responsibilities. To carry out the mandate of change, reorganizations have been designed to bring about greater efficiency in command, closer supervision of personnel, projects, and duties, and elimination of the conditions that breed community distrust of the police. Improved communications among police personnel and with the public are a primary goal of this restructuring. Such restructuring has taken place recently in Arizona, Florida, and Minnesota.[4]

Many of the problems at the state police level are shared by the municipal police and the sheriff: recruitment, training, selection, tenure, and fringe benefits. Governmental leadership in many states is attempting to help with the problems:

> In at least 30 states, requests were made for an increase in patrol strength, either by the governor, by legislative committees, or by safety agencies. Collec-

[4]Council of State Governments, *The Book of the States—1970–1971*, XVIII (Lexington, Kentucky), 421.

tively, specific requests were made in 21 states for nearly 3800 troopers to be added to the patrol strength within the next four years. . . . [This] would increase patrol strength by an average of 23 percent.[5]

HISTORICAL DEVELOPMENT

The state police have developed primarily during the twentieth century. They were formed mostly as a result of societal distrust of special interest groups, especially labor organizations. In one sense, the public had lost confidence in municipal and county policing and looked for something to take its place. Frequently given specific reasons for development of state police agencies are:

1. Necessity of some mechanism to coordinate state and local law enforcement agencies
2. Need for uniformity of law enforcement practices in the state rather than widespread dissimilarities
3. Frequent lack of even a minimal amount of police protection and services in rural areas
4. Inability of local police, sheriffs, and constables to cope with the crime problem
5. Hesitancy of local law enforcement to enforce laws that are unpopular
6. Lack of coordination of enforcement for crimes that are characterized by mobility, such as fraud and false representation by professional criminals
7. Political influence exerted on local law enforcement
8. Mismanagement, corruption, and waste that characterize many local police departments
9. Rise in the volume and complexities of the automobile and concomitant traffic accidents and enforcement problems[6]

As mentioned, state police are a development that occurred, in the main, after the turn of the century, although the Texas Rangers were organized in 1835 by Stephen Austin to supplement the military forces of Texas.[7] Their primary function was to patrol the Mexican-Texas border although they possessed statewide authority. Arizona and New Mexico formed short-lived bor-

[5]Edward Gladstone and Thomas Cooper, "State Highway Patrols: Their Function and Financing." (Paper read before the 45th Annual Conference of the Highway Research Board, January 1966.)

[6]Gladstone and Cooper, "State Highway Patrol"; Bruce Smith, *Police Systems in the United States* (New York: Harper and Brothers, 1960), *et passim;* The President's Commission on Law Enforcement and Administration of Justice, *Task Force Report: The Police* (Washington, D.C.: Government Printing Office, 1967), p. 6.

[7] *Task Force Report: The Police,* p. 6.

der patrols in 1901 and 1905 respectively. They passed from the scene because of political interference.

It was not until 1905 that the first formal state police department was established, in Pennsylvania, by the governor because of the lack of an effective sheriff-constable system. Its primary purpose was to cope with a public dispute between labor and management. The state police experiment developed rapidly in other states as a result of the inadequacy of local sheriffs and constables and the inability of the municipal police to cope with crime and to pursue criminals beyond their own jurisdictional limits.[8] The creation of state police organizations increased rapidly after World War I to deal with the increasing problem of automobile traffic and the accompanying increases in auto thefts.

ORGANIZATION AND ADMINISTRATION

State police and highway patrols are highly bureaucratic organizations. As a consequence, there is a great deal of delegating of decision-making powers, increasing the difficulty of supervision, management, and control. The decentralized units may be known as troops, barracks, regions, posts, or zones. The number of personnel assigned to each subunit varies from a single resident post to a complex division headquarters acting as the administrative head of several posts, substations, or similar units. For example, the California Highway Patrol in 1970 had 52 resident posts, 14 substations, 54 barracks, and a total of 150 decentralized units in the entire department. The Kansas Highway Patrol had 115 decentralized units whereas Texas and Minnesota had none. Those states having state police departments rather than highway patrols were also greatly decentralized. For example, Alaska had 24; Arkansas, 14; Michigan, 68; and New York, 665.[9]

Budgets for the state highway patrol and public agencies range from a high of over $116 million in California (5,674 sworn personnel) to a low of slightly over $1 million in North Dakota (80 sworn personnel). Both of these states have highway patrol organizations. The highest budget for state police departments and/or highway patrols was New York with almost $50 million (3,410 sworn offices). The lowest in 1970 was $1.8 million for Idaho (400 sworn officers). On the average, state police departments spent about 71 percent of the budget on personnel, and highway patrols spent about 68 percent. This compares to 80–90 percent allocated for this purpose in municipal police agencies.[10] It is reasonable to have such a gap because the geographically

[8]Elmer D. Graper, *American Police Administration* (New York: Macmillan Co., 1921), pp. 109–10.

[9]*Comparative Data Report—1970*, p. 12.

[10]*Comparative Data Report—1970*, p. 12.

widespread operations of state agencies, for one thing, require highly sophisticated communications equipment. The largest state law enforcement agency is the California Highway Patrol with 7,423 authorized police and civilian personnel. Texas has the next largest highway patrol with 3,698. The smallest highway patrol is in North Dakota with 96; Wyoming has 98. Among those states designating their state agencies as state police departments, Pennsylvania has the largest with 4,056 authorized police and civilian personnel; New York's department is second with 3,932. The smallest of these departments is in Rhode Island, 176, followed by New Hampshire with 189 personnel.[11]

In 1970, the actual numbers of full-time sworn and civilian personnel are reflected in Table 3–1.[12]

TABLE 3-1   State Police Agency Personnel

	Officers	Civilians	Totals
Highway patrol	18,934	8,727	27,661
State police	20,018	5,576	25,594
Totals	38,952	14,303	53,255

The salary schedules for state law enforcement agencies vary widely. In 1970 of those states having highway patrols, California had the highest beginning salary for the patrolman, from $9,720 to $11,244 after six years of service. Missouri paid $12,480 after thirty years of service although the entry salary was $7,800, somewhat below that of a number of states. Minnesota paid $8,004; Nevada, $8,841; and Washington, $8,952. Georgia had the lowest salary to beginning troopers, $4,575, the top being $9,075 after thirty-five years. The median entry salary in 1970 was about $7,249, a figure about which most entry salaries tended to cluster. For the patrolman to reach top salary, requirements ranged from a term of service of a little less than two and a half years in Kansas to thirty-five in Georgia. The number of patrolmen at this level ranged from 59 in North Dakota to 4,930 in California.

In the twenty-three states having state police departments, the median entry salary in 1970 was slightly over $7,400. Beginning patrolmen were paid $5,640 in Arkansas (the lowest), and Alaska paid $10,956, the highest entry salary paid in state police departments. Alaska also paid the top salary to patrolmen after five years of service, $13,104. Illinois was next with $11,760, followed by Michigan with $11,317. At the other end of the scale is Arkansas, $7,572 after seven years and Idaho, $7,692. To reach top salary, the term of

[11] Comparative Data Report—1970, pp. 12–15.
[12] Comparative Data Report—1970, p. 4.

service requirements ranged from three and a half years in Rhode Island to twenty years in West Virginia.[13] Only two states, Connecticut and Massachusetts, employed women as sworn personnel, and both of these were in state police departments.

As a general rule, state police departments follow the traditional military rank system: corporal, sergeant, lieutenant, captain, major, and lieutenant colonel. Furthermore, they do so with more regularity than highway patrols. Only five states have the corporal rank in the highway patrol, whereas fifteen of twenty-three state police departments have this rank. Just the opposite is true, however, with the rank of inspector. Six highway patrols, in contrast to only one state police department, have this rank. Detectives, so much a part of police departments, are found in only two highway patrols, Nevada and Tennessee, and neither has state-wide police authority. Nine state police departments utilize detectives to carry out their functions: Connecticut, Kentucky, Maine, Michigan, New Hampshire, Pennsylvania, Rhode Island, Vermont, and Virginia. Only Kentucky has no state-wide police authority.[14]

In 1970 the salary range for the director of highway patrol offices was from $12,636 in Wyoming and $12,720 in South Carolina to $30,000 in California and $25,792 in Ohio. The service necessary to reach the top ranged from three years in Utah ($15,000) to thirty years in Missouri ($24,000). In the states having state police departments, the salary range was from $11,041 in Louisiana and $11,904 in Idaho to high of $35,875 in New York and $29,500 in Michigan.[15]

As may be expected, the overwhelming expenditure of time in highway patrols is devoted to providing traffic services. In state police agencies, the amount of time for this is somewhat less with a corresponding increase in the efforts directed toward crime-related activities.

Selection procedures for highway patrol and state police departments are similar. Residency requirements range from six months in Rhode Island to five years in Mississippi. Most states specify twelve months. Minimum age is twenty-one. Illinois specifies twenty; Arkansas, Washington, Montana, Kansas, and Iowa, twenty-two; Alabama (unless hired from the state cadet program), Colorado, Oklahoma, Utah and Wyoming, twenty-three. The maximum age for selection is from thirty-nine years in Georgia and forty in Alaska to a low of twenty-eight years in Rhode Island. The maximum age is waived for veterans in seven states. All states require at least a high-school diploma or the G.E.D. equivalent. In addition, Washington requires two years of college, and Delaware, at least six college credits in the behavioral sciences above the high-school diploma. Most states require a minimum height of 5 feet

9 inches. The maximum ranges from 6 feet 3 inches to 6 feet 6 inches. The weight must be between 135–242 pounds. Uncorrected vision varies between 20/20—20/50, although Oregon sets its minimum uncorrected vision at 20/100. A written examination is mandatory in all states except Washington and Rhode Island. Psychological/psychiatric testing is required except in Kansas, Minnesota, Missouri, North Carolina, North Dakota, Texas, Wisconsin, Delaware, Indiana, New Jersey, Rhode Island, and West Virginia. Polygraph examinations are mandatory in Colorado, Georgia, Iowa, Nebraska, Connecticut, Illinois, Maine, Maryland, New Hampshire, New Mexico, and Vermont. Physical examinations must be passed in every state although physical agility tests are required in only 60 percent of the states. Every state agency requires completion of a comprehensive character background investigation prior to appointment.[16]

All states have some kind of retirement plan for state police agencies whether or not it is separate from the plans in operation for other government employees in general. The earliest age for retirement benefits varies widely from state to state. For example, Washington allows retirement benefits at age twenty-five; Montana, thirty-two; and South Dakota, twenty-one. The maximum retirement age is predominantly sixty, but it ranges from a low of fifty-five years to a high of seventy in Wyoming, Connecticut, and Idaho. Georgia and Nevada set the maximum retirement at thirty years of service and Rhode Island and Mississippi mandate retirement at twenty years of service. All states but six (Florida, Iowa, South Carolina, Texas, New Mexico, and Rhode Island) have plans for compulsory retirement upon reaching a specific age or length of service.[17]

Regarding recruitment procedures, ten state police agencies use the state governmental personnel board and seven, the civil service board. Thirty recruit through their own program. Six use a combination of these three common methods to secure their personnel. The scope of the recruitment effort is a large undertaking. For example, in 1970, a high of 12,000 persons applied in California for sworn highway patrol positions; 7,000 were screened; 1,500 passed the examination; and 538 were appointed. Illinois: 2,350 was the high for the state police applicants; 1,621 screened; 854 passed; 193 appointed. Wyoming was the lowest in the country for both highway patrols and state police with 34 applicants for state police; 32 screened; 16 passed; 13 appointed. A number of state law enforcement agencies have an organized and active departmental cadet program to assist in their recruiting. Cadet programs are found in Alabama, Arizona, Ohio, Washington, Indiana, Kentucky, Maryland, New Hampshire, and West Virginia.[18]

[16] *Comparative Data Report—1970*, pp. 18–21.
[17] *Comparative Data Report—1970*, p. 22.
[18] *Comparative Data Report—1970*, pp. 23–24.

OPERATIONAL FUNCTIONS

The range of functions performed by state police is wide and extremely varied. Once again using the state police/highway patrol categorization, one finds that the highway patrols in Arizona, Nebraska, and North Dakota enforce state liquor laws. Of the state police departments, a similar function is performed only in Alaska. Twelve of twenty-six state highway patrols conduct drivers' license examinations, whereas only five of twenty-three state police agencies engage in this activity. Motor vehicle inspections are performed by seventeen highway patrols and eleven state police departments. Only ten highway patrols serve traffic and criminal warrants but this function is performed by about 78 percent of state police departments. Only the Alaska State Police serve civil warrants.

Enforcement of commercial vehicle regulations is performed by eighteen of the twenty-six highway patrols and twenty-three state police agencies. Suspension and revocation notices are handled by only six state police agencies: Alaska, Arkansas, Kentucky, Louisiana, Oregon, and Pennsylvania. Of the highway patrols, only nine do not provide this service. Every state police agency and highway patrol is responsible for traffic supervision on almost all state highways, county roads, and controlled access roads.

Criminal investigation is carried out by every state police department but only eight of the highway patrols do so. Only four highway patrols furnish investigative services in rural areas but all but two of the state police agencies do this. Crime laboratories are found in eight highway patrols and seventeen state police departments. A majority provide fingerprint and other field identification services. If not accomplished by either, it is the responsibility of the county sheriff. Two highway patrols, North Dakota and Oklahoma, enforce marine regulations as do the following state police: Alaska, Kentucky, New York, and Vermont.[19]

TRAINING

Proceeding on the assumption that a department pays "either for training or for the lack of training," highway patrols and state police agencies have expanded their training capabilities both within and outside their organizations. According to statistics compiled by the International Association of Chiefs of Police (IACP) in 1970, forty-two of the forty-nine state police and highway patrol agencies actively encourage college attendance; twelve of these agencies assist the officer in payment of tuition (three highway patrols and nine state police). Thirty-five agencies reported that they assist students to attend

[19] *Comparative Data Report—1970,* pp. 36–37; 54; 55; 57.

college by arrangement of work hours to fit individual class schedules. The Minnesota Highway Patrol and Louisiana State Police grant special credit on promotional examinations for college attendance.[20]

Training budgets vary greatly, from $4,780,826 in California to $6,900 in New Hampshire. The total budgets include salaries for administrative and clerical staff, instruction, students, equipment, building operations, audio-visual equipment and materials, books and publications, and general supplies.[21] In-service refresher training for patrolmen is provided in forty of the forty-nine state agencies. The total hours range from a low of twelve hours per year to eighty, with one state police agency having an indefinite number. In-service training is also provided for other ranks on a regular basis in a majority of the agencies. Roll call training (short training periods of fifteen to twenty minutes conducted prior to starting or sometimes after completion of a work shift) is rarely conducted. Only the California Highway Patrol and the state police agencies in Connecticut, Oregon, Pennsylvania, and Vermont reported, in 1970, that they conducted roll call training.[22]

All police agencies require recruits to attend training schools. Five (Minnesota, Illinois, Indiana, Kentucky, and Rhode Island) require attendance before appointment. All but three state agencies (Tennessee, Utah, and Idaho) operate their own recruit training schools. The hours of training devoted to classroom work for highway patrol agencies range from 890 hours in California and 850 hours in Missouri to 120 hours in Wyoming and 200 hours in Utah. The range for state police departments is from 1,031 hours in West Virginia and 993 in Maryland to 200 hours in New Hampshire and 275 in Oregon. Field training varies greatly, from a maximum of one year in West Virginia and Missouri to a minimum of 30 hours in New Hampshire and 40 hours in Alabama, South Dakota, and Wyoming. Nineteen agencies indicate that junior colleges grant transfer credit for successful completion of the recruit training school. Also, all states but four, Kansas, North Carolina, South Carolina, and Louisiana, report that they provide training services and programs for other agencies. Only Alaska reports, in the 1970 IACP *Comparative Data Report,* that its training program does not utilize outside instructors or speakers.[23]

Training needs frequently are very difficult to ascertain. As emphasized by the president's Crime Commission in 1967, training must be geared to job requirements. In spite of this crucial observation, only nineteen of the forty-nine (39 percent) state law enforcement agencies report that their departments have formal systems to determine training needs.[24]

[20] *Comparative Data Report—1970,* p. 51.
[21] *Comparative Data Report—1970,* pp. 47–48.
[22] *Comparative Data Report—1970,* p. 51.
[23] *Comparative Data Report—1970,* pp. 52–54.
[24] *Comparative Data Report—1970,* p. 54.

STATE LAW ENFORCEMENT SERVICES

Twenty-six of the forty-nine state law enforcement agencies have centralized records systems. Seventy-five percent maintain accident records. About 80 percent maintain criminal and arrest records. Only four maintain motor vehicle registration records: the highway patrols in North Carolina and Wyoming and the state police in Kentucky and Vermont. Drivers' license records are kept in ten state highway patrols and two state police agencies, Alaska and Louisiana. Conceivably, this can be attributed to the importance of the traffic responsibility and orientation of the highway patrols. State police more likely are concerned with their statewide law enforcement function. Still, the IACP study, in 1970, found that about eight out of all the agencies maintained criminal and arrest records.[25]

Sixty-six percent of the highway patrols and 30 percent of the state police maintain vehicle inspection records. Most state police departments maintain statistical summaries of the following kinds: complaints, criminal arrests, juvenile arrests, felonies reported, traffic summonses issued, persons arrested on warrants, and court dispositions. Most do not maintain statistical summaries on numbers of prisoners jailed and parking tickets issued. A majority of highway patrol agencies maintain statistical summaries on criminal arrests, juvenile arrests, traffic summonses issued, and court dispositions. Most do not maintain summaries of complaints received, prisoners jailed, felonies reported, parking tickets issued, and persons arrested on warrants. Once again, the types of statistical summaries produced reflect the basic differences in the functions performed by the state police and highway patrols.[26]

Ninety-six percent of the state police agencies maintain fingerprint files; 87 percent, physical description and photograph files; and 39 percent, *modus operandi* files. The corresponding percentages for highway patrols are 26, 30, and 11 percent respectively.[27]

Eight highway patrols and seven state police departments utilize civilian courtesy patrols, with varying degrees of frequency, in such areas as mountain passes, toll roads, interstate highways, and, in Alabama, on all roads. Statewide crime laboratories are not used by the Alaska, Delaware, Idaho, and Virginia state police. The highway patrols in Montana, Nevada, North Dakota, Utah, Washington, and Wyoming also report no statewide laboratory use. The annual case loads for those highway patrols with statewide crime laboratories range from 150 in Oklahoma to 2,200 in Arizona for narcotics analyses; from 300 in Arizona to 5,596 in Texas for investigations; and from

---

[25] *Comparative Data Report—1970*, p. 68.
[26] *Comparative Data Report—1970*, p. 70.
[27] *Comparative Data Report—1970*, p. 70.

24 in Missouri to 10,370 in Georgia for toxicology examinations. State police were primarily involved in narcotics cases, from a high of 3,458 in New York to a low of 139 in Vermont and in criminalistics investigations, with Oregon requesting 12,410 as compared to 260 in Kentucky. The numbers of personnel in crime laboratories for all agencies ranged from highs of forty-two in Texas and Massachusetts to two in Arkansas and New Hampshire.[28]

Intelligence units are found in eighteen state police agencies and nine highway patrols. Texas, with the high, has fifty-two persons assigned and the low is one, found in the three states of Mississippi, California, and Kentucky. Planning and research units are found in seventeen state police agencies and sixteen highway patrols. The California Highway Patrol has the most personnel assigned to this, twenty-five, and Indiana has the least. Of the eighteen state police departments, the eighty-one personnel assigned to the narcotics in New York is the greatest for both state police and highway patrols in the country. Eight highway patrols have narcotics units, with Missouri having the lowest number of personnel, two. Four highway patrols and four state police agencies have internal affairs units. Only the Nebraska Highway Patrol and the state police in Delaware, Michigan, and Pennsylvania report the instance of a juvenile unit.[29]

LOOKING TO THE FUTURE

In the criminal justice complex, the problems facing the police in general are many and multifaceted. Problems experienced by one element in the total process have an adverse effect upon the other stages of the process. Thus, should the state police increase the number of personnel in narcotics enforcement units, the question arises whether the statewide laboratory can absorb the increased workload or must turn to city police or county sheriffs for assistance. A chain reaction frequently is created that perpetuates conditions that the system was designed to eliminate.

It is essential to have a total systems approach to criminal justice problems in each state. The primary responsibility for control of crime and violence rests with the state. It should have the tools and planning that will enable it to identify the problems, locate the needs, and isolate the issues involved. The state police can assist by developing a statewide crime reporting systems. A need also exists for state police agencies to have statewide jurisdiction over offenses and enforcement of related laws in order to provide the supportive services so badly needed by local police agencies.

[28] *Comparative Data Report—1970*, pp. 78–79.
[29] *Comparative Data Report—1970*, pp. 80–82.

State police must place a high priority on establishing communications among the state level, local level, and the public. Public relations programs are not enough; the state police have a responsibility to encourage a partnership between police agencies and the citizens. If this does not happen, then all the reforms, hardware, and additional manpower will not do the job of assuring law with justice in the United States.

SUMMARY

Management of state police resources is a crucial problem. Continuing efforts to upgrade supervisory and lower level management personnel are required. Much of the training is aimed toward line personnel, but managing and supervising require a different set of skills. These skills can be developed by imparting knowledge through statewide workshops, conferences, and seminars.

There is little doubt that the police, as well as the other agencies concerned with law and societal order, are changing. The change is accelerating at the state level and is evident because of the ever-increasing necessity to provide statewide coordination and services to local police agencies. The crime challenge is demanding. It requires strong leadership to cope not only with crime, but also with the rising traffic carnage, modern high-speed freeways, and increasingly complex traffic legislation.

QUESTIONS

1. Describe the seven basic kinds of state police agencies.
2. Is state involvement in enforcing fish and game and alcoholic beverage control actually a police function? Discuss the pros and cons.
3. Describe the general distinctions between state *highway patrol* and state *police* agencies.
4. Is there a need to have an organization with state-wide police powers, or should the state agency be limited to traffic control? Discuss the pros and cons of each position.
5. Discuss the statement that "many problems at the state police level are shared by the municipal police and the sheriff."
6. Describe the historical development of the state police.
7. Describe the organization and administration of state police agencies. Compare the organization of true state police agencies with state highway patrols.
8. What are some of the general selection criteria for entry into a state police agency? Should the criteria differ depending on whether or not the agency is oriented toward police functions or highway patrol?

9. What are the traditional functions normally associated with the state police agencies? Describe the functions in general and comment on whether or not you believe the functions should be expanded in our present society.

10. Discuss the statement that within a state police agency, training needs are frequently very difficult to ascertain. Why?

11. What do you believe are the future needs of state police agencies? Do you foresee a change in their primary responsibilities?

THE SHERIFF

HISTORICAL DEVELOPMENT

The office of the sheriff is a development of the two words *shire* and *rieve; shire* is the counterpart of county, and *rieve* is the chief enforcement officer in the county. These two terms were used by the Normans shortly after their conquest of the English in 1066 A.D. Although the terms were separate, constant usage over several hundreds of years permitted the terms to run together to become *sheriff.* In the early development of the office, the sheriff's principal duties were to apprehend and punish criminals and to collect taxes for the king.

The term *constable* came into being at about the same time. The constable actively assisted the sheriff as a law enforcer, although officially he was the keeper of the stables. It is interesting to note that today all the police in England are known as constables, and there are no sheriffs.[1]

As the English were the predominant people in the early settling of the United States, they transplanted the terms with which they were most familiar. The sheriff was, in effect, a county officer representing the executive or administrative power of the state within his county. His enforcement powers were exercised in the counties, and in the towns, the enforcement officer was the constable.[2] During the settlement of the West, sheriffs and constables exercised similar authority in frontier towns and counties. As states joined the Union, police functions were provided for in the state constitutions.[3] In

[1]Raymond E. Cliff, *A Guide to Modern Police Thinking,* 2nd ed. (Cincinnati: W. H. Anderson, 1965), p. 4.

[2]Cliff, *Guide to Modern Police Thinking,* p. 11.

[3]Cliff, *Guide to Modern Police Thinking,* p. 10.

California and Alabama, for example, the sheriff emerged as the chief law enforcement officer in the county.

In order to reserve control over the sheriff's department and its police functions, the people made the sheriff an elective officer. Depending on the state, he is also the chief magistrate of the county,[4] a constitutional officer,[5] or a county officer.[6] Furthermore, he is an officer of the court subject to its orders and directions,[7] and is responsible by common and statutory law for conservation of the peace within his jurisdiction.[8] In some states, the sheriff must be elected every two years. This requirement exercises control over the sheriff but poses a serious question of whether such a person is a true law enforcement professional. Anyone meeting general elective qualifications can run for the office, and, more important, there can be a new incumbent with each election. However, in many states the problem has been partially solved because the reality is that once elected to the position, reelection time after time is assured, and thus he remains in office for many years. State constitutions or statutes usually require the office to be filled by a person chosen by the people of the county at an election held under the general rules relating to popular elections. Either by common law or by statutes or state constitutions, certain general qualifications are specified as prerequisite for holding the office of sheriff. He normally is required to be a resident of the county, twenty-one years of age, an elector, and a citizen. Most states also indicate that an individual may be disqualified from being the sheriff if he is unable to account for public money previously in his trust, if he has been convicted of an infamous crime, or has held a federal office.

In some states, sheriffs are prohibited from holding the office of sheriff for two successive terms. However, this has been interpreted to apply to two full terms, not to the situation where an individual was specially elected or appointed as the sheriff to fill an unexpired term. In law enforcement work, it is almost mandatory as a practical matter that there be some stability in the office of the sheriff to permit a working partnership between various peace officer organizations and the sheriff. In the huge urban societies of today, partnership between state and local police agencies is instrumental for attacking organized crime and improving the performance of other aspects of the police functions at the local level.

Throughout U.S. history, the sheriff has remained the principal law enforcement officer in the county. As cities began forming their own municipal police departments, sheriffs' offices confined their duties to the unincorporated

[4] *In re Olson*, 211 Minn. 114, 300 N. W. 398 (1941).
[5] *State* v. *Knox County*, 165 Tenn. 319, 54 S. W. 2ᴰ973 (1932).
[6] *In re Opinion of Justices*, 225 Ala. 359, 143 So. 345 (1932).
[7] *Sparks* v. *Buckner*, 14 Cal. App. 2ᴰ213, 57P2ᴰ1395 (1936).
[8] *Sweat* v. *Waldon*, 123 Fla. 478, 167 So. 363 (1936).

areas of their counties. It should be borne in mind, however, that the sheriff has county-wide jurisdiction and he normally limits his performance of police functions to unincorporated areas, "except when the county contracts with a municipality to provide police services."[9]

POLICE POWER AND THE SHERIFF

Police power is a rather nebulous term frequently misused, misunderstood, or both. Because the states delegate their police powers to counties and cities, and because the sheriff is the chief law enforcement officer in the county in the United States system of criminal justice, the term should be defined.

Webster's dictionary defines police power as "the inherent power of a government to exercise reasonable control over persons and property within its jurisdiction in the interest of the general security, health, safety, morals, and welfare except where legally prohibited."[10]

Police power has been a point of controversy many times in the history of the United States. Perhaps the broadest latitude was expressed in 1839 by Justice Taney of the United States Supreme Court: "The object and end of all government is to promote the happiness and prosperity of the community by which it is established; and it can never be assumed that the government intended to diminish its power of accomplishing the end for which it was created."[11]   Through such broad interpretations, the term meant not only legislative authority to remove government-granted privilege, but also to sanction laws having broad social purposes. Police power has been used by legislatures to suppress business and industrial conditions regarded as offensive to the public welfare.

In 1896, a Louisiana police power statute was upheld by the Supreme Court, requiring separate but equal accommodations on railroads as a means designed to preserve public peace and order.[12]   There were many more such decisions involving state use of its police powers to regulate commerce and industry within the state until the Supreme Court decided in the 1930s to concentrate more on individual rights. By its use of the due process clause of the Fourteenth Amendment to the United States Constitution, a much more restrictive view of state police powers was taken. In 1954, the Supreme Court finally recognized that no persistent discrimination can occur without the assistance of the state's enforcement powers.[13]

---

[9] *Sweat* v. *Waldon,* p. 19.

[10] *Webster's Seventh New Collegiate Dictionary* (Springfield: G. & C. Merriam Co., 1963), p. 656.

[11] *Charles River Bridge* v. *Proprietors of the Warren Bridge,* 11 Peters 420 (1837).

[12] *Plessy* v. *Ferguson,* 163 U.S. 537 (1896).

[13] *Brown* v. *Topeka,* 347 U.S. 483 (1954).

Still other decisions have delineated and limited state police power by granting persons national citizenship and free passage from state to state.[14] Another constraint on state police powers is found where there has been a preemption or occupation of a field by the federal government thereby preventing the state from enforcing state laws on the same subjects.[15]

A practical definition for local police power generally must be the police function of meeting society's demands for order as activity, growth, and development of the community take place. Special emphasis must be given to the wise and appropriate use of this power. "All employees in all governmental units should have a great responsibility for guarding against the overzealousness of public employees that cause excessive curtailment of the average citizen's freedom of action."[16] As a consequence, the police and, especially, the sheriff must apply the enforcement powers of their office to areas that genuinely affect the health, morals, safety, general welfare, and prosperity of the citizen and the state.[17]

POWERS AND DUTIES OF A SHERIFF

Recent studies have pointed out that there is a gigantic struggle to maintain a reasonable balance between effective law enforcement practices and the often expressed concern for the rights of the individual that is evident through the entire criminal justice system.[18] The first step is to provide for local law enforcement. Most state constitutions provide such a basis and further define the duties in detail in state statutes. As a general rule, the sheriff answers to the attorney general for his activities even though the constitutions and statutes list him as a county officer with his compensation provided by the governing body in the particular county. It becomes clear that the sheriff is answerable not only to the public, but to both elected state and county officials.[19]

Because the sheriff is normally enumerated as a county officer, just how is the position of a county officer defined? A usable definition is "a public officer who fills a position usually provided for in organizations of counties and county governments, and is selected by the county to represent it continuously

[14]*Edwards* v. *California,* 314 U.S. 160 (1941).

[15]*Pennsylvania* v. *Nelson,* 350 U.S. 497 (1956).

[16]John M. Pfiffner and Robert Presthaus, *Public Administration,* 5th ed. (New York: Ronald Press Co., 1967), p. 7.

[17]Cliff, *Guide to Modern Police Thinking,* p. 263.

[18]The President's Commission on Law Enforcement and Administration of Justice, *Challenge of Crime in a Free Society* (Washington, D.C.: Government Printing Office, 1967), p. 1.

[19]For a typical state code provision relating to powers, elections, compensation, and so on, see California: *West's Annotated Codes,* II, 501.

as part of the regular and permanent administration of public power in carrying out certain acts with the performance of which it is charged on behalf of the public."[20]

A frequently found duty of a sheriff is administering and certifying oaths. More important, however, is a certain core of other duties that the sheriff performs. Primarily, he is charged with preserving the peace. In order to accomplish this task, he may sponsor, supervise, or participate in almost any project devoted to crime prevention, crime detection, rehabilitation of persons previously convicted of crime, or the suppression of delinquency. In the performance of his duties, it must be borne in mind that the sheriff is solely a ministerial or executive officer and not judicial.[21] Accordingly, a sheriff is charged with the responsibility of arresting and taking before a magistrate or other judicial officer for examination all those persons who attempt to commit or do commit public offenses.

The sheriff also has the duty to prevent and suppress any affrays, breaches of the peace, riots, and insurrections that come to his attention and to investigate public offenses that have been committed in his area of jurisdiction. These duties present an awesome task in today's turbulent society.

Usually he is responsible for handling the bailiff duties in courts within his county and for enforcing all lawful orders and directions of these courts. In addition, the sheriff is assigned a multitude of civil duties as a ministerial officer of the court. Although the duties may go on ad infinitum, a few of the more common are:

1. Certifying lists of jurors' names drawn for jury duty
2. Conducting civil executive sales of confiscated and unclaimed property
3. Arresting and detaining civil prisoners
4. Serving civil writs and legal processes
5. Executing court orders such as attachments, seizures, and sequestering property
6. Endorsing processes and various kinds of legal notices

It must be remembered that these are examples of only a few of the civil duties of the sheriff.

The state's police powers are used to invest the sheriff with the right of the *posse comitatus,* empowering him to command the aid of as many male inhabitants of his county as he believes necessary to cope with a given situation. Although the idea of the *posse comitatus* summation is of early origin, the mandate has been voiced by a recent court pronouncement.

[20] *Coulter* v. *Pool,* 187 Cal. 181 (1921).

[21] *People ex rel Attorney General* v. *Squirel,* 14 Cal. 12 (1859); *Merritt* v. *Gorham,* 6 Cal. 41 (1856).

... All citizens are under statutory duty to assist in maintaining peace and suppressing crime, a historical duty as common laws, which includes furnishing information about crime on request to public authorities.[22]

An almost universal duty of sheriffs in the United States is the care and upkeep of the county jail and its prisoners. In conjunction with this duty, the sheriff must maintain custody of each inmate's property and transport him to and from the jail when he is required to be in court. In many jurisdictions, the sheriff serves as either a full or ex officio director of the county civil defense office. Some sheriffs have the additional responsibility of providing special search and rescue services, including rescues at sea if such are the geographical conditions in the county.

By statute, the sheriff and his deputies are designated *peace officers,* and as such he frequently has the authority to enforce the law anywhere in the state. State laws set forth various administrative duties of the sheriff: delivery of a sentenced prisoner to state prison; making demand for expenses, bond, or deposit when a civil prisoner is committed to jail; acceptance of bail; and special escort duties, such as protection of public personalities. The arrest powers of the sheriff are those of the peace officer and are carefully spelled out in the applicable state law.

As one final note on the general duties of the sheriff, it is important to note that the sheriff has the power to take charge of a municipal police department "if in his judgment, there has been a breakdown in the performance of the police function."[23]

To sum up very briefly, the sheriff and his deputies perform all the functions of a police department in unincorporated areas and cities that contract for their services *plus* the previously described handling of civil processes and custodial functions.[24]

TERMS OF OFFICE AND VACANCIES

As a general rule, the term of office for the sheriff is fixed either by statute or constitutional provision. If the term of office is found in the state constitution, it cannot be changed by the state legislature although it may be changed by amendment of the constitution. If the office and length of term are created by the legislature, then the legislature may abolish it or fix the term of office.

[22] *People* v. *Ford,* 234 Cal. App. 2ᴰ480 (1965).

[23] *Kenney, op. cit.,* p. 19., *California Constitution, Art.* XI, secs. 7.5 and 4.5; *State on Inf. of McKittrick* v. *Williams,* 144 S. W. 2ᴰ98, 346 Mo. 1003 (1940), *State* v. *Reichman,* 188 S. W. 225, 135 Tenn. 653 (1916).

[24] The President's Commission on Law Enforcement and Administration of Justice, *The Police and the Community* (Washington, D.C.: Government Printing Office, 1966), I, 14–15.

In some states, the term of the sheriff begins on his election and runs for a specified period of time, usually four years.[25] In other states, the term of office may start a specified number of days after the election. A person who is elected to be sheriff is entitled to hold the office until removed, he resigns, or his term expires. An interesting situation arose in Mississippi where a constitutional provision that sheriffs shall hold their offices for two years meant that the term of the sheriff was to be from one general election to another and not for exactly two calendar years.[26] However, in Tennessee it was held that an election gave a right to be inducted into the office and that where a sheriff's term of office was specified as two years, this meant two calendar years.[27]

When a change in the law or constitution causes a time interval between the expiration date of one sheriff's term of office and the election or seating of another, in the absence of statutory or constitutional provision, the incumbent is entitled to hold the office until his successor is officially elected or installed. This is the situation even though the effect of such a holdover continues him in office longer than the time permitted by the constitution or statute.[28]

When a sheriff-elect is entitled to hold office for a specific time but something prevents him from doing so even though he meets all qualifications, a constructive or virtual vacancy exists in the office for the length of the entire term. It has been held that such a vacancy is as effective a reason to appoint a new sheriff as if the sheriff-elect had died. If the sheriff-elect dies after the term of his predecessor has expired, the previous incumbent is still not entitled to hold over for the succeeding term.[29]

The expiration of a term creates a vacancy in the sheriff's office even though the legislature has not prescribed by law the office to be vacant at the expiration of such a term. The term *vacancy* refers both to the office and the term for which the appointment is made. Under various state laws or constitutional provisions, the office of the sheriff may be declared to be vacant because of the ineligibility of the sheriff, his failure to give required bond, conviction of a felony or crime involving moral turpitude, or unauthorized and protracted absence from the county. Acceptance by a sheriff of another position that is incompatible with his office also creates a vacancy in his office.[30]

Death of a sheriff in office creates a vacancy; however, a vacancy in the office is not deemed to have occurred where there is the death of a sheriff-elect between the election and final swearing in.

[25] *Garner* v. *Clay*, (Ala.), 1 Stew. 182 (1827).

[26] *Thornton* v. *Boyd*, 25 Miss. 598 (1853).

[27] *Burt* v. *Bobo*, (Tenn), 4 Sneed 234 (1856).

[28] *State* v. *Vincent*, 104 N. W. 914, 20 S. D. 90 (1905); *Pruitt* v. *Squires*, 68 P. 643, 64 Kan. 855 (1902); *State* v. *Harris*, 83 N. E. 912, 77 Ohio St. 481 (1908).

[29] *Maddox* v. *York*, 54 S. W. 24, 21 Tex. Civ. App. 622 (1899).

[30] *Shell* v. *Cousins*, 77 Va. 328 (1883).

Once a vacancy occurs, if there is no provision in the constitution to fill the vacancy, it is within the legislative power and discretion to fill the office. When the term of office of the sheriff corresponds with general elections and there is no constitutional provision for filling vacancies that occur during the term, the legislature determines the mode of filling the office.[31] In Louisiana, the governor has authority to fill a vacancy in the office of the sheriff for an unexpired term of office of less than one year if approved by the state senate.[32] In most instances, however, state constitutions and statutes provide that under certain circumstances the sheriff's office may be filled by (1) county commissioner, (2) court commissioner, (3) the governor, (4) district judge, (5) clerk of the county, (6) judge of the local probate court, (7) county prosecuting attorney, and (8) the county court judge. In many situations, the chief deputy sheriff succeeds the sheriff upon his death, but if he is prohibited from doing so by statute, the governor usually appoints another incumbent. In those states providing that the sheriff must be elected in the event of a vacancy, the governor usually has the power and duty to appoint a temporary sheriff. It is the policy of the states to fill vacancies in elective offices as soon as practicable.[33] Ordinarily, this election to fill the unexpired term occurs at the first general election after the vacancy.

A vacancy exists in the sheriff's office when he resigns and, once his resignation has been presented to the proper authority, he usually cannot legally withdraw it although the governing authority may not accept it immediately.

Normally, a governor cannot suspend a sheriff except on specific constitutional or statutory grounds. However, a sheriff may accept an office with the proviso that he may be suspended by the governor for specific reasons.[34] In the situation where a governor can remove a sheriff for nonfeasance or malfeasance, he also can suspend him for the duration of the removal proceedings. If the hearing decides that there are no grounds for suspension, the sheriff has the legal right to return to his office.

The removal of a sheriff is regulated by the constitution or state statutes. In the event that the constitution does not cover removal grounds, then the legislature may provide for removal or removal by judicial proceedings. A governor cannot remove a sheriff from office unless he is given this power either by statute or the constitution.[35] Impeachment and removal are used in some

---

[31] *State* v. *Crow,* 20 Ark. 209 (1859).

[32] *State ex rel Palfrey* v. *Judges of Council District Court of Parish of Orleans,* 5 So. 2D 756, 199 La. 232 (1942).

[33] *In re Mitchell* 114 N. E. 382, 219 N.Y. 242 (1916).

[34] *State ex rel Hatton* v. *Joughin,* 138 So. 392, 103 Fla. 877 (1931).

[35] *State* v. *Hough,* 87 S. E. 436, 103 S. C. 87 (1915).

states with the state supreme court hearing the impeachment proceedings.[36] Among some of the more frequent grounds found for removal are:

1. Corruption in office
2. Conviction of a felony or crime involving moral turpitude
3. Misfeasance, nonfeasance, or malfeasance in office
4. Chronic absenteeism from the county
5. Intemperance in the use of drugs or alcohol
6. Failure to perform statutory duties adequately and correctly

DEPUTY SHERIFFS AND DEPARTMENTAL ORGANIZATION

The sheriff has the responsibility for organizing and staffing his office although his freedom is somewhat constrained by budgetary and political considerations that are discussed in subsequent sections. The purpose of this section is solely to identify the key personnel who do the work in the department, analyze their specific duties, and present a short explanation of the organization of the department, especially the unique feature of civil responsibilities.

The deputy sheriff is the backbone of the department. His main function is to patrol an assigned area of the county for the prevention of crime and enforcement of the law. He also serves civil processes and performs other related work. He may be supervised by a sheriff's sergeant, an undersheriff, or an assistant sheriff. The specific duties performed by the deputy sheriff are much the same as those of the police officer. He receives and responds to complaints of law violations in county areas. He serves citations, makes arrests, receives and reports descriptions of wanted persons and stolen property, and maintains close surveillance of known trouble spots in his assigned area. On occasion, senior deputies act as first line supervisors and trainers of newly employed deputies. One of the more delicate tasks that a deputy must perform is to intervene in public and private disputes to maintain the peace and protect the public in general.

In addition to the above tasks, the deputy sheriff:

1. Keeps contact with juveniles in his assigned area
2. Appears in court as a witness
3. Assists in investigation of criminal violations
4. Serves warrants and other legal documents

[36]Alabama: *Constitution* Sections 173, 174; North Carolina: *Statutes of North Carolina* Section 128–16; New Mexico: *Statutes Annotated,* Section 40–101.

5. Escorts and transports prisoners to and from jail, courtrooms, and state institutions

6. Conducts water and land searches for lost persons

7. Serves subpoenas, summonses, garnishments, court orders, executions, attachments, and other civil notices

In some jurisdictions, the sheriff also has the responsibility for furnishing bailiffs for the local courts, but this duty varies widely throughout the United States. Graduation from high school or some educational equivalency is normally required to be appointed as a deputy sheriff. Physical qualifications vary greatly and are set up by the local civil service commission personnel board.

The first level supervisor in the sheriff's office is the sheriff's sergeant. He has the general responsibility for supervising patrol activities on an assigned shift and conducting investigations of complex felony cases. How his work is performed is usually left to his judgment with a higher level supervisor available if needed.

Examples of the specific tasks performed by the sheriff's sergeant are:

1. Conducting investigations into felony crimes against persons and property

2. Questioning crime victims and preparing detailed case reports

3. Assigning patrol units to specific patrol zones and supervising and participating in patrol activities to aid in the suppression of criminal activity

4. Ensuring that proper patrol coverage is maintained in assigned areas

5. Supervising all of the deputies assigned to him for proper performance of their duties

6. Reviewing all cases processed for conformance with departmental policies and instructions

7. Counseling juveniles and parents

Qualifications to be a sergeant require high school graduation or its equivalent plus a specified amount of law enforcement experience, normally in the same sheriff's office. In addition, the incumbent must know the general principles of effective supervision and general law enforcement methods, equipment, and procedures. At present, the trend is to encourage sergeants to secure at least two years of college although this is by no means mandatory.

The next person in the chain of command in the sheriff's office is the sheriff's lieutenant who is responsible for the activities of the sheriff's patrol on an assigned shift. He is also required to plan and supervise the activities of a major function such as civil processes. A few of his general tasks are:

1. Assignment and supervision of the work of deputies in performing patrol, investigation, and crime prevention work on a shift

2. Giving general advice and guidance to precinct or substation personnel

3. Assisting deputies by transmitting communications, interpreting policies, instructing subordinates on proper law enforcement techniques, and actively assisting his personnel on all calls of a serious nature

4. Making assignments to subordinate personnel and reviewing finished work for conformance to policy, instructions, and legal requirements

5. Advising deputies on the more difficult types of civil processes to be served or cases to be handled

6. Ensuring that all fees are collected for service of civil process and that accurate accounting and depositing systems are maintained, especially when various types of sheriff's sales are conducted

Depending on the size and complexity of the department, a sheriff's deputy may be the head of communications, the criminalistic laboratory, records and identification, or a similar organizational component. In addition to the general qualifications to be a deputy sheriff and supervisor, a sheriff's lieutenant is frequently required to have an associate of arts degree in criminal justice or administration and considerable experience related to his work.

The sheriff's captain is responsible for the work performed by a major organizational component in the sheriff's office, such as the patrol division, civil division, and so on, as depicted in Figure 4–1.

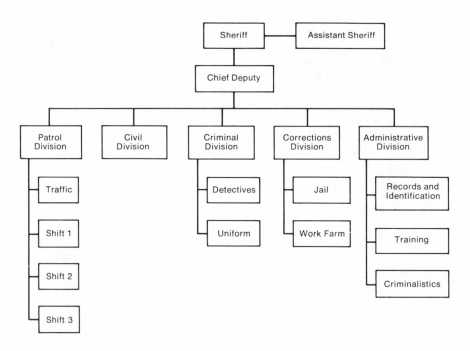

FIGURE 4–1

Administrative Organization of a Medium-Sized Sheriff's Department.

The captain assists in the overall command of the sheriff's responsibilities. His methods of performing tasks are his responsibility so long as they are within established policies and procedures in the department. His work is monitored only periodically to ensure general conformity and to measure results.

Some of the specific responsibilities of a sheriff's captain are:

1. Supervising and directing the activities and personnel within a division or major organizational component
2. Conferring with superiors relative to operating procedures and problems
3. Training subordinate personnel on new police methods and procedures
4. Supervising and evaluating subordinates and maintaining discipline in his organizational component
5. Reviewing arrest records, reports, and complaints to assist other officers in preparing cases for prosecution
6. Planning, estimating, and presenting his arguments for requirements in manpower and equipment
7. Performing administrative tasks such as composing correspondence, maintaining and compiling a variety of reports and records, keeping current on new laws pertaining to the department, and maintaining good public and community relations

Generally, the sheriff's captain should have a college education or the equivalent in an appropriate curriculum, plus a thorough amount of experience.

Some of the larger sheriffs' offices have additional levels in the chain of command. For instance, there are the inspectors in charge of groups of major organizational components and chiefs who have direct responsibility for the management of several major operations, such as chief of administration, chief of all communications, chief of detectives, chief of corrections, and chief of civil matters. It must be emphasized that the sheriff's office would have to be large and complex to have such a complicated chain of command.

The civil process responsibilities of the sheriff are unique to his office. The execution of civil processes is the first and foremost duty of the sheriff. All civil actions in courts of record, except where changed by statute, are commenced by the filing of a summons and complaint or the statement of the plaintiff's cause of action. The summons is secured by the clerk of the court and must be accompanied by the complaint of the plaintiff signed by him or his attorney, setting forth the cause of action.

Copies of the summons and complaint on the defendant are then served by the sheriff, his deputy, or another officer of the court. The sheriff must return to the court with evidence, a signed statement, that the process has been served. The sheriff is required by law to exercise due diligence in the execution of all legal processes rendered to him, whether it be serving the summons or some other kind of civil papers, or attaching property. He is not required in a particular case to use all possible efforts to serve process but must, by law, use reasonable diligence. For service of civil process, the sheriff receives a fee that helps to defray the expenses of his office. In counties that have large populations and, subsequently, great numbers of civil cases filed in county courts, the civil aspects of the sheriff's duties are indeed staggering.

Now that the various components of a typical sheriff's office have been presented, it is important to understand the constraints on this vast bureaucracy.

CONSTRAINTS ON ACTIVITIES AND POWERS OF THE SHERIFF

The powers and duties of the sheriff as presented might seem quite impressive and almost unlimited. However, a number of checks and constraints on the sheriff's activities have been built into state constitutions and statutes. Usually, the sheriff is prohibited from practicing law although he is not prohibited from being a lawyer. In the same vein, he is not allowed to be partner in a law firm or collection agency, nor is he allowed to act as a collector of civil debts. Criminal liability attaches to breaches of the public trust given to the sheriff and this appears to ensure that he effectively will carry out the duties of his office.

The sheriff normally has the power to appoint as many deputies as are necessary for the prompt and faithful discharge of the duties of his office. To the lay person, it would appear that such a mandate, either statutory or constitutional, grants unlimited appointment powers.[37] This is not the case. For example, appointment of deputies was curtailed by both the California Constitution and court decision.

> ... Allowance and compensation of these extra deputies and assistants out of the treasury was prohibited as being in violation of the Constitution Article XI, Section 13, providing that no person shall be granted power to control, appropriate, supervise or in any way interfere with county funds.[38]

It may be summed up by stating that the budgetary and fiscal powers of the sheriff are constrained by statute. Furthermore, he often uses money provided by the state and federal government. For example, federal prisoners jailed and maintained by the sheriff are supported by the United States government. The funds are paid into the county treasury, and the sheriff must file a claim with the county for expenses incurred in the maintenance of the federal prisoners.

State statutes frequently provide that the sheriff is liable for failure to pay over money collected by virtue of his office, to enforce gambling laws, or to prevent a prisoner from escaping. It is unlawful for him to permit or delegate

---

[37]For example, see *California Government Code* Section 24101.
[38]*City and County of San Francisco* v. *Broderick,* 57 P. 1098 (1899).

to a prisoner or group of prisoners authority to punish any other prisoner or group of prisoners in a place of detention. These are merely examples of constraints on the exercise of authority by a sheriff. Should the question arise, "To whom is the sheriff accountable?" the answer would be that he is accountable to the public, the county governing authority, and to the state (usually the attorney general).

At any point in administration, the budgetary process is a central theme. Those who control the purse strings possess the most effective tool of coordination. They are in a position to determine the entire scope and nature of government. In the county, the government authority (for example, Board of Supervisors, County Council) is in the driver's seat. That authority is empowered to regulate compensation of all county officers with the possible exceptions of the district attorney, judges, and themselves. It is traditional that the governing authority regulates the number, method of appointment, terms of office or employment, and compensation of all deputies. It can be seen that the provision for the sheriff to appoint deputies, although not invalid, does depend upon a source of appropriation. As a result, it appears that a sheriff does not have the unlimited powers and authority regarding manpower that some people believe exist.

In regard to equipment and facilities, the sheriff is in much the same position. The county governing body provides the funds to run the jails, purchases supplies and equipment, and audits the accounts of county officials on a periodic basis. Finally, the sheriff's use of appropriations is precisely defined by law. For example, in California he may use appropriations for expenses incurred in criminal cases arising in his county; expenses necessarily incurred by him in preserving the peace; and expenses necessarily incurred by him in the suppression of crime.[39]

Frequently, concern is expressed regarding the enforcement powers of the sheriff. Sometimes, the public believes that because the sheriff is an elected official, he and his deputies scamper about arresting and locking people up at random. General statutes governing the conduct of the sheriff and deputies have been discussed. However, two main figures in the overall system of criminal justice appear on the scene.

The first of these is the district attorney, who is in a position to exercise broad functional constraints on the activities of the sheriff in his county. The prosecutor has the power to determine what crime is to be charged or if any crime is to be charged at all. Consequently, the sheriff's enforcement activities must be sound or at this point he may find himself and the prosecutor at loggerheads.

The second of the two figures is the state attorney general who is usually designated the chief law officer in the state. In some states, the attorney general

---

[39]California, *Government Code* Section 29435.

has the power to step in and assume the functions of the district attorney or sheriff if either is not performing his functions properly.[40] The chapter on the attorney general discusses his duties in detail; however, more will be said later about the attorney general and his relationship to the sheriff and the police.

A third factor that acts as a constraint on the sheriff is the court system which is in a position constantly to review enforcement practices and scrutinize the sheriff's operations.

It becomes clear that the office of the sheriff does not exist in a vacuum. Throughout history, there has been a great concern to control the exercise of state police powers. As a result, sheriffs and all other law enforcement officials as well must find ways to perform their tasks in the most effective manner and still remain within legal boundaries and administrative constraints.

THE SHERIFF AND COUNTY GOVERNMENT

In practically all states, the county is the largest political subdivision. The time is fast approaching, however, in large metropolitan areas, when several counties may merge to form one great area government. Nevertheless, most states today provide, by law, that the office of the sheriff be located in the individual county. Sheriffs' offices are very similar in most counties as are his powers and duties even though minor differences may exist in the nature, organization, or legal structure of his office in the county government. As a general rule, the sheriff exists on the same plane as all other elected county officers. Figure 4–2 illustrates the normal county governmental configuration.

However, a more realistic view is that the sheriff's status, as well as that of many others, changes, depending on the strength of his personality, political astuteness, and his ability to bargain for a favorable power position with other departments. Sometimes, not only does the office of the sheriff become subordinate to other elected officials, but also at times is below that of some appointed officials. For example, in a major city where there is large-scale civil unrest and rioting, the governor may place the sheriff's manpower under the control of an appointed police chief for the containment and suppression of the riot. Another example is that of an appointive county administrator being employed to assist the county governing body in wielding its administrative authority. In this situation, all county officers must go through this agent to get to the purse strings. It should also be clear that, in practice, the governing authority (board of supervisors, county council, and so on) is at the top of the county

---

[40]John C. Bollens and Winston W. Crouch, *The Governments of California* (San Francisco: Wagner, Co., 1966), p. 69.

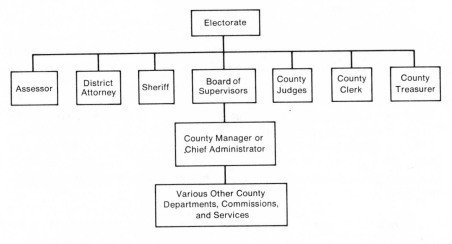

FIGURE 4–2
County Government Organization.

hierarchy. This body is required by law to provide appropriations to the sheriff, but the amount is at its discretion.

It is not the purpose of the author to judge whether this kind of situation is good or bad but to point out that it exists, because many important political implications for the sheriff are the outcome.

County governing bodies administer to the executives of the various segments of county government, and, for the most part, these segments are not organized on an integrated basis.[41] Coordination and cooperation between various independent units of county government generally must be voluntary and usually result from negotiation. The observation has been made that:

> Except for limited and sporadic supervision of the state legislature, units of local government are allotted spheres of authority where they may carry on the function of government delegated to them without reference to the activities either of adjacent communities or of the states themselves.[42]

This may be true for some functions of county government even today. However, in the realm of law enforcement, as pointed out previously, there seems to be an ever-increasing effort at teamwork throughout the governmental and criminal justice system.

[41]Schuyler C. Wallace, *Federal Departmentalization: A Critique of Theories of Organization* (New York: Columbia University Press, 1941), p. 30.

[42]Wallace, *Federal Departmentalization,* p. 25.

THE SHERIFF IN THE STATE PICTURE

The key to an effective approach to efficiency in the administration of criminal justice is teamwork. A state government must encourage organizational relationships that assure the primary police agencies of the support they need for the good of society.

As mentioned previously, the attorney general often is designated as the chief law officer in the state with specific powers under the state constitution. He is sometimes given the authority to call district attorneys, sheriffs, and police chiefs into conferences to discuss the duties of their respective offices. One example of the strength of the attorney general's position in relation to the sheriff in the total state picture is:

> The attorney general has direct supervision over the sheriffs of the several counties of the state, and may require written reports concerning the investigation, detection and punishment of crime in their respective jurisdictions. Whenever he deems it necessary in the public interest he shall direct the activities of any sheriff relative to the investigation or detection of crime within the jurisdiction of the sheriff, and he may direct the service of subpoenas, warrants of arrest, or other process of the court in connection therewith.[43]

Nevertheless, the sheriff cannot evade or avoid his duties by substituting the judgment of the attorney general for his own. In this respect, even though a state has a statute or a policy similar to the one just quoted, no absolute control by the attorney general is contemplated. However, if a sheriff is not doing his job in a particular matter, the attorney general has the power to appoint a competent person to perform such investigations into the area as he considers necessary. The power is seldom used.

With teamwork the keynote, the state and local law enforcement officials must develop a functional partnership through an institutionalization of relationships. In many areas of the county, the sheriff has recognized this need for coordinated activities. In fact, a neat schematic diagram could be drawn of the state system of criminal justice, placing the sheriff below the attorney general and above the local chiefs of police. However, from an overview, the diagram should look more like a football team, with the attorney general as the quarterback and the sheriff in a central position on the front line.

POLITICAL ASPECTS OF THE
SHERIFF'S OFFICE

The sheriff is the object of many varied political currents; however this does not imply political corruption. A sheriff is in a position where he must interact with many elected officials. Others, appointed functionaries, are in a

[43]California: *Government Code,* Sections 12524, 12560; *Penal Code,* Section 480.

position of administration, possibly in the area of goods and services needed by the sheriff. Finally, there is the public who elected him to office and who need his services.

The sheriff must operate within the realm of county government. He is not in a position to dictate what he believes is necessary for the immediate fulfillment of his goals. In fact, the sheriff may never be in that position. As a consequence, he must learn to bargain with people. If newly elected, the sheriff may indeed find himself in an atmosphere where he must overcome apathy or outright distrust by other elected or appointed officials.

The sheriff is a policy maker. By virtue of his position he will find himself impelled, influenced, and restrained from both inside and outside of his office. The influence may be as small as that of a single individual or as large as public opinion.[44] Emmett S. Redford has stated in regard to this dilemma that, "The attainment of the democratic ideal in the world of administration depends much less on majority vote than on the inclusiveness of the representation of interests in the interaction processes among decision makers."[45]

The sheriff will find his role and his policy making are influenced by the attitudes and standards of conduct prevailing in society at any one time. Even though the sheriff's official role has a foundation in a formal allocation of duties, it will be influenced by the habits of the system in which it functions.[46] The sheriff frequently is in a position to take dynamic leadership in developing training, community programs, and teamwork among local police agencies in his county.

On the other hand, a sheriff can escape such a course of action, if he so desires, by concentrating on maintenance of the status quo. One does not have to look far to find this type of sheriff. However, with the turbulence, turmoil, and political activism in contemporary society, such lack of leadership by a sheriff will contribute little.

Charles E. Lindblom sums up this political aspect with the idea that actual and potential policy makers and people in strategic positions constantly engage in partisan mutual adjustment with each other, both bilaterally and multilaterally in all possible combinations. He states:

> There is no highest prescriptive authority in government; no agency, legislator, executive, or continuing collectivity of legislators can prescribe to all others yet concede no authority to any other, even if direct prescription is allowed for. No allocation of authority or function can be found that eliminates interdependence among participants in partisan mutual adjustment.[47]

[44]Emmett S. Redford, *Democracy in the Administrative State* (New York: Oxford University Press, 1969), p. 42.

[45]Redford, *Democracy in the Administrative State,* p. 46.

[46]David B. Truman, *The Governmental Process: Political Interests and Public Opinion* (New York: Alfred A. Knopf, 1951), p. 157; Redford, *Democracy in the Administrative State,* p. 47.

[47]Charles E. Lindblom, *The Intelligence of Democracy: Decision Making Through Mutual Adjustment* (New York: The Free Press, 1965), p. 98.

No matter in what kind of political system the sheriff operates, he is involved in a central, often critical, role. The sheriff must be responsive to the political implications of the role he performs and assume active leadership in those functions that are attributed to him. One of the major factors in the sheriff's political power lies in the fact that he is elected from the county at large rather than districts, as, very frequently, is the case with the members of the governing body. Even though the sheriff is, in reality, just another executive officer of a county agency, he is elected; and, because his power base is countywide, he is in a position that may be utilized effectively to persuade members of the governing body to adopt his point of view. Hopefully, a sheriff will use his political power only when a need exists to further the efficient performance of his official duties.

SUMMARY

The role of the sheriff has been compared to that of an urban police administrator. As a result, the sheriff gives the appearance of using less formal means of law enforcement. His role is often seen as that of a social intermediary rather than as a crook catcher.[48] This idea seems to hold true today, especially in the smaller counties. However, one can find some startling contrasts where sheriffs departments are urbanized, highly proficient organizations, as in Los Angeles County, California; Cook County, Illinois; or Dade County, Florida.

Trends seem to indicate that, with increasing urbanization of vast segments of the country, large numbers of sheriffs' departments will have to adopt one of three possible methods of operation. First is the idea of contract law enforcement in which cities employ the sheriff to provide law enforcement services for the city. Second is the formation of metropolitan police agencies under the sheriff, as in Suffolk County, New York.[49] The third method is found in San Francisco City and County, where the sheriff limits his activities to civil and custodial functions and a police department handles the law enforcement activities.

It must be remembered that any public agency is vulnerable to political criticism. Consequently, a sheriff should not just meet the minimum qualifications to hold county office. He must be an experienced administrator in law enforcement or possess administrative experience in some other field. He must have an appreciation of his role in society. In addition, for practical reasons, he must be a man who commands political respect and is politically astute. A person occupying the office of sheriff today is in a

---

[48]J. C. Esselstyn, "The Social Role of a County Sheriff," *Journal of Criminal Law, Criminology and Police Science,* XLIV (1953), 174–84.

[49]The President's Commission on Law Enforcement and Administration of Justice, *Task Force Report: The Police* (Washington, D.C.: Government Printing Office, 1967), pp. 99, 104.

position to increase the spirit of teamwork and cooperation and to aid in raising the level of efficiency and quality of the personnel in his organization. In this chapter, it has been pointed out that a sheriff must wear a number of different hats because his functions range over a great number of duties. He must also operate in a number of different systems in state and county government and the courts.

QUESTIONS

1. Describe the historical development of the sheriff's office.
2. Discuss the general constitutional requirements necessary in order to be elected sheriff in the United States.
3. What is meant by the phrase "police power" of a state?
4. Describe the powers and duties of the sheriff. Are the traditional powers and duties largely outmoded by current societal conditions?
5. What is meant by *posse comitatus?* Do you believe that a modern day sheriff would have to make use of this device?
6. Describe the various duties performed by deputy sheriffs and sheriffs' sergeants.
7. Describe the administrative organization of a typical sheriff's department.
8. Identify and discuss the various kinds of restraints placed upon a sheriff either by statute, constitution, or custom.
9. Describe the relationship that the sheriff has with other elements of county government.
10. Discuss the political aspects of the job of the sheriff. Do you believe that the sheriff should or should not be an elective office? What are your reasons for the position you take?

THE CRIMINALIST
AND
CRIMINALISTICS

INTRODUCTION

Mankind's battle against the social problems he has created has
often left him baffled, frustrated, and helpless. The problem of
crime is a huge burden upon the populace and the government.
However, man has gained an ally in combating crime that helps
establish the existence of a criminal offense, reconstruct the situation, and
identify the perpetrator. This friend and ally is the applied technology and
inventiveness devoted to solving the problems generated by the investigation
of criminal activity—the field of criminalistics. Criminalistics provides factual
and opinion evidence intended to advance the pursuit of the truth. Generally,
the criminalist deals with physical rather than sociopsychological evidence.
But this is not to say that an understanding of criminal behavior and social
responses can be ignored. The results of scientific analysis may be meaningless
unless interpreted in the light of the possible actions of the criminal mind.
Criminalistics presupposes that the approach to evidence should be one of
scientific objectivity. The investigator must also be guided by the requirements
of criminal law in directing his attention to items that can establish or refute
an allegation. Finally, the criminal scientist must present his findings to the
investigator, prosecutor, and court because they do not have the scientific
background possessed by this specialist.

Science was applied to the investigation of crime in Europe around the
turn of the twentieth century. In the United States at a later date, only a few
police departments made use of scientific investigation by employing city
chemists or other analysts to aid in the collection and study of evidence. After

the early 1930s, the tide turned and crime laboratories were established in rapid succession until nearly all states and most major cities had at least one facility for examining evidence. Because no model existed for proper development, many laboratories were inadequate. Organization was the result of local whim and limited resources. In many places, the laboratory was merely a small step beyond the lifting of latent fingerprints and the use of a photographic setup, adequate for simple and common evidence collection but unsuited in equipment and staff to accomplish real scientific investigation.[1]

Since the beginnings, large, highly technical laboratories have developed throughout the United States. The field of criminalistics is ever-expanding. Especially with the development of highly centralized records and data collection systems, evidence can be stored and retrieved in a short time, greatly streamlining the investigative operations of the police department and criminalistics laboratory. New techniques of disseminating evidence and new equipment have increased accuracy in solving cases and determining the true facts for criminal proceedings.

Criminalistics is a profession and scientific discipline that deals with the investigation of physical-legal problems. The criminalist is one of the experts in this field. The terms *criminalist* and *forensic scientist* are frequently used to designate the same person or function. Both of these individuals interpret, handle, and analyze physical evidence. Likewise, both testify in court as expert witnesses. However, an important distinction must be made. The criminalist is a scientific investigator concerned with *all* legal physical evidence problems. The forensic scientist specializes in a specific area of this knowledge. For example, the criminalist investigates all matters relative to physical cause: blood tests, automobile accidents, airplane accidents, glass fractures, explosions of gasolines, and so on. The forensic scientist would be competent to perform specific blood tests; but the criminalist would go more extensively into the matter, for instance, by studying splatter patterns in order to determine density and flow of blood that might reveal the actual placement of the victim. In short, the forensic scientist is a highly skilled and specialized individual in a single area of physical investigation; the criminalist is a highly skilled and competent generalist.[2]

---

[1]The President's Commission on Law Enforcement and Administration of Justice, *Task Force Report: The Police* (Washington, D.C.: Government Printing Office, 1967), pp. 90–91; U.S. *The FBI Laboratory* (Washington, D.C.: Government Printing Office, 1969); Paul L. Kirk and Lowell Bradford, *The Crime Laboratory, Organization and Operation* (Springfield: Charles C. Thomas, 1965), p. 5.

[2]Paul L. Kirk, *Crime Investigation* (New York: Interscience Publishers, Inc., 1953), p. 511; William W. Turner, ed., *Criminalistics* (Rochester: Aqueduct Books, 1965), pp. 1–6; William W. Turner ed., *Crime Investigation*, Part I (San Francisco: Bancroft-Whitney, 1965), pp. 104–5. See also: *American Jurisprudence*, Vol. I (San Francisco: Bancroft-Whitney, 1964).

The criminalist, however, is not limited to the criminal aspects of the law. He is just as at home in civil cases involving product warranties, personal injury suits, and automobile accident cases.

There are so many types of physical evidence that are involved in criminal cases that it would not be feasible, or even possible, to describe them in this chapter. This work may be set apart by noting that, regardless of the criminal or civil nature of the case, the criminalist proceeds by applying the laws of natural science to his evaluation, isolation, identification, and recognition of physical evidence as well as utilizing the scientific methods of criminal investigation.

In criminal matters, the expertise of the criminalist is sought both by the prosecution and by the defense. His services are so important that most urban police departments and state law enforcement agencies employ literally hundreds. As a member of the police department, the criminalist becomes a specialist, similar to the forensic scientist, in such criminal matters as ballistics, photo interpretation, or voice identification. He has the expertise to cast a tire imprint left at the scene of a crime in the manner of a forensic scientist. However, the criminalist retains and uses his more extensive ability to examine the imprints for traces of material that might yield a peculiar dirt composition and further aid the police investigation. In the same context, in a robbery, a police investigation may need the services of a ballistics expert, handwriting expert, and fingerprint examiner. The criminalist is able to furnish all of these services in place of three specialists.

As mentioned previously, the criminalist is often deeply involved in civil litigation that may range from the sale of adulterated foods to the ingredients used to freeze ice on a hockey rink. In numerous instances, the criminalist is contacted by the plaintiff to help ascertain the composition and safety qualities of a product. For example, should a person suffer an eye injury while wearing a pair of supposedly shatterproof glasses that shattered and pierced his eye, the plaintiff's attorney may very well call in a criminalist to determine whether the glass was defective and, consequently, the liability of the manufacturer of the glass or even the optometrist who recommended the glasses. The criminalist is able, by conducting tests, analyzing the composition of the materials, subjecting the glass to various stress examinations, and similar techniques, to ascertain possible defects.

Another example would be that of the plaintiff who was injured by a gas explosion in a stove he recently purchased. The criminalist is called upon to test the parts of the stove to ascertain whether the design is defective, workmanship shoddy, or instructions given for usage of the stove inadequate for safe operation. This type of investigation involves materials testing, microscopic examinations, and a knowledge of the physical properties of gas and metals. Recognition, identification, and evaluation all are part of the skills of the criminalist.

TRAINING AND EDUCATION FOR A CRIMINALIST

Criminalistics, to be effective, demands broadly educated and trained personnel. The criminalist may be a highly skilled specialist in one or two fields, but it is more accurate to describe him as having the capability to use various scientific techniques in any investigation. He has the educational and training background needed for application to the specific problem at hand.[3]

Because of the breadth and scope of the matters that may come to the attention of the criminalist, it is unreasonable to expect competency in all fields of physical evidence. However, being a specialist in one or two fields, to the exclusion of an extensive educational background and training in physical-legal evidence, does not make a criminalist. There is no concensus among criminalists as to what a complete and detailed training program should be, but a partial categorization of the areas in which the criminalist must have training include the following skills:

1. An expert knowledge of identification methods and their significance.

2. A wide background in the natural sciences sufficient to support him in reaching logical and reasonable conclusions and then uphold him in court.

3. Advanced knowledge in the areas where the major part of his work is expected to be performed.

4. Expertise as a witness in court. The criminalist must be able to present facts clearly and convincingly so as to prevent errors or loopholes in his testimony that can be challenged by an opponent, whether such challenge is warranted or not.

5. An adequate knowledge of the law of evidence and expert testimony in order that he will understand the significance of his testimony and present it so that it will withstand attacks on its legality and admissibility.[4]

It is clear that the generalist in physical-legal evidence, not the forensic scientist, was in the mind of Paul Kirk, when he wrote this list. He is setting forth broad guidelines for education and training. The breadth of a liberal academic education is much more important to the criminalist than the forensic scientist.

Because the criminalist is concerned almost daily with the various laws of the physical sciences, he must possess a thorough understanding of physics that includes the basic laws of mechanics and their application, optics, magnetism, and electricity. The criminalist comes into constant contact with such optical instruments as the microscope, spectrograph, and refractometer. Because he may be called upon to test metals, a background in metallurgy is highly desirable.

Measurements and testing likewise are important to permit the criminalist to examine physical evidence and testify concerning it in court. Many

[3]Turner, *Criminalistics*, pp. 7–9; William Dienstein, *Techniques for the Criminal Investigator* (Springfield: Charles C. Thomas, 1952), pp. 210–11.

[4]Kirk, *Crime Investigation*, p. 512.

courses are offered in chemistry and physics to enable the criminalist to adopt the techniques of the microchemist when handling evidence. A basic background in biology is indispensible. Some experienced criminalists indicate that a minimum of one year each in both botany and zoology is mandatory in a proper curriculum for a criminalist. Still others emphasize the desirability of courses in anatomy and physiology as well as in other biological subjects.

Because the criminalist is called upon to analyze dirt, rocks, and minerals during his criminalistics career, at least a one-year course is often recommended in minerology or geology. It is indeed rare to find a criminalist who is not frequently involved in a specialized examination of gasolines and oils, other petroleum products, and various kinds of soils. Some knowledge of chemistry is mandated for the criminalist to aid his understanding of the physical properties of various substances that are likely to be encountered, such as poisons, blood, and other fluids found at a crime scene.

It is difficult to name all the other subject areas with which a criminalist must be familiar. In Kirk's five guidelines for education, one can note immediately the desirability of having courses in police administration and organization because a majority of the criminalist's efforts will involve interaction with law enforcement agencies. Because practically all of the criminalist's efforts have legal action as an end result, some knowledge of criminal law, court procedure, evidentiary rules, torts, and various legal subjects is highly desirable. Courses in political science, business, and public speaking serve to broaden the academic background and general knowledge of the professional criminalist. Statistics and mathematics frequently are useful even though the physical sciences presuppose this kind of background.[5]

A criminalist's education and training never end. He is, in reality, the proverbial *professional student.* New theories, techniques, modifications of former practices, and so on are commonplace. With the proliferation of new ideas, the criminalist who does not constantly review his knowledge not only stands still, but slips further behind.

Ideal education for a criminalist has been covered in the preceding paragraph. How does the ideal compare with reality? A comprehensive study of California criminalistics laboratories in 1969[6] revealed a wide variation in the educational achievements and experience of criminalists assigned to these laboratories. The study, although somewhat unclear as to the number of actual criminalists employed, was rather disheartening. In some instances, criminalists were only sworn police officers without a complete college education. Master's and doctorate degrees were rare.

Eleven of the twenty-seven publically funded criminalistics laboratories required at least a bachelor's degree in criminalistics or the physical sciences

[5]Kirk, *Crime Investigation,* p. 513–15.

[6]Ronald Rogers, "Report on Criminalistics Laboratories" (unpublished document prepared for the California Council on Criminal Justice, n.d.), *et passim.*

but required no previous crime laboratory experience. Thirteen required the bachelor's degree plus from one to three years experience. One of the laboratories required training and experience equivalent to a degree in criminalistics but did not require any kind of formal academic training or a university degree. Still another laboratory required only an associate of arts or science degree with no experience necessary. It would appear that the study identified individuals used as evidence technicians, rather than criminalists, because there was such a lack of specificity in qualifications.

Once a criminalist is affiliated with a crime laboratory, he is governed by personnel policies that often leave much to be desired. Once again turning to the California experience, one finds several procedures in effect. Most individual laboratories provide for promotions either within each pay grade or to higher pay grades only by the candidate's passing a written examination. In some jurisdictions, promotions are obtained by petitioning the appointing authority. In still others, promotion is within the discretion of the laboratory director who is responsible for evaluation of the applicant's capabilities as a criminalist. It was found that in about 70 percent of the laboratories, no promotional policy was in existence. It is likely that the California experience can be transposed to other states.

THE CRIMINALISTICS LABORATORY[7]

Because the criminalist is a scientist, the laboratory is his work environment. How elaborate it is depends on a multiplicity of factors, among which are: (1) the scope of the major services he will provide; (2) space available for a laboratory; (3) storage space available for equipment and materials; (4) photographic (darkroom) requirements; (5) evidence locker and storage space; (6) services available to ensure that the laboratory is functional, such as gas, electricity, water, flume hoods; and (7) administrative demands for offices and records. Another important consideration is the kind of equipment that will be needed for the majority of the cases that the laboratory will be called upon to handle. For example, crime laboratories, in recent years, have been inundated by requests for analysis of blood, drugs, and alcohol. It would, therefore, be essential to plan to have sufficient space and equipment initially to perform these basic services adequately even though it might mean the exclusion of exotic tests involving the use of expensive, complex, and large equipment.

As a minimum, however, a laboratory should have at least enough work space for each criminalist so as not to impede his productivity. Tables for microscopes should be provided for each worker as well as large table work

[7]See generally Harry Soderman and John J. O'Connell, *Modern Criminal Investigation,* (5th ed.) (New York: Funk and Wagnalls, 1962), pp. 463–65; Kirk, *Crime Investigation,* pp. 529–34; Dienstein, *Techniques for the Criminal Investigator,* pp. 211–16.

areas to examine bulky pieces of evidence. Additional tables, such as work benches, are required for any special instruments the laboratory will house: comparison microscopes, ballistics firing chambers, spectrographs, x-ray refraction cameras, stereomicroscopes, drying ovens, refrigerators, chromatography equipment, centrifuge equipment, various balancing devices, ultraviolet lamps, photomicrography and macrophotography equipment, to name but a few.

In order to perform the tests, investigations, recognitions, and evaluations, the criminalist must have specific services available in the laboratory much like those the housewife needs in order to manage the home.

1. A vacuum system is essential in most well-equipped and staffed offices.

2. Compressed air serves many useful purposes.

3. Not only is adequate illumination essential, provision must be made also for highly concentrated light fixtures as well as a high level of illumination in the work areas.

4. Sources of electricity are critical, especially with the large amounts of equipment in a laboratory. High voltage lines are mandatory, as are a large number of outlets to prevent overloading.

5. Illuminating gas is virtually indispensible at each workbench and microscope place.

6. In a modern laboratory, large flume hoods are essential to remove fumes and vapors from the laboratory as various examinations are performed.[8]

In addition, every crime laboratory must provide both secure storage of its equipment and special chemical storage areas. This space may be on shelves for nonpoisonous materials, but there also must be a secure cabinet for toxic chemicals and the large amounts of narcotics used by contemporary laboratories.

Evidence storage is mandatory. A small secure room is desirable as a minimum, with bins secured by locks to hold the evidence from each case. It must be kept so that it is not intermingled with like evidence in other cases. Where such individual storage is unavailable, the evidence may be stored with other items but must be carefully wrapped, labeled, and otherwise identified. It is always desirable to have the evidence room designed as a safe and fireproof vault. Adequate locking devices should be provided. A favorite avenue of assault on the introduction of evidence during a trial is of charging that the custody of the evidence cannot be adequately traced because it was out of the control or custody of a proper person at some time during the investigation of the case.

[8]John W. Gunn and Richard S. Frank, "Planning a Forensic Science Laboratory," *The Police Chief,* XXXIX (January 1972), 36–41.

Ideally, the custodial chain should include as few individuals as possible. Usually there will be the investigator who recovers the evidence and transmits it to the crime laboratory. The evidence specialists or criminalists examine the evidence and give testimony, if required, at the trial. Personnel not engaged in a specific investigation who take custody of the evidence between its initial recovery and introduction in court tend to break the custodial chain. In fact, the greater the number of persons who are required to take the witness stand in order to account for the custody of any piece of evidence, the greater the possibility the chain will be attacked. To limit the custodial chain, it is a good rule that only the initial investigator and the criminalists who are involved in the examination have access to the material.

No criminalistics laboratory is complete or even functional without a photographic darkroom not only for photographic work but also to examine various evidence under ultraviolet lights. It must be large enough to permit the usual photographic equipment to be installed: enlarger, sinks, various electrical outlets, dryers, and similar equipment.

Each laboratory should have a reference library with text books and other materials on criminalistics subjects. The reference texts serve as source material on any problems the laboratory personnel may encounter in the analysis of crimes, ranging from possession of narcotics and dangerous drugs to the kinds of gunpowder used in a homicide. Particularly in drugs and narcotics that have caused so much concern over the past decade, is it imperative that crime laboratory personnel have up-to-date reference material to help them make accurate analyses of all evidence submitted to them.

SPECIFIC FUNCTIONS OF THE CRIMINALISTICS LABORATORY

The work of the laboratory criminalist and other technicians includes recognition, identification, and evaluation in some of the following areas of specialization:

1. *Hairs and Fibers.* Textile fibers and hairs can be found and used almost everywhere. Identification and matching often play a part in litigation. Hair can be traced to man or animal and, in the case of a human being, it can identify his race. The technician can then discover whether it was pulled out, fell out naturally, was cut, or crushed.

Fibers found in fabric abrasions or caught in torn metal on hit-and-run vehicles are important evidence for the criminalist. Examination of fibers is conducted to determine type and color. Fibers and threads also can be compared to determine whether or not they could have come from the same clothing. In special cases, it may be possible to demonstrate contact between persons and some object, such as between victim and car seat in a rape case, by comparing transferred fibers.

2. *Soil.* The criminalist conducts various studies of soil evidence including microscopic examination, density tests, and contamination studies (cement mixtures or vegetation impurities). If the soil is unusual in any way, comparisons are always helpful.

3. *Glass.* Frequently, windows are broken in crimes and fragments are left on personal belongings of subjects involved. In cases where there are large enough fragments, studies of the physical properties of glass may show whether two samples have the same origin. The best evidence, however, is larger fragments that can be physically matched.

4. *Blood Samples for Alcohol Analysis.* The criminalist may be called upon to conduct tests that determine intoxication in drunk-driving cases or other crimes. The tests may involve urine or blood samples.

5. *Urinalysis.* The criminalist must be competent to conduct analyses of urine because evidence of drugs appears only in urine.

6. *Blood Stains.* In criminal offenses involving injuries to persons (homicide, rape, assaults with deadly weapons), blood is usually found in the form of stains or smears. It can be typed if enough is submitted, and it may provide valuable evidence that either exculpates a suspect from or associates him with an offense. Laboratory examination of all body fluids may also produce significant information in certain criminal investigations.

7. *Seminal Stains.* In sex cases, semen stains are often found on clothing, blankets, sheets, seats, or other materials. The victim can be examined for seminal fluid from the suspect. Such evidence may implicate or exclude a suspect.

8. *Paint.* Paint evidence is often encountered, as in such instances as hit-and-run cases and on burglars' tools. Sometimes, whole chips of paint will be transferred to clothing. Several layers on a suspect's car may confirm a repaint job in a hit-and-run case. Large chips of paint can be matched to the fracture line of a car involved in an accident.

9. *Metals.* It is possible for the criminalist to compare metals on the basis of composition. Such laboratory techniques as the application of metallography, emission spectrography, crystallography, and x-ray refraction make it possible to identify minute metal fragments. Questioned metal fragments may frequently be fracture-matched with the object from which they originated. Frequently, serious accidents result from metal failure, such as structural failure in an airplane, which, in some instances, indicates negligence.

10. *Firearms and Ammunition.* The criminalist may be able to obtain information regarding the type of firearm and projectile that inflicted an injury by examination of x-rays of metal particles along the wound tract in the victim's body. Often, it is possible to restore manufacturer's serial numbers, property marks, or other die-stamped markings that have been altered, obliterated, or removed.

11. *Documents.* Questioned documents may be analyzed for comparison of handwriting, ink, typewriting, paper, and related materials. It can often be determined whether or not handwritten or typewritten alterations have been made on documents. A questioned document may be a will, check, contract, or the like that allegedly is forged or altered. The criminalist will attempt to confirm or deny the allegation.

Such a list of evidence is not all-inclusive but serves to show the breadth and scope of the work carried on in the laboratory, especially by the criminalist. All in one day, he may be called upon to analyze an explosive substance, examine fingerprints, identify a poison, and compare burglary tool makings. He must be competent to perform these operations or else he cannot be called a true criminalist.

THE CRIMINALIST'S JOB DESCRIPTION

To better understand the tasks and functions performed by a beginning and advanced criminalist, a typical job description for each is presented below in extract form, labeled CRIMINALIST I and CRIMINALIST II.

CRIMINALIST I

Definition

This is responsible professional work in microscopic analysis and comparison of physical evidence as it relates to scientific criminal investigation.

Employees in this class perform a wide variety of microscopic, physical and some chemical identification and comparison of trace evidence on firearms, burglary tools, weapons, clothing, automobiles, buildings, etc. Work involves both laboratory and travel to crime scene to collect the evidence deemed necessary for testing. Work involves the supervision of professional and clerical assistants. Assignments are usually received with limited instructions in the case of routine work; however, detailed instructions may accompany unusual problems. Finished work and reports are checked upon completion by a superior.

Examples of Work Performed

Inspects crime scene for evidence falling within his scientific specialty along with other investigators; collects items and materials for laboratory inspection.

Makes decisions as to what tests are to be applied to specific items of evidence, and performs or supervises others in performing these tests; checks results, and makes proper photographic record of these findings.

Tests and fires weapons in evidence for identity and function; identifies burglary tools and connects these by proper physical and chemical tests to burglary scene or to suspects; makes microscopic preparation and study of textile fibers, hair, soil, dust, etc., related to crimes; selects, examines, tests and photographs materials used as evidence in automobile death cases.

Performs special and non-routine physical and chemical tests to determine identity of stains, dusts, soil, fibers, etc.

Designs and prepares photographic exhibits of laboratory or other findings, prepares his findings and materials for proper court presentation at criminal trial wherever required.

Performs related work as required.

Required Knowledge, Skills, and Abilities

Considerable knowledge of principles and practices of scientific-legal work.

Considerable knowledge of principles of physics and chemistry.

Considerable knowledge of principles and application of microscope and other optical instruments in field of specialty.

Considerable knowledge of principles of photography, including the ability and talent to produce good color transparencies.

Demonstrated skill in handling and preserving trace evidence in specialized field of assignment.

Ability to do original research work and devise new procedures for identification and comparison.

Ability to supervise work of subordinates in criminalistic work.

Ability to present scientific information in clear, understandable manner to lay persons and legal personnel.

Ability to understand and follow complex written and oral instructions.

Qualifications

Graduation from a four-year college or university with courses in general and analytical chemistry and physics, preferably with some graduate work in one of the above or related scientific fields.

Experience in criminalistics or related areas of scientific criminal investigation desirable.

Revised November 5, 1970

Alabama State Toxicologist, Birmingham, Alabama

CRIMINALIST II

Definition

This is highly responsible technical and professional supervisory work in the area of criminalistics in a crime laboratory.

Employees in this class are responsible for planning and supervising the work of other employees doing criminalistic procedures on many kinds of physical evidence related to crimes. Duties involve supervision of technical and professional personnel doing forensic work in a specialized area of crime laboratory activity. Certain evidence materials are received or obtained by personal crime scene search, and assignments are made to employees who perform analytical studies somewhat independently according to established policies. Work also involves responsibility for planning the processing procedures for evidence in each case in his scientific area, and in checking results obtained for accuracy and interpretation. Employees supervise those graduate college students doing their thesis problems with the laboratory in the area of criminalistics. Duties are performed with considerable independence under departmental policy.

Examples of Work Performed

Plans, organizes and develops procedures into a working program for the criminalistics division of a crime laboratory.

Supervises and performs various identification, comparative, and analytical procedures covering drug dosage forms, blood and seminal stains, tool marks, firearms, hairs, fibers, paints, soil residues, etc. presented by various items of physical evidence related to crimes.

Advises employees and directs development of laboratory procedures for identification of unusual unknown marks, paint residues, stains, etc.

Coordinates criminalist responsibilities and activity of the crime laboratory with law enforcement agencies and investigators. This duty may involve activity at the crime scene as well as laboratory investigation.

Reviews and approves reports of other employees under his direction.

Performs related work as required.

Required Knowledge, Skills, and Abilities

Thorough knowledge of the principles and practices of chemistry and the biological sciences.

Thorough knowledge of microscopic techniques as applied to identifications and comparisons of a wide variety of substances and objects constituting physical evidence in criminal cases.

Considerable knowledge and skill in applying specialized instrumental analysis to the identification of drugs, paint residues, fibers, plastics, tool marks, stains, etc.

Working knowledge of mathematics, chemistry, physics, criminal investigation and legal principles.

Ability to coordinate criminalistics services and maintain effective working relations with other functions of the same or other division of the crime laboratory, other officers, and law enforcement agencies. This also includes the giving of lectures to officers in law enforcement schools.

Ability to testify as an expert witness and to explain scientific and applicable legal matters in understandable manner.

Ability to supervise and direct a division or regional laboratory supplying scientific services in criminalistics, and to coordinate these activities with the parent crime laboratory, the courts, and the public.

Qualifications

Any combination of training and experience equivalent to:

Graduation from a four-year college or university with major course work in chemistry or a related field, preferably supplemented by one or more courses in law.

Considerable progressively responsible experience in scientific criminal investigative work in criminalistics, or forensic science.

Approved November 5, 1970

Alabama State Toxicologist, Birmingham, Alabama

THE CRIMINALIST AS AN EXPERT WITNESS

The criminalist will be expected to testify on all topics relative to physical-legal evidence. His qualifications as an expert must be shown, however, before he may testify regarding his opinion.

To establish his qualifications, the counsel must show that the expert possesses unusual skill and knowledge gained from study and experience. As a practical matter, the counsel sponsoring the criminalist will establish expertise by showing the amount of training, education, and experience the criminalist has. He also will point out the professional groups to which he belongs, such as the State Association of Criminalists, American Academy of Forensic Sciences, and the American Society of Questioned Document Examiners.

The number and title of books, articles, monographs, and other publications written by the criminalist add to his stature as a witness. Of extreme importance is the educational background of the criminalist. His scientific academic achievements are emphasized. Advanced degrees should be brought out in the questioning of the expert. If the criminalist teaches at a college or university, the court is interested in this background, especially if it is in one of the scientific disciplines such as physics, criminalistics, or chemistry.

On-the-job experience as a forensic scientist, laboratory technician, and criminalist fortifies his previous qualifications. An expert may testify as an expert based on training and education alone. As a practical matter, however, when listening to the expert testimony, the audience is likely to give more weight to the person who has education, training, and experience in his background.

PREVALENCE OF CRIME LABORATORIES

As has been seen, scientific analysis has become essential to the detection of crime and identification of offenders. It has been pointed out by Supreme Court decision that the police must rely on new and better investigation techniques rather than on confessions. The International Association of Chiefs of Police[9] classified state crime laboratories by the function they performed. No functions were shown for nine states: Colorado, Idaho, Montana, Nevada, New Mexico, North Dakota, South Dakota, Utah, Washington. The following breakdown was listed for the types of functions performed:

1. Firearms identification, 34
2. Polygraph examination, 34
3. Film development, 37
4. Photography, 38
5. Tool mark identification, 34
6. Document analysis, 28
7. Chemical analysis, 27 ·

[9]International Association of Chiefs of Police, *Comparative Data Report*—1969, (Washington, D.C.: IACP, 1969), p. 37.

The IACP report further noted that thirteen states had mobile crime laboratories to process crime scenes. Local police agencies in thirty-five states were furnished state crime laboratory assistance.

A John Jay College of Criminal Justice study[10] attempted to draw up a model laboratory incorporating the following *principles:*

1. Each crime laboratory should serve a minimum of five hundred thousand people with at least five thousand FBI Part I crimes: murder, forcible rape, robbery, and aggravated assault, burglary, auto theft, and larceny ($50 and over). If a community has less than five thousand crimes regardless of population size, whether or not a laboratory were maintained would be a policy decision. If a community has less than five hundred thousand people but nevertheless is a victim of the five thousand crimes, a criminalistics laboratory would most likely be justified.

2. It should have a capital budget of about $200,000.

3. It should employ twelve to twenty scientific employees.

4. It should offer most of the services previously mentioned in this chapter.

SUMMARY

In our modern society with the emphasis on protection of civil rights in criminal procedures, the system of criminal justice has come to depend on extrinsic evidence independently secured through careful investigation and improved scientific techniques. More and more, the solution of offenses will hinge upon the discovery and analysis of such evidence at crime scenes as blood stains, body fluids, fingerprints, and voiceprints. As a result, the criminalist working in the crime laboratory will play an even greater part. The familiar cliché that *crimes are solved by hand digging* is still accurate, but the highly trained criminalist is now included in the digging crew.

QUESTIONS

1. Describe the field of criminalistics. Discuss its historical development.

2. Distinguish a criminalist from a forensic scientist.

3. Describe the kinds and amount of training and education a criminalist possesses.

4. Discuss the various, generally recognized skills which a criminalist should have.

[10]John Jay College of Criminal Justice, *Study of Needs and the Development of Curricula in the Field of Forensic Sciences in Crime Laboratories—Three Study Reports, Office of Law Enforcement Assistance* (Washington, D.C.: Government Printing Office, 1968), p. 9.

5. It is sometimes stated that a criminalist's home is in the laboratory. What does this mean?

6. What factors aid in determining how elaborate a criminalistics laboratory will be?

7. Describe the evidence storage responsibility of the criminalist. What is meant by the custodial chain of evidence?

8. Discuss some of the specific functions performed in a criminalistics laboratory.

9. Describe the role of the criminalist as an expert witness. What is meant by the statement that the criminalist must be qualified as an expert?

10. How have recent United States Supreme Court decisions increased the importance of the tasks performed by the criminalist?

BIBLIOGRAPHY

LEONARD, V. A., *Criminal Investigation and Identification.* Springfield, Ill.: Charles C. Thomas, 1971.

O'HARA, CHARLES E., *Fundamentals of Criminal Investigation.* Springfield, Ill.: Charles C. Thomas, 1971.

O'HARA, CHARLES E., and JAMES W. OSTERBERG, *An Introduction to Criminalistics.* New York: Macmillan, 1949.

OSTERBERG, JAMES W., *Crime Laboratory: Case Studies of Scientific Criminal Investigation.* Bloomington, Ind.: Indiana University Press, 1968.

The President's Commission on Law Enforcement and Administration of Justice, *The Challenge of Crime in a Free Society.* Washington, D.C.: Government Printing Office, 1967.

WALLS, H. J., *Forensic Science: An Introduction to the Science of Crime Detection.* New York: Praeger, 1971.

POLICE
LEGAL ADVISORS

HISTORICAL PERSPECTIVE

There is a lack of material on the police legal advisor primarily because only in recent years has there been a growing recognition of the need for this type of advice in a police department. Secondarily, because the office is so new, there has been little pressure to ascertain exactly what is required of a legal advisor.

6

According to the International Association of Chiefs of Police (IACP), the first legal unit in a law enforcement agency was established in 1907 in the New York Police Department. The unit initially was known as the *Law Library* because it was to be an office for legal research on matters affecting the police department. Years later, the name of the unit was changed to the *Legal Bureau.* The bureau grew from one attorney in 1907 to five supervising attorneys, eleven police officer attorneys, three civilian attorneys and eight clerical personnel in 1970. It is known as the *Legal Division* and operates under the general supervision of a Deputy Commissioner of Legal Matters.[1]

The FBI has preferred agents with a law background who can solve their own legal problems. As law became more complex, the bureau established its own *Legal Research Unit* in its training division in 1961. The unit assisted in the training of FBI agents, taught at FBI police schools, and helped the bureau with its own legal problems. In 1971, this special form of legal advisor became

[1]International Association of Chiefs of Police, *Guidelines for a Police Legal Unit* (Washington, D.C.: Police Legal Center, Research Division, 1972), p. 7.

the *Office of Legal Counsel* under an assistant director of the FBI with a staff of five lawyers.[2]

Since 1941, the Indiana State Police also has had a legal unit. The unit is now known as the *Legal License Section* and is staffed with attorneys who formerly were police officers.[3]

The need for continuing legal advice within a police department has been recognized by police authorities. This is especially true in light of the great interest the courts have exhibited toward police practices. O. W. Wilson, the former dean of the school of criminology at the University of California, Berkeley, and chief of the Chicago Police Department, spoke about the need for a legal unit in a police department to review departmental practices and procedures with an eye toward necessary changes.[4] However, the President's Crime Commission reported that in 1965 only 14 of 276 departments in a national survey reported that they employed attorneys, and 6 of these were part-time.[5]

Because of the foresight and urging of O. W. Wilson and Professor Fred Inbau of Northwestern University Law School, a *Police Legal Advisor* program was started in 1964 at the Northwestern Law School under a Ford Foundation grant. Selected lawyers are given fellowships to study criminal law and spend a year's internship with the Chicago Police Department and another year with a selected police department. At the end of the two years, a thesis is prepared and the attorney is awarded a Master of Law degree.[6]

In 1970, the legal advisor program moved to the IACP where it is designated the *Police Legal Center.* It serves the entire police community, not just those large enough to hire a legal advisor. Through a monthly training bulletin, participating police departments obtain up-to-date legal materials, advice, and legal training for its officers even in the absence of an on-the-scene advisor. As of May 1972, there were a total of 137 police legal units in the United States, classified as follows:

> City, 89
> County, 16
> Regional, 8
> State, 17
> University, 1
> Federal, 6[7]

---

[2]Edwin D. Heath, Jr., "The Police Legal Unit," *FBI Law Enforcement Bulletin,* 41 (August 1972), p. 23.

[3]*Guidelines for a Police Legal Unit,* p. 8.

[4]O. W. Wilson, *Police Planning,* 2nd ed. (Springfield: Charles C. Thomas, 1962), p. 11; O. W. Wilson, *Police Administration,* 2nd ed. (New York: McGraw-Hill, 1963), p. 60.

[5]President's Commission on Law Enforcement and Administration of Justice, *Task Force Report: The Police* (Washington, D.C.: Government Printing Office, 1967), p. 50.

[6]*Guidelines for a Police Legal Unit,* p. 8; *Task Force Report: The Police,* pp. 66–67.

[7]Report from the IACP, "Roster of U.S. Police Legal Units (May 1972)," n.d.

MANPOWER

(The following section is primarily from the *Task Force Report: The Police.* See footnote 8.) It is impossible to calculate with confidence the number of advisors needed by police agencies across the country. An estimate of the outer limits of manpower needs is dependent upon the knowledge of the functions the legal advisor will perform; these necessarily will vary, often substantially, from department to department. In some places, the advisor will be responsible for training, or legislative relations, or policy planning; in others, he will perform none or all of these duties. A reasonable estimate of minimum needs may be made, however, even though it is difficult to specify underlying criteria. The following estimates represent the best guess of those most experienced.

There are five police departments servicing cities in excess of one million population. At least five legal advisors may be needed to meet minimum needs of these departments, and even this figure is probably very conservative. Based on his experience as deputy commissioner for legal matters in the New York Police department, Franklin Thomas feels that "twice the number recommended would be the absolute minimum to fulfill properly the functions required of such advisors."

Approximately seventeen cities range in population between 500,000 and 1,000,000. At least three advisors should be available. There are about thirty-three cities within the 250,000 to 500,000 range. At least two advisors should be budgeted. There are nearly eighty cities under 250,000 and over 100,000 population. At least one advisor would fulfill minimum standards.

Smaller cities, such as those below 100,000 and over 50,000 that may not need an advisor full-time may, however, be able to justify employing one by pooling arrangements with several police agencies in a given area to share a single police legal advisor. Fragmentation of police services is notorious and the common use of a legal advisor could be a device not only for acquiring counsel, but also for achieving greater coordination among separate police departments.

All of the states, except Hawaii, maintain state police or highway patrol organizations. These departments range in serving membership from 50 men in Nevada to 2,795 men in California. Total personnel in all the states, as of December 31, 1964, was 26,784 men. At least one advisor should be budgeted for each state, and the largest states, such as New York (2,464 men) and Pennsylvania (2,015 men) should employ several advisors. In addition, there are about 773 counties that operate road patrols, about 100 of which have uniformed forces of over 100 men. Each of these should employ a full- or part-time advisor.

Totaling these figures, the manpower needed to supply minimum needs ranges from 250 to 400 men skilled in criminal law, administrative law, and police science.[8]

[8] *Task Force Report: The Police,* p. 66.

The IACP suggests that one advisor is needed for each 500 police officers, although it is recommended that there be a second advisor for departments having less than a thousand officers but more than two or three hundred.[9] The IACP also lists the following considerations bearing on manpower needs:

1. Whether the county prosecutor's office is located in or near the police head-quarters

2. Whether assistant prosecutors have the time and willingness to discuss pending cases with arresting officers prior to trial

3. Whether the county prosecutor's office can be consulted routinely on planned enforcement actions prior to arrests

4. Whether the prosecutor's office is willing and able to draft arrest and search warrants on an around-the-clock basis

5. Whether the city attorney's staff is willing to answer routine questions

6. How promptly the city attorney responds to requests for written opinions, and how detailed these are regarding the subject matter of the inquiry

7. How vigorously the city attorney defends suits against the department and its members, and how experienced his staff is in matters of criminal law and police liability

8. Whether the staffs of the prosecutor and city attorney are full- or part-time, and whether they are permitted to practice on the side

9. The length of preservice training given the officers and the quantity and quality of in-service programs

10. The educational level of the department

11. The number of square miles in the police jurisdiction

12. The willingness of the city attorney to file suits needed by the department

13. Whether the city attorney and the county prosecutor have effective legislative programs

14. Whether specialized enforcement units like gambling and narcotics can select detectives for their ability or must accept men from a civil service detective grade

15. The average age of detectives, patrol supervisors, and commanders[10]

GOALS OF A POLICE
LEGAL ADVISOR PROGRAM

The mounting crime rate in the United States has greatly increased public demand for enforcement of the criminal law. Simultaneously, the courts have expanded their interests in law enforcement by increasing their surveillance over the procedures involved in routine police practices. As a conse-

[9] *Guidelines for a Police Legal Unit,* p. 10.
[10] *Guidelines for a Police Legal Unit,* p. 10.

quence, police tasks have become more difficult and complex as new constitutional and procedural rules govern the day-to-day conduct of police operations. Of a more pressing nature is the interpretation of these court-imposed rules that often are difficult to understand and carry out.

The police officer of today often is unable to accept the fact that, on one hand, he must maintain a balance between liberty and justice as defined by the courts, and, on the other, be a police-public relations personality in the community he serves. The police function is hindered by the persistent and even bitter cultural conflicts in our society.

Police response to the legal demands has been to provide better training in the law for its men and to sensitize them to judicial pronouncements. The police legal advisor has a key role in this effort. He is like a general who is directly responsible to the police chief and is permitted a great deal of flexibility in regard to movement and responsibility in the department. He has three major goals:

1. To assist the chief of police in formulating public policies for implementation
2. To advise the police officers assigned to the department of proper operational practices and development of legal alternatives to current police practices
3. To assist in recruit and in-service training programs and the preparation of roll call training bulletins on recent judicial decisions

The introduction of a lawyer into the law enforcement process results in a new way to familiarize officers with current trends in judicial decisions and legislative enactments, thus assisting in warding off overly restrictive court decisions.

The legal advisor also develops alternative noncriminal procedures for solving law enforcement problems usually handled by the criminal justice system. Because total enforcement of the criminal law is neither practical nor desirable, discretion in the enforcement of the law must be exercised.

Of equal importance is the absolute necessity of translating judicial decisions into workable operating procedures. A problem that impedes decision-making in this regard by policemen, prosecutors, defense attorneys, judges, and probation officers is the lack of information about the offense and the offender. The legal advisor helps by supplying this information.

Probably the most dramatic result of having a police legal advisor in a department is the increased sensitivity within the department in regard to the complexity of the law. The police officers and administrators have a place where they can seek advice and test their own judgments with that of the legal advisor. Such sensitivity quite likely results in the enormous power and responsibility of the police being exercised more effectively, efficiently, and discriminately. The advisor also provides a valuable liaison channel with the prosecution and the courts which, in many police departments, did not exist previously, or if it did, was on a superficial basis.

The qualifications for police legal advisor may vary, depending upon a particular police department, but generally are:

1. Graduation from an American Bar Association or state bar accredited law school
2. Membership in the bar of the state in which the advisor is employed
3. Possession of good moral character and professional ability
4. Possession of a minimum amount of experience in the practice of law or in related law enforcement activity as required by a particular department

NATURE AND PURPOSE OF SPECIFIC FUNCTIONS

A primary program that is of immediate interest to the prosecutor is the *protection of the constitutional rights of all citizens.* In this program, the legal advisor, through his constant observations in the police department, effects this goal by ascertaining that the department's relations with the public conform to the requirements of the law and remain cognizant of the rights of the individual citizen. In our present societal environment, the citizens are concerned with the ever-increasing crime rate and violence in the streets. They encourage direct and positive action by police officers to solve these problems. Within such circumstances lies the possibility for the police to abuse the public support they enjoy. The community must be guaranteed that its police officers will operate in a proper and legal manner. The legal advisor serves an important function in this program by constantly monitoring the departments' operations and assisting in the in-service training program to assure that the individual officer is informed of the changes in the law that bear directly upon the rights of citizens. Certainly, one ramification of this interaction between the police legal advisor and the police will be increased acceptance of the police officer by segments of the community that, in the past, have considered him indifferent to some of their rights.

A second program is *providing advice on police-related legal matters to private citizens.* The police officer may refer legal questions, which he is frequently asked while on duty, to the police legal advisors who then can either answer the question or suggest that the person contact a private attorney if the matter is significant. The officer alone cannot provide his community with the more sophisticated level of approach to police-related legal problems that it requires today.

By being available for consultation with members of the public on police-related matters, the legal advisor often is able to assist citizens in finding solutions to their problems. If nothing more, the legal advisor is able to refer indigent citizens with civil problems to the various free legal aid offices or consumer protection agencies of which the person is often unaware. The advisor also is able to answer questions regarding the carrying of weapons and their registration, operation of motor vehicles, conduct of bingo games, and various police-legal matters.

A third major area of the advisors' responsibility is *liaison with the bar and the courts.* Because the members of the bar and the courts represent a very specialized segment of the community, in the past, they have been frustrated by the lack of a legal liaison person operating within the law enforcement agency. This situation often has bred ill will on both sides. There is an overpowering need for effective communications between the police officer and members of the bar in the private sector of the community. The legal advisor is in a unique and crucial position to articulate the problems and frustrations of the police officer to the court and bar. The legal advisor can perform a valuable service by informing the police officer of legal matters in enforcement-oriented language.

A fourth major program in which the legal advisor plays a key part is *providing services to other governmental and criminal justice agencies.* As examples, only two will be mentioned, but the list is much larger. The legal advisor is intimately involved with the office of the attorney for the city, county, or region, whether this be the city attorney, county counsel, or regional general counsel. The purpose of this program is to reduce the amount of time that the office of the governmental counsel is required to spend on matters concerning the police department or other law enforcement agencies.

The legal advisor may implement this program by using several techniques such as (1) preparing requests for formal opinions of the governmental counsel, (2) consultation with the governmental counsel on civil suits involving the law enforcement department, (3) consultation on claims filed against police department officers, and (4) cooperation with the governmental counsel in drafting of proposed ordinances that will be beneficial to law enforcement.

The legal advisor is also concerned with *improvement of relations with the prosecution.* For the police department, its ultimate goal of enforcement activity is successful prosecution. However, this goal is sometimes a barrier between the prosecutor and the police department. Too often, the police officer is concerned only with the problems as they occur in the streets and consider a valid arrest to be the end of his effort. The prosecution, on the other hand, is often so involved with work in court that he fails to take notice of the problems that the police officer has. The legal advisor is able to convey these feelings to the prosecutor. If, for example, the prosecutor determines not to prosecute a case, too often the police officer is not advised in layman's language of the reason. The failure to communicate is likely to create ill will. The legal advisor can take the time to explain to the officer the reasons for the decision and, by doing so, increase the effectiveness of the individual officer's future activities.

Frequently, where an enforcement activity is questioned and ruled against by a court, the prosecution might be tempted not to appeal the decision because of overwork and understaffing. The legal advisor can help him make the decision about whether to appeal by providing appropriate justification for the particular law enforcement technique under question.

In addition to these specific programmatic responsibilities, a great deal of the legal advisor's time is devoted to a broad spectrum of duties that, for want of a better term, will be designated as the *general duties work program.* Under this broad umbrella are found the duties that take up about 75 percent of the advisor's time.

To begin with, he drafts formal requests for legal opinions as needed from the city attorney, district attorney or county prosecutor, and the state attorney general. Where appropriate, the legal advisor files a detailed memorandum of law pertaining to the subject matter of the request. He also attends all departmental staff meetings to report to the staff on legal decisions that affect day-to-day operations of the office. In addition, as he becomes more familiar with departmental procedures, he may counsel the staff on the legal aspects of problems occurring in the department.

The legal advisor is available to any member of the department for the purpose of providing guidance on field operations. He is merely to be asked and he will be present to observe any operation. As part of this duty, he maintains constant observation of all departmental procedures for the purpose of determining that they comply with existing legal requirements. He maintains constant communications with all members of the department to determine the existence of any legal problems and their solutions.

In the event of a riot, civil disturbance, or disorder, the police legal advisor is present, either at the departmental command post or in the field, for the purpose of promulgating any legal directives necessitated by the emergent situation. He often finds that he must advise the chief, his staff, and the department with respect to any court decisions or legislation having an effect on the operations, practices, and policies of the department.

The advisor is always available for consultation on specific enforcement questions such as the validity of arrests, probability of proving guilt of suspects, anticipated charges, legal methods of questioning, search and seizure, lineups, handling evidence, and similar issues. Legal research is undertaken with reference to criminal statutes, ordinances, and court decisions, as well as drafting proposed legislation that is believed to be necessary by the department. Legal memoranda are issued in answer to specific inquiries. General research is also undertaken and periodic bulletins issued to keep all personnel abreast of current and changing court decisions and criminal legislation.

In this same context, the legal advisor reviews the curriculum of the department's training academy or in-service training program and advises its supervisor on the legal aspects of the training efforts. He is available for the purpose of giving lectures to the trainees on subjects within his area of expertise. The advisor also assists the academy in obtaining the services of qualified guest instructors.

In police departments, the legal advisor almost always has the responsibility of publishing summaries of all pertinent case decisions and legislative enactments. In cooperation with the training academy, he writes and publishes a legal training bulletin for the department.

The legal advisor is available to review all proposed standard operating procedures, bulletins, and general orders prior to publication for the purpose of determining legal sufficiency. The problem of civil liability for illegal police activities is always in the background in police operations. He must constantly be aware of potential situations that may cause such liability to arise and so inform the chief. He should also bring the concept of civil liability and how it affects the efficiency of police operations into the training program.

Liaison duties are an important aspect of the general duties of the legal advisor. When necessary, he provides relevant information to the office of the county prosecutor for case preparation, and he checks on the quality of courtroom testimony of police officers for needed improvements. The police legal advisor conveys departmental policies to the prosecutor and has the reciprocal responsibility of advising the chief concerning suggestions made by the prosecutor. The legal advisor consults with the city attorney concerning legal problems within his purview, including problems of civil liability and possible judicial attacks on city ordinances. He likewise acts as the chief's legal liaison with the court system, striving to improve court-police relations, as discussed previously. When feasible, the advisor explains the rationale for a court decision to members of the department.

With the consent of the city attorney or other appropriate body, the legal advisor may file a civil action against a person for damages to police equipment. In addition, the advisor may assist municipal offices in their interactions with the police. Improvement of police relations with the bar is always pursued. Because the advisor is a member of the bar, he may seek to be put on various criminal law or procedure committees for the purpose of liaison. In appropriate cases, the legal advisor will file *amicus curiae* (friend of the court) briefs on behalf of the department. This approach will, at the least, present the police point of view to the review courts and the various bar associations.

ORGANIZATIONAL CONSIDERATIONS

Controversy may develop when consideration is being given to the operation of a police legal advisor office. Resistance usually comes from the city attorney who presents the argument that his office has exclusive responsibility for providing advice and legal assistance to the police department. However, the general duties and functions of the police are much beyond the scope and capabilities of the city attorney. For example, what city attorney could provide twenty-four hour legal advice for officers in a police department? The objections by the city attorney sometimes have caused the police legal advisor to camouflage his title by calling himself a research analyst or research director but nevertheless performing the job of a police legal advisor.[11] Neither can the prosecutor, who sometimes objects to the creation of such an office, provide adequate counsel to the police department. The President's Crime Commission noted:

> Very few prosecutors' offices endeavor systematically to provide legal counsel to the police. Save for those few departments which employ legal advisors, most police forces receive only sporadic counsel from the prosecutor's office or from individual prosecutors who have developed a special relationship with certain squads or officers. As the American Bar Foundation researchers noted:
>
>> While private counsel representing a business client would believe it to be of the utmost importance to consult fully with his client, prosecutors commonly proceed on the assumption that the police need not be consulted. A prosecutor who understood the problems of the police ... could better decide what issues are in greatest need of clarification. .... [Commonly] communications between the prosecutor and the police chief [are virtually] nonexistent.[12]

It is suggested that the police legal advisor be a civilian rather than a policeman or prosecutor because, as such, he is likely to be more sensitive to the peculiarities and needs of other such governmental agencies as welfare, education, and housing that should coordinate their efforts with law enforcement.[13]

In the police department, the legal advisor's office should be an entity and not belong to some other division, bureau, or detail, such as planning and research or training. O. W. Wilson recommends that the legal advisor report directly to the chief.[14] Most police organizations follow this advice.[15] The reasons for creating an autonomous advisory unit near the chief are: (1) On many occasions, the advisor may be called on to make decisions and issue orders in the name of the chief. For this, he must have a degree of independence and be responsible to the chief for his actions rather than to a deputy chief or commander of some lower level organization entity. (2) The breadth and scope of the advisor's duties are as complex and all-inclusive as those of an attorney. For this reason, it is unwise to narrow his scope of operations to those services provided by a single organizational component in the depart-

---

[11] *Task Force Report: The Police,* p. 67.
[12] *Task Force Report: The Police,* pp. 50–51.
[13] *Task Force Report: The Police,* pp. 50, 65.
[14] O. W. Wilson. *Police Administration,* p. 38.
[15] *Guidelines for a Police Legal Unit,* p. 9.

ment. (3) A morale problem may arise when an advisor is located in a component where his pay scale is higher than that of most of the other personnel.
Furthermore, treatment as a professional attorney may differ greatly. Con-
versely, the advisor may resent the fact that his professional legal status is
being removed or degraded by assignment to a subordinate position. (4) Communications between an attorney and his client are privileged in the rules of
evidence. The party asserting the privilege must establish that the attorney is
functioning as such. The police chief is in the role of the client. On frequent
occasions, the legal advisor will prepare confidential written materials between
the chief and himself or other officers. An attorney for the defense may move
for discovery of these in court unless the legal advisor is a police attorney and
has a legal title.

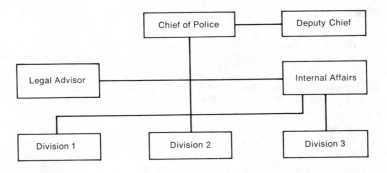

FIGURE 6–1
Location of the Police Legal Advisor in the Police Organization.

FEDERAL-LEVEL LEGAL ADVISORS

Legal advisors are found in six federal agencies: Federal Bureau of
Investigation; Bureau of Narcotics and Dangerous Drugs; Naval Investigative
Service; Alcohol, Tobacco, and Firearms Bureau of the Internal Revenue
Service; Washington, D.C., Police Department; and the Secret Service. The
functions and tasks of the advisors here are similar to those of the legal advisor
in police departments. There are some differences, however. The federal advisors primarily are concerned with the enforcement of federal statutes or regulatory rules. In order to give the reader an overview of the kinds of duties
performed by an advisor at the national level, the Secret Service has been
selected because it represents a typical law enforcement agency.[16]

[16]Letter from Robert O. Goff, Legal Counsel, The Department of the Treasury, United
States Secret Service, Washington, D.C., June 23, 1972.

The Secret Service attorney-advisor has the general responsibility for providing legal advice and counseling to Secret Service officers. He has wide latitude for the exercise of independent judgment and receives his assignments and policy guidance in general terms. His completed work is usually assumed to be accurate with regard to legal matters, such as case facts and legal citations.

The advisor is required to exercise a considerable degree of originality and initiative in handling Secret Service matters because of the uniqueness, complexity, and different legal interpretations that may be given to any factual situation. The Secret Service legal advisor confers with officials in his department, lawyers in the Department of Justice, private attorneys, and representatives of other agencies interested in, and affected by, the activities of the Secret Service.

Specific duties that the attorney-advisor performs are:

1. Preparation of correspondence answering inquiries from the public relating to counterfeiting statutes and other laws that are the responsibility of the Secret Service.

2. Preparation of memoranda on the interpretation of counterfeiting statutes and laws governing the protection of the president and other high federal government officials.

3. Informing field personnel of changes in criminal law and procedure that may affect the department's operations in discharging its obligations. He is required to keep abreast of current developments in the laws of arrest, search and seizure, confessions, criminal evidence, defendants' rights, as well as counterfeiting and related federal statutes.

4. Formulation of decisions and judgments with reference to seizure of contraband, counterfeiting paraphernalia, vehicles, vessels, and aircraft. He also examines petitions for the remission or forfeiture of counterfeiting paraphernalia seized by the department for legal sufficiency as required by law. In these cases, he prepares the necessary reports setting forth the position of the Secret Service.

5. Preparation and presentation of course outlines and classes for the Executive Protective Service Training School on the statutes and laws relating to the protection of the president and foreign embassies. As part of the duty, he keeps the Executive Protective Service informed of changes of criminal law and procedure that may affect the discharge of its duties.

6. Preparation of litigation reports and other documents at the request of the Department of Justice Civil Litigation section for the trial of civil actions involving the activities and employees of the department.

7. Investigation of formal complaints of discrimination and evaluation of affirmative action taken by the department. He serves as the advisor on the departmental body that supervises the implementation of the Equal Employment Opportunity program and, as such, lectures to Secret Service officers on their responsibilities.

8. Participation in planning decisions and judgments with reference to settlement and compromise of claims for and against the government that arise out of Secret Service activities. Review for legal sufficiency of administrating regulations, contracts, and other matters relating to the operation and administration of the service are also handled by the advisor.

As the Secret Service legal advisor, the individual is constantly relied upon for accurate, timely, and dependable advice on departmental matters assigned to him. Errors in judgment or determination of applicable legal principles could result in improper Secret Service actions and cause considerable embarrassment for the organization.

SUMMARY

The concept of the police legal advisor is not new but has only come into relatively widespread use since 1967, primarily because of the increasing complexity of the criminal laws and the efforts to which the courts have gone to ensure the protection of individual rights. Police behavior is now scrutinized at the earliest stages of the invocation of police investigation and arrest powers. To ensure increased effectiveness of the police responses, the introduction of an attorney, the police-legal advisor, into the law enforcement process is now increasing. The duties of the advisor are myriad, interesting, and crucial for the police department of today. The primary resistance to hiring legal advisors in the cities has come from the city attorney or, on occasion, the district attorney who believes that the office is an infringement on his area of responsibility. However, once the need for the advisor is established and it is shown how the advisor helps in the effective functioning of the criminal justice system, most objections can be overcome.

QUESTIONS

1. Describe the historical development of the police legal advisor.
2. Discuss the general police legal advisor manpower criteria for the various sized police departments as recommended by the President's Crime Commission.
3. The IACP suggests certain manpower considerations be kept in mind when contemplating the use of police legal advisors. What are they? Discuss them fully.
4. Discuss the general goals of a police legal advisor unit.
5. Why is it important for the police legal advisor to translate court decisions into workable police operating procedures?
6. What is probably the most dramatic result from having a police legal advisor? Discuss fully.
7. One of the specific functions of the police legal advisor is the protection of the constitutional rights of all citizens. Discuss this fully.
8. Describe some of the techniques with which the police legal advisor maintains liaison with the courts and bar.
9. "In appropriate cases the legal advisor will file *amicus curiae* (friend of the court) briefs on behalf of the department." What does this mean?
10. Discuss the various organizational considerations when a police agency contemplates hiring a police legal advisor.

FEDERAL
LAW ENFORCEMENT
AGENCIES

For those who are interested in criminal justice, jobs at the federal
level are expanding both in numbers and complexity. Changes in
laws and enactment of new laws create new enforcement, research
as well as inspection, corrections, and scientific problems. As the
federal government becomes more involved in the problems of environment,
there will have to be persons who work in the compliance and enforcement
areas of that field.

7

    This chapter will present an overview of the qualifications, kinds of jobs,
and federal agencies that utilize individuals with an education in the broad field
of criminal justice. The plan of this chapter will be to present the general
qualifications for various positions and then detail the specific requirements
and responsibilities for each position.

GENERAL REQUIREMENTS[1]

    This discussion, although it does not pertain to specific criminal justice
oriented jobs with the federal government, does establish for the student the
general guidelines and requirements for various levels of positions. Jobs with

[1]The general position requirements in this section and the specific job qualifications for
each have been derived from correspondence with personnel members of the appropriate federal
agencies as well as job announcements furnished by the agency.

the federal government are organized by grades on a general schedule with each grade (GS-1, GS-2, and so on) having certain general requirements. Salaries correspond to the requirements and increase as the grades go higher. Many of the jobs in the federal criminal justice field have special requirements. For example, a special agent for the Internal Revenue Service must have at least twelve hours of college accounting in his background. Before a person is appointed to a federal job, his qualifications are evaluated on education and experience requirements. The more qualified an applicant is, the higher the grade level he can attain.

For federal level jobs, a distinction is made between generalized and specialized experience to qualify for a particular GS rating. Generalized experience refers to a géneral background of responsible employment. Specialized experience is actual work of a particular type that provides knowledge directly applicable to the job. Based on this broad categorization, jobs in the criminal justice field are rated as follows:

GS-5 Three years of acceptable general experience or four years of college or an equivalent combination of both.

GS-6 Two years of acceptable general experience plus two years of specialized experience.

GS-7 Four years of college plus one year of graduate study or four years responsible experience or an equivalent of both.

also:

An applicant can qualify for a GS-7 in several other ways, including a high college grade point average or a high score on the written test.

GS-9 Four years of college or three years general experience or equivalent combination plus three years specialized experience or two full years of graduate study.

GS-11 Four years of college or three years of general experience or equivalent combination plus three years of specialized experience or three full years of graduate study.

GS-12 Same as GS-11, except one year of the specialized experience must be at a level comparable to the GS-11 in the federal service. The quality of the experience is important.

GS-13,14,15 Although a minimum of six years of experience or appropriate combinations of education and experience are needed, senior level applicants are evaluated on the basis of a clearly demonstrated ability to perform high level work, rather than solely on the basis of years of experience.

The job levels indicated above are to be found in all civil service positions at the federal level for positions that normally are of interest to those in criminal justice.

The following sections discuss the criminal justice functions in the major federal agencies and the kinds of personnel required. Although there may be minor modifications of the listed functions in a particular job, all types of personnel and their work in criminal justice will be presented. It should also be observed that some of the agencies, such as the FBI, do not recruit through the Civil Service Commission. This will be noted for the particular job.

DEPARTMENT OF JUSTICE

Bureau of Narcotics and Dangerous Drugs (BNDD)

A special agent of the BNDD finds a wide range of activities in which to become involved. The BNDD is responsible for enforcing registration provisions of federal drug laws. The agent is in close contact with the drug industry, from retailer to manufacturer. Enforcement of criminal provisions of the various laws requires a general knowledge of the principles of criminology and practical law enforcement at both the federal and local levels.

The agent will be required to act as an undercover agent to locate sources of illicit narcotics traffic and illegal distribution of dangerous drugs. A knowledge of the powers of arrest, searches, and seizures will be developed. In addition, there is always the opportunity to use both traditional and new enforcement procedures and to gain experience before federal and local courts.

The BNDD special agent will be required to participate in public education on the drug and narcotics problem with a large number of civic groups who are deeply interested in the social problems created by drug and narcotic abuse. He is, in fact, a valuable and valued member of the community dedicated to the eradication of drug and narcotic abuse and the protection of all persons against its consequences.

The Job of BNDD Compliance Investigator. In addition to the BNDD special agent, one of the most challenging jobs with the bureau is that of compliance investigator. This position, along with that of the special agent, is the backbone of the bureau. Compliance investigators conduct industry audits to assure that controls on production and distribution of narcotics and dangerous drugs into legitimate channels are adequate to prevent diversion. This requires initial on-site study of official records to determine that incoming raw materials, production records, and shipping documents are consistent and that physical security is sufficient. Alertness is required to spot any evidence of falsification or manipulation of records, dual sets of books, or use of control documents other than those expressly authorized by the company.

Formal reports of an investigation must be well documented and supplemented by exhibits substantiating conclusions reached, because they may be used as government evidence in court trials and administrative hearings. Compliance investigators will be required to testify in a professional manner at court trials and administrative hearings. As circumstances dictate, investigators are required to maintain liaison and work closely with state and other federal agencies who have related interests and common regulatory responsibilities.

Shortly after employment, compliance investigators undergo a formalized training program at the BNDD's National Training Institute in Washington, D.C. The training involves investigative techniques, drug pharmacology, drug abuse education, drug identification, legal procedures, industrial security, manufacturing techniques, and physical training.

Compliance investigators are hired at GS-5, 7, and 9. Promotions are likely to be rapid. (See page 138.)

Border Patrol Agents

The entrance grade for border patrol agents is GS-7, with appointments made from a list of eligibles established as a result of a competitive civil service examination given for the position. The U.S. Border Patrol is located in the Immigration and Naturalization Service, (INS), an agency in the Department of Justice. The INS is responsible for administering the immigration and naturalization laws of the United States. Its officers serve throughout the United States and at stations found in Europe, Bermuda, Nassau, Puerto Rico, Canada, Mexico, and the Philippines. INS officers perform a wide variety of duties including (1) investigations, (2) detecting law violations, (3) determining whether aliens may enter the country or may remain here, (4) collecting and evaluating evidence, (5) adjudicating applications for benefits, such as petitions for visas, and (6) presiding over or presenting the government's cases at various hearings. Additionally, the INS officer prevents illegal entrance of aliens into the United States and makes recommendations to the courts in such matters as petitions for citizenship.

New officers enter the INS through appointment to the position of border patrol agent in the INS Border Patrol. Its principal purpose is the prevention of smuggling and illegal entry of aliens into the United States and the initiation of departure of aliens illegally in this country.

Border patrol agents are assigned along international boundaries and coastal areas. They also may be assigned to areas within the country. A sampling of the law enforcement functions of the agent include:

1. Patrolling areas to apprehend persons seen crossing the border
2. Stopping vehicles on highways and inquiring about the citizenship of the occupants
3. Inspecting and searching trains, buses, airplanes, ships, and terminals to detect aliens entering the country illegally

4. Checking the citizenship and immigration status of farm and ranch workers
5. Apprehending and interrogating persons suspected of violating immigration laws
6. Performing other duties to enforce the immigration and naturalization laws
7. Ability to apply criminal law
8. Competence in field evidence
9. Understanding of court procedure
10. Enforcing the Immigration and Naturalization Service regulations
11. Ability to speak the Spanish language
12. Fingerprinting
13. Report writing
14. Marksmanship
15. Caring for and using firearms
16. Judo

The beginning agent is appointed at GS-7 and attends three months of intensive training. Each agent serves a one-year probationary period. The journeyman grade level is GS-11.

Immigration Inspector

Also in the INS is the position of immigration inspector. These positions start at the GS-5 level. The incumbent has the responsibility of detecting people who are in violation of immigration and nationality laws. The inspector works with border patrolmen and other investigators and determines through interview and evidence whether an applicant may enter the United States. The work may be hazardous, as when dealing with dangerous criminals. Most of the agents' posts are located in small communities.

Federal Bureau of Investigation (FBI)

Within the FBI are numerous functions in the criminal justice field. The FBI is an investigative agency charged with the detection of those who break any of many different laws of the United States, including such crimes as kidnapping, extortion, and bank robbery. In all, the bureau has jurisdiction over some 185 investigative matters. It is also responsible for protecting the security of the United States and ferreting out subversive activities, spies, and saboteurs.

All of the investigative work in the FBI is performed by special agents. There are, however, many other law enforcement related functions performed by persons with specialized skills: fingerprint technicians, translators, photographers, and laboratory technicians. Additionally, there are numerous administrative and clerical positions in the bureau.

Special Agents. The special agent is not a civil service position. All appointments are made on a probationary basis that may become permanent upon satisfactory completion of a one-year period. Each special agent must complete a fourteen week training course at the FBI Headquarters in Washington, D.C. and the FBI Academy at Quantico, Virginia. Upon successful completion, the agent is assigned to one of about sixty field offices in the United States.

Among the qualifications are general physical requirements, but education is pertinent at this point. The applicant must be a:

1. Graduate from a state-accredited resident law school. Such graduates must have completed successfully at least two years of resident undergraduate college work; or,

2. Graduate from a resident four-year college with a major in accounting with at least one year of practical accounting or auditing experience; or,

3. A person who meets qualifications set out under FBI special considerations. The bureau presently is considering special agent positions for applicants possessing a four-year resident college degree with a major in a physical science, fluency in a foreign language that the bureau needs, or three years of specialized experience of a professional, executive, or complex investigative nature. No assurance can be given that this category will remain in effect.

Translators. The FBI employs translators who are thoroughly qualified in more than one foreign language, generally romance, germanic, and Slavic. The position requires a knowledge of three or more languages. The translator must be able to translate successfully and interpret correctly both into and from English.

Photographers. The FBI photographer must be knowledgeable in the areas of camera equipment, contact printing, enlarging, filter work, and lighting effects. He must have three years experience and a general knowledge of chemicals used in making developers and other formulas.

Laboratory Positions. The FBI laboratory makes extensive use of employees to assist chemists, physicists, metallurgists, document examiners, cryptanalysts, and other scientific examiners. Such positions require specific scientific backgrounds, and the higher grades generally require both experience and degrees in science from recognized colleges and universities.

Bureau of Prisons

The Bureau of Prisons was established in 1930 by congressional legislation that directed the bureau to develop an integrated system of institutions that would provide custody and treatment based on the individual needs of the offender.

Subsequent legislation approved open camps for inmates, employment of prisoners on military reservations, construction of numerous facilities, and a program of diversified industrial employment within the institutions.

As the Bureau of Prisons entered its fifth decade of service, it was faced with some serious problems, as pointed out by the President's Commission on Law Enforcement and Administration of Justice and the Joint Commission on Correctional Manpower and Training. In 1969, the president of the United States issued a directive to improve the federal correctional system and have it serve as a model for state and local systems. The ten-year plan included thirteen points:

1. Develop a ten-year plan for reforming correctional activities.

2. Explore the feasibility of pooling the limited resources of several governmental units in order to set up specialized regional treatment facilities.

3. Give special emphasis to programs for juvenile offenders.

4. Expedite the design and construction of a federal psychiatric study and treatment facility for.mentally disturbed and violent offenders.

5. Develop recommendations for revising the federal laws relating to the handling of the mentally incompetent charged with a federal crime, serving a sentence for a federal crime, or found not guilty solely because of a mental condition.

6. Expedite the planning and construction of federal demonstration centers for urban areas that would provide comprehensive, community-oriented facilities replacing the traditional jails.

7. Expand the federal program of technical assistance in corrections to state and local governments.

8. Provide new vocational, educational, and employment opportunities for persons on probation, in prison, and on parole, enlisting the cooperation of private agencies.

9. Expand training programs for correctional personnel at the federal, state, and local level.

10. Study the feasibility of making the federal correctional system more effective through closer coordination of existing programs.

11. Expand the use of *half-way house* community treatment centers to include offenders on probation and parole, and assist in the development of similar programs at state and local levels.

12. Institute a comprehensive program of research, experimentation, and evaluation of correctional methods.

13. Coordinate and consolidate correctional programs among federal agencies.

Correctional Officer. The function of the correctional officer is especially important in the federal criminal justice system. Although the functions may vary, they remain very similar to the state and local levels. The correctional officer is, in effect, the mainstay of the corrections system. He enforces the rules and regulations governing the operations of a correctional institution and is responsible for the confinement, safety, health, and protection of inmates. On occasion, this requires arduous physical activity to control inmates.

The officer supervises work assignments of inmates and counsels them on personal and family goals and problems. He is a member of the treatment team of social workers, psychiatrists, psychologists, teachers, and others working to modify the behavior of the individual offender.

One of the greatest opportunities of the correctional officer is to assist in the social change of offenders. He exerts considerable influence over the committed offender. Through constant contact, the correctional officer has the opportunity to demonstrate the habits and traits that are necessary for adjustment to society. In addition, he can encourage work habits and skills that are necessary in maintaining a job. Women also are employed as correctional officers in the Bureau of Prisons.

The beginning correctional officer is employed at the GS-6 level. In order to be so employed, however, an applicant must show that he has a minimum of three and a half years experience in one or more of the following fields:

1. Supervisory or leadership experience
2. Teaching or instructing, especially with adults or advanced groups
3. Enforcement of rules or regulations relating to safety, health, or protection
4. Rehabilitation or corrections
5. Counseling in a welfare or social agency
6. Interviewing and counseling
7. Sales work involving extensive person-to-person relationships

Educational Requirements. Education successfully completed in an accredited college, university, or resident school above the high-school level may be substituted, as indicated below:

1. Two years of study successfully completed in a resident school above high school may be substituted for general experience.
2. Successful completion of a full four-year course of college study may be substituted for three years of general experience.
3. One full semester of graduate study in correctional administration, criminology, penalogy, sociology, or social work successfully completed in an accredited college or university may be substituted for six months of general experience and is fully qualifying for grade GS-6.

Correctional Treatment Specialist. Correctional treatment specialists perform many of the functions that also are assigned to social workers. The primary difference for beginning positions is that a correctional treatment specialist can be appointed with a bachelor's degree that has included twenty-four semester hours of course work in the social sciences, but a social worker must have a master's degree in social work. Social workers also are assigned to supervisory roles, including the training of students in graduate study programs in social work and the social sciences.

Approximately one hundred thirty treatment specialists are assigned to a wide variety of correctional institutions, including major penitentiaries, juvenile and youth offender institutions, narcotic rehabilitation units, correctional facilities for women, medical centers, and community treatment centers. They work with the Bureau of Prisons, D.C. Department of Corrections, and for the U.S. Parole Board.

Correctional treatment has its own particular challenge. As one specialist remarked, "My clients are here by court order, not because they choose to be." The work often consists of intra-institutional and community contacts designed to aid in correcting offenders. They must deal with many types of offenders, including first commitments, mentally and emotionally ill, major custody risks, sex offenders, and notorious criminals.

Many kinds of programs and approaches are used by correctional treatment specialists to solve problems in which they are involved. For example, a federal reformatory was experiencing considerable friction between staff and inmates, including problems of interracial relationships. A comprehensive training program for seventy-two staff members and fifty-four inmates was developed that included *sensitivity* and *encounter* concepts. Correctional treatment specialists contributed to the success of this program that resulted in a better working relationship in the institution.

Correctional treatment specialists continually are called upon to involve the community in the treatment processes and to counsel state and local governments on treatment practices.

United States Marshals

United States Marshals are appointed by the President by and with the advice and consent of the Senate for each of the 93 judicial districts except the Virgin Islands where the Marshal is appointed by the Attorney General. They are appointed for a term of four years except in the Canal Zone where the term is eight years.

The authority of United States Marshals extends to all areas of federal law enforcement except those delegated by law to other federal agencies. United States Marshals execute lawful orders and commands of the federal courts and the United States; serve process issued by Congressional Committees and government agencies and by federal courts on behalf of the United States and private litigants; attend sessions of the district courts and courts of appeals, when so required; handle juries; and protect witnesses, judges, and others when necessary. They arrest, guard, and transport federal prisoners, seize, guard, and sell, or otherwise dispose of personal or real property pursuant to federal court orders; and serve as disbursing officers for the Department of Justice and the United States courts. Marshals sometimes face danger in the performance of their duties. Most notable are the dangers they bravely faced in enforcing federal court orders issued in civil rights suits in the past few years in such places as Little Rock, Arkansas; New Orleans, Louisiana; Montgomery and Selma, Alabama; and Oxford, Mississippi.

The Executive Office for United States Marshals, directed by the Chief Marshal, provides general executive direction and assistance to all Marshals' offices, and serves as liaison between those offices, elements of the Department of Justice and other federal agencies.

Deputy United States Marshals

These officers are immediately subordinate to the United States marshal. The deputy occupies a job that is primarily law enforcement oriented, rather than investigative. He serves processes, makes arrests, transports prisoners, seizes and disposes of property under court orders, maintains order in federal court rooms, protects key figures in court cases, and prepares vouchers, reports, and correspondence. The deputy marshal is a civil service position with appointment based upon competitive examination. The entry level is grade GS-6.

In the Department of Justice are several divisions that are important and involve functions and operations in the total criminal justice system.

Criminal Division

The Criminal Division has general direction and supervision over the enforcement of more than nine hundred federal criminal statutes with responsibility extending to all federal violations except for a small number of specialized criminal statutes assigned to other divisions. The Criminal Division also handles civil matters that are closely related to its criminal jurisdiction, principally those covered by the Immigration and Naturalization laws, extradition proceedings, and seizure actions under the Federal Food, Drug, and Cosmetics Act.

The Organized Crime and Racketeering Section. Largest of the division's seven operating sections, it coordinates the government's fight against organized crime. The section was established in 1954 by the then attorney general, Herbert Brownell, Jr. The section has grown and the scope of its work expanded as further recognition has been gained of the extent of syndicated crime and its national significance.

The program of this section has two basic thrusts. First, the section receives, analyzes, and correlates a mass of intelligence information submitted to it by at least twenty-six federal investigative agencies as well as various local law enforcement sources. This intelligence has enabled the section to determine the structure of the principal criminal organizations and their fluid interrelationships. Major racketeers have been identified and their positions in the crime hierarchy charted.

The second aspect of the war on organized crime is the actual use of the accumulated data to prosecute the offenders. Specific investigations are initiated to determine violations of federal criminal laws by these individuals. The section has successfully prosecuted not only leading figures—such as Raymond Patriarca, reputedly the head of Cosa Nostra in New England—but large numbers of their lesser associates. New legislation and new knowledge have made possible a massive drive on organized crime. The recent development of the strike force technique, which combines the efforts of several federal investigative agencies under the direction of veteran section prosecutors in those areas of the nation in which organized crime is most prevalent, has proved to be a highly effective weapon. In 1968, more than eleven hundred individuals were indicted under racketeering statutes, compared to nineteen, eight years earlier; more than five hundred racketeers were sentenced, compared to forty-five in 1960.

The Administrative Regulations Section. This section supervises the enforcement of the statutes through which federal departments and agencies regulate private activity. Prominent in the scope of its jurisdiction are prosecutions under the Federal Food, Drug, and Cosmetic Act; customs violations; Selective Service offenses; and violations of the immigration and naturalization laws.

The General Crimes Section. Its jurisdiction includes the many offenses against the integrity or the operations of government and the courts, common crimes on federal property, and statutory offenses, such as interstate auto theft, kidnapping, and bank robbery.

The Fraud Section. Supervises and assists in the enforcement of a broad range of criminal statutes proscribing fraud against the government, and commercial frauds affecting private parties that involve the use of the mails or facilities of interstate commerce. These include violations of the securities acts, bankruptcy frauds, mail frauds, election frauds, and banking violations.

The Narcotic and Dangerous Drug Section. Supervises and assists in the enforcement of statutes pertaining to narcotics and to those drugs classified as dangerous. This section also has supervisory jurisdiction over litigation to condemn vehicles and other property forfeited as a result of violations of federal liquor, narcotics, and gambling laws.

Other sections handle appeals, legislation, and many special projects associated with the responsibility for the administration of federal criminal laws and criminal justice.

Office of Criminal Justice

The Office of Criminal Justice was established in 1964 in the office of the deputy attorney general. In 1969, its function was reoriented and its status upgraded when it was placed under the direction of the associate deputy attorney general for the administration of criminal justice, a newly created position. The mission of this small staff office is to assist the attorney general in the overall direction of the criminal justice responsibilities of the department. It has both a criminal justice planning and implementation function. It works with the judiciary, the bar, the law enforcement and corrections agencies, law schools, and the criminal justice research community.

The office coordinates and implements special presidential criminal justice programs that cut across department components or affect interdepartmental responsibilities. The office uses expert personnel both within and outside the department to design action programs. Early in 1969, the office was charged with the implementation of the president's eleven-point program for curbing crime in the District of Columbia, including court reorganization, bail and correctional system reform, expansion of the Washington, D.C. Metropolitan Police Department and United States attorney's office, and reform of narcotics and juvenile law enforcement.

In the past, the office assisted in planning for the National and D.C. Crime Commission, for the Law Enforcement Assistance Act of 1965, and the Omnibus Crime Control and Safe Streets Act of 1968 which established the Law Enforcement Assistance Administration in the department. It helped implement and it oversees the operation of the Bail Reform Act of 1966, and it continually studies (in conjunction with the Judicial Conference of the United States), and proposes amendments to the Criminal Justice Act of 1964.

The office analyzes the performance of the criminal justice system, affording its expertise and advice to the attorney general and deputy attorney general in their policy-making roles. It evaluates criminal justice objectives, identifies problems and their tractability, plans a course of action consistent with fiscal constraints, executes or assists others in executing the plan, reviews the effectiveness of actions taken, and proposes plan adjustments to improve performance. The office's analytic role is oriented to action: legislation, demonstration projects, conferences, revision of policy, and experimentation throughout the system. Illustrative of some outputs of the office are:

1. Its publication, *Criminal Justice in a Metropolitan Court* (1966)—analysis of the processing of criminal cases in the District of Columbia Court of General Sessions

2. Development of a criminal process curriculum for Southwestern Police Academy

3. Development of procedures for administering justice during civil disorders

4. Development of planning standards, with LEAA, to assist comprehensive law enforcement planning by states and localities

5. Liaison with such departments as Treasury; Health, Education, and Welfare; Labor; and Housing and Urban Development regarding interrelated programs for crime reduction

6. Production of substantial proposals of major court reorganization in the District of Columbia and for significant revision of the federal bail law

Law Enforcement Assistance Administration

The Law Enforcement Assistance Administration (LEAA) was created by the Omnibus Crime Control and Safe Streets Act of 1968 to help improve the nation's criminal justice system—police, courts, and corrections.

A major responsibility of LEAA is the award of financial grants to assist all of the states—and cities and counties within the states—to strengthen their law enforcement and anticrime programs.

The goal of this federal partnership with state and local governments is to make the United States safer and more just for all of its people.

Prior to passage of the Omnibus Crime Control Act in June, 1968, no national strategy existed to fight crime, and most states had no statewide planning or anticrime programs. However, within a year after enactment, a national strategy did evolve. LEAA awarded a total of $19 million in planning grants to the fifty states, Washington, D.C., Puerto Rico, and the Virgin Islands for planning comprehensive law enforcement improvements. The states then began submitting their plans, and action grants were awarded to carry them out.

The action grant funds for fiscal 1969, the program's first year, totaled $29 million. Most of that, about $25 million, was for the states. The remainder was for LEAA to award at its own discretion for a variety of priority projects.

The act specifies that the states receive block grants. Each state must, in turn, make 40 percent of its planning funds and 75 percent of its action funds available to city and county governments.

Action funds may be used for a wide variety of purposes: programs for public protection, including development of new methods and equipment;

recruitment and training of police and corrections personnel; public education programs relating to crime prevention; construction of facilities for the criminal justice system programs to combat organized crime; police salaries; programs for prevention and control of civil disorders; improvement of corrections facilities; new programs for rehabilitation of offenders; programs for improvement of court systems; and police-community relations projects.

State and local governments provide matching funds under several different formulas.

One of the major divisions of the LEAA is the Office of Law Enforcement Programs, which administers the block grant program. It also includes programs in which LEAA experts give assistance to state and local enforcement agencies in such fields as organized crime, civil disorders, corrections, and a variety of police functions.

Another major division is the National Institute of Law Enforcement and Criminal Justice, the research body of LEAA. It sponsors and conducts research on such things as the causes of crime and means of prevention, new techniques for quicker detection and apprehension of offenders, management of the criminal justice system, rehabilitation of offenders, development of new equipment.

The Academic Assistance Division of LEAA gives funds to colleges and universities that, in turn, award grants and loans for degree studies by law enforcement and corrections personnel and other promising students preparing for careers in those fields.

The LEAA is under the general authority of the attorney general. The agency is directed by an administrator and two associate administrators, who are appointed by the president and must be confirmed by the Senate. The act specifies that no more than two of the three administrators may be from the same political party.

The Department of Justice is also composed of the following offices that are intimately involved with the day-to-day operations of the criminal justice system: (1) deputy attorney; (2) solicitor general; (3) assistant attorneys general that include the antitrust, civil, civil rights, internal security, land and natural resources, office of legal counsel, tax, and administrative divisions; (4) board of immigration appeals; (5) board of parole; (6) community relations service; and (7) pardon attorney.

DEPARTMENT OF THE TREASURY

In 1775, the first United States currency was printed. Shortly afterward, the Department of the Treasury was formed. From a handful of persons, the department has grown to over a hundred thousand employees throughout the world. As the department's responsibilities have grown, so has the need for effective law enforcement. The curtailment of counterfeiting, tax fraud, and illicit distilleries; the prevention and detection of smuggling; the protection of the president and his family; and countless other vital enforcement activities have become the responsibility of more than five thousand Treasury enforcement agents. These personnel are found in the Bureau of Customs; Alcohol, Tobacco, and Firearms Division; Internal Security; Intelligence; and the Secret Service. The enforcement officers are known as Treasury enforcement agents.

Treasury Enforcement Agent

A new Treasury enforcement agent quickly steps into a carefully planned training and development program emphasizing investigative and law enforcement techniques and the special skills and knowledge related to the branch he has joined. He joins with agents from the other branches of the Department at the Treasury Law Enforcement School for approximately six weeks of intensive, highly specialized training in basic investigative and law enforcement techniques. There, under skilled instructors, he will study such subjects as rules of evidence, surveillance techniques, incognito operations, courtroom demeanor and the use of firearms.

This classroom work will be supplemented by continued training on the job and in class, carefully planned to sharpen his professional skills and develop his ability to perform work of greater responsibility. This additional training varies, depending upon the type of enforcement work the agent will do.

Alcohol, Tobacco, and Firearms Special Investigator

Special investigators of the Alcohol, Tobacco and Firearms Division of the Internal Revenue Service have an exciting and challenging job within the federal law enforcement community. Operating from more than two hundred offices throughout the United States, special investigators are dedicated to providing assistance to other federal, state, and local law enforcement officials in their fight against crime and violence.

The *revenooer,* as he has come to be known, is responsible for the investigation, detection, and prevention of violations of the liquor, explosives, and firearms laws. These agents are called upon to perform a variety of investigation and enforcement duties, ranging from raiding a distillery to preparing material for court proceedings.

The illicit distillery operators are often clever and hardened criminals. Their arrest and apprehension may involve years of dangerous and strenuous work including extended surveillance of suspected criminals and the use of modern scientific equipment.

Agents have masqueraded as criminals for months at a time in order to carry out their assignments. On occasion, the agent also investigates reputable distilleries, breweries, and manufacturers, to ensure compliance with laws concerning alcohol and tobacco products. An agent comes into contact with a variety of people, ranging from executives of a large company and mob bosses to small-town storekeepers and petty moonshiners.

Special investigators also enforce federal laws relating to the sale, transfer, manufacture, importation, and possession of firearms and explosives. Investigations may go from checking the background of an applicant for a firearms or explosives license to one involving the illegal acquisition of fully automatic or other gangster-type weapons for use in furthering illegal purposes. Investigators inspect firearms licensees' records to ensure compliance with firearms laws and to obtain evidence of unlawful acts by licensees and/or purchasers of firearms or explosives. Special investigators must develop an extensive knowledge of firearms and explosives so they can classify weapons according to laws and regulations. They must maintain close liaison and working relationships with other federal, state, and local law enforcement agencies to assure maximum enforcement of the laws at all levels of government.

The special investigator's job is diversified, challenging, and anything but routine. The alcohol, tobacco, and firearms special investigator is devoted to strict law enforcement and the hard but exciting work that goes with it.

Alcohol and Tobacco Tax Inspectors

The alcohol and tax inspectors are involved in the day-to-day government supervision of facilities that produce, process, or distribute industrial alcohol, alcoholic beverages, tobacco products, and related industry products. Their job includes spot-checking the records system, interviewing people, and examining operations.

Bureau of Customs Special Agent

Smugglers have gone modern. The hollow shoe heel has been replaced by the imported car tire, but ingenious as the smuggler may be, he is confronted by the special agent of the Bureau of Customs.

These agents make certain that the government gets its revenue on incoming goods, and that narcotics, drugs, and defense materials neither enter nor leave our borders illegally.

The Bureau of Customs special agent pits intelligence and courage against a group of devious and clever criminals. A network of highly trained investigators spans ocean and continent to prevent and detect attempts to defraud the country at its borders and ports. The special agent in today's customs service must employ every modern detection device to intercept resourceful criminals and detect improper claims, undervaluation of merchandise, and other frauds against the Treasury. The agent also is in a prime position to aid in curtailing illicit drug traffic.

Customs Inspectors

Customs inspectors check cargo, baggage, mail, and articles worn by people entering or leaving the United States, in an effort to prevent smuggling and illegal importing or exporting of merchandise. The work involves continual contact with travelers, importers, crew members, and carrier employees.

Import Specialists

Bureau of Customs import specialists are specifically trained in examining commercial shipments. They must be well versed in the complex aspects of a product that may affect the duty to be paid on it.

Customs Patrol Officers

The Bureau of Customs patrol officers maintain uniformed and plain clothes surveillance at docks and airports to prevent pilferage of cargo. The job performed is similar to that of the municipal police patrolman.

Customs Security Officers

Customs security officers or *Sky Marshals* are newcomers on the scene, the result of the great number of aircraft highjackings beginning in the latter part of the 1960s. These personnel are assigned to detect and prevent criminal acts, including highjacking, at major gateway airports and during flights. The work requires a great deal of travel but is a valuable and worthwhile kind of position.

Internal Security Inspectors

Internal security inspectors make up the Internal Revenue Service's own investigative unit. They aid the entire service by investigating prospective IRS employees and by investigating information and allegations concerning serious misconduct or illegal activities involving Service employees or outside parties.

Because the United States tax system depends on the honesty and integrity of its citizenry, the Internal Revenue Service must maintain the highest standards of character and integrity among its employees. The security inspector accomplishes an important part of this vital mission by conducting background investigations of prospective and new employees so the service and the public can be assured that only persons of high integrity are employed.

The internal security inspector must be alert to discover or act upon information or allegations that may involve serious misconduct or illegal activity on the part of employees.

On occasion, a dishonest taxpayer or other person may seek to gain improper advantage by attempting to bribe or otherwise corrupt an employee to commit crimes against the United States government through its revenue system. If a prospective employee has established an integrity pattern below the high standards demanded of service employees, or if an employee is vulnerable to temptations or proffers to defraud the revenue, the reputation and integrity of the entire service, as well as his own, could be in jeopardy. For this reason, the work of the internal security inspector involves as much prevention as cure. By careful preliminary investigation, only persons of suitability are appointed to positions of trust.

The internal security inspector may be called upon to conduct all phases of investigative work. Inspectors must nip illegality in the bud, remove doubts, resolve accusations, and get the facts.

Internal Revenue Agents

The Internal Revenue agents are essentially professional accountants who examine taxpayers' accounting records and investigate other sources required to determine correct federal tax liabilities. Progressively more difficult assignments and training opportunities in the higher positions develop the need for greater and more varied skills. The IRS agent can move into specializations such as fraud investigation, internal audits, and appeal adjudication.

Internal Revenue Service Special Agents, Intelligence Division

The special agent of the Internal Revenue Service's Intelligence Division investigates the facts in cases involving tax fraud and other related criminal violations. This may take an agent into many paths, from examining books in the back room of a tiny cigar store to interviewing the president of a state's largest corporation. Following hours, days, or weeks of investigation, it would be the agent who makes the report that serves as the basis for the government's prosecution in a federal fraud case. The special agent assists the United States Attorney and is often the government's key witness in prosecution cases.

The work of the special agent is unique in the field of criminal investigations. Unlike the usual criminal offense that involves a single instrument of crime such as a murder weapon and frequently is a single occurrence, tax frauds often involve violations that consist of many acts committed over a period of years.

The investigation is complicated by the vast number and variety of past business transactions, the varied methods of evasion, and the voluminous records that must be analyzed. No book entry can be accepted at face value; the special agent checks accounting transactions behind all suspected entries and obtains corroborating statements, evidence, and records. Special agents must interview persons in all walks of life, many of whom will be reticent, openly hostile, or previously persuaded by the taxpayer to give false testimony. Agents are highly skilled in the techniques of surveillance of racketeers, interrogating suspects and witnesses, making arrests, and participating in raids.

Secret Service Special Agent

The responsibilities of the Secret Service are twofold: protective and investigative.

The protection of the president of the United States, a duty performed since 1901, is its primary responsibility. Since that time, Congress has assigned other protective duties, so that today the Secret Service provides protection for members of the immediate family of the president, the vice president, the president-elect, the vice president-elect, former presidents, and major presidential candidates during presidential campaigns.

The Secret Service also is charged with the responsibility of suppressing the counterfeiting of United States currency and other securities, the purpose for which the service was established in 1865. The effectiveness of the Secret Service in this phase of its operation is measured by the small loss sustained by the public from counterfeit money.

In addition, the Secret Service conducts the investigation of thousands of forged government checks and bonds, leading to the arrest of persons responsible for these crimes. The Secret Service agent participates in raids and apprehends and arrests persons suspected of offenses against the counterfeiting and forgery laws. He also locates persons wanted as witnesses or accomplices.

Secret Service Document Analyst

The Secret Service document analyst conducts examinations and analyses that include: (1) resolving questions about alterations where skillful efforts have been made to conceal their presence; (2) developing evidence to establish the genuineness of a signature or to expose evidence of forgery and show the identity of the forger; (3) studying a variety of elements of documents, including watermarks, ink, and paper.

The analyst testifies in court or gives depositions that might be used in criminal or civil proceedings in connection with cases that are typical of the difficulty at this level and prepares to withstand rigorous cross-examination.

Secret Service Fingerprint Examiner
(Ninyhdrin Specialist)

The fingerprint examiner makes identification of latent fingerprints and compares them with prints of individuals already on file.

He prepares necessary photographic reproductions of fingerprints and documents, makes photographic charts of fingerprints, and prepares evidence to be used as exhibits in courts of law.

The examiner conducts examination of documents to find, and make intelligible, indented writing and makes necessary photographs of this writing using complex photographic and lighting techniques. He also consults with expert photographers and develops new methods of photographing latent fingerprints.

The fingerprint examiner prepares detailed laboratory reports on his examination and testifies as an expert witness as to his conclusions and opinions in courts of law.

Executive Protective Service

The protection of the White House buildings that house the presidential offices, the president, and his family; foreign embassies in Washington, D.C.; and other places directed by the president is the responsibility of the uniformed Executive Protective Service. Its officers are not subject to civil service testing but must pass a written test and pass a strict physical examination administered by the U.S. Secret Service.

Bureau of Engraving and Printing

Although the security investigators employed by the Bureau of Engraving and Printing maintain liaison with representatives of private investigative, municipal, and law enforcement agencies on personnel matters of mutual concern, the investigators are primarily engaged in personnel and plant security. Their duties include the conduct of investigations of bureau job applicants, incumbents, and nongovernment personnel from a standpoint of industrial security suitability for assignment and/or employment by, or in, the bureau; and direct and/or conduct investigations involving special inquiries, various administrative matters, thefts, and other criminal offenses. They also are responsible for conducting surveys to determine the adequacy of existing security measures and to ensure continued effectiveness of plant security controls.

In practically all of the criminal justice oriented positions in the Treasury Department, competitive civil service examinations are mandatory, with appointments made from registers of eligibles. The starting grade for most of the jobs is at the GS-5 or GS-7 level.

DEPARTMENT OF TRANSPORTATION

Federal Highway Administration

The Federal Highway Administration (FHWA) is primarily a civil engineering organization that works in cooperation with state highway departments in building and improving the nation's highways. The FHWA does, however, employ investigators who plan and conduct investigations of allegations of irregularities, fraud, land speculation, bribery, and so on, on the part of FHWA employees, state and other political personnel, or any violation or noncompliance with the requirements of legislation and administrative rules and regulations pertaining to programs administered by FHWA. It also employs highway safety specialists who check on drivers' qualifications and their hours of service on the road, analyze accident reports, make carrier and vehicle inspections, control the movement of such dangerous cargoes as explosives, and conduct demonstration clinics on safety.

National Highway
Traffic Safety Administration

In the National Highway Traffic Safety Administration (NHTSA), the Traffic Regulations and Adjudication Division is responsible for developing and improving highway traffic safety program standards relating to police traffic services, traffic law enforcement, accident investigation, codes and laws, and adjudication.

One position in the NHTSA that is available to criminal justice-educated personnel is the highway safety management assistant. The incumbent is successively assigned to the several offices of the traffic safety programs where he performs tasks selected, in part, to familiarize him with the program activities of the office and to provide experience in formulating judgments on simple program matters when precedents are available. Such work includes drafting responses to written inquiries on substantive program matters after discussion with program specialists and review of program materials in the office; assisting program specialists on projects by compiling and summarizing data, developing charts and graphs; and preparing initial drafts of reports relating to the program of the office to which assigned. This person is requested to have college or higher educational achievement with study relating to evaluation and analysis of problem aspects in traffic safety activities.

DEPARTMENT OF AGRICULTURE

Department of Agriculture
Criminal Investigator

Within the Department of Agriculture is the Office of the Inspector General. One of the criminal justice oriented positions in the department is that of the criminal investigator.

This position is located in a regional office of the Office of the Inspector General (OIG). The Office of the Inspector General has responsibility for (1) developing, directing, and carrying out a broad comprehensive program of internal audit (including appraisal of all department programs and activities), and audit of all external activities over which the department has jurisdiction; (2) investigating all personnel and program irregularities, violations of laws administered by the department, and other matters of interest to the department for which it has responsibility; and (3) providing appropriate audit and investigative services to agency heads and staff offices of the department.

The criminal investigator independently carries out a variety of investigative, compliance, and operational survey assignments of highly complex and difficult nature relating either to a large number of the department's programs within his assigned region or, on a nationwide basis, to segments of special assignments programmed from the national headquarters office. These assignments may involve activities in which prescribed or standard procedures, methods, techniques, precedents, and practices require broad adaptations.

He makes recommendations to his superiors regarding formulation, development, and revision of investigation policies, programs, standards, requirements, methods, procedures, precedents, and techniques. The investigator participates in technical aspects of training conferences, workshops, and so on, as required.

The incumbent independently plans, conducts, or is responsible for directing complete investigations of matters relating to various organizations and programs of the department, including transactions of its agents, contractors, and cooperating state and local agencies and others, and of functional programs or activities that cross agency lines. He conducts investigations of regional, interregional, or nationwide character. These investigations are wide in scope and diversity and may be such that interrelationships are difficult to establish; or a large number of separate and distinct matters may grow out of the original case assignment; or they may involve a high degree of sensitivity or controversy. Assignments involve: (1) responsibility for investigative problems of a highly complex nature that require discovering and developing sources of information; obtaining facts or evidence; anticipating and coping with emergency situations; and preventing invalidation of the government's position; (2) dealing with circumstances involving delicate matters having significant political, economic, or social implications; (3) handling unusual situations or unexpected developments that require informed interpretation of basic guides, procedures, and techniques, and demand a great deal of ingenuity, resourcefulness, and creative thinking.

The investigator also is assigned to cases where a high degree of personal responsibility in overcoming hostility is needed and person-to-person relationships are important. He formally testifies to, or advises others on, investigation findings. He carries out cooperative investigations with other agencies. When assigned, he assists or directs others in providing assistance on program audits, surveys, special studies, and so on, where investigative techniques are required. He also appears as a government witness or representative before courts or grand juries in connection with matters investigated by him. The incumbent prepares recommendations to his supervisor for corrective action or disposition of cases based on his findings, as required. He confers with and discusses investigations and reports with responsible administrative officials.

The criminal investigator starts at the GS-5 level for those without experience.

DEPARTMENT OF THE INTERIOR

In the Department of Interior, the majority of personnel involved in criminal justice functions are primarily in law enforcement and investigative work.

United States Game Management Agents

U.S. game management agents have responsibility for the enforcement of various federal statutes and regulations enacted for the protection and conservation of wildlife, including birds, mammals, and certain fishes. Their duties include: (a) investigating criminal cases involving violation of federal conservation laws within the enforcement jurisdiction of the U.S. Department of the Interior; (b) detecting and apprehending persons responsible for violations; (c) recognizing, preparing, and presenting facts and evidence in orderly form to federal and state prosecuting officers and courts of law; and (d) appearing as a witness and otherwise aiding in the prosecution of cases.

U.S. game management agents make investigations covering a wide range of subjects relating to the functions of the Bureau of Sport Fisheries and Wildlife, such as: (a) investigating applicants for federal permits to take and/or possess protected species of wild birds and mammals for scientific or propagating purposes; (b) conducting and participating in making surveys and censuses of wildlife populations; (c) engaging in migratory game bird banding operations; (d) investigating, suggesting, and instructing others in methods of abating damage to agricultural crops caused by wild birds protected by federal statutes; (e) disseminating information pertaining to fish and wildlife conservation through radio, television, newspapers, personal contacts, and group meetings.

U.S. game management agents in charge of districts serve as field liaison representatives for the Bureau of Sport Fisheries and Wildlife in their respective districts, with the state conservation department, other federal agencies, and private organizations on migratory bird management and federal conservation enforcement matters. They confer with and advise bureau personnel of the Division of Wildlife Refuges, Federal Aid, Wildlife Services and Realty relative to local conditions affecting programs under their jurisdiction. The starting grade for the new agent is GS-5.

United States Park Police

The United States Park Police is a unit of the Office of National Capital Parks, National Park Service, Department of the Interior. Jurisdiction extends to property administered by the Office of National Capital Parks located in the District of Columbia and the surrounding five counties of Maryland and Virginia. The force has jurisdiction on certain other federal lands such as the Agricultural Research Center in Beltsville, Maryland, and the Arlington National Cemetery in Virginia. The force has the same police powers within the District of Columbia as the metropolitan police.

Each member of the United States Park Police is charged with the responsibility of providing a wide variety of effective police services. In addition to the primary protection and investigative services, force members must deal with complex problems typical of our changing society and behavioral patterns today. Many of these tasks require full application of social skills in dealing with people under many different circumstances in order for the best interests of society and the individual to be served.

In addition to the primary protective responsibilities, force members act as host to millions of park visitors, annually serving as guide and information specialists. Other police services are also provided for the many notable civic events conducted within the national capital parks such as the National Cherry Blossom Festival, The National Independence Day Celebration, the President's Cup Regatta, and the Presidential Inaugural.

To be successful in meeting these responsibilities, a member of the force must possess the following qualities:

1. Initiative
2. The ability to carry a great deal of responsibility and to handle difficult emergency situations alone
3. Social skills and the ability to communicate effectively with persons of various cultural, economic, and ethnic backgrounds
4. The mental capacity to learn a wide variety of subjects quickly and correctly
5. The desire and ability to adapt his thinking to technological and sociological changes
6. An understanding of his fellow man and a desire to help those in need
7. The emotional maturity to remain calm and objective and provide leadership in emotionally charged situations
8. The physical strength and endurance to perform these exacting duties

Also found in the Department of Interior, National Park Service, are the following kinds of law enforcement related positions:

Park aids
Park technicians
Park guards

The starting level is either GS-5 or GS-7.

DEPARTMENT OF STATE

Agency for International Development

The Office of Inspections and Investigators in the Agency for International Development (AID) is involved in law enforcement investigative services. Two criminal justice related areas are found in the agency.

Public Safety Advisors. These persons work in police agencies in developing countries. Their activities cover every law enforcement function. They advise the host country's police officers on the concepts and principles of police organization, administration, and management; basic police operations; investigative techniques, including scientific and technical aids; border control; police instruction training; and other internal security subjects. They also participate frequently in training civil police personnel at all levels.

To carry out these responsibilities, the public safety advisor preferably has an academic degree in police administration or related fields (law, international affairs, criminology, and so on). A minimum of five years of professional experience at the command or executive level in federal, state or local law enforcement is required. (In some cases, major responsibility may be acceptable.) The typical public safety advisor has expertise in one or more of these disciplines: police administration and organization; criminalistics; communications; records and identification; immigration; customs; border control; criminal investigations; patrol operations; rural policing; and training program development.

Criminal Investigator. About forty criminal investigators are found on the AID Inspections and Investigations staff. The investigators are responsible for investigating violations of AID regulations and the criminal and civil fraud statutes of the United States government that involve AID financed transactions or AID employees. They also conduct inspections to ensure compliance and integrity of the agency's programs and to identify, deter, or prevent operational irregularities.

The person who becomes an AID criminal investigator performs the following functions:

1. Based on a broad and intensive knowledge of AID policies, regulations, and established procedures, initiates and participates in inspections to evaluate and review agency programs to ensure compliance and integrity of operations.

2. Prepares comprehensive inspection reports reflecting findings, differences of opinion, action recommended and/or the corrective action initiated during the inspection.

3. Analyzes reports or allegations of malfeasance, fraudulent, or other criminal activity primarily related to the laws of the U.S., or personal misconduct that have been directed to his attention by agency personnel, through personal contacts, or developed as the results of self-initiated inquiry.

4. On the basis of the source and the significance of the allegations, determines the type and the scope of inquiry to be conducted and assumes personal responsibility for a thorough and timely investigation.

5. In conducting an investigation, is required to exercise a full range of investigative techniques to develop confidential and other informational sources in the interview of witnesses and in securing depositions and statements or documents sufficient in content and structure to be admissible as evidence in criminal or civil proceedings.

6. In highly complex or technical enquiries, may be required to utilize the services of experts in these fields. In so doing, he is responsible for the establishment of a definitive scope of work to be performed and supervises the expert's activities in the achievement of the required objectives.

7. Is responsible for the preparation of documented and comprehensive investigative reports that, if need be, can be transmitted to the Department of Justice for consideration as to criminal or civil prosecution without further investigation.

8. May be required to serve as a witness before a grand jury or in a trial proceeding conducted by the U.S. government.

9. Where the investigation reveals misconduct or criminal activity on the part of nationals or business firms under the jurisdiction of foreign governments, consults with and renders assistance to local and national officials in the initiation of prosecution or other action and the presentation of evidential materials. He may also act as a witness on behalf of the foreign government in such proceedings.

Special Agent, Office of Security

The State Department has investigative positions in the Office of Security. The positions are special agent security investigative jobs and are not law enforcement oriented. However, there are a few persons involved in protective security of important persons. There are about one hundred forty special agent positions in the United States and about ninety overseas. Primarily, the agents conduct full background investigations.

The personnel who become agents must have a four-year college degree and be willing to spend a great amount of time overseas. About ten to eighteen special agents are hired each year. The positions are not filled through civil service registers.

DEPARTMENT OF HEALTH, EDUCATION, AND WELFARE

Consumer Safety Officer

The Food and Drug Commission in the Public Health Service has one investigatory position, the consumer safety officer.

Consumer safety officers' professional work enforces laws and regulations that protect consumers from foods, drugs, cosmetics, fabrics, toys, and household products and equipment that are impure, unwholesome, ineffective, improperly labeled, or dangerous. They apply scientific knowledge to a variety of functions including: inspecting food and drug manufacturing establishments; investigating complaints of violations, injuries, and illnesses caused by regulated products; planning and directing regulatory programs; initiating actions against violators and coordinating activities associated with their prosecution; developing inspectional and laboratory analytical methods, procedures, and techniques; and advising industry, state and local officials, and consumers on enforcement policies, methods, and interpretation of regulations. Applicants for the entry-level position (GS-5) of consumer safety officer must have a bachelor's degree with appropriate coursework or have thirty semester hours of such courses plus additional experience and/or education to total four years of experience and education. The thirty hours of coursework must include any combination of biological sciences, chemistry, pharmacy, physical sciences, food technology, nutrition, home economics, epidemiology, and engineering.

Internal Security Office

This office does investigations but has no law enforcement responsibilities or functions. The investigative personnel are limited to areas of employee loyalty, personnel security and suitability, safeguarding and protection of classified information, and facility protection.

DEPARTMENT OF DEFENSE

Department of the Air Force

Within the Department of the Air Force, several law enforcement functions may be found. The Air Force Office of Special Investigations utilizes personnel in investigative functions. However, this is primarily a military organization and the number of civilian investigative positions is small. These positions are filled through civil service competitive examination.

The Security Police of the Air Force Inspector General is also primarily a military organization, but it does have a small civilian work force who are security specialists. These highly specialized positions are at grades GS-13 and above.

Air Force Investigator. Investigators plan and conduct investigations relating to the administration of, or compliance with, federal laws and regulations. The duties performed typically include: collecting facts and obtaining information by observing conditions, examining records, and interviewing individuals; writing and securing affidavits; administering oaths; preparing investigative reports to be used as a basis for court or administrative action; testifying before administrative bodies, courts, or grand juries; serving as a witness for the government. The work occasionally may involve criminal investigations.

Performance of these duties may require work at irregular hours and considerable travel.

Air Force Criminal Investigators. Criminal investigators plan and conduct investigations relating to alleged or suspected violations of federal laws. The duties typically include: obtaining physical and documentary evidence; interviewing witnesses; applying for and serving warrants for arrests, searches, and seizures; seizing contraband, equipment, and vehicles; examining files and records; maintaining surveillance; performing undercover assignments; preparing investigative reports; testifying in hearings and trials; and assisting U.S. attorneys in the prosecution of court cases. Most criminal investigators are required to carry firearms and to be proficient in their use. The work occasionally may involve noncriminal investigations.

These duties frequently require irregular, unscheduled hours, personal risks, exposure to all kinds of weather, considerable travel, and arduous exertion under adverse environmental conditions.

The kind of investigative work performed varies with the investigative jurisdictions and functions of the employing agencies. The grade levels of the positions depend on the scope, complexity, and importance of investigations and the degree of individual responsibility required. At the higher grade levels, investigators may also serve as team leaders, group supervisors, case reviewers, or unit coordinators, with responsibility for supervising the work of other investigators; or, they may be responsible for the management or direction of an investigative program or program segment.

Air Force Security Specialists. Security specialists or officers direct, plan, develop, coordinate, control, inspect, or execute programs designed primarily to protect the national security against espionage, sabotage, and related threats in cases of: persons employed or to be employed by the government; industrial facilities and personnel entering into contracts with agencies of the government; safeguarding of official information in the interests of the defense of the United States. In performing these duties, they are typically responsible for participating in formulating policies, standards, procedures, and methods, and for their application. Security specialists or officers participate in the promulgation of regulations and rules, and in the preparation of instructional and training information and of other material for use in security programs and systems. They plan, organize, and conduct training programs to acquaint and instruct government personnel and industrial management and employees in security matters and to alert them to the dangers of espionage and sabotage; and they maintain personnel security records, files, reports, and forms. Some security specialists or officers in the higher grade levels also present cases.

Within the broad security specialist category are:

> Personnel security specialists
> Industrial security specialists
> Security classification specialists
> Foreign exchange security specialists
> Visit control security specialists

Internal security specialists
Physical security specialists
Security specialists (general)

Department of the Army

Most criminal justice oriented functions in the Department of the Army are filled by commissioned officers. A few civil service positions in the provost marshal general's office do exist, however, and are summarized below.

Security Officer. Serves as chief, Industrial Defense Branch, and as program manager for the Department of Defense, Industrial Defense Survey Program.

Industrial Security Officer. Staff advisor and action officer on Department of Defense industrial defense matters.

Physical Security Officer. Staff advisor and action officer on Army physical security matters.

Supervisory Clemency Officer. Coordinates and supervises the Army clemency actions program in considering military prisoners for restoration to duty, parole, and clemency.

Case Analyst. Reviews and analyzes case histories of military prisoners in order to obtain necessary information on which to base recommendations for clemency and parole.

Correctional Institution Administrative Specialist. Staff advisor and action officer on custody and correctional treatment of military prisoners.

Military Personnel Management Specialist. Coordinates the military police absentee and deserter apprehension program.

Criminal Investigation Command. Seventeen civilian investigative positions are in this Army organization. The civilian investigator in this command initiates, directs, and coordinates Army-wide accomplishment of criminal and character investigations. He reviews preliminary and criminal investigative findings, compiles reports, and advises his supervisor on decisive factors involved. The investigator plans, advises on, and coordinates recruitment, utilization, training, and career development of investigative personnel. He formulates and staffs new directives or changes to existing Department of the Army regulations. He maintains top-secret *limited access* files pertaining to special criminal investigations. He also procures, processes, and accounts for files, including *top-secret* files required for background and other investigations, from the Army Intelligence Command. In addition, the incumbent maintains suspense files and records to ensure proper maintenance and return.

Department of the Navy

The criminal justice oriented functions are performed almost entirely by military personnel. There are, however, four highly specialized, one-of-a-kind, civilian positions involved in the criminal justice functions. These positions are occupied by personnel who have specialized experience; they offer little in the way of immediate career opportunities for college graduates at the bachelor's level.

DEPARTMENT OF COMMERCE

Within the Department of Commerce is found one criminal justice oriented function. The Department of Commerce criminal investigator conducts investigations involving fraud against the United States in the export field. This function includes investigation of actual or suspected violations of export control laws and attempts at bribery of export licensing officials. The duties of the criminal investigator include preparation and presentation of cases for administrative and/or criminal action.

UNITED STATES CIVIL SERVICE COMMISSION

The Civil Service Commission employs general investigators who conduct background investigations on federal employees and applicants for federal jobs. These investigations are noncriminal in nature and involve personal contact with witnesses as well as the review of official records. Applicants for investigator are selected from eligibility lists developed through the Federal Service Entrance Examination.

The C.S.C. investigative staff has about 650 investigators. New investigators attend a concentrated one-week training course in Washington, D.C.

The course covers the basic techniques of conducting investigations, with primary emphasis on full field investigations because these make up the largest part of the workload. Following the class instructions, investigators are returned to the field and join experienced investigators for training on the job to bring them rapidly into production. This is followed by continued training through supervisory review of reports, periodic supervised investigations, group meetings of investigators, and biennial training conferences in which the bureau director or other high-level Washington staff members, a commissioner, or a representative of the executive director participates.

UNITED STATES CAPITOL POLICE

The uniformed United States Capitol Police is a force of about a thousand personnel having primary jurisdiction within the District of Columbia. Members of the force serve in a variety of positions and perform the functions expected of a police department operating in a large city. Most positions are in patrol work. The responsibilities of the capitol police are restricted somewhat in that their duties and jurisdiction are closely involved with the Washington, D.C., metropolitan police, park police, White House police, security forces of the General Services Administration, and other federal law enforcement agencies having specified responsibilities.

TENNESSEE VALLEY AUTHORITY

The Tennessee Valley Authority (TVA) has a minimum amount of activities related to criminal justice, and these activities relate to protection of TVA property, investigation of theft and damage to property, and official misconduct of TVA employees. Few positions in TVA are concerned primarily with such activities; thus, the Authority is interested in candidates with more general qualifications rather than with specialized training in criminal justice. In fact, TVA investigations for security clearances and suspected criminal activity that require more than can be accomplished as part of regular jobs are done by other federal agencies specializing in these fields.

TVA does have a large force of employees, called public safety officers, who patrol TVA property to prevent and deter theft, vandalism, and fires and make arrests as required; receive and conduct visitors over the property; observe and report property conditions that are unsightly, unsanitary, or hazardous; and cooperate with outside law enforcement agencies in making investigations and arrests, especially in cases involving TVA interest. Preferred qualifications include ability to meet the public and convey information about TVA, knowledge of applicable fire and police regulations, proficiency in the use of firearms and self-defense techniques, and the ability and initiative to act in emergency situations.

A small number of property protection specialists are employed to develop and update the industrial defense program for property security. These employees are generally focused on material steps to protect property and draw upon the expertise of others for counsel in matters of criminal justice.

UNITED STATES POSTAL SERVICE

The Postal Service was set up as an independent establishment in 1971. Formerly, it was the Post Office Department. The criminal justice oriented functions in the service are found in three primary sections.

Postal Inspectors

Postal inspectors represent the investigative arm of the Postal Service. The position of inspector involves the highest type of investigative endeavor, demanding absolute integrity, and the ability and dependability to determine, assemble, and present, under any and all conditions, factual and absolutely reliable findings. The position is one of unusual trust and responsibility, requiring, after special training and development, a thorough basic knowledge of all phases of the postal service and specialization in several important areas. The inspection service is a separate bureau of the United States Postal Service, headed by the chief postal inspector, who is personally responsible for the selection, appointment, training, and general management of the bureau and all field elements of the inspection service. Field supervision, under the chief postal inspector, is managed by fifteen inspectors in charge, each of whom is assigned a geographical area.

Duties of postal inspectors are varied and are divided into broad categories: (1) criminal investigations, relating to all types of postal offenses, which involve apprehending violators, seizing evidence or illegal material, and appearing before grand juries and courts as witnesses; (2) service investigations to determine whether postal revenues are being properly protected, appropriated funds are expended economically, and the service operated in conformance with the postal operating laws and regulations and in the best interests of the public. Both categories of work include such duties as auditing accounts and preparing written reports and accurate evaluation of facts and circumstances and necessitate extensive study of rules, regulations, instructions, and practices.

Investigators

These individuals formerly were called investigative aids. They assist the postal inspector.

Security Force Technicians

The security force technicians are a uniformed force that provides security at postal installations and at buildings where federal courts are located.

Postal Service jobs are classified on a Postal Service grade schedule rather than the general schedule. The entry level rating is PS-8 for Inspectors, PS-7 for Investigators, and PS-5 for Technicians.

UNITED STATES COURTS

Within the judicial branch, but outside the judges and federal public defender positions, only the *federal probation officer* is directly concerned with the criminal justice system.

Growing problems of correcting offenders have led judicial and correctional leaders to seek new alternatives to jail and prison. The federal probation system is active in newer community-centered activities such as aftercare programs for narcotic addicts and graduated partial release programs such as furlough, work release, and halfway house placement.

United States probation officers also serve the United States Board of Parole and the Bureau of Prisons as parole officers. Persons under their supervision now may be assigned temporarily to community treatment centers operated by the Bureau of Prisons. This enhances the use of probation as an alternative to prison and often helps integrate the offender into the community.

For many released offenders, readjustment to life in a free community is a continuing series of crises. Coping with such emotion-laden events calls for creative use of the probation officer's ability and the utmost in self-control. The ultimate product is reclaimed human lives.

Many offenders are already rejects and failures in home, school, work, and leisure-time activities. Once they become labeled *criminal* or *delinquent,* and, particularly, once they have been imprisoned, their estrangement increases and a sense of powerlessness takes over. In addition, society often reacts to offenders' misbehavior by walling them off from the help they need most if they are to turn away from crime.

The probation officer works with people who need help. He is involved with them, with their lives, problems, and concerns.

In this work, the probation officer has autonomy, independence, and professional freedom to match the task. Much work is done away from the office and decisions must be made on the scene. Great reliance is placed on each officer's wisdom, judgment, and ability to make decisions.

As a most important aid to his work, the probation officer must know his community—its culture, traditions, institutions, and welfare agencies. He must have knowledge of vocational counseling resources, medical help, and educational facilities. He should be a community leader in promoting participation of all citizens in the solution of community problems and take a leading role in delinquency prevention activities.

In encouraging the offender to share normal community activities, the probation officer must help him to learn how to get along with others, get and keep a job, use leisure hours constructively, and other skills necessary to get along in fast-paced modern life. The learning is complicated by the fact that persons do not come to the probation officers for assistance. If the community accepts them at all, it is only on condition that they comply with specific rules ordered by the court or parole board. Thus, the probation officer must keep informed of their whereabouts and activities and take prompt action in the event of any violation of the conditions imposed upon each offender.

Probation and parole also mean helping the community learn to accept the offender and give him a fair chance to live and work productively.

On any day, the probation officer may be called upon to counsel a disturbed family and deal with the tense and highly charged feelings of that group. At the same time, he must represent the best interests of one family member whose criminal acts resulted from the unwholesome relationships at home. The officer deals with uncounted resources offering education, therapy, medicine, welfare, vocational training, or employment placement assistance. Later in the same day, he may lead a group therapy session with a dozen probationers and five parolees for an hour of no-holds-barred give-and-take.

Probation officers stay in touch with prison inmates' families, help with preparations for release, and supervise persons following release from federal institutions.

Probation officers are appointed by the federal district courts they serve. Recruiting generally is conducted locally by the chief probation officers. Currently, the entering level for probation officers is grade nine of the federal scale and progresses to grade twelve by promotion.

To qualify for this position, a person must also demonstrate that he possesses:

1. A substantial knowledge of the philosophy, theories, and practices of the correctional field with a knowledge of law, psychology, sociology, and criminology as these disciplines are related to the duties and responsibilities of the correctional profession

2. A devotion to the principles of public welfare

3. The ability to meet people, inspire confidence, and secure cooperation

4. A knowledge and understanding of both normal and abnormal behavior

5. An understanding of the relationship of family life to the community and its import for the offender

6. Unquestioned integrity

7. The ability to exercise initiative in handling problems encountered while performing assigned duties

8. Maturity of judgment and tact

9. A knowledge of the Federal Criminal Code and sentencing procedures

10. The ability to make thorough investigations of ordinary cases and make sound evaluations and recommendations

11. A knowledge of all available community resources and the understanding and skill necessary to use them

FEDERAL TRADE COMMISSION

The Federal Trade Commission is constantly working to stop practices that deceive customers. The *consumer protection specialist* is the agent used to halt this activity.

The consumer protection specialist usually begins his career as a member of a team responsible for enforcement of the Truth in Lending Act. He visits retail stores, small loan companies, automobile dealers, and other credit-granting firms to make sure that the creditors' advertising and loan forms properly disclose the information needed by consumers to make informed judgments in comparing credit sources. He provides guidance to consumers, consumer groups, state and local officials, and the business community on consumer credit matters; conducts conferences and prepares correspondence to explain the requirements of the law and regulations to businessmen; obtains assurances that improper practices will be corrected; and gathers evidence for use where legal action is necessary.

After he has acquired expertise in the consumer credit field, the consumer protection specialist, through a planned program of formal training and job enlargement, is given an opportunity to develop a broad knowledge of all aspects of the commission's consumer protection work. For example, a consumer protection specialist may be called upon to:

1. Visit mills and retail stores to encourage advertising, invoicing, and labeling practices that provide accurate information for the consumer on the fiber content of wearing apparel and other textile and fur products

2. Initiate the removal of dangerously flammable fabrics from store shelves

3. Advise local businessmen in the preparation of advertising to ensure accuracy and honesty of claims

4. Investigate business practices that stifle competition or deceive consumers

5. Use various means to educate the public on unfair practices so that the consumer is in a position to help himself

Ultimately, a consumer protection specialist will be working with state and local officials, advisory groups, and other organizations at the local and regional levels in an effort to resolve all types of consumer problems in their incipiency.

A four-year college degree qualifies the individual for initial appointment. However, applicants are selected from high scorers on the Federal Service Entrance Examination. Initial appointment is usually at the GS-5 or GS-7 level.

FEDERAL MARITIME COMMISSION

In the Federal Maritime Commission are several positions involved with the enforcement or investigative functions.

Bureau of Enforcement

This office is responsible for program development, administration, and activities in connection with the investigation of common carriers by water in the foreign and domestic offshore commerce of the United States. Program activities of the Bureau of Enforcement are carried out by the Office of Investigation and the Office of Informal Complaints.

Office of Investigation

This bureau conducts investigations of the activities and practices of common carriers by water in the foreign and domestic offshore commerce of the United States, conferences of such carriers, freight forwarders, terminal operators, and other persons subject to the regulatory jurisdiction of the FMC. In collaboration with the Office of Informal Complaints, the Office of Investigation makes recommendations as to prosecution or other appropriate action where violations of the shipping acts or rules and regulations of the commission have been developed. This office consults with and advises the bureau's hearings counsel and the office of the general counsel in preparing formal hearings before the commission or actions in federal court.

The Office of Informal Complaints

This office reviews informal complaints or protests against the practices, methods, and operations of common carriers by water in the foreign or domestic offshore commerce of the United States and other people subject to the regulatory jurisdiction of the Federal Maritime Commission. It is responsible for recommending further action that may include further field investigation, or recommendation for formal action by the commission as to prosecution, or other appropriate action where violations of shipping acts or rules and regulations of the commission have developed.

GENERAL SERVICES ADMINISTRATION

The General Services Administration (GSA) has an investigative function in regard to violations of criminal statutes that affect the operations of the agency. The criminal investigator is the primary investigator.

The Criminal Investigator

This person independently plans and conducts complete criminal and civil investigations that involve substantial and varied ramifications and, frequently, a high degree of controversy. The investigator's results, recommendations, and consequences to a major degree, constitute deterrents to violations of criminal statutes and regulations; establish bulwarks against recidivism; influence remedial action, such as changes in regulations, policies, practices, and operations, regionally or agency-wide; and serve as precedents for future actions. These may include matters and issues of substantial delicacy; broad interpretation of basic guidelines, practices, and techniques to meet unusual conditions; and the exercise of a high degree of initiative, ingenuity, resourcefulness, versatility, imagination, and creative thinking. The incumbent will deal with widely diversified types of cases, requiring personal contact with individuals from the lowest to the highest social, business, professional, and governmental levels and will meet a substantial variety of investigative areas, each requiring extended specialized experience and training, and knowledge of applicable rules, regulations, and statutes.

Investigations encompass:

1. Complaints and reports indicating collusion, bribery, favoritism, conflict of interest, and violations of federal statutes covering fraudulent activities, thefts of government property in the custody of GSA, thefts of personal private property in areas under GSA jurisdiction, and the majority of crimes falling within the purview of Title 18, United States Code, including assaults, sex violations, numbers games, and confidence games committed in areas under GSA jurisdiction

2. Alleged violations of the Copeland Anti-Kickback Act, the Eight-Hour Law, the Davis-Bacon Act, the Walsh-Healey Act, the Buy American Act, the regulations of the secretary of labor, and the criminal statutes relating to the falsification of payrolls, and the fraudulent deviation or failure to comply with specifications contained in GSA contracts

3. Alleged violations of laws and regulations covering GSA responsibilities for the physical security of its facilities, particularly those for the storing of strategic materials for the national defense

4. Allegations of discrimination involving employment within GSA, because of race, creed, or color

5. Contingent fees, contractor responsibility, debarred bidders or similar lists, alleged violations of the GSA standards of conduct, personal security investigations of GSA applicants as requested by the GSA personnel security officer

6. Inquiries and surveys relating to GSA operations requested by members of Congress, congressional committees, the administrator and other responsible GSA officials

CENTRAL INTELLIGENCE AGENCY

Intelligence Specialists

Such specialists collect, produce, and disseminate information on foreign and domestic areas that has direct or indirect effect on national security. The primary intelligence collection agency is the Central Intelligence Agency, although intelligence specialist positions may be found in the:

National Security Agency
Department of State (Special Agents and Security Officers)
Federal Bureau of Investigation
Atomic Energy Commission
United States Postal Service
Defense Intelligence Agency
United States Army Security Agency
Naval Intelligence Command
U.S. Air Force Security Service
1127th United States Air Force Field Activities Group

DRUG ENFORCEMENT ADMINISTRATION

Congress recently consolidated five existing drug-control agencies into a single Drug Enforcement Administration (in the Department of Justice). The new agency will combine the drug control functions of the Bureau of Narcotics and Dangerous Drugs, the Bureau of Customs, the Office of Drug Abuse Law Enforcement, and the Office of National Narcotics Intelligence. LEAA drug-law enforcement research and other agencies will also be transferred to the DEA.

The reorganization of drug control programs will give the new DEA responsibility to develop overall federal drug-law enforcement programs, planning, and evaluation; to investigate suspects for violations of federal drug-trafficking laws; to conduct all U.S. relations with drug-law enforcement officials of other nations; to coordinate and cooperate with state and local enforcement officials or joint drug-enforcement efforts; and to regulate the legal manufacture of drugs under federal regulations.

SUMMARY

This chapter has attempted to identify criminal justice related functions and positions at the federal level, thereby giving an idea of the scope and breadth of federal involvement in the fields of law enforcement, corrections, courts, and prosecution. The student has been given a view of the specific functions as well as the qualifications of the personnel who occupy the positions.

As has been previously mentioned, the field of criminal justice is dynamic. Functions die and new ones arise, especially at the federal level. The sincere criminal justice student should have no difficulty in finding a fascinating and rewarding career in federal criminal justice work.

QUESTIONS

1. For federal level jobs there is a distinction made between generalized and specialized experience. Discuss the distinctions between the two.
2. What agencies make up the Drug Enforcement Administration?
3. What does the work of the Border Patrol agent entail?
4. What are the general responsibilities of the FBI? What are the qualifications of FBI Special Agents?
5. In 1969 the president of the United States issued a directive to improve the federal correctional system. What points are covered by the directive? Discuss each one.
6. Discuss the general requirements and tasks performed by a federal correctional officer; the federal probation officer.
7. Describe the functions, organization, and operations of the Law Enforcement Assistance Administration.
8. Name the law enforcement oriented jobs in the Department of the Treasury. Discuss the general tasks performed by each.
9. Describe the job of Department of Agriculture criminal investigator.
10. What are U.S. Park Policemen?
11. What are the three military departments found in the Department of Defense? Describe the kinds of jobs found in each department.
12. What kinds of investigations are performed by the criminal investigator found in the General Services Administration?

PROSECUTION

THE PROSECUTOR

The prosecutor may be called an enigma, no matter what his title
—county solicitor, county prosecutor, commonwealth attorney, or
district attorney. He is highly political because of the manner in
which he gains office. He is elected in all states except New Jersey,
Connecticut, Rhode Island, and Delaware, where he is an appointed officer.[1]
As a consequence, he is sensitive to the political winds in his jurisdiction and
needs great delicacy in the enforcement of the highly technical criminal laws.
Political expediency frequently comes into contact with the prosecutor's sworn
duty to prosecute violators.

For example, he must decide whether or not housing or welfare laws are
to be enforced, what type of enforcement of the state prostitution laws is to
take place, and how vigorously Sunday closing laws are to be enforced. Also,
the prosecutor's policies on arrests, searches, and seizures significantly affect
the law enforcement efforts of local police agencies.

THE OFFICE

County prosecutors are public officers, elected or appointed as provided
in state statutes or constitutions. They can be considered part of the judicial

---

[1]Jay A. Sigler, *An Introduction to the Legal System* (Homewood, Ill.: The Dorsey Press,
1968), p. 79; Duane R. Nedrud, "The Career Prosecutor," *Journal of Criminal Law, Criminology,
and Police Science,* LI (September-October 1960), 343.

system or, at least, officers in the judicial part of the government. The prosecutor is not an ordinary legal attorney. He is a sworn officer of the court who represents the county that he serves, but he is not part of the court. Ideally, his ethics should correspond to those of the judiciary. The prosecuting attorney is a public officer also because he represents the sovereignty of the state in whose name all criminal prosecutions must be commenced, and has often been called the enforcement power of the executive branch of government.

In those states in which the office of the district or prosecuting attorney is created by the constitution, the incumbents are considered to be constitutional officers. In other states, they are creatures of statute. Occasionally, the question arises whether prosecuting attorneys are state or county officers. The answer is found in the constitutions and statutes. Under some statutes and constitutions, the prosecutors are held to be state officers not withstanding that their duties are confined to the specific counties in which they are elected or appointed. Even their salaries are paid by the county, which may provide as many prosecuting attorneys as are necessary for the work at hand, the limitation generally being the budget. In some instances, the prosecutors are regarded as neither state nor county officers but as district officers.

In most, if not all, jurisdictions, the general qualifications for the office of the county prosecutor also are specified in the state constitution or statutes. It is almost universally required that a county prosecuting attorney be an attorney or a person *learned in the law.* The requirement that the prosecuting attorney must be learned in the law is satisfied by admission to the bar in any state provided he has a license to practice law in his own state.[2] Should the constitution or statute state that only attorneys at law or persons learned in the law may be a prosecutor, no one other than this class may be eligible. One Illinois case has even held that in the absence of a specific constitutional or statutory requirement the incumbent must be an attorney at law or learned in the law because the duties of the position itself demand that he possess such qualifications.[3] At present, all states require prosecutors to be lawyers.[4] Residence requirements within the county are usually necessary to make a person eligible to be a county prosecutor. Sometimes, residence for a specified length of time is required.

The term of office of the prosecutor usually is fixed by the state constitution or statute. Prosecutors generally serve for a term of four years where the position is elected. In the appointive offices where there is no tenure specified, the term is at the pleasure of the appointing authority. However, a prosecutor whose office is fixed by law may not be removed except as provided by applicable constitutional or statutory provisions. If no specified term of office is fixed

[2]*Howard* v. *Burns,* 85 N.W. 920, 14 S.D. 383 (1901).
[3]*People ex rel. Elliot* v. *Benefiel* 91 N.E. 2d 427, 405 Ill. 500 (1950).
[4]Nedrud, "The Career Prosecutor," p. 344.

by law, the appointive authority may remove and appoint others without assigning a reason.

Although mere misconduct in office not constituting official misconduct is not sufficient for removal of a prosecutor, a few of the grounds that various courts have held to be adequate for removal include: incompetence, habitual intoxication, gross immorality, and official misconduct. Ignorance of the law has been held by a New York court not to be sufficient cause for removal.[5] Official misconduct has been interpreted to mean such activities as those in which the prosecutor fails or refuses to institute or conduct criminal investigations or prosecution; fails to give legal advice to county officers; renders professional assistance to a defendant in a criminal prosecution; disobeys an order of the court; is guilty of extortion in office; or accepts unauthorized fees.

POWERS AND DUTIES

Prosecutors exercise the powers conferred on them by constitutional and statutory provision, usually only within the county they serve. At common law,[6] an individual interested in punishing an accused carried the prosecution by hiring a private prosecutor who laid the case before the grand jury and prosecuted the charges before the petit jury. The public was not involved in the prosecution. It is also a common rule that counties may employ special counsel to assist the county prosecutor in representing the county. In any case, the prosecutor has wide discretion in the manner in which his duties are to be performed. The courts will not interfere unless he acts in excess of his jurisdiction or completely without jurisdiction.

A duty rests with the prosecutor to prosecute the violators of criminal laws of the state when he knows or has reason to believe a violation has been committed. The duty, however, is not absolute. He is required only to exercise sound discretion and is permitted to refrain from prosecuting or, once he commences, to enter a *nolle prosequi* whenever he has a good faith belief that the interests of the state are best served, that the guilt of the accused is doubtful, or that no conviction is possible. But the fact that he is given this discretion does not permit him to fail to prosecute in order to conform to the sentiments of the people living in his county. Likewise, the belief of the prosecutor that the jury will not be likely to return a verdict of guilt because of prejudice against such prosecution, should not excuse him from performing his duty. In any case, his discretion must always be exercised in good faith, in

---

[5] *People* v. *Jackson* 48 N.Y.S. 2d 401 (1944).

[6] A system of unwritten law governing the rights and duties of individuals that was developed in Great Britain. The unwritten law and appropriate English statutes were brought with early settlers to the American colonies and, with modifications to fit the conditions in the New World, were adopted as law by the various states. Common law is frequently distinguished from statutory or written law.

accord with the dictates of his own good judgment. He has a high and difficult responsibility to act according to established principles of law fairly, wisely, and with professional skill and reason.

The prosecutor is also the attorney and legal advisor to county officials in criminal matters unless the law disqualifies him. Depending on the specific jurisdiction, the county prosecutor may appear in proceedings in respect to real estate, divorce proceedings, habeas corpus hearings, abatement proceedings, and adjudication of matters concerned with the constitutionality of statutes. He cannot, however, act as a purely private prosecutor. The duties of the prosecutor do not normally include the arrest and apprehension of an accused. He cannot enforce laws solely for his own benefit.

A prosecuting attorney is not prohibited, in the absence of a statute, from representing private parties where there is no duty to the state. In some jurisdictions, the prosecutor therefore is not prohibited from practicing law as long as no conflict exists between his public duty and private enterprise. The entire problem rests with the legislature which can regulate the activities of a public officer, including the prosecutor. Such statutes have been upheld by the county under the theory that there is a need to protect the public by ensuring that the prosecutor's duties will not be influenced by his personal activities.

In the United States, the greatest number of crimes are committed against the state and the accused is most often subject to state prosecution. The prosecutor is the country's most powerful and influential law official. He has the initial authority, as mentioned above, to involve himself significantly in police procedures regarding arrests. His actions in this single area can reduce case loads in his office, change police training techniques, reduce or increase court proceedings, alter the population in the correctional system, and bring about needed coordination between the police, courts, corrections, and the prosecution. Second, the prosecutor has the responsibility of representing the government in court on criminal matters. As a consequence, he must be a skilled trial lawyer, not only to present the best possible evidence for the government but also to portray accurately police practices that may come under judicial scrutiny. Third, investigation of criminal cases before initiating them in court is a common function of the prosecutor. Often, carefully selected professional investigators are part of the permanent staff in the prosecutor's office. Because the investigations involve complicated issues of proof, responsibility, and procedures, the effective presentation of the prosecutor's case depends on the diligent efforts of his investigative staff.[7]

Because of the vast powers given to the public prosecutor in initiating criminal cases, control over his authority is only slight. Perhaps the two most

[7]The President's Commission on Law Enforcement and the Administration of Justice, *Task Force Report: The Courts* (Washington, D.C.: Government Printing Office, 1967), pp. 72–73.

effective, once he is elected or appointed, are the minor restraints of the grand jury which has the responsibility to initiate prosecutions and independently investigate matters on its own and the judiciary which constantly is in a position to scrutinize the prosecutor's criminal enforcement activities.

Judicial scrutiny of the prosecutorial function is sometimes camouflaged by the actions of the law enforcement agencies when a statute is struck down by a court. Statutes that set up particular offenses are created by the legislature, which establishes the categories of activities identified as being criminal and the procedures that aid the police and prosecution in enforcing those laws. Many times, the statutes are so vague that the police and the prosecution have little guidance in determining what acts are prohibited by the statute. As a consequence, the courts must interpret the statute in regard to actual situations. These interpretations and judicial rules therefore are of great impact in the rules and policies in the prosecutor's office. In effect, the prosecutor may attempt to evade judicially set standards, but he cannot avoid them.

One of the primary restrictions placed on the prosecutor is the Bill of Rights of the national Constitution. The framers of the Constitution undoubtedly had some control of the prosecutorial function in mind but obviously could not set forth a detailed set of rules in a single document. Therefore, the rights of an accused person were protected in very general and quite vague language in Amendments Four, Five, Six, Seven, and Eight. The rights are basically procedural and are designed to restrict the arbitrary execution of judicial processes by the prosecutor.

Decisions of the Supreme Court of the United States as well as lower federal and state courts have mandated that the prosecutor's function be held to the highest ethical standards practicable. The county prosecutor, for example, is bound by rules of evidence regarding searches and seizure resulting from an unreasonable arrest.[8] The rule that restrained federal officials from using illegally secured evidence in federal trials is now the same rule that guides county prosecutors.[9]

The Supreme Court has also provided numerous examples of guidance to the prosecutor. The gradual unfolding of the rights of an accused has been felt at the state level in the enforcement of the criminal law much more profoundly than at the federal levels. But the essential point for the prosecutor to bear in mind is that continually higher standards of responsibility are demanded of him to make the U.S. system of justice equal for all individuals.

One major drawback to becoming a prosecutor is that the position often is part-time and ill-paid. Frequently, it is used only as a springboard to higher office. Joseph A. Schlesinger found that in a twenty-year period, thirty-five

[8] *Weeks* v. *U.S.* 232 U.S. 383 (1914).
[9] *Mapp* v. *Ohio* 367 U.S. 643 (1961).

public attorneys became governors.[10] In 1964, a survey by the American Bar Association reported that a high proportion of county prosecutors reported that their salary was inadequate. The Baltimore state attorney's office's highest paid assistant, in an office with thirty-two assistants, was approximately $10,000. Comparatively low salaries were common in other areas. An earlier study, by Nedrud in 1960, reported that some prosecutors in the twenty-one states studied had incomes less than $4,200 per annum.[11] A 1968 study[12] of the prosecutors in Southern California counties reported that the salary of deputy district attorneys reflected a relatively high level of compensation when compared to the average annual income of other professional persons with a comparable amount of experience. In 1968, the median income for white families where the head of the household had four or more years of college education was $13,589 but the mean annual salary of the prosecutors in the study was $17,449. Table 8–1 reflects the salary schedule.

TABLE 8-1   Salary Schedules of Prosecutors in Three Counties

	X county	Y county	Z county	Total
Less than 12,999	8	3	3	14
13,000–15,999	27	5	7	39
16,000–18,999	10	1	2	13
19,000–21,999	8	1	0	9
22,000–24,999	8	1	0	9
25,000 or more	10	1	0	11
MEAN	$18,221	$15,968	$14,426	$17,449

The study further established that in County X, a prosecutor with a mean experience of 52.8 months was earning $18,221; one in County Y with an average of 20.6 months experience earned $15,968; and in County Z, a county prosecutor with a mean experience of 19.3 months collected $14,426 per annum. It is highly doubtful, however, whether a significant number of prosecutors' offices reach the compensation scale.

[10]Joseph A. Schlesinger, *How They Became Governor* (East Lansing, Michigan: State University Press, 1957), p. 94.

[11]Nedrud, "The Career Prosecutor," p. 343.

[12]George T. Felkenes, "A Sociological Study of the Prosecutor's Office" (unpublished Doctor of Criminology dissertation, School of Criminology, University of California, Berkeley, 1970), pp. 98–99.

SOME MAJOR CONCEPTIONS AND CRITICISMS
OF THE PROSECUTOR

A conceptualization of the role of the prosecutor has some obvious limitations and *caveats.* Some generalizations can be made. The prosecutor is in a critically important position in the criminal justice system. Because he works in close cooperation with the police, courts, and corrections, he is in an excellent place to lend leadership to coordinate the activities of the various other agencies in the system. It has been suggested that

> if the prosecuting attorney is to fulfill the potentialities of his office adequately, he must be a criminologist rather than merely a prosecutor. He must understand the purpose and method of crime prevention activities and techniques of criminal investigation. He and his staff must know when to be lenient as well as when to be severe in the disposition of the case and must be thoroughly conversant with the purpose and utility of the devices of probation and parole.[13]

Assertions like this point up the need for an agency with a broad operating overview and sense of responsibility concerning the whole criminal process. The prosecutor must interact with other agencies in the criminal justice system. He must be responsive to the needs and demands of the police courts and corrections functions as well as to the practical limitations of his office. When the prosecutor must make a decision on whether to charge a person with an offense, the degree to which the prosecutor seeks to accommodate to the problems of other agencies, or whether the actions of other agencies impose upon and sometimes restrict the prosecutor's activities is indicated by the following relationships.

Relationships with the Police

The prosecutor's office is heavily dependent upon the police in three major respects. First, the police, by answering complaints, detecting and investigating suspicious circumstances, and deciding whether to take suspects into custody, regulate the cases that come to the prosecutor for a charging decision. Except for a few crimes where complaints come directly to the prosecutor's office, such as nonsupport and business fraud, and except for a few instances when the investigators of the prosecutor's office participate in crime detection programs, the prosecutor's office has little practical operational control over

---

[13]Newman S. Baker and Earl H. DeLong, "The Prosecuting Attorney and His Office," *Journal of Criminal Law and Criminology,* XXV, No. 1, (March-April 1935), 888.

the invocation of criminal cases. One deputy prosecutor described the police function:

> The laws passed by the legislature, local government or even by Congress are meaningless without law enforcement officers to carry them out. The traditional cop on the beat—whether he's a city policeman, deputy sheriff, state trooper, game warden or FBI agent—is the basic element in our system of laws. No district attorney can prosecute; no court can try; no jury can convict criminals of breaking our laws without an arrest first being made by a law enforcement officer.

Second, the quantity and quality of evidence considered, including its admissibility as determined by the procedures used in obtaining it, are, as indicated, primarily police responsibilities over which the prosecutor has little control in routine cases. Third, for most minor offenses, the charging decision is delegated to the police. The preparation of the charge and presentation of evidence in court against drunks, vagrants, disorderly persons, prostitutes, and traffic offenders are commonly police responsibilities. If an assistant prosecutor is assigned to the lower criminal court adjudicating low misdemeanors, his role is typically a minor one. Delegation of this power to the police is doubtless made because the majority of minor offenses present no serious evidentiary or procedural problems and can be conveniently and summarily disposed of by a direct interchange between the court, police, and defendant, leaving the county prosecutor free to deal with serious crime.

Relationship with the Trial Court

In a sense, the prosecutor's office operates as an adjunct to the trial court. Assistant prosecutors assigned to a court develop a close professional and personal relationship with the judges because of their continuing daily contacts. From this relationship, there also develops effective communication and mutual understanding of legal and administrative problems routinely encountered in processing cases. Inexperienced prosecutors also receive guidance from criminal court judges, who, in many instances, began their careers in the prosecutor's office.

Inasmuch as the judge is the dominant figure in the adjudication process and, as such, has administrative control over his workload and the disposition of routine cases, the prosecutor's decisions tend to conform to the court's predispositions or temperaments. Courts, for example, are often loathe to force testimony from complainants who have a change of heart in assault cases. Likewise, in an effort to modify police practices, courts frequently dismiss cases grounded on detection methods that, although not illegal, are felt to be improper. Cases of this sort are often screened out as a preliminary matter by the prosecutor even though his personal feelings may run counter to those of the judge. In many instances, informal efforts in the prosecutor's office to effect restitution for crime victims and to arrange for psychiatric care in lieu of prosecution are designed to relieve the courts of performing these same functions. In short, the criteria for screening many cases is significantly influenced by the court and particularly by the attitudes and predilections of the trial judges in the community.

One prosecutor described the realities of the court-prosecutor relationship as "bread and butter, where the judge must be buttered up in certain instances by showing him that the prosecution has considered various kinds of civil treatment but still believes the accused will respond only to criminal punishment."

The criteria for charging a *lesser offense* or reducing the charge in plea negotiation are also formulated to coincide with judicial policy. If the prosecutor's office fails to charge lesser offenses or negotiate pleas to accommodate to the inclination of the court, the court may, at its own instance, make such an arrangement at the preliminary hearing or arraignment, or even suggest informally that the most serious charge seems inappropriate in order to induce the prosecutor to amend the charge.

Relationship with Defense Counsel

Before a decision to charge has been made, defense counsel sometimes influences the decision by meeting with the prosecutor and pointing out weaknesses he has detected in the state's case and relating his knowledge of mitigating circumstances. *Precharge* conferences, however, are relatively infrequent in most jurisdictions.[14] Instead, negotiations between the prosecutor and counsel normally occur after the charge has been filed. Persuading the prosecutor to reduce the charge, or less frequently, to drop the case is, therefore, the primary role of defense counsel in the charging process.

It is conceivable, and sometimes actually occurs, that defense counsel might influence basic charging policies by insisting on going to trial in a sizable number of cases where negotiations fail to produce the desired result. This tactic seems particularly applicable in metropolitan areas where caseloads are high and at times unwieldy because such pressure might seriously disrupt the often archaic methods of the prosecutor's office in maintaining an even, expeditious flow of cases. In this connection, the office of the public defender, because of its control and management over large numbers of criminal cases, may be

---

[14]President's Commission on Law Enforcement and the Administration of Justice, *The Challenge of Crime in a Free Society,* (Washington, D.C.: Government Printing Office, 1967), pp. 11, 135–36; *Task Force Report: The Courts,* p. 34. The reason for the lack of the precharge conference is found in Jerome H. Skolnick, *Justice Without Trial: Law Enforcement in a Democratic Society* (New York: John Wiley and Sons, Inc., 1966), pp. 191–92.

better able to apply this kind of pressure than are relatively unorganized individual defense practitioners. In some instances, this may result in the establishment by the public defender's office of its own institutional policy. As one public defender commented,

> Our four trial deputies have often threatened to request jury trials in all cases if the trial prosecutor does not go along with our concerted opinions on certain important prosecutions. He knows we can cause the prosecutor's office to collapse if we carried out our threat.

Relationship with the Grand Jury

State statutes generally are worded to permit the attorney general, whenever he considers that the public interest requires it, with or without the concurrence of the prosecutor, to direct the convening of the grand jury for the investigation and consideration of such matters of a criminal nature as he desires to submit. The statute allows the attorney general to take full charge of the presentation of such matters, issue subpoenas, prepare indictments, and do all other necessary things to the same extent as the prosecutor may do. It would appear that the purpose of this section is to prevent the prosecutor from misusing the authority of his office but it is questionable whether the grand jury serves as a significant bulwark against unwarranted or frivolous prosecutions. Charging practices that are or that are alleged to be abusive appear to be no different in states with and without a grand jury system. For all practical purposes, the grand jury, with few exceptions, is under the control of the prosecutor, meaning that its decisions mainly affirm the prosecutor's decision on whether to charge. In a direct reference to his importance in forming the decisions of the local grand jury, a senior trial prosecutor once remarked:

> The grand jury is chosen without much concern for individual judgment and independence. The age of most of them makes them easily susceptible to hidden persuasion, especially when we are able to present only enough evidence to raise a good suspicion to believe that X committed a crime. It is very easy to convince a grand jury of almost anything, particularly when some newspaper coverage publicizes the incident.

The comment may have been made from an inflated ego, but similar references to the malleability of grand jurors have been made on numerous occasions.

There are situations, however, in which the grand jury assumes the major responsibility for the charging decision and hence relieves the prosecution of pressure. The grand jury may be important, for example, in resolving doubtful cases where a decision not to charge seems appropriate but because of the notoriety of the crime, such a decision would likely result in criticism of the prosecutor. Additionally, the grand jury may be relied upon to take unpleasant actions otherwise faced by the prosecutor, as with a decision to charge an influential politician or businessman. The prosecutor then has the guidance and support of an agency not involved in partisan politics. It is not clear in the literature when and how often the grand jury is relied upon in such instances.[15]

Relationship with the Attorney General

In some states, the attorneys general have significant power and influence over the local prosecutor's office, not only on the appointment of personnel but also in the control of office policy and practice.[16] The more pertinent constitutional and statutory provisions regarding the duties and responsibilities of the attorney general and the prosecutors in general, and the consultative and advisement mandates of the attorney general in particular, are found in the laws of all states. The extent of interchange and consultation between county and state prosecution agencies is, according to some studies,[17] less than might be expected and, in any event, is not a routine practice of these prosecuting agencies.

There are other more specific relationships between the attorney general and prosecutor. A review of *prosecution* statutes in a few states reveals that many offenses may be prosecuted by either the attorney general or local prosecutor.[18] In particular, statutes often give the two agencies prosecution responsibilities for both the enforcement of regulations of departments at the state level and of civil rights acts.[19] How these responsibilities are divided or shared is not clear, nor does one find satisfactory policy statements or studies of the power of the attorney general to intervene in local prosecution when, under the wording of one constitution, the attorney general determines whether or not *laws are being adequately enforced.*[20]

The Sentencing Hypocrisy

The dominant characteristic of the prosecutor's decisions is their quasi-judicial nature; when he analyzes evidence and the suspect's personality traits to determine both the chances of conviction and how the suspect will respond to

---

[15]California, Department of Justice, Bureau of Criminal Statistics, *Crime and Delinquency in California—1968* (Sacramento: State Printer, 1969), pp. 91–96. The California report indicates that during the past several years, grand jury filings consistently made up about 3½ percent of the total filings of criminal cases. Drug offenses accounted for about half of the grand jury indictments.

[16] *Task Force Report: The Courts,* p. 76.

[17] *Task Force Report: The Courts,* pp. 75–78.

[18] *Task Force Report: The Courts,* pp. 75–78.

[19] *Task Force Report: The Courts,* pp. 75–78.

[20]California, *Constitution,* Art. 5, sec. 13.

punitive or therapeutic measures, he is considering matters commonly associated with judicial responsibilities; but the decision is based on unconscious and personal predilections. The unknown in this equation is the extent to which the prosecutor's decisions are dominated by his quasi-judicial role. The term *quasi-judicial* itself, like *discretion,* does not convey an acceptable understanding of a decision by the prosecutor unless placed in the context of the circumstances of that decision and the objective the prosecutor is seeking.

It is difficult to comprehend the prosecutor acting as a quasi-judicial officer and at the same time functioning under the label so frequently placed on him of *advocate for law enforcement.* It is, therefore, important that there be less concern with descriptive phrases and more attention to the dynamics of what he does and why. For example, it is true that the prosecutor acts as an advocate in the traditional sense, just as an attorney represents a private litigant, once the issue of guilt or innocence has been drawn and he is fully committed to presentation of the case for conviction. This conception is reinforced by the very human desire of the prosecutor to win the cases he tries and by public expectations that he do so. Even here, however, the description must be qualified. All advocates have responsibility to see that *justice is done,* even if it means losing their cases. With the prosecutor, this theoretical obligation is probably greater than that of private counsel, because the prosecutor is a public official who must have concern for the effect his decisions will have throughout the system.

It is also a fact that only a small fraction of criminal cases actually goes to trial. This means that the prosecutor's activities as an advocate should be seen in the context of the kinds of interests he is representing when handling the majority of cases, which are settled without resort to a formal judicial hearing.

Further, it should be noted that the prosecutor, even more than the judiciary, has a direct, although imprecisely defined, responsibility for the overall effectiveness of the criminal law system. The pattern may vary with the jurisdiction and with the individual, but the prosecutor everywhere has a variety of administrative and executive responsibilities, extending from preventive law enforcement to rehabilitative measures. It is these less conspicuous functions, performed outside the judicial forum, that require the greatest examination and analysis if there is to be a meaningful grasp of the impact of the prosecutor's office. Without such an understanding, it is impossible to accurately assess the power of that office in the administration of criminal law.

The courses of action the prosecutor might take against a suspect who is probably guilty range from dropping the matter altogether to pressing the most serious charge possible. Between these extremes lie several additional possibilities. To illustrate, the suspect may be charged with an offense less serious than the one for which he was arrested or for which he could be convicted; prosecution may be abandoned in favor of a civil remedy such as the initiation of civil commitment procedures; or procedures, often informal or extralegal in nature, may be initiated to provide restitution to the victim or conciliation between the aggrieved party and the accused.

With regard to *charge reductions* as a means of inducing pleas of guilty and of expeditiously disposing of large caseloads, some information is available; but analyses of this process have been made primarily from the vantage point of the judiciary.[21] The exploration of several factors that impinge upon the possible settlements indicate more clearly what is meant by the quasi-judicial nature of the prosecutor's decision because the degree of their influence in the prosecutor's office is not known.

Sentencing laws often lack sufficient flexibility to permit the court, upon conviction, to fit the personal characteristics of the offender or any mitigating circumstances of the crime to the statutory sanctions. The difficulty is exemplified by excessive mandatory sentences that preclude probation. Charging a *lesser offense* or reducing the charge are often done to accommodate unrealistic sentencing restrictions. Because there is no formalized or systematic recognition of this practice, the result is wide disparity within a jurisdiction in the selection of charges involving similar, if not identical, criminal behavior.

The Crime Victim and Restitution

Charge reductions or the decision not to charge, especially if the crimes border on civil wrongs and are not regarded as serious threats to the community, often result when restitution or a promise of restitution is made to the victims. When the chief concern is providing restitution—as in cases of larceny by trick or device, business fraud, and bad checks—formalized procedures and special bureaus within the prosecutor's office have been established to achieve this goal. Settlement by informal mediation or arbitration may also be used in minor neighborhood and family squabbles. Greater understanding of the deterrent and rehabilitative aims of these procedures may portend modification of the handling of other and even more serious offenses where satisfying the victim is the primary aim.

Decisions often are based on the personal and social characteristics of the accused. Factors such as these are taken into account in the charging decision. It is here that the prosecutor's decision most closely resembles the sentencing function of the court. Both functions focus attention on committing the accused (if he is dealt with at all) to the appropriate correctional resource. But there is no fair comparison between the quantity and quality of back-

[21]Donald Newman, *Conviction: The Determination of Guilt or Innocence Without Trial,* A Report of the American Bar Foundation's Survey of the Administration of Justice in the United States (Boston: Little, Brown and Company, 1966), pp. 106–30.

ground data considered at the charging and sentencing stages. Except for a minority of cases where the accused receives psychiatric evaluation before the trial, the prosecutor has little or no information provided to the sentencing judge by the probation department. Information about the suspect's background during the charging process sometimes is limited to what is contained in the investigating officer's write-up. Psychiatric, social service, and other community-based correctional resources, even when available, are seldom used by the prosecutor in making evaluative decisions about the accused, but, instead, are called upon only to administer therapy to the convict. Many of the deputies interviewed recognized and stressed the need for this kind of information, especially before charges are formally made. An empirical analysis of such specific factors as these should make it possible to present a more sharply defined perspective of prosecution. The development of such a perspective should, in turn, lead to the more intelligent assessment of the overall objectives of criminal law and, hence, to a better considered and more responsible system.

Characteristics of the Prosecution Office

The American Bar Association has stated that

> ... the power of the prosecutor to initiate criminal prosecutions rests in him an authority in the administration of criminal justice at least as sweeping as, and perhaps greater than, the authority of the judge who presides in criminal cases. ... the prosecutor is vested with virtually unreversible power as to the persons to be prosecuted or not.[22]

In European systems, the entire criminal investigative and prosecution process is under the central authority of the state. In the United States, the prosecutor is peculiarly a local function. The concept of local prosecution is diffused among county or district prosecutors who are primarily concerned with local matters. As stated in State v. Finch, "the office of prosecuting attorney has been carved out of that of Attorney-General and virtually made an independent office."[23] It is unlikely that this characteristic of the U.S. prosecutor will change. Of the fifty states, only Alaska, Delaware, and Rhode Island do not have local prosecutors, twenty-nine have county prosecution, twelve have districts, and seven have both county and districts. For example, Texas has the largest number of county prosecutional units, 254; Kentucky is next with 120 county prosecutors but, in addition, there are forty-three com-

[22]American Bar Association, Project on Standards for Criminal Justice, "Standards Relating to the Prosecution Function and the Defense Function," Tentative Draft, 2 (March 1970), p. 19.

[23]128 Kan. 665, 280 P. 910 (1929).

monwealth attorneys who are elected for six years and prosecute cases in their respective districts. In those states having prosecuting attorneys for judicial districts, the judicial districts may encompass several counties as is the case in Oklahoma, for example, where there are fifty-eight counties and thirty-six judicial districts each with its own elected district attorney.[24]

Although the county has been the traditional unit for the prosecutor in the United States, there appears to be a trend toward the district system. The President's Crime Commission on Law Enforcement and Administration of Justice said that "in smaller jurisdictions, where the case load does not justify a full-time criminal prosecutor, consideration should be given to use of prosecutors representing larger districts."[25] The main problem with the county prosecution unit is that it is too small to provide adequate services.

> One Idaho county, for example, has no attorneys living there, although the law specifies the county attorney must be a resident. Two of Idaho's counties have less than 6,000 population. Only two prosecutors in the state serve full time. Oklahoma adopted a district system in 1965, following an election in which there were no candidates for county attorney in a majority of the counties. Vermont has fourteen states attorneys, seven of whom are full time. One prosecutor is not a member of the bar, and the state must contract with an attorney in this district to handle trial matters. The Attorney General's office favors fulltime prosecutors "who would not leave the office due to financial pressure as is presently the case" which would require larger districts. These examples are typical.[26]

Another characteristic of the prosecutor's office is the almost universally inadequate training, although the situation may have improved somewhat since 1967 when the President's Crime Commission noted that:

> There has been deplorable inattention to the development of curricula and training techniques in the investigative, administrative, and broader law enforcement policy roles played by the prosecutor. These matters have not been seen as suitable subjects for the attention of law schools and the legal scholarly community. . . . Large metropolitan prosecutors' offices should develop a training program for new assistants. . . . There is also a need for training programs on a state or regional level to reach prosecutors and assistants in small offices.[27]

In a survey of eighteen prosecutors' offices, only four indicated that there was a formal training program for new prosecutors. Six of the eighteen did not even offer on-the-job training. Only eight reported that they had a staff devoted to training Because these were all large offices, it is entirely likely that smaller prosecutors' offices have even less training.[28]

---

[24]National Association of Attorneys General, Committee on the Office of the Attorney General, *The Office of the Attorney General,* (February 1971), pp. 106–7.

[25] *The Challenge of Crime in a Free Society,* p. 148.

[26] *The Office of the Attorney General,* p. 109.

[27] *Task Force Report: The Courts,* p. 75.

[28] *The Office of the Attorney General,* p. 110.

The Conviction Psychology

Professional ethics and court decisions dictate that the primary responsibility of the prosecuting attorney is not to convict, but to see that justice is achieved. The majority of the prosecutors queried in a 1970 study expressed this concern for fairness and impartiality, but nearly one-third essentially indicated that their major function is to secure convictions, thus exhibiting what may be termed the *conviction psychology.*[29]

The development of this conviction psychology seems to be directly related to the length of experience as a prosecutor. Those district attorneys expressing a concern for conviction had, on the average, about twice as much experience on the job as those who mentioned a concern for justice. Exposure to the prosecutorial system, therefore, may in itself tend to alter one's perceptions and beliefs, eroding the idealism that generally characterizes the more inexperienced prosecutor.[30]

The conviction psychology may also be attributed to organizational pressure to visibly demonstrate efficiency by means of *hard* criteria, to justify the public expenditures made on this tax-supported office as well as the continued political life of an elected prosecutor. The office of the county prosecutor is under a self-imposed pressure to justify its budget, to get the most for each prosecution dollar, and to demonstrate the superiority of the public service model, all of which serve to justify utilization of the number of convictions (or guilty pleas) as the criterion of office efficiency.[31]

Additionally, an individual's success as a prosecutor may be measured by the number of criminal convictions that he has been able to secure. If too many accused persons *slip through his fingers* and manage to win their cases and thus avoid punishment, it may be considered an adverse reflection on his skill as an attorney and he may be labeled *inefficient.* If a prosecutor is using his position as a stepping stone to a political office or to private practice, as the data seem to indicate is often the case, he is even more dependent upon his superiors for their support and recommendations when he moves to a new position. It is unlikely that he will obtain their cooperation if, while a prosecutor, he did not fulfill their production expectancies.

The appearance of the conviction psychology may also be due in part to the concurrent role the prosecutor must play as both a quasi-judicial officer and an advocate in the trial proceedings. As a quasi-judicial officer of the court, he is required to be impartial and must attempt to determine whether the

---

[29]The remainder of the chapter on the prosecutor is based on the research conducted by the author. See fn. 11.

[30]Cf. Howard S. Becker and Blanche Geer, "The Fate of Idealism in Medical School," *American Sociological Review,* XXIII (April 1958), 50–56.

[31]Abraham Blumberg, *Criminal Justice* (Chicago: Quadrangle Books, 1967), p. 46.

accused is guilty or innocent of the crime charged. If, during a trial, he uncovers evidence that tends to negate the guilt of the accused, mitigate the degree of the offense, or reduce the punishment, he is obligated to disclose that information to the defense. As an advocate and an integral part of the adversary court proceedings, he is required to present persuasively all the evidence favorable to the government's case. To do anything less is to abridge his responsibility of public office.

The attorneys who displayed the conviction psychology may have experienced a rather severe role conflict because compliance with one role would make it more difficult to comply with the other. In this instance, being an advocate in court and trying to gain a conviction would be difficult, if not impossible, if, as a quasi-judicial officer, he was required to acknowledge evidence that would damage his case. Consequently, the anomie that results may cause him to ignore his quasi-judicial role altogether, or he may play this role only when he makes the initial charging decision. If he is forced to choose only one of the two roles, it is highly unlikely that he will choose the quasi-judicial role because, as was pointed out earlier, the criterion by which his efficiency is judged is probably his conviction record. A former United States attorney has advanced the possibility of ignoring the quasi-judicial role, or of relegating it only to the charging decision.

It is essentially true that a prosecutor is a "quasi-judicial officer." But the reference is usually made as a term of criticism thrown up during a trial when the prosecutor is fighting his hardest to protect the government's case. At this time, most of the prosecutor's quasi-judicial functions have long since passed, and he is an eager lawyer trying to protect his client's interest.

We believe that our primary duty is not to convict, but to seek justice. This definition principally comes into play, however, when a case is first brought into the office and is being readied for Grand Jury presentation. This is where we exercise our judicial role in making our decisions as to whether to prosecute or decline.

When we decide to prosecute, it is because we decide that this is how justice will be done. The decision is reached only after we have satisfied ourselves of the defendant's actual guilt.[32]

The conviction psychology may be made more common by the availability and prevalence of plea bargaining. This practice, which offers undeniable advantages to both parties in certain circumstances, assures the prosecutor of a conviction when a trial might result in acquittal. Plea bargaining epitomizes the conviction psychology as a prosecutor bargains for a plea when he feels that his case is not strong enough to obtain a conviction at trial.

[32]Whitney N. Seymour, Jr., "Why Prosecutors Act Like Prosecutors," *Record of the Association of the Bar of the City of New York,* II (June 1956), 312–13.

Whatever the reasons for the use of this practice, 80 percent of the respondents in the study indicated a feeling that plea bargaining is justified and is utilized quite commonly in the prosecution process, which may show that the conviction psychology is more pervasive than the prosecutors would care to admit.

SUMMARY

The prosecutor as a public officer is the person in the criminal justice system charged with the responsibility of presenting the evidence that the state has against a defendant. He is normally considered to be an officer of the court, but, in fact, most of his responsibility is directed to performing the executive function of prosecuting violations of the law. The powers and duties of the prosecutor are defined by constitutional, statutory, and common law provisions. Likewise, the prosecutor is also the attorney and legal advisor to county officials.

The office of the county prosecutor in many parts of the United States is part-time, poorly financed, and frequently used as a stepping stone for higher political office. Because of the crucial position the officeholder occupies in the total criminal justice system, this must be viewed as a major defect. It requires a true professional to maintain adequate realtionships with the police, trial court, defense counsel, grand jury, and state and federal attorneys general.

The prosecutor frequently operates in extremely controversial areas of the law in such matters as plea bargaining, charge reductions, and decisions not to prosecute in favor of civil restitution. Such decisions closely resemble the sentencing function of the judge. In any event, the largest responsibility of the prosecutor revolves around the trial; as such, his role in the judicial procedure becomes paramount.

QUESTIONS

1. In what four states is the prosecutor appointed?
2. What is meant by the "adversary system"? the "inquisitorial system"?
3. Discuss the varying terms of office of the prosecutor. What are the arguments favoring two-year terms? four-year terms?
4. Describe the constitutional and statutory powers which a prosecutor commonly exercises.
5. Why is it often asked "What should a person become a prosecutor for if the job is only temporary and for ambitious men"?
6. Describe the general relationship which a prosecutor should have with the police, the trial courts, the defense counsel, grand jury.

7. Distinguish the functions of the prosecutor from those of the state attorney general.

8. Describe the general characteristics of the prosecutor's office as discussed by the American Bar Association.

9. Compare the European system of criminal investigation and prosecution with the system found in the United States.

10. What is meant by the statement "the prosecution's conviction psychology"? Discuss this concept.

THE ATTORNEY GENERAL

Among the most striking characteristics of the political system of the United States are the state and federal offices of the attorney general. Despite some differences in functions, both share a common core of authority and activities. Some aspects of each office are unique because of the separate governmental levels that the offices serve and also because position of the state attorney general varies from state to state in the amount of power it offers. This chapter briefly discusses the United States attorney general. Most of the material will cover the attorney general in the states.

HISTORICAL DEVELOPMENT OF THE ATTORNEY GENERAL

The attorney general's office originated centuries ago in England. In the Middle Ages, the king appointed attorneys, sergeants, and solicitors to represent the crown by performing the same general functions that the modern attorney general performs. The first use of the term *attorney general* appears to have been in 1398 by the English Parliament. The exact date of the first office of attorney general is uncertain. Hugh Bellot stated that in 1472, William

Husse was appointed the attorney general in England with the power to appoint assistants to act for him.[1]

By the sixteenth century, the king's attorney became the most important person in the legal department of the state. Gradually, the office of the attorney general began to assume political importance. The king's attorney would represent the crown in all tribunals. During the American Revolution, the English attorney general emerged as the legal adviser for the government, not just the king. He appeared on behalf of the crown in court, advised the various governmental departments, and even represented them in court. He became the government's advocate.

In colonial America, the attorney general came into being either by legislative or executive action. Most often, however, his duties were vague and uncertain. He was, in a sense, the delegate of the English attorney general. Early records indicate that the attorney general was engaged in such activities as preparing indictments for such charges as piracy, murder, and theft; appearing before the grand jury; and acting against persons for disrupting religious services.

An attorney general was appointed in the colonies as follows: Virginia, 1643; Rhode Island, 1650; New York, 1674; Massachusetts, 1680; Carolina, 1697.[2]

Study of the development of the state office of the attorney general reveals that thirty-four of the fifty states either continued the office by law or created it with the first state constitution. Eight others established the offices by law when statehood was accorded. Eight states did not have attorneys general at the time they became states. Georgia did not create a unified office of the attorney general until 1868, operating since colonial days with two attorneys general and a solicitor general. Iowa created the office seven years after statehood; Oregon, twenty; Ohio, thirty-three; Tennessee, thirty-five. Vermont did not create the office of its attorney general until one hundred and thirteen years after it joined the Union in 1791.[3]

UNITED STATES ATTORNEY GENERAL

The attorney general of the United States is the chief law officer in the president's cabinet. His position is somewhat unusual historically. Unlike the

[1]Hugh Bellot, "The Origin of the Attorney General," *Law Quarterly Review,* XXV, (1909), 405.

[2]Oliver W. Hammonds, "The Attorney General in the American Colonies," *Anglo-American Legal History,* Series 1, No. 3 (1939), pp. 6–20; Committee on the Office of the Attorney General, National Association of Attorneys General, *The Office of the Attorney General* (February 1971), pp. 14–17.

[3]*Office of the Attorney General,* pp. 17–18.

state governments, the United States government was not the natural successor of another government. The federal government rose completely new out of the Revolution. The office of attorney general has no common law authority, being created solely by statute.[4] The Constitution, in Article II, Section 2, provides that the attorney general is to advise the president on matters relating to his duties, but, other than this, his role is not defined.

In 1781, a committee of the Continental Congress recommended that an attorney general be appointed to prosecute all suits on behalf of the United States and advise Congress on matters it refers to him: the recommendation was not followed. The First United States Congress passed the Judiciary Act of 1787, authorizing the president to appoint an attorney general. It also provided for appointment of district attorneys, but they were not under the supervision of the attorney general. In 1861, when the attorney general was given power to appeal in inferior courts, the office was also given power over the district attorneys.

Even though the Constitution provided for the office of attorney general and mentioned *heads of departments,* the attorney general did not head a department until 1870, eighty-one years after the Departments of State, War, and Treasury were established. He was required to be a person knowledgeable in the law. Edmund Randolph became a member of President George Washington's cabinet as it developed, primarily because of the growing legal problems and also because of personal friendship with the president. Personal friendship and political obligations still play a part in selection of the president's cabinet. Until 1853, the attorney general was paid less than secretaries of other departments even though he carried an equal position in the cabinet.[5]

The duties of the United States attorney general have grown during the almost two hundred years since the Judiciary Act of 1789. He now heads major federal departments with thousands of personnel and highly complex responsibilities. He is required to manage a far-reaching bureaucracy composed of several diverse and politically sensitive divisions.

Organization of the United States Department of Justice

All functions of officers of the Department of Justice and of the agencies and employees thereof are, with four exceptions, vested in the *United States attorney general.* The exceptions are: (1) certain duties of hearing examiners employed by the department, (2) Federal Prison Industries, Incorporated, (3) Board of Directors and officers of the Federal Prison Industries, Incorporated, and (4) the Board of Parole.

---

[4]Judiciary Act of September 24, 1789, Statute 93.
[5]Richard Fenno, *The President's Cabinet* (Cambridge: Harvard University Press, 1959), p. 17.

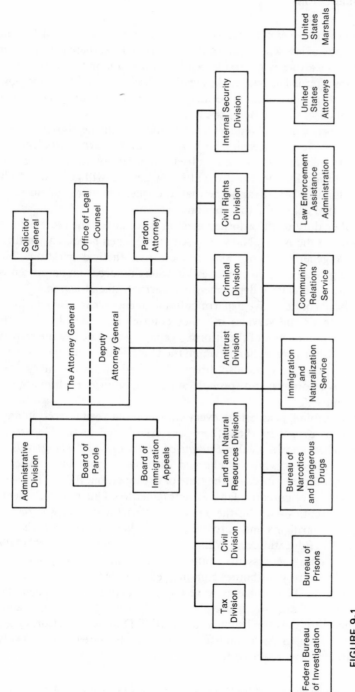

FIGURE 9-1

Organization Chart of the United States Department of Justice.*

*Source: *United States Government Organization Manual—1971/72,* Office of the Federal Register, National Archives and Records Service, General Services Administration (Washington, D.C.: Government Printing Office, 1971), p. 620.

The attorney general advises the president on questions of law and on matters outside of law when required. As a normal rule, there is rarely a proper occasion for the attorney general to render an opinion on the constitutionality of a measure after it has become law. He likewise does not have the power to declare an act unconstitutional because he would be invading the province of another branch of government, the courts.

The attorney general renders legal opinions to the heads of other departments, upon request, concerning both internal and external problems. Under this statutory mandate, he is not required to render opinions on areas outside of his legal duties. Furthermore, the attorney general will generally decline to give an opinion where it appears that the question does not arise in the department that asked for the opinion.

Another duty of the attorney general is to advise the secretaries of the Departments of the Army, Navy, and Air Force when necessary. In this area, the attorney general will not answer mere hypothetical questions. He will likewise not give an opinion on a question where no occasion has arisen within the requesting secretary's department to warrant official action.

The heads of executive departments and agencies can also give investigative assistance or the services of other counsel requested by the attorney general. A major concern of the attorney general is that he has the responsibility for supervising all litigation to which the United States, an agency, or officer thereof is a party. He must also direct all United States attorneys, assistant United States attorneys, and specially appointed counsel in discharging their respective duties.[6]

In the criminal justice field, every student has a keen interest in narcotics and dangerous drugs. In 1968, there was established in the Department of Justice an office known as the *Bureau of Narcotics and Dangerous Drugs* headed by a director who was charged with performing such duties as the attorney general prescribed. At the time of organization, federal investigation and enforcement of narcotics laws were fragmented. One major element—the Bureau of Narcotics—was in the Treasury Department and was responsible for control of marijuana and narcotics, such as heroin. Another, the Department of Health, Education, and Welfare, was responsible for control of dangerous drugs including depressants, stimulants, and hallucinogens, such as LSD. The separation of responsibilities complicated and obstructed the enforcement of drug controls. The problems were compounded when the agencies were confronted by well organized, disciplined, and resourceful criminals, and organized crime. With the establishment of the BNDD under the attorney general, federal laws were to be administered by a single bureau. Specifically, the BNDD director was required to:

[6]For the general duties of the United States Attorney General see Title 28, *United States Code Annotated,* Sections 509–19.

1. Consolidate the authority, experience, and personnel of the former Bureau of Narcotics in the Treasury Department and the Drug Abuse Control in the Department of Health, Education, and Welfare

2. Work with the states and local government in their crackdown on illegal trade in drugs and narcotics, and help train local agents and investigators

3. Maintain worldwide operations that work closely with other nations, to suppress the trade in illicit narcotics and marijuana

4. Conduct an extensive campaign of research and a nationwide public education program on drug abuse and its effects[7]

As this book is being produced, there is a proposal before Congress to further consolidate and refine the drug enforcement capabilities of the federal government.

Still another little known major responsibility of the attorney general is to prepare a national emergency plan and develop preparedness programs concerning law enforcement functions of concern to the executive branch of the federal government except where such functions are vested in other agencies by statute or executive order. The attorney general assists in developing preparedness programs covering law enforcement functions, provides liaison, guidance, and assistance to state and local government, maintains contact with the federal judicial system, and develops liaison channels with Congress.[8]

In the Department of Justice, a major part of all criminal prosecutions are performed by *United States attorneys* who are charged with the duty of prosecuting all crimes against the United States committed within their districts. To fulfill this obligation, the United States attorneys and their assistants must rely heavily on informed and efficient grand juries.

The United States attorney or an assistant usually presents the evidence to the grand jury. In an extreme case, however, the grand jury may decide to exclude the United States attorney, thereupon calling for questioning and otherwise conducting its own investigation.

The U.S. attorney is also the legal advisor of the grand jury. He is always prepared to explain the law but should never be asked for opinion as to the facts except for the legal ramifications of testimony or other evidence.[9]

Where the grand jury decides to indict, the U.S. attorney prepares the indictments although he may not be present when the grand jury decides whether or not to return an indictment. Once it is returned, however, further prosecution is within his control because the grand jury cannot withdraw it nor has it any further authority over it. In cases where the defendant waives

[7]Title 28, *United States Code Annotated;* Section 509, *Federal Register,* XXXIII (1968), 5611.

[8]Executive Order 11310, October 11, 1966, *Federal Register,* XXXI (1966), 13199.

[9]*Federal Rules of Criminal Procedures for the United States District Courts,* Rule 6 (d) (Washington, D.C.: Government Printing Office, 1966).

prosecution by grand jury indictment, he may be prosecuted by an information that is a statement of the offense charged and filed by the U.S. attorney. In all cases at the federal level, if the offense is punishable by death, prosecution must be by indictment.[10]

The office of the attorney general as seen in Figure 9-1 includes the *deputy attorney general,* who assists the attorney general in the overall supervision and direction of the department. He has specific responsibility for the executive office of United States attorneys, office of criminal justice, and office of the director of United States marshals. He is the chief liaison officer between the office of the attorney general and other governmental offices and handles matters pertaining to presidential and judicial appointments.

The *solicitor general* is the representative of the United States in the United States Supreme Court. He is the government's advocate or defender. In addition, he has sole jurisdiction to decide which of these cases lost in lower courts are to be appealed by the government. The office of the legal counsel is charged with drafting formal opinions of the attorney general and with assisting as legal advisor to the president. Executive orders of the president are reviewed prior to presidential execution. This office coordinates federal-state legal relations to the extent of having problems handled by the states rather than by the federal government. The office also coordinates the attorney general's responsibilities with respect to treaties, executive agreements, and international organizations.

The *pardon attorney's office* performs a specialized service for the attorney general dealing with receipt, investigation and disposition of applications for presidential pardons or acts of executive clemency.

The *Community Relations Service* was created by the Civil Rights Act of 1964 to assist communities, either upon request or at its initiative. It helps in solving disputes and difficulties and in avoiding racial upheavals. Its goal is to bring about progress toward securing justice, equality of opportunity, and human dignity for Americans.

The *Law Enforcement Assistance Administration* helps state and local governments reduce crime and improve law enforcement by providing support for improving the police, courts, corrections, and other criminal justice agencies.

The *assistant attorney general in charge of the criminal division* supervises and directs United States attorneys in criminal matters and litigation involving about 900 federal statutes, including the more commonly known criminal statutes on kidnapping, extortion, bankruptcy, fraud, forgery, counterfeiting, illegal trafficking in narcotics and dangerous drugs, among others. The Criminal Division supervises international extradition proceedings as well as criminal litigation arising under immigration and naturalization laws. It

---

[10] *Federal Rules of Criminal Procedures for District Courts,* Rule 7.

also coordinates the fight against organized crime, from initial detection through prosecution and appeal. The division maintains a number of metropolitan-based strike forces for this purpose. Should the solicitor general desire, he can assign to the division preparation of government briefs in its criminal cases before the Supreme Court and presentation of oral arguments. Preparation of the government's legislative program relating to criminal law is another major function. The activities touch on all aspects of criminal justice and crime.

The Federal Bureau of Investigation and Bureau of Narcotics and Dangerous Drugs are covered elsewhere in this book. However, one other bureau is intimately involved in the criminal justice system. *The Bureau of Prisons* has general supervision over the operations of federal correctional and community treatment facilities. Included are commitment, management, confinement, and support of federal prisoners. The five divisions in the bureau are (1) Institutional Services, (2) Community Services, (3) Administrative Services, (4) Health Services, and (5) Federal Prison Industries, Incorporated.[11]

ATTORNEY GENERAL IN STATE GOVERNMENT

The office of the attorney general is constitutional in forty-three states and Puerto Rico. The office is based on statute in Alaska, Connecticut, Hawaii, Indiana, Oregon, Vermont, and Wyoming, and in the territories of Guam, Samoa, and the Virgin Islands.

Relationship with State Government. The position that the attorney general occupies in the state government is unique in that it is a bridge between the executive and legislative branches. He advises both. The Florida Supreme Court commented that although the attorney general "in many respects is judicial in character," he is "intimately associated with the other departments of Government, being as well the proper legal adviser of the Executive and Legislative departments."[12]

Relationship with the Legislature. Primarily, the attorney general furnishes services to the legislature preparing legal opinions for the body, and rendering advice and opinions to individual legislators.

Relationship with the Judiciary. It is agreed by most authorities that the attorney general is an executive officer, not judicial, even though he does render advisory opinions that are quasi judicial in effect. For example, the

[11] *United States Government Organization Manual, 1971/72,* Office of the Federal Register, National Archives and Records Service, General Services Administration (Washington, D.C.: Government Printing Office, 1971), pp. 192–211.

[12] *State ex rel. Landis* v. *S. H. Kress Company,* 115 Fal. 189, 155 So. 823 (1934).

attorney general rendered over six hundred formal opinions in Arkansas and Kentucky in 1968. Idaho and New Jersey, although preparing only a few formal opinions, issued between one to three thousand informal opinions that year.[13] The attorney general plays a role in some states in disciplining members of the bar. It has likewise been held that the judiciary may discipline the attorney general for misconduct as an attorney even though the attorney general is in another branch of government.[14]

In California, the relationship of the attorney general to the judiciary is quite close. If a vacancy occurs in higher judicial offices, it is filled by the governor. The appointments, however, are not effective until confirmed by the California Commission on Judicial Appointments of which the attorney general is a member along with the chief justice of the state supreme court and other individuals.[15] Such responsibilities as these help create a close relationship between the attorney general and the judiciary.

Relationship with the Executive. The office of the attorney general is normally considered to be in the executive department. His duties as part of the executive branch primarily consist of advising its officers and agencies, approving various contracts, and occasionally supervising bond issues. He serves on boards or other commissions that direct varied governmental programs. In some states, he is appointed by the governor and may be removed by him.[16] The Council of State Governments reported that twenty-six jurisdictions have a governor's cabinet of which only sixteen include the attorney general as a member. The survey also indicates that the attorneys general view themselves as executive officers. They also indicate that their most important functions, in their opinion, are representing the state governmental agencies and serving as the attorney for the people.[17]

Common Law Powers of the Attorney General

State attorneys general derive their powers from constitutional, statutory, and common law. There is no clear division among the three. Each supplements the other. Because the powers of the attorney general, whether written or not,

---

[13]*Office of the Attorney General*, p. 251.

[14]"Court May Discipline State Attorney General for Professional Misconduct," *Harvard Law Review*, LXXIII (1960), 773.

[15]California: *Constitution*, Article VI, Section 7.

[16]Alaska, Guam, Hawaii, New Hampshire, New Jersey, Pennsylvania, Puerto Rico, Samoa, Virgin Islands, Wyoming.

[17]*Cabinets in State Government*, The Council of State Governments RM-436 (October 1969).

are primarily based upon the common law, we will now examine those powers as generally found throughout the United States. One must remember that the common law is different in every state. Nevertheless, there is a general similarity even though there may be no generally accepted delineation. In the following listing are the more usual common law powers.

1. The attorney general may act to protect the public interest by institution of civil actions on behalf of the state for the protection of the state's rights, interests, and well-being of its citizens. Such protection may be involved in the attorney general's suing to purge fraudulent individuals on voters lists; restraining a party performing an act without proper safety precautions where the public may be involved; or suing to prevent a corporation from doing business in the state without having first put up bonds to protect the citizens.

2. The attorney general has the standing to challenge the constitutionality of state legislation. He also has the power to attack actions by administrative agencies that, in his estimation, are injurious to the public interest, as in the instance where a state tax assessment office attempts to lower assessment rates. The attorney general may very well challenge the action because of the damage reduced taxes could have on the economy of the state.

3. The attorney general may intervene in public utility rate cases as a defender of the public interest. He may question the reasonableness and lawfulness of rate increases and may represent the state in litigation involving these rate increases.

4. He has the power to sue to remove public officers from offices wrongfully held by them. In this situation, for example, the attorney general may seek to remove an officer who fails to report criminal violations or institute proceedings to oust a treasurer for malfeasance in office. Under this general power, he may seek to have public officers perform duties they owe to the public. He may likewise seek recovery of money that public officials convert to their own use.

5. The common law also gives to the attorney general the power to challenge whether corporations may operate in a state. The attorney general is prohibited from doing this for a private complaint and can do so only when the public interest dictates.

6. The attorney general is vested with the power and duty of enforcing state antitrust laws.

7. One of the common law powers of the attorney general has been to prevent or abate public nuisances and, as a consequence, he may seek to enjoin nuisances in the form of water or air pollution. For example, he might seek an injunction against a mining company or a chemical corporation that discharges debris into a stream. He may proceed to prohibit the discharge of noxious fumes into the atmosphere in his efforts to protect the public.

8. Abatement of public nuisances against morality is an important common law power of the attorney general. He may initiate proceedings against gambling premises, bawdy houses, loud or boisterous business enterprises, and similar activities.

9. The power to institute and prosecute a suit to establish and effectuate a charitable donation resides with the attorney general. He can secure an accounting of a charitable trust fund.

10. He may intervene in an action contesting the existence of a valid will, especially where the property would escheat to the state if the deceased died with heirs.

11. At common law, the attorney general has had the exclusive power and duty to render legal counsel to the government. From this practice, several courts have held that agencies of the state government may not hire private counsel but must rely on the attorney general for advice and assistance. Statutes in many states have also been used to permit hiring of counsel by various agencies.

12. The office of the attorney general existed at common law. That of the local prosecutor did not. The office of the prosecuting attorney was carved out of that of the attorney general and virtually made an independent office. In exercising his common law powers, the attorney general undoubtedly may advise the prosecuting attorney as he does other officers, because he is regarded as the chief law officer of the state. However, by practically all jurisdiction either by constitution or statute, the offices are separate. Certain powers and duties are vested in the prosecutor and impose functions that cannot be increased nor decreased by the attorney general.

In most states, there is a considerable body of law defining the relationship between the two. Generally, however, where the attorney general is empowered either generally or specially in criminal cases, he may do any act the local prosecuting attorney may do in order to prosecute successfully.

In some states, the courts have said that the legislature may deprive the attorney general of certain common law powers by statute, such as giving the power to its local prosecutor to intervene in rate cases instead of to the attorney general. Still other courts have taken the opposite position.

13. Some states have given the attorney general the authority, by statute, to intervene in proceedings initiated by the local prosecutor. In specific circumstances, he may supersede him entirely, the rationale being the attorney general has the duty to do so if he believes that the government will be hindered in the lawful conduct of its affairs to the detriment of the peace, and good order of the state.

14. The attorney general has the power to appear before the grand jury, even though the power is also assigned to the local prosecutor (district attorney). Once again, this power sometimes has been changed by statute. If there is no statute in existence, then because the grand jury investigation is deemed to be as much a part of a criminal proceeding as an actual trial, the attorney general has the power to supersede the district attorney in a grand jury investigation where he has a good reason for so doing.

15. The common law established that the attorney general has the power to dispose of cases instituted by him in practically any way so long as he acts in good faith and in the public interest. He may make compromise agreements in cases, turn them over to local prosecutors for disposition, seek dismissals, or the like.

16. In a number of states, the attorney general may enter a *nolle prosequi* (decline to prosecute). This common law power has been recognized even where he intervenes or supersedes in a case.

Selection

The selection of the attorney general varies widely in each state. He is elected by popular vote in forty-two states; appointed by the governor in six states, three territories, and the Commonwealth of Puerto Rico; selected by the legislature in Maine; and, finally, by the supreme court in Tennessee.[18] It is likely that the attorney general will someday become the most common *single* elected official if the trend to elect the governor and lieutenant governor together on a single ballot continues to grow. Historically, the contrary is true —the attorney general has been appointed to his office. In England, he was appointed by the crown; in colonial America, by the governor. Even now, the attorney general of the United States is appointed by the president.

There is a running argument whether the attorney general should be appointed or elected. Proponents of the appointive procedure argue primarily that the executive is strengthened by placing the administrative power and responsibility in his hands. He can then appoint persons to carry out the policies upon which he was elected. Most recent studies on administrative organizations have argued for appointment of the attorney general. They contend that fragmentation, due to election of numerous officials, each with his own political philosophy, leads to irresponsibility, but that a single executive can be held responsible through periodic elections. Because the job of the attorney general is to advise the governor, he should be permitted to select his advisor. One other prevalent argument for appointment of the attorney general is that the elective process does not assure professional competence. The function of the attorney general is primarily to interpret the law, a technical task not to be involved in the electoral process.

The proponents of the elective system for the attorney general argue strongly that the appointed general owes his allegiance to the appointing official (usually the governor) and that he has no direct responsibility to the public. As an elective officer, he can be creative and exercise broad initiative. He is free of the fear of dismissal should he disagree with other political elective officers. In his advisory function to the governor, his elected position permits him to render impartial advice to the governor as well as to the state agencies, the legislature, and to the judiciary in those states where he has this responsibility. He can, in effect, represent the people without fear or favor.[19]

In the six states where the governor appoints the attorney general, the appointment is subject to confirmation by the senate or some other state body (New Hampshire). There is a lack of research and literature on this method of selection of the attorney general.

Terms of Office

Tennessee has an eight-year term of office for the attorney general. New Hampshire, five; Samoa, a minimum of two years; Alaska, Guam, Puerto Rico, and the Virgin Islands, an indefinite term. The remainder of the states set the

---

[18] *Office of the Attorney General,* p. 63.

[19] Louis J. Lefkowitz, "Position Paper of Louis J. Lefkowitz, Attorney General to Constitutional Convention, Committee on the Executive Branch," June 1, 1967, Albany, New York.

term at four years.[20] The attorney general may succeed himself in office without restriction in every state and territory except Alabama, Kentucky, and New Mexico. Only Kentucky prohibits immediate succession. New Mexico restricts the attorney general to two successive two-year terms; Alabama, to two successive four-year terms.[21]

The trend is toward longer terms. For example, the number of attorneys general serving two-year terms declined from twenty-one in 1937, to eighteen in 1950, to nine at present.[22] One of the major problems of the two-year term is that there is a lack of meaningful continuity, especially where a new incumbent assumes office after only a two-year term of his predecessor. Also, the time spent in campaigning and the costs involved mitigate against securing the most competent person to fill the job. The main argument favoring restrictions is the fear of *bossism* or self-perpetuation. This is possible with any political office. However, it would appear that summarily restricting an attorney general to a limited term may affect his ability to develop and implement long-range plans.

Once he is in office, how is the attorney general removed? First of all, impeachment is provided in thirty-six states and territories, twenty-one of which indicate it is the only method of removal. Impeachment is not a common means of removing attorneys general. Some of the alternative methods for removal of the attorney general include removal by the governor when he has the power to appoint. Hawaii indicates that the senate must consent to the removal. Various other governor-legislative removal procedures are followed in other states. In eight states, the legislature alone may remove other than by impeachment. In Arizona, Colorado, Louisiana, North Dakota, Oregon, Washington, and Wisconsin, where the attorney general is an elective office, he may be removed by recall. Louisiana indicates that the district court can remove an attorney general, and in Maryland, conviction in any court of law results in removal. In general, vacancies are filled by appointment, either by the governor, the legislature, or the supreme court; or by the elevation of a deputy.

Qualifications

In only two jurisdictions, no qualifications of any kind are required for the attorney general. Seventeen jurisdictions have no minimum age requirement. Twelve jurisdictions set a minimum age of twenty-one; nine, twenty-five years; two, twenty-six years; six, thirty years; one, thirty-one years.

Residence and citizenship are required, except in Guam, Nebraska, New

---

[20] *Office of the Attorney General,* p. 63.

[21] *Office of the Attorney General,* p. 70.

[22] *The Book of the States–1937,* The Council of State Governments II, 163 and *1950–51,* VIII, 629 (Chicago: Council of State Governments).

Hampshire, and Pennsylvania. Some jurisdictions do not require citizenship but do require the attorney general to be an elector, or an elector with a specific number of years residence in the jurisdiction.

Admission to the bar sometimes is not required. However, many jurisdictions stipulate bar membership by constitutional or statutory law. In others, bar membership is implied from statutory or a case law. For example, New Jersey prohibits the attorney general from practicing law privately. The implication of this prohibition is that he must be a member of the bar. In Minnesota, only members of the bar can appear in court as an attorney; because the duties of the attorney general require court appearance, it is implied that he must be a member of the bar.

The educational background, age at assumption of office, public offices held prior to taking office, and tenure of office are set out in Tables 9-1 through 9-4.[23]

TABLE 9-1   The Attorneys General: Educational Background.

Degree Held	Number of Attorneys General Holding Degree					
	1963	*1964*	*1965*	*1966*	*1967*	*1968*
L.L.B.	53	50	52	51	50	50
A.B. and L.L.B.	26	22	19	21	24	25
B.S. and L.L.B.	6	8	12	9	5	5
J.D.	1	1	0	0	1	1
B.S.L. and L.L.B.	0	0	1	1	1	0
A.A. and L.L.B.	0	0	0	0	1	1
Ph.B. and L.L.B.	0	2	1	1	1	1
B.B.A. and L.L.B.	0	0	1	0	1	1

From National Association of Attorneys General, Committee on the Office of Attorney General, *The Office of Attorney General,* February 1971, p. 77.

TABLE 9-2   Age at Assumption of Office.

Year	Age at Assumption of Office		
	Range	*Arithmetic Mean*	*Mode*
1963	32–63 years	47.2 years	48 years (freq. of 6)
1964	32–63 years	45.0 years	49 years (freq. of 7)
1965	29–63 years	46.4 years	49 years (freq. of 9)
1966	29–63 years	40.4 years	49 years (freq. of 8)
1967	29–63 years	44.1 years	41 years (freq. of 7)
1968	29–63 years	44.8 years	none discernible

From National Association of Attorneys General, Committee on the Office of Attorney General, *The Office of Attorney General,* February 1971, p. 78.

[23]Tables 9-1 through 9-4, as well as Figures 9-2 through 9-4, on the following pages, are reprinted from *Office of the Attorney General,* a report by the National Association of Attorneys General, Committee on the Office of Attorney General, pp. 77, 78, 183, 184, 187.

TABLE 9-3 Public Offices Held Prior to Taking Office.

Office	Number of Attorneys General Having Held Position					
	1963	*1964*	*1965*	*1966*	*1967*	*1968*
City or County Attorney	16	22	22	22	20	22
Municipal Judge	2	2	5	4	4	4
State Judge	3	4	4	4	4	4
Federal Judge	0	0	1	1	1	1
State Agency Head	3	2	4	3	5	5
Governor	1	1	1	1	1	1
State Senator	5	4	2	3	6	6
State Representative	16	14	13	13	13	14
Floor Leader	3	2	2	4	4	4
Asst. or Dep. A.G.	14	11	13	13	15	13
U.S. Attorney	6	7	7	7	6	6
Assistant to Governor	1	0	2	2	2	1
City Elected Official	2	1	1	1	2	2
Lieutenant Governor	1	1	1	1	1	1

From National Association of Attorneys General, Committee on the Office of Attorney General, *The Office of Attorney General,* February 1971, p. 78.

TABLE 9-4 Tenure of Office.

Years of Tenure	Number of Attorneys General Holding Given Tenure					
	1963	*1964*	*1965*	*1966*	*1967*	*1968*
One or less	16	7	4	4	0	0
Two	14	10	15	5	14	4
Three	5	7	3	15	3	12
Four	5	10	10	7	15	3
Five	5	6	5	4	1	13
Six	2	4	5	4	4	4
Seven	1	2	2	5	5	1
Eight	1	0	2	2	4	5
Nine	0	3	1	2	1	4
Ten-Fourteen	3	4	5	4	5	5
Fifteen-Twenty	1	1	1	1	1	1

From National Association of Attorneys General, Committee on the Office of Attorney General, *The Office of Attorney General,* February 1971, p. 78.

Organization of the Office of the Attorney General

The duties and functions that the attorney general must perform dictate to a substantial degree how the office will be organized. The organization is not rigid or peculiar to one state. The organization of the office of an attorney general follows several different patterns. At one pole, there may be no formal division of work although there may be specialization. For example, Nevada has attorneys who specialize in the major areas of concern to the state: Colorado River Commission, motor vehicles, gaming commission, and so on. In some offices, the major portion of the staff work directly under the attorney general, but there may also be a few highly specialized divisions. For example, Mississippi has no statutory divisions but there is a Civil Rights Division and a Criminal Division in the office. There has also been organized a Federal Litigation Division. See Figure 9-2.

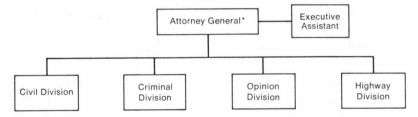

*The Attorney General is also the State Securities Commissioner.

FIGURE 9-2

Organization of the Alabama Office of the Attorney General.

Another kind of organization has almost all staff members working within divisions, but the divisions are few and broad in the function each performs. There are, for instance, the appeals, criminal, civil, and legal affairs divisions. A fourth group of jurisdictions has a highly structured organization with divisions that perform both general and specialized functions. Highly specialized personnel are assigned to these specialized divisions. Figures 9–3 and 9–4 illustrate this kind of organization.

Authority of the Attorney General to Initiate Prosecutions

Only six states do not allow the attorney general to initiate prosecutions under any circumstances. In six jurisdictions of the United States, the attorney general is responsible for all or most local prosecutions (Samoa, Guam, Virgin Islands, Alaska, Delaware, Rhode Island). It will be noted that these jurisdictions are atypical. They are small in populations and area, except for Alaska. They do not have strong county governments. In four of the six, the attorney general is appointed. The incidence of criminal cases is probably relatively small.

Some fourteen states authorize their attorneys general to initiate prose-

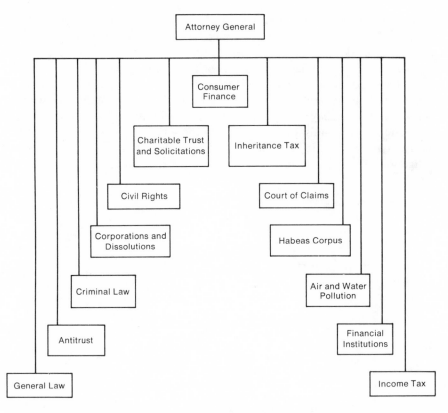

FIGURE 9-3

Organization of the Illinois Office of the Attorney General.

cutions at their discretion.[24] A few states give the attorney general either exclusive or concurrent jurisdiction to initiate prosecutions under certain statutes. For example, in Indiana, he may commence prosecution for violators of the lobbyist statute and antitrust acts, for tax frauds, and against a sheriff who permits a lynching. In Kentucky, only the attorney general is permitted to initiate criminal actions under laws relating to unemployment compensation and a few other miscellaneous subjects. On the other hand, Arizona, Colorado, Maryland, Minnesota, Ohio, Oklahoma, Oregon, Wisconsin, and Wyoming permit the attorney general to initiate prosecutions only at the request or under the direction of another state officer. A few states deny the attorney general

[24]California, Georgia, Hawaii, Iowa, Nebraska, New Hampshire, New Jersey, New York, Maine, Michigan, North Dakota, South Carolina, South Dakota, Vermont.

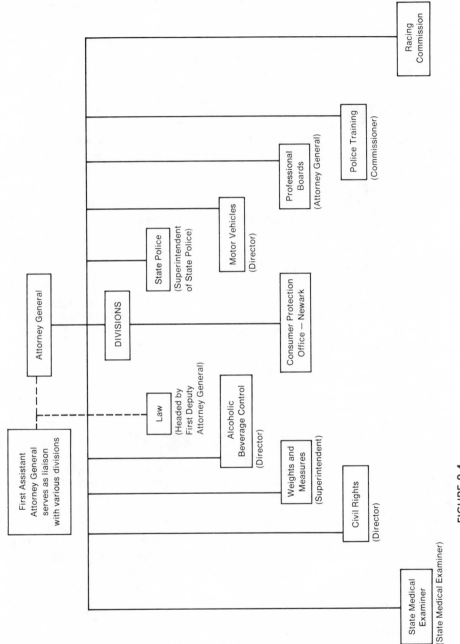

FIGURE 9-4
New Jersey Department of Law and Public Safety Headed by the Attorney.

any authority to initiate prosecutions. In some, he can only handle cases on appeal.[25]

Relationship of the Attorney General to State Law Enforcement Agencies

The attorney general has a close and continuing relationship with the agencies that are part of the criminal justice system. Many attorneys general have at least some direct law enforcement duties in the various jurisdictions. They may have organizational divisions set up specifically to handle organized crime matters. These divisions may possess peace officer powers in performance of their duty; have responsibility for criminalities functions on a statewide basis; or serve as a criminal investigation body statewide. In some jurisdictions, the attorney general supervises the state fire marshal. As a general rule, however, attorneys general do not have charge of a significant number of law enforcement personnel. One major exception is New Jersey where the state police are the attorney general's responsibility.

The attorney general is commonly considered a part of the courts in our system of criminal justice. He is seen as a law officer rather than a law enforcement official, if one accepts the trichotomy of courts, corrections, and police as comprising the criminal justice system.[26]

Do the attorneys general want to have a greater voice and control over state police? One recent comprehensive study concluded:

> Incumbent Attorneys General were asked whether the Attorney General should have authority to direct the state police, or highway patrol. Seven said he should have full authority, seventeen that he should have limited authority, and sixteen that he should have none. Sixteen thought that the state police should be accountable to the Attorney General with regard to enforcement of criminal laws, while eighteen thought they should not. Of one hundred and four former Attorneys General, fifteen felt that the Attorney General should have complete authority over state police, thirty-seven that he should have limited authority, and fifty-two that he should have none.[27]

It is noted, therefore, that a majority of current and former attorneys general believe they should have some control over state police.

One of the new areas in which most attorneys general are involved results from the enactment of the Omnibus Crime Control and Safe Streets Act passed

---

[25] *Office of the Attorney General,* p. 28.

[26] The President's Commission on Law Enforcement and the Administration of Justice, *The Challenge of Crime in a Free Society* (Washington, D.C.: Government Printing Office, 1967), p. 7.

[27] *Office of the Attorney General,* p. 484.

by Congress in 1968. The attorney general has a direct interest in this act. In only two states, Kentucky and West Virginia, is he or one of his staff not a member of the State Planning Agency (SPA), the office set up to administer federal grants made to each state.[28]   Charles Rogovin, Administrator of the Law Enforcement Assistance Administration, deplored the fact that some of the SPAs did not include the attorney general.

> ... An attorney general has special abilities of great value to bring to the L.E.A.A. program regardless of whether his official duties include law enforcement or strictly legal work.
>
> I do not know all of the reasons why some attorneys general are not represented on state supervisory boards. If partisan considerations are even a factor, I would urge that they be forgotten. Congress clearly intended that it be nonpartisan and that is the way it is being operated by the L.E.A.A. staff.[29]

The importance of having the attorney general on the SPA appears to be recognized by the several states. In fifty-two separate United States' jurisdictions, the attorney general or a member of his staff is on the SPA. In thirteen, he is the chairman, and in two more, a member of his staff heads the board. In four of the fourteen, the attorney general is appointed by the governor.[30] The long-range impact to the Omnibus Act and the importance of the attorney general serving on the SPA can be seen from the purposes for which Congress enacted the act:

> 1. To encourage states and units of general local government to prepare and adopt comprehensive plans based upon their evaluation of state and local problems of law enforcement
> 2. To authorize grants to states and units of local government in order to improve and strengthen law enforcement
> 3. To encourage research and development directed toward the improvement of law enforcement and the development of new methods for the prevention and reduction of crime and the detection and apprehension of criminals[31]

SUMMARY

The attorney general is important in the system of criminal justice because through his office he is in a powerful political position to lend support to other criminal justice agencies. He has the capability, in most

[28] *Office of the Attorney General,* pp. 515–16.

[29] *1969 Report of Conference Proceedings,* National Association of Attorneys General, p. 21.

[30] *Office of the Attorney General,* pp. 515–16.

[31] United States: Title I, 82 Statutes 197, Public Law Number 90–351, Ninetieth Congress.

states, to help these other agencies by providing staff support such as attorneys, criminalists, forensic scientists, evidence technicians, investigators, and other professionals. The assistance may be to the courts, corrections, or police depending on the need. He generally has the authority to initiate prosecutions and assist local prosecutors in conducting investigations. In many areas, the powers of the attorney general in administration are unclear and he can carve out the role he wishes to perform. This is especially true in the State Planning Agencies provided for by the Omnibus Crime and Safe Streets Act of 1968. Because of the uniqueness of his office statewide, he can strengthen efforts of local police, prosecutions, and corrections offices. We have discussed in some detail in this chapter who the attorney general is, what he does, and how he can become more effective. The attorney general can play an important role in developing a strong, viable criminal justice system, provided he is energetic enough to exert the necessary leadership.

QUESTIONS

1. Describe the historical development of the Attorney General.
2. What is the specific national responsibility of the United States Attorney General? Discuss the development of the office of the U.S. Attorney General.
3. Describe the organization of the office of the United States Attorney General. What are the overall responsibilities of the U.S. Attorney General?
4. The office of the state attorney general is constitutional in how many states? What states and territories base the office on statutory mandate?
5. Describe the relationship of the state attorney general with the chief executive of the state.
6. Discuss the general common law powers of the state attorney general.
7. Describe the various methods of selecting state attorneys general.
8. Summarize the arguments for and against elected versus appointed state attorneys general.
9. What are the various ways in which a state attorney general may be removed?
10. Discuss the relationship of the state attorney general in your state with state law enforcement agencies.

DEFENSE ATTORNEY

The role of the lawyer came into existence in the ancient Greco-Roman world. The Athenians are credited with being the first to establish regular processes of law. Their familiarity with the subject of law plus the vigorous political activity of the times initiated considerable court action. They were, in effect, a country of litigants. In those days, citizens were their own prosecuting and defense attorneys. The most famous trial of the period was that of Socrates, initiated by one of the citizens who undertook a prosecution to force Socrates out of Athens. He was formally indicted for not believing in the Athenian deities and for corrupting the young. The penalty demanded was death. Socrates appeared in court with his famous defense speech, the Apology, but was found guilty. Where penalties were not fixed by law, the condemned had the right to propose an alternative to that demanded by the prosecution, and the jury had to choose between them. Socrates suggested a fine he could not pay, and the jury, through a majority vote, chose the death penalty.[1]

With the development of English law, the defense attorney was unknown. At the time of the signing of the Magna Carta, individuals who were suspected of committing crimes were charged by jury presentment. This is not intended to mean that the person so denounced was entitled or required to

[1]Robert J. Bonner, *Lawyers and Litigants in Ancient Athens* (New York: Benjamin Blom, 1969), pp. 5, 101; A. R. Burn, *The Pelican History of Greece* (Baltimore: Penguin Books, 1966), pp. 305–9.

submit to a jury trial to prove his innocence. He could purge himself from his alleged wrongdoing by submitting to *ordeals* or to compurgation.

The ordeal was a method of judging guilt or innocence based on superstition and used fire or water. When tried by the ordeal of fire, the accused either walked barefoot over hot stones or carried red-hot irons in his hands. In the water ordeal, the suspect was simply thrown into a river or lake; if his body floated to the surface, it was a sign of rejection and, hence, he was guilty. Another common variation of these ordeals was to thrust the hands of the accused into scalding water. If he came away from either the scalding or the fire ordeal with injury he was guilty because God would have protected him from injury if he were innocent.

In compurgation, the accused would solemnly swear before a judge that he was innocent of the charges. After this purging himself by his oath, he would call on some of his friends and neighbors, called compurgators, to swear that they believed him. If the compurgators would not so swear, trial by ordeal followed with predictable results.[2]

The inquest or petit jury trial in preference to the ordeal was considered, in the early Anglo-Saxon legal development, to be an unusual privilege. In order to obtain such treatment, the king was paid a substantial fee. Later, trial by ordeal was abolished. With the loss of this means of punishment, other, more horrible ones arose to arrive at the truth, such as being pressed to death and branding. Methods such as these led to the realization that it was necessary to have someone to plead the case of the accused in court.

SOLICITORS AND BARRISTERS IN ENGLAND

The earliest division of the practice of law was based on a separation between the legal tasks of representation of a client in a trial and advocacy in higher appellate courts. The profession of the lawyer came about when it became acceptable to permit an accused to employ another, a *solicitor,* to plead his case in court. The second group, *barristers,* were employed to represent a client in cases on appeal when there was no need for the litigant himself to be present.

The right of advocacy in the royal courts was not granted by legislation or edict. Individual judges in each court decided who would be allowed to represent a litigant. It was therefore to their own advantage that the counselors be well trained. Soon it became the custom that those who appeared in court first be declared fit to practice before the bar by senior members already experienced as judges and advocates.

[2]Julius Marke, *Vignettes of Legal History* (New York: Fred Rothman and Company, 1965), pp. 208–16, 313–23.

Faced with shady practices by some of the solicitors, often caused by ignorance of the law, the judges gradually provided that the function of initiating litigation could only be performed by a person certified by the court. The necessity for this control was evident: solicitors were found to be embezzling money from clients, extortionate fees were charged for unnecessary litigation, and vexatious litigation was commenced against clients who were tardy in payment of money.

In 1729 the forerunner of the modern bar examination came into being. The English law provided that before one could be approved as a solicitor, he had to serve a period as a law clerk and then be examined by a judge. In 1830, oral examinations were inaugurated that solicitors were required to pass before being admitted to practice law. There were still no statutes in existence governing the rights of barristers nor qualifications for admission to practice law. In 1887, the Solicitor's Act set up a procedure for the Council of the Law Society to act as a disciplinary committee with power to refer breaches of ethics and law to the courts for appropriate disposition.[3]

Throughout the years, the control over the legal profession in England was provided to protect the people from being persecuted by those members of the legal profession who preyed upon the poor and the ignorant. The development of the legal profession in the United States took a similar tack.

DEVELOPMENT OF THE U.S. LEGAL PROFESSION

Until the end of the Civil War, the lawyer in the United States typically had a face-to-face relationship with his client and, as a rule, handled all of the legal problems in a community. He often acted as the counselor and arbiter in his village. The war and the gigantic growth of large business corporations dramatically changed these relationships. As Adolphe Berle said, the lawyer became "an intellectual jobber and contractor for business matters."[4] The lawyers assumed the task of remolding the legal framework from that suited to an agrarian society to one for a corporate state.

We have seen that, during the formulative years of the legal profession in England, lawyers were trained by fellow practitioners in law offices rather than by attending a university. This was generally the practice followed in the United States through the middle of the nineteenth century, at which time formal legal education started to come into existence. The coming of age of university legal education dates to 1870 when Christopher Columbus Langdell

[3]Brian Abel-Smith and Robert Stevens, *In Search of Justice* (London: Penguin Press, 1968), pp. 16–25, 50–63, 199–205.

[4]Herman Prickett, *Courts, Judges, and Politics* (New York: Random House, 1961), pp. 120–25.

was appointed the dean of Harvard Law School. It was not until the last decade of the nineteenth century, however, that the law schools required the law student to have some college education. In 1921, the American Bar Association stated that two years of college would be mandatory for a student who wishes to be admitted to an approved law school.

At present, every state has set up standards for admission to the state bar. Although the individual state standards vary, each draws essentially from an English statute promulgated in 1402:

> All attorneys should be examined by the judges, and in their discretion, only those found to be good and virtuous, and of good fame, learned and sworn to do their duty, be allowed to put upon the roll and all others put out.[5]

Admission to the bar means no more than that the lawyer is permitted to practice law in the courts of the admitting state or other jurisdiction. The standards of conduct for the professional lawyer are high, almost idealistic. Should ethical problems arise, each state provides a scheme for disciplining attorneys. Some states leave the matter of discipline to the professional bar association; some require the court to do the disciplining.

COUNSEL FOR THE DEFENDANT

The need for counsel for a defendant was expressed four decades ago:

> The right to be heard would be, in many cases, of little avail if it did not comprehend the right to be heard by counsel. Even the intelligent layman has small and sometimes no skill in the science of law. . . . Left without the aid of counsel, he may be put on trial without a proper charge and convicted of incompetent evidence, or evidence irrelevant to the issue or otherwise inadmissible. He lacks both the skill and knowledge adequately to prepare his defense, even though he may have a perfect one. He requires the guiding hand of counsel at every step in the proceedings against him. Without it, though he is not guilty, he faces the danger of conviction because he does not know how to establish his innocence.[6]

Subsequently, the United States Supreme Court held that the Constitution mandates that a felony defendant in both federal and state courts be afforded the right to be represented by counsel. It is only recently that the Supreme Court of the United States revolutionized criminal proceedings by ruling that a free attorney must be provided to any person tried for a petty offense even if he is jailed only for one day. Today, there is agitation for the appointment

[5]Prickett, *Courts, Judges, and Politics,* pp. 120–25.
[6]*Powell* v. *Alabama* 287 U.S. 45, 68–69 (1932).

of counsel for the poor in civil cases because the results of civil trial are often financially devastating for a defendant.

It is necessary to understand the importance of the defense counsel to the defendant. An adequate defense does not commence when the defendant and his attorney enter the court room. There should be an attorney present at the earliest point in the legal process. The Supreme Court has held that counsel must be provided at critical stages of the criminal process—arraignment,[7] preliminary examination,[8] and at the police interrogation of a suspect who is in custody.[9] Constitutionally, appointment is required by the state as a matter of right for an indigent defendant who is granted an appeal from a conviction.[10] Probation and parole revocation hearings, although somewhat different from the legal technicalities of a trial, still involve disputed issues of fact, gathering evidence, and investigation. Therefore, a lawyer for the defense is needed to represent the person adequately.

THE ROLE AND DUTIES OF THE DEFENSE COUNSEL

The defense counsel has a primary obligation to his client within very broad guidelines set out by court rules, law, case decisions, and legal ethics. He will work to discover any legitimate angle he can to protect his client. He will attempt not only to secure the acquittal of his client, but, if that is not realizable, will make every effort to have the defendant convicted of some lesser offense or to mitigate the sentence imposed by the court.

The counsel for the defense is a peculiar breed. He is quite likely to have compassion for the downtrodden and a deep feeling for the welfare of the individual. He is interested in the slightest infringement of the legal rights of anyone. This is not to say that the same is not true of many prosecutors, but they have different and conflicting roles to perform that create pressures upon them to prosecute and secure convictions. The defense attorney operates as a free agent with allegiance only to his client. The commonly heard comment that the defense attorney is a "bleeding heart," and the prosecutor is "too calloused," stems from this type of role conflict.

The next important duty, once the preliminary investigation by the defense attorney has been accomplished, is the commencement of the trial. In U.S. trials, the defendant may elect trial by court or by jury. If jury trial is

---

[7] *Hamilton* v. *Alabama* 368 U.S. 52 (1961).

[8] *White* v. *Maryland* 373 U.S. 59 (1963).

[9] *Miranda* v. *Arizona* 384 U.S. 436 (1966).

[10] *Douglas* v. *California,* 372 U.S. 553 (1963).

selected, the first step is the selection of the individuals who will serve as jurors. In most jurisdictions, there are varying degrees of permissible questioning of these individuals, but nevertheless, the defense attorney has a valuable role to perform in questioning the prospective jurors. The procedure of *voir dire* (preliminary) examination of jurors is an important factor in the outcome of the case. The defense attorney is vitally concerned with this phase.

It is during the *voir dire* examination that the counsels for both parties attempt to feel out the attitudes of the jurors toward problems that are detrimental to one side or the other. For example, the defense attorney is familiar with any criminal record that his client might have. As a consequence, he may want to know how individual jurors react to having a one-time convict being tried on another criminal charge. The problem of jurors' prejudices against former offenders is very important in securing an impartial jury. It is incumbent upon him to ascertain prejudice before the final jury is impaneled.

As a second point, the defense attorney wants to meet the prospective jury members and to create a favorable impression upon them. Extreme care must be exercised to ensure that his questioning is not carried out in such a manner as to antagonize the jurors. Courtesy in questioning jurors and requesting that individual members be excused no matter what the cause can create an atmosphere of cooperation between the jury and the defense attorney by indicating that both want to have an impartial body decide the fate of the defendant. The defense attorney must not attempt to humiliate individual jurors nor should he seek the dismissal without due cause of certain classes of jurors, such as all Protestants, Negroes, Caucasians, or blue-collar workers.

The defense obviously desires to have a jury finally sworn that is favorable to his case. Quite often one hears or reads that a certain attorney has a knack for selecting favorable jurors because he knows human nature or because he knows that all Catholics are more conservative than low-income blacks and that they favor big business. Probably the real reason for his success in selecting jurors is because of careful analysis of the backgrounds of the jurors. Intuitive selection or exclusion is no substitute for knowledge and defense attorneys are aware of this. Simplistic generalizations are notoriously inaccurate and for a defense attorney this is a deadly vice.

Once the jury members are finally agreed upon and sworn, the opening statements of the counsel for both sides are made (1) to acquaint the jury with testimonial evidence that may be detrimental to one side or the other; (2) to forewarn the jury of the general tenor of the evidence to be presented; and (3) to create a favorable atmosphere to acquit or convict. The statements are short, clear expositions of what will follow when there is the presentation of evidence. The prosecutor precedes the defense attorney. In many cases, the defense may reserve his opening statement until he is ready to present his evidence. He does this to keep his case always fresh in the minds of the jury members rather than take a chance that they will forget, especially when the prosecutor intends to present a lot of evidence. This technique is also used when the defense is not going to present any evidence but still wishes to address the jury after the prosecutor presents his evidence. As a practical matter, a large number of defense attorneys reserve their opening remarks until after the prosecutor has completed his case.

In his opening statement, which is normally short, the defense attorney will quite likely interject matters extraneous to the evidence to be produced, in order to cloud the primary issues in the case. Underlying this technique is an effort to arouse sympathy for the defendant by such comments as: "It could have happened to anyone," or "It was simply an innocent mistake." If successful, the attorney has taken a big first step toward the defense of his client.

PRESENTATION OF
EVIDENCE AT THE TRIAL

During this phase of the criminal proceeding, the role and conduct of the defense attorney to a large extent determine the success or failure of the entire endeavor. Remember, the primary task is to secure an acquittal. Sympathy plays a large part in an acquittal according to the many experienced defense attorneys who state that they can frequently predict the outcome of a case by the amount of sympathy that a defense attorney creates.

How does the defense attorney create the aura of sympathy that is so necessary? One way is to develop a picture of the victim of the alleged offense as being the real culprit in the case. In this kind of situation, the defense attorney attempts to put the victim on trial in the mind of the jury. His every undesirable trait and characteristic is brought out by the defense who hopes to generate hostility on the part of the jurors toward the victim and sympathetic understanding toward the defendant. Once the jury can be made to accept the victim as the "bad guy," the defense lawyer has, to a great degree, accomplished his job. Take the case where a defendant is on trial for murdering an acquaintance he allegedly found in cohabitation with his wife. The defense will undoubtedly gather evidence to prove that the victim was in the habit of promiscuously seducing women. He may also attempt to prove that his client's wife actually invited such conduct.

Still another favorite trial tactic to arouse sympathy is to picture the defendant as an object that the police and the state want to get because of prior record, unpopular association, or whatever. Every effort is made to place the police and the prosecutor in a position of discredit because of the way the defendant was arrested (harassment), the evidence secured (illegal), and a confession obtained (coerced); or because of the fact that the defendant furnished incriminating information (he was promised leniency).

The defense attorney may show that his client was merely a victim of circumstances where a series of completely unrelated circumstances occurred and the defendant just happened to be present. If one juror can say to himself, "It could have happened to me!" the defense attorney can say he has done a good job.

Frequently, the defense attorney attempts to muddle the main issue by keeping it as vague as possible. He may do this by showing that the bias of the various witnesses toward the defendant is the real cause for his being on trial, not the fact that there is hard evidence pointing toward his guilt. *They* are the ones responsible because of their prejudice toward *my client.*

Sympathy can also be encouraged by the manner in which the defendant is physically presented to the court. If deformed, the jury is made aware of this fact. If the defendant has a wife and children, the attorney makes sure that they are in the courtroom lending moral support to the poor, unfortunate defendant. If he suffers from a disease, an attack from the symptoms in front of the jury never hurts. In addition, the defense attorney maintains the impression of a spring under tension—always ready to uncoil for the benefit of his client should he be falsely or improperly maligned by the prosecutor.

The defense attorney has the responsibility of thwarting the overzealous prosecutor by preventing the introduction of evidence that has no relevance toward proving the prosecutor's case, but is aimed solely at painting a picture of the defendant as a "bad guy."

More and more in trials, the defense of insanity in some form is being raised. It may take the forms of temporary or permanent insanity or diminished capacity. The entire subject of legal insanity is fraught with emotion, uncertainty, conflict, and dramatics. If the background and character of the defendant have been placed in a favorable or sympathetic light, the jurors may look for a way to acquit the defendant because of low intellect or temporary insanity and not because of the evidence presented by the prosecution to establish guilt.

During the trial, the defense attorney must be alert to challenge the legality of evidence whether it be because of an illegal search and seizure, irrelevancy, hearsay, or other valid reason. His attention to detail during the trial itself is of utmost importance in representation of his client. The duty of the defense attorney is to use every reasonable and available defense to protect his client. He dare not be remiss in this obligation.

The final argument to the jury is but another chance to reinforce the points and evidence brought out during the presentation of the evidence phase. Once the defense rests its case after introduction of its evidence and there is no rebuttal evidence offered by the prosecution, the stage is set for final arguments. In this phase, the procedure might seem odd to the layman: the prosecution opens and closes with the defendant's final argument sandwiched in between.

During the presentation of evidence in the trial, much testimony is elicited. Because the exchanges are frequently hot and heavy, salient points that are pertinent to the defendant's case slip by the jury's attention. The defense attorney now uses these innocuous bits of testimony and evidence to weave his version and stress the importance of both as they pertain to the innocence of his client. Remember that the prosecutor has previously reviewed the same evidence and arrived at an opposite conclusion. The defense attorney, however, need not have as neat and logical a presentation as the prosecution. His main objective is to convince the jury that a reasonable doubt exists as to the guilt of the defendant. The defense attorney is not too interested in rebutting point by point the arguments put forth by the prosecutor.

The defense attorney must avoid alienation of any of the jury by talking down to them. He is the voice of morality who desires to right a wrong done to a fellow member of the human race. He emphasizes that part of the testimony and evidence, no matter how fragmentary, that supports his client. Evidence that is damaging is omitted or presented in a light that is favorable to the defendant. He hammers at the weak points in the evidence presented by the prosecution; he attacks the credibility of prosecution witnesses while emphasizing the truthfulness of the testimony of defense witnesses. In attempting to establish a reasonable doubt, the defense attorney does not always appear as cool and dispassionate as the prosecutor. After all, he is defending an innocent man whom the state is attempting to make a criminal. Emotional sobs and frenzied pleading are often tools used to implant the seed of a reasonable doubt.

The case presentation comes to an end. The judge now instructs the jury on the law that is to be followed and the jury retires to reach a verdict. The defense attorney has performed his duty. The fate of the defendant is now out of his hands.

COURT-APPOINTED COUNSEL

Court-appointed counsel for an indigent with the judge appointing an attorney for a defendant is the most widely used method of providing representation. The attorney usually is selected at random or on a rotating basis from members of the local bar. As the system would have it, a high percentage of younger attorneys take the cases because they frequently have the time and wish to gain experience. Judges, however, usually appoint the more experienced, more competent attorneys in serious or capital cases. Compensation, as a rule, is quite low and completely inadequate. Reimbursement for investigative assistance is often unavailable. In California, however, the state does provide attorneys' compensation, funds for investigation, and trial and appeal monies.

The assigned-counsel system developed when the United States had many small communities in rural areas. There were few criminal cases, and the ones there were attracted wide attention. From the many attorneys who would volunteer their services, one was assigned. The success of the assigned counsel system depended on the relative infrequency of criminal cases. In this environment, the few criminal cases relieved attorneys from the burden of frequent, nonfee court appearances.[11] Presently, the inducements for accepting assigned cases usually involve singly, or in combination, any of the following:

1. Receiving compensation
2. Getting referrals as a direct result of being assigned the case
3. Creating a good relationship with judges that could prove useful in future cases
4. Fulfilling professional and social obligations
5. Enhancing one's reputation as a skilled defense lawyer by taking highly publicized cases
6. Gaining trial experience, wherein beginning attorneys, fresh out of law school, take the assigned cases to develop the skill of advocacy.

It is unlikely that any of these inducements attract the more competent attorneys; hence, the cases are defended by those least competent to do so.[12]

The system of assigned counsel originally developed in the idea that the bar had the obligation to provide free legal services to selected needy defendants. The situation today is vastly changed. As a consequence, the number of cases requiring counsel has risen rapidly, at a rate disproportionate to the availability of attorneys. If the assigned counsel system is to be used, then it is unfair to require attorneys to be called upon time and again without adequate compensation whether it be for investigation, trial, or appeal.

The merits of the assigned-counsel system are usually pointed out by emphasizing the defects in the public defender system. Some insist that the assigned counsel is more responsive to his client because his complete allegiance is to him and not to an outside public defender agency. Because the assigned counsel does not depend on the assigned case for his livelihood, he is free to decide on the best legal advice he can give the defendant, not being under pressure, he can defend the interests of his client. It is then argued that assigned counsel makes a better adversary and battles more tenaciously for his client than the public defender who is more directly dependent upon the establishment for his position.[13]

[11]Herman I. Pollock, "Equal Justice in Practice," *Minnesota Law Review*, XLV (1961), *et passim*.

[12]"Representation of Indigents in California—A Field Study of the Public Defender System and Assigned Counsel Systems," *Stanford Law Review*, XIII (May 1961), 522.

[13]Edward J. Dimock, "The Public Defender: A Step Toward a Police State," *American Bar Association Journal*, (1956), p. 219.

This argument lacks merit. First, most cases are generally not contested in open court but are settled by deals made between the prosecutor and defense attorney. Too frequently, cases that go to trial are already lost. Even conceding that assigned counsel may be a better system, it is not at all clear that it is in the best interests of the client to go to trial, especially if he is guilty. It might be of more importance for the assigned counsel to be an "assigned bargainer" to negotiate with the prosecutor to secure the best deal for his client. The bargainer function would ensure that the defendant is not excessively punished.

One could argue that the public defender could make the same deals. But because he has such heavy case loads he might be less willing to bargain aggressively for his client. He might prefer to keep his calendar open for more important cases.

The assigned-counsel system has certain limitations. It is based on the assumption that all lawyers are qualified to handle criminal cases. This assumption is false. As presently administered, the assigned-counsel system fails to "afford representation which is uniformily experienced, competent and zealous."[14]

A serious problem arises with the assigned-counsel system in courts in large metropolitan areas. It fails to provide adequate representation in inferior and lower courts of limited jurisdiction, the primary reason being the large number of cases. At least part of the reason stems from economic functions, wherein assignment of compensated counsel to all indigent defendants would quickly become a costly proposition even though compensation today is so low. Now that the United States Supreme Court has mandated that counsel be provided to indigents if the potential punishment involves loss of freedom for even one day, the costs are likely to rise.[15]

The assigned-counsel system fails to benefit those persons who are confined, not awaiting trial as criminal defendants, but as mental cases, material witnesses, or prisoners held in lieu of fines. A person unjustly committed to a mental institution or languishing in a county jail is sorely in need of representation, but the assigned counsel system is not designed to handle this kind of situation.

Available money is frequently insufficient to pay for a skilled, detailed investigation into the facts of the case. Indeed, if an investigation is made at all, it must be paid for by the assigned counsel who is already inadequately compensated. Other services also frequently not available to assigned counsel might be the physicians, psychiatrists, criminalists, handwriting experts, and so on. These difficulties are not the theoretical results of the assigned-counsel

[14]Special Committee to Study Defender Systems, *Equal Justice for the Accused* (New York: Doubleday and Company, 1959), p. 64.

[15]*Argersinger* v. *Hamlin* 40 L.W. 4679 (June 12, 1972).

system, but the practical consequences of the system. If the assigned-counsel system were provided adequate financial resources, these difficulties might be overcome.[16]

As a general rule, the assigned counsel's duty ends after conviction. If an appeal is attempted, new counsel is assigned and he must start from the beginning to familiarize himself with the case. This difficulty may be alleviated by extending the original appointment to cover the first appeal. But, once again, a source of adequate funding would be essential.

It has been estimated that the costs of providing assigned counsel for adequate representation from the arraignment through the appeal would be great indeed, considerably outstripping the cost of a public defender system.[17] It may very well be that, in an attempt to remedy the ills of the assigned counsel system, the desirability of a public defender system becomes more attractive. As Reginald H. Smith commented in 1919, "The defender idea, in last analysis, is nothing more revolutionary than a plea for the extension of what is the best in the assignment system and for reorganization along modern lines of efficiency."[18]

PUBLIC DEFENDER

The public defender is a publicly employed attorney who has the task of being the legal counsel for indigent defendants. He is a professional, skilled in the law, just like the prosecutor. Usually, he is a county official although, as the need for and desirability of the public defender are recognized, statewide public defender offices will become a necessity. For example, as a result of having to provide attorneys to all indigents who face a potential jail sentence, Alabama is contemplating a statewide system funded from state and federal funds. The usual public defender currently is found at the county level. In large counties, he is employed full-time. In some counties he is elected and, in others, he is appointed from lists of qualified candidates compiled by local civil service procedures. His primary duty is to ensure that indigent defendants always receive the fundamental right, under law, to counsel.

The failure of the assigned-counsel system caused the development of the public defender's office. The failure was not solely due to incompetent or inadequate representation but also to the rapid growth of population and large metropolitan areas during the twentieth century. The failure was recognized

---

[16]Pollock, "Equal Justice in Practice," p. 737, in general.

[17]This conclusion is supported by: Pollock, "Equal Justice in Practice," *Equal Justice for the Accused,* and "Representation of Indigents in California."

[18]Reginald H. Smith, *Justice and the Poor* (New York: Scribner, 1919), p. 116.

early: "The truth about the assignment system in criminal cases is that, as a whole, it had proved a dismal failure, and that at times it has been worse than a failure."[19] With the mushrooming of population centers and the resulting rise in the numbers of criminal cases, new methods were sought to correct the problem of sheer numbers. A public defender system resulted.

In addition to population pressures, social changes also acted to encourage new techniques that would make possible the dream of justice for all. The development of the right to counsel in *Powell* v. *Alabama*[20] in 1932, extending the absolute right to counsel in all capital cases, smoothed the way for development of a public defender system. This case also set the stage for an extension of such a right to all criminal defendants in *Gideon* v. *Wainwright*[21] which held that for felony cases, the Fourteenth Amendment's due process clause extended the Sixth Amendment's guarantee of the right to counsel to state courts. *Argersinger* v. *Hamlin*[22] further extended the right to all indigent defendants who were charged with any offense that could result in a loss of freedom.

A frequent argument against the public defender system concerns the possibility of political and/or judicial corruption. However, the arguments are seldom accompanied by supporting data or facts of any kind. For instance:

> Falling back then on pure reason, it teaches that the adoption of the public defender system would bring our government so close to the police state that we ought to shun it like the plague.[23]

Another criticism of the public defender system is that because the office is employed by the state to defend a person who is prosecuted by the state, a conflict of interest arises that must work against the interests of the defendant. One might also argue that the structure and relationship of the public defender's office to the prosecutor and the court, coupled with the pressure to settle multitudes of cases, preclude the defender from effective representation of the defendant in a high percentage of his cases. Judges in districts with heavy case loads are interested in clearing the docket by settlements out of court. In the case of assigned counsel, the judge may see the attorney in court infrequently, whereas he probably has a close relationship with the public defender. A judge realizes that he has no right to pressure counsel into plea bargaining with the district attorney, and he realizes that the assigned defense attorney probably would resent a covert suggestion on his part to have a defendant "cop a plea." The assigned counsel has the one defendant. The public defender has many;

---

[19]Smith, *Justice and the Poor,* p. 103.
[20]*Powell* v. *Alabama.*
[21]*Gideon* v. *Wainwright* 372 U.S. 335 (1963).
[22]*Argersinger* v. *Hamlin,* 407 U.S. 25 (1972).
[23]Dimock, "The Public Defender," p. 221.

the argument goes that, because of the defender's close relationship with the judge, high case loads, and frequent appearances in court, an understanding is possible so that hopeless cases are moved without the necessity of tying up court. The criticism continues that these surely can be settled by guilty pleas in which the prosecutor is expected to play his part of offering deals and public defender is expected not to hold out for too much when the offers are made.

One final argument sometimes posed against the public defender system is that he has too many cases to handle and consequently cannot perform an adequate job. William Scott Stewart has written that "The defense of a criminal case is a great responsibility. No lawyer would undertake to defend properly the volume of cases put upon the public defender. Why should any defendant be so handicapped?"[24]

The advantages of the public defender system are impressive because it incorporates many of the positive factors of the assigned-counsel system besides having several that are not available in the assigned-counsel system. Generally, the public defender system provides an efficient and economic tool by which society fulfills its duty to indigent defendants. Ideally, the defendant should have access to an attorney when he is interrogated in custody.[25] The public defender does enter the case at a very early point and as a result can make the proper motions regarding bail, release, pleas, and so forth. If a defendant is not charged with a serious offense and can be released within a relatively short time, taxpayers are saved costs of incarceration as well as welfare costs frequently necessary to support a defendant's family during this period.

The public defender system is economical. A California study found that the average cost per case for several counties ranged from a low of twenty-five dollars in one county to a high of sixty-two dollars in another.[26]

The public defender's office is organized and staffed as a criminal law firm quite comparable to the office of the local district attorney. The resulting specialization, especially in criminal procedure, makes for efficiency and helps reduce such expenses as research as well as lending itself to competence. The public defender has a defense training program similar to that of the prosecutor and provides an environment in which the beginning public defender receives his training in the lower courts, thoroughly analyzing and familiarizing himself with the procedures *before* he is permitted to handle a felony case. Specialization soon results, as is mandatory in public defender offices set up in high volume criminal case areas. The President's Crime Commission stated that in all states combined, defender offices are probably handling about 35 percent of indigent felony trials, with assigned counsel taking care of the

---

[24]William Scott Stewart, "The Public Defender System is Unsound in Principle," *Journal of the American Judicature Society,* XXXII (December 1948), 118.

[25]*Miranda* v. *Arizona, supra.*

[26]"Representation of Indigents in California," p. 540.

remainder, despite the fact that 2750 of its 3100 counties in the country use some form of the assigned-counsel system.[27]

The public defender performs certain additional services for the community. He serves as a constant check on the police as well as the prosecutor. His responsibility extends beyond defending particular indigents. He helps establish and modify criminal law and its procedures for the total benefit of society as well as the defendant. He is always interested in bringing about beneficial changes within the substantive criminal law and its proceedings.

In handling cases, the public defender has a staff of trained investigators and funds for hiring consultants and experts for the proper defense of a case. You might recall that assigned counsel can normally obtain these services only by contract and the costs of doing so are often forbidding.

One final argument in support of the public defender is that because it is a public agency, it is constantly open to public scrutiny. In itself, it is no more free from possible corruption than any public agency (including the prosecutor and the courts). But then neither is the assigned-counsel system. However, because the funds come from public sources, the force of operating in a fishbowl has a great restraining effect on the public defender.

The public defender system is under the constant scrutiny of the American Bar Association which has set up certain standards pertaining to defense services. The standards, in general, sum up the desirability of having a professional public defender's office:[28]

1. The objective of the bar should be to assure that all persons receive necessary counseling in criminal proceedings and that the public be educated regarding this objective.

2. Counsel should be provided in a systematic, well publicized way.

3. Each jurisdiction should require by law the adoption of a plan for the provision of counsel and the law allow selection from a range of plans suitable for varying local needs.

4. Integrity of the lawyer-client relationship should be guaranteed.

5. Plans should provide for hiring of investigative experts and other necessary defense services.

SUMMARY

In a criminal trial, a human being's freedom is at stake. The defense of this person is in the hands of the defense attorney. His history to the present is characterized as a defender of individual liberty. During the total criminal process, his presence is evident whether it be in investigating

[27]President's Commission on Law Enforcement and Administration of Justice, *Task Force Report: The Police* (Washington, D.C.: Government Printing Office, 1967), pp. 58–60, 158–60.

[28]Committee on the Office of the Attorney General, National Association of Attorneys General, *The Office of the Attorney General* (February 1971), pp. 303–4.

evidence, challenging law enforcement practices, presenting testimony, cross-examining witnesses, summing up his case in the final argument, or acting as the attorney on appeal. As our society grows larger and more complex, the role of the defense counsel also will grow in importance.

QUESTIONS

1. Describe the historical development of the role of the lawyer as a defense attorney.
2. In early English law the role of the defense attorney was nonexistent. What were the various methods of deciding how a dispute was to be settled?
3. Distinguish the English solicitor from barrister. What are the functions of each in the English court system?
4. Describe the early English system used to qualify persons to practice law in English courts.
5. Describe the development of the legal profession in America prior to and after the Civil War.
6. Describe the role and duties performed by a defense attorney.
7. What is *voir dire* examination? What is its main purpose? Why is *voir dire* examination so important to a defense attorney?
8. Once the jury is impaneled and sworn, what is the usual order in which a trial proceeds?
9. What is meant by the statement "the defense attorney must be alert to challenge the legality of evidence"?
10. Distinguish court-appointed or -assigned counsel from the public defender system.
11. What are the limitations of the assigned counsel system?
12. Describe the office of the public defender.
13. What is the holding of the following court decisions:
    Powell v. *Alabama*
    Gideon v. *Wainwright*
    Argersinger v. *Hamlin*
14. What are the arguments in favor of the public defender system?

IV

COURTS

JUDGES

GENERAL CONSIDERATIONS

A judge is the officer of a court who presides over a court or
tribunal organized for the purpose of hearing facts and ensuring
that justice is administered. For the purposes of this introduction
to the functions and persons who make up the criminal justice
system, the activities of the judge will be related to his work with criminal
cases, but in practice the same judges often hear civil cases as well. Although
the term *judge* is broad enough to include members of commissions, agencies,
boards, and other quasi-judicial bodies, it is used in a restricted sense in this
chapter as the officer who is named in his commission as a judge and who
presides over a court.

Judges are public officers. They include individuals having such titles as
associate judge, justice, chancellor, circuit judge, district judge, presiding
judge, senior judge, judge *pro tempore,* probate judge, law judge, supernumer-
ary judge, to name some of the more common. The judge must be appointed
by a proper authority. In many instances the term *judge* is used interchange-
ably with *the court.* Many statutes intend the terms to be synonymous.

Judges of courts of general jurisdiction are usually held to be state
officers. The same also applies to county court and probate judges, whereas city
or municipal court judges are most frequently not state officers.

Frequently, there is some confusion over whether or not the term *magistrate* is synonymous with *judge.* Usually, a magistrate is regarded as a public
officer but of an inferior judicial status, similar to that of a justice of the peace.
Commonly, like the judge, he is given the power to issue a warrant for the

arrest of a person, but he does not have the power to try cases. Also, the magistrate, unlike the judge, is given only the powers provided by the government appointing him.

DUTIES AND POWERS OF JUDGES

The statutes and applicable constitution, plus the powers inherent in his office, determine what powers the judge actually has. His duties include all of those within the scope of his judicial position, those that are essential to the accomplishment of the office that he occupies, and those powers that are collateral but nevertheless serve to promote or carry out the principal purposes of the judicial office. Because these are his official duties, he is obligated to carry them out to the best of his ability.

Where the judge's office is created by the constitution, he is considered to be a constitutional officer; where it is created by statute, he is a statutory officer and not a constitutional officer. Local judicial officers are normally statutory officers. When a judge acts, his acts must be done within his area of jurisdiction, and because judicial powers are predominantly local in nature, they must be exercised in the areas over which the judge can act. Usually, unless changed by statute, a judge has no authority to perform judicial duties or exercise judicial functions outside of the territorial limits of the county or district in which he was elected or appointed. If he does, any decision he renders is a nullity.

However, frequently due to statute and constitutional provisions, judges of different counties are permitted to hold court for each other or, under specified circumstances, assist one another in performing duties that he would otherwise be unqualified to perform. Where judges in state courts are members of a statewide court system, although they are assigned to a particular county to perform their functions, they may be required to perform duties in other counties even though they may have been elected by the citizens of the county in which they sit. Federal judges, on the other hand, are not constitutionally restricted to a particular territorial area in which to hear and decide cases. Congress has provided areas of jurisdiction by statute that authorizes federal judges to act temporarily in other districts.

APPOINTMENT AND REMOVAL OF
COURT OFFICERS, REMUNERATION

As a general rule, a judge cannot be compelled to perform duties at the request of the appointing body or person, where such duties are not part of or incidental to the judicial function, especially when the duties are within the scope and responsibility of other branches of government. In other words, a judge can not be required to perform nonjudicial duties. After the assassination of President John F. Kennedy, Chief Justice of the United States Earl Warren was asked by President Lyndon Johnson to organize and conduct an investigation of the tragic events leading to the death. Under his general duties, the chief justice could have refused the president.

Occasionally, the question arises as to whether or not judges may make appointments of other judicial officers. Although the exact limits of their appointing powers have not been delineated, it is rarely challenged when a judge appoints inferior officers, especially those who are under the control of the court making the appointment, such as referees, receivers, commissioners, clerks, bailiffs, administrative aids, and court employees. The same applies to the judge's power to remove.

Generally, salaries for appointed personnel are set by the legislature. However, in some states, by statutory authorization the judge can fix the salaries of specified employees, such as the clerk of the court.

RIGHTS AND PRIVILEGES OF JUDGES

The nature of the judge's office is unique in the system of criminal justice. He is generally immune from liability for acts performed incident to his office. Under certain circumstances, he is immune from arrest and from the service of civil process. Because of the nature of his duties, he may be assigned protection by the executive.

A judge, however, is not exempt from disciplinary proceeding for deficiencies while he is in office. Acts of immorality, fraud, or other crimes may result in his license to practice law being revoked. The deviant act, however, must be intentional. Errors in the exercise of his judicial discretion or the failure to exercise a legal mandate alone are insufficient to be the basis of such disciplinary proceedings.

It is a common requirement, either by statute or constitutional provision, for a judge to be prohibited from practicing law while he is appointed as a judge. In some instances, it has been held that even without a legal request, he is prohibited from practicing law. Once he resigns or retires, he is not so prohibited. At common law, a judge could not hold another office that was incompatible with the judge's functions and it is a common requirement, by statute or constitutional permission in many states, to follow the common law. The purpose is to free the judge from the taint of bias and permit him impartial exercise of discretion. Likewise, it has always been regarded improper for a judge or a candidate for a judicial position to serve on political party committees or make partisan speeches. However, one statute making it unlawful for a judge to participate in partisan activities was declared unconstitutional as an infringement of freedom of speech.[1]

TRAINING FOR JUDGES

The newly appointed judge assumes the bench without more than cursory knowledge of what a judge is to do. He undoubtedly has had some experience as an attorney, but because of other more lucrative areas of law he probably has had only a very minimum of experience in the criminal law.

In the United States, there is a growing recognition that specialized training for judges is mandatory both before he actually assumes his duties and, periodically, afterwards. His need for in-service training is every bit as great as that of the police officer, prosecutor, or correction officer. In 1967, it was reported that only about 12 percent of judges received any training or orientation when they assumed their offices. Recognition of this situation has been slow in coming, however. It is only in recent years that there has been any kind of concerted effort toward judicial training and this has come mainly from the Joint Committee for the Effective Administration of Justice.

This group has assisted in organizing seminars, training programs, and other sessions in which a new judge is exposed to the criminal justice aspects of his new position. It may sound rather extraordinary for a person who is appointed as a judge to receive instruction on empaneling a jury, handling courtroom decorum, expediting cases appearing on a docket, instructing a jury, handling intricate problems of evidence (especially in the area of searches and seizures), sentencing, preparing questions for appeal, and ruling on objections; but the fact remains that there has been no systematic approach to preparing appointees in the art of judgeship.

The National College of State Trial Judges was established in 1964. A permanent academic base was established in 1965 at the University of Nevada, in Reno. In 1971, the name was changed to National College of the State Judiciary. Judges from throughout the United States presently attend a four-week summer session each year. Since 1964, over seventeen hundred general jurisdiction judges have received certificates of graduation. Since 1969, four one-week graduate sessions have been conducted each year. Approximately two hundred alumni have completed these sessions. Faculty members include professors of law and senior judges who lecture on the law and more practical aspects of the judge's duties. The Socratic and seminar approaches are followed, the catalyst being the judge himself seeking to perfect his role as a lawgiver and public servant. The college also provides seminars on legal topics

[1] *Louthan* v. *Commonwealth,* 79 Va. 196 (1884).

to be held throughout the United States to aid trial judges in ke
the law. Workshops on crime and corrections have been held
of state judiciaries by the college. Special courses and studies on co
ment for judges of courts with limited jurisdiction have been offered, anu
Judges Journal, a quarterly publication, also aids in the training of judges.

The curriculum at the college is carefully designed to provide a thought-
ful and pragmatic blend of solutions to problems, as well as broad considerations of the style, role, and function of the judge. A sampling of the topics
covered in the four-week program are court administration, civil proceedings
before trial, judicial discretion, family law, evidence, special problems in the
judicial functions, jury, community relations, sentencing and probation, criminal law, new developments in civil law, and the inherent powers of the courts.
The judges who attend these sessions can compare problems and how each
attempted to solve them.

State-level training is almost nonexistent. Probably the most active endeavor has occurred in California where seminars, special juvenile institutes,
and legal education programs are provided for from state, county, and private
funds. Regional, state, and local bar associations are a source of educational
programs for judges when periodic meetings are held. On many occasions,
these meetings are structured to court changes in statutory law, recent decisions, and procedural modifications. Law schools occasionally sponsor programs for judges, but it is entirely clear that judicial training and education
in the United States is in its infancy.

There is general agreement in the legal profession that the administration
of criminal justice could be greatly improved if there were adequate judicial
training programs. The improvement can only come about, however, if new
judges are required to attend a training program prior to assuming office or
within a short period thereafter. As conditions are now, attendance is voluntary, programs infrequent and few, and funds scarce. A central training office
in each state, with funds appropriated by the legislature, may be a start.

THE ROLE OF THE JUDGE

The judge is a problem solver and decision maker involving legal matters.
He is called upon to decide such issues as the insanity of a defendant, admissibility of a confession, legality of a written document, ownership of an automobile, custody of a child, and, in situations where he tries criminal cases without
a jury, the guilt or innocence of the defendant. The judge sits in the center of
a vast network of criminal processes. In this position, he can exercise a great
amount of influence over the various components in the total criminal justice
complex.

His decisions, for example, on the admissibility of certain kinds of evidence can radically alter police investigative procedures and proof of facts by the prosecution during a trial. A decision by a judge concerning conditions in a correctional institution has far-reaching effects. Likewise, his requiring an attorney to be present at a probation revocation hearing would create a ripple effect throughout the total complex.[2] The public views the role of the judge with a feeling of respect. Therefore, his actions and demeanor both inside and outside of courts help shape a favorable or unfavorable public attitude toward the criminal justice effort as a whole.

To most Americans, the judge is a living symbol of justice. He is the wise, impartial arbiter between two warring counterparts in a criminal case. He is expected to be neither rude, unduly apologetic, arbitrary, servile, demeaning, nor unduly laudatory. Fairness is his chief attribute in the mind of the public.

The judge in the system of criminal justice determines the rules and general principles that govern the future of the law. Whether he is a trial or appellate judge, his dignity and fairness are crucial. If he serves on an appellate court, the principles that are established must be implemented on the trial level. Primarily at the trial level, the judge possesses a great deal of autonomy. For example, when he decides on the admissibility of search and seizure evidence, his decisions are not overturned except in the infrequent instances where he grants a new trial after ruling that he has made an error and where his decision is reversed on appeal. When serving as the sole appraiser of fact, he alone determines the credibility of witnesses, and when he acquits a defendant, there usually is no appeal by the state. Where there is a jury trial, his behavior is an important influence on the jury even though this factor will not be found in the transcript should there be an appeal.

In regard to the power the judge has in the sentencing of defendants, the President's Crime Commission stated in 1967:

> The power of the trial judge in sentencing is another example of virtual autonomy. In most jurisdictions today, the trial judge's sentence cannot be adjusted by an appellate court if it is within the statutory limits, no matter how harsh or arbitrary it appears to be. Even an appellate review of sentences . . . for correcting unjust sentences, would leave the trial judge with broad discretion in most sentencing decisions.[3]

The sentencing function is of great importance because of the impact it has on the entire system of criminal justice. If the judge imposes a sentence that is too lenient, it may not act as a deterrent and will greatly upset the police. If the sentences a judge imposes imprison a high percentage of those convicted, the impact on the corrections component may well be staggering because of the increased number of inmates, as well as the costs involved.

---

[2]See *Mempa* v. *Rhay*, 389 U.S. 128 (1967).

[3]President's Commission on Law Enforcement and Administration of Justice, *Task Force Report: The Courts* (Washington, D.C.: Government Printing Office, 1967), p. 65.

The cause for disparity in sentences, often a hot issue of debate, is, however, often not the direct fault of the judge. One of the most chaotic aspects of the law relating to sentencing is the condition of the penal codes which define the permissible penal sanctions without any rational basis. For example, a report by a legislative council in Colorado found that a person convicted of first-degree murder must serve ten years before he becomes eligible for parole; a person convicted of a lesser degree of murder may, however, be compelled to serve fifteen years or more.[4]

By reducing these apparently unessential differences in penalties, much of the illogic in the judge's sentencing function may be eliminated. However, that task is for the legislature.

The President's Commission on Law Enforcement and Administration of Justice suggested that legislatures can best arm the system by the power to deal individually with each defendant. It can establish institutions and programs, provide funds, and set goals; but it cannot determine, in advance of the event, sentences to be imposed. The theory in modern corrections is that the sentence should assist in the rehabilitation and return of the miscreant to his lawful place in society. Providing the judge with a range of tools to effect this is mandatory. Therefore, the legislature should not list specific sentences that must be imposed regardless of the circumstances of the offense. The judge must be given discretion, for example, to determine whether a defendant is a suitable subject for probation without confinement in an institution. Mandatory sentences deny the judge the authority to accomplish the best rehabilitative program for the offender.

The sentencing dilemma currently is being studied widely by those responsible for effective promulgation of the rules of sentencing under which judges operate—the individual legislatures. States are reexamining the appropriate provisions in the penal codes to simplify sentencing by removing mandatory minimum prison sentences, excessively long maximum sentences, and ineligibility for probation or parole. The studies are aimed at providing more effective handling of defendants by giving judges more discretion to sentence or otherwise impose sanctions that will rapidly, safely, and effectively reintegrate the person into society. To accomplish this end, the indeterminate sentence that provides a maximum amount of discretion and flexibility to the judge or sentencing authority is being adopted, increasing the options available within the corrections component of the criminal justice system.

A major role in the system that falls on the judge is the negotiation of pleas between the defendant and prosecution. In a large number of cases, the role of the judge is to sit in court while the defendant enters a guilty plea that

[4]Colorado Legislative Council Report, *Report to the Colorado General Assembly,* Preliminary revision of Colorado Criminal Laws, Research Publication, No. 98, (1964), quoted in "Disparity and Equality of Sentences—A Constitutional Challenge," *Federal Rules Decisions* 40:55–56 (1966).

was a result of bargaining between the parties. The plea entered by the defendeant was agreed upon under expectation of a certain outcome if the case went to trial, such as reduced sentence or recommendation of probation. The prosecutor agreed to suggest certain punishments to the judge who, as final arbiter, decides whether or not the recommended penalty is fair. Normally, however, he follows the request of the prosecutor. The Supreme Court of the United States has approved the plea negotiation concept.[5]

It can be seen that the role of the judge is crucial and, as a result, our society must make every effort to select the best qualified persons and provide for effective removal of those who are unfit to serve. In regard to the competence of judges, the President's Crime Commission in 1967 made this observation:

> The first step is to employ selection procedures that will bring to the bench lawyers who are likely to be excellent judges. Although it is impossible to identify such factors as professional competence, laziness or intemperance, which should disqualify a lawyer from becoming a judge, it is much more difficult to choose confidently the potentially superior judge from among a number of aspirants who appear generally qualified. And many of those who can become excellent judges come to the bench without certain skills and experience. Therefore it is important to provide training for judges especially for those who are newly selected. Finally, there must be fair and expeditious procedures for disciplining or removing judges who are unwilling or unable to perform their duties properly.[6]

SELECTION OF JUDGES:
PROCESSES AND CONSIDERATIONS

There is no single system for selecting judges in the United States. The choosing of judges varies greatly between the federal and state levels and still more widely among individual states. But no matter how, by whom, or from where he is selected, the choice is based on politics. Partisan activities are always helpful in securing an appointment, whether by a governor or the president. In large urban areas, appointment to a judgeship is a highly sought after prize.

Selection of federal judges is quite simple in format—neither the United States Constitution nor federal laws set any particular qualifications. Informal criteria serve as guidance but the president uses whatever criteria are expedient to him. Federal judgeships carry a lifetime tenure. Because of this, the president, by astute selection, can influence the path of law for many decades after he leaves office. Political infighting to receive a presidential nomination is

---

[5]*North Carolina* v. *Alford* 400 U.S. 25 (1970).
[6]*Task Force Report: The Courts,* p. 66.

sometimes fierce. Once the nomination for a federal judgeship has been made, it is sent to the Senate which, under the Constitution, can withhold its consent from the nomination. First, though, the Senate gives the nomination to the Judiciary Committee which asks a smaller subcommittee to hold hearings and make a report to it. The subcommittee is a strong influence on the outcome of the nomination because it is almost certain that the Committee on the Judiciary will adopt the subcommittee's recommendation.

According to Joseph P. Harris, the Senate has rejected about 20 percent of the nominations sent to it. However, this percentage is small. Nominations to the Supreme Court, in spite of long drawn-out debates, opprobrious allegations, and sly innuendoes, are seldom rejected.[7]

The practice of *senatorial courtesy* has been the custom ever since the administration of George Washington.[8] Under this political device, before the president nominates a person for a federal judgeship below the appellate court level, he consults with the appropriate senators from the state in which the vacancy is located. This procedure is politically expedient because, in effect, it allows the senators to reject a presidential choice before the nomination is submitted to the Senate. Senators from both parties are consulted because of the feeling of the entire Senate that they should be approached on such important matters. If the President refuses to consult the senator from the opposite party, the Senate will consider it an infringement of one of the prerogatives of the office and may attempt to embarrass him later for this affront.

In order for the President not to be embarrassed, his nominees must meet standards of competence and certain qualifications. To assure the proper selection, the attorney general is normally given the task of investigating potential nominees. He then recommends the appointments to the president.

Independent advice is also sought by the president and Senate from outside organizations such as the American Bar Association to assist in determining proper qualifications and competence.[9]

As a general rule, appointments to federal appellate courts are by elevation of judges from the federal district courts. As one consequence, there is a dissolution of senatorial power because the appellate bodies serve several states. However, the nominees will normally have senatorial support.

Selection of state judges follows a variety of procedures.

1. Judges are selected by popular election in more than half of the states. In about ten of these states, the elections are partisan affairs after the nominee has

---

[7]Joseph P. Harris, *The Advice and Consent of Senate* (Berkeley: University of California Press, 1953), pp. 302–24.

[8]Harold W. Chase, "Federal Judges—The Appointing Process" *Minnesota Law Review,* LI (December 1966), 218–21.

[9]Joel B. Grossman, *Lawyers and Judges* (New York: John Wiley and Sons, 1965), *et passim.*

been nominated at a political convention or survived party primaries. In the other states, the elections are nonpartisan. Usually, the applicants are placed on the ballot at their own initiative. In many instances, the elections occur after initial appointment of the incumbent judge was occasioned by death or retirement. The nonpartisan election of judges has been called the traditional method used in this country.

2. Approximately ten states permit the merit selection of judges. This procedure follows the so-called Missouri Plan which calls for the nomination of qualified candidates by a nonpartisan commission, selection by the governor from the list, and final approval of the appointee by the electorate in an election in which the appointee faces no opposition—the voters merely indicate yes or no.

3. The legislature elects judges in five states. Appointment by the governor is permitted in seven states.[10]

The President's Commission on Law Enforcement and Administration of Justice, dismissing the two most popular methods of judicial selection at the state level, favors the merit selection method.

In sum, merit selection provides a more rational procedure for selecting judges than popular election alone. The essential elements of merit selection are that the qualifications of prospective judges are screened and the field is narrowed to a panel of a few nominees whose legal training, character, and temperament mark them as potentially superior judges. Whether the ultimate method of selecting a nominee from this panel is appointment or selection by the voters, a good judge is likely to be selected. Because the nominating commission plays an important role, it should be a professional agency with a professional staff. The members of the commission should be drawn from a wide varity of disciplines and backgrounds including the legal profession and should be representative of the entire community. They should serve for terms that are sufficiently long to give them a chance to become sensitive to the qualities of good judges.

The most difficult problem involved in merit selection is the development of standards on which to choose nominees for the bench. The New York Mayor's Committee relies on several broad categories of criteria: a prospective nominee's personal qualities, his character, patience, and industry; his education and training; and his professional attainments and specialized experience. Trial experience is not a *sine qua non* for nomination, but it is a qualification of major importance. Political activity is regarded as being in a lawyer's favor, and in no sense is it a disqualification or demerit. These factors are illustrative of the type of criteria which a nominating commission should consider. But no way has been found to give a uniform meaning to imprecise terms such as "character" and "patience," and there is no agreement on the relative importance of, for example, trial experience or age. These problems may never be resolved; therefore the success of the merit system depends largely on the intelligence and wisdom of the nominating commission and the appointing official.

Another way to remove judges from undue political influence and to increase their independence is to provide lengthy tenure. Yet in a number of States the judges or major criminal trial courts must seek reelection as frequently as every four years. Federal judges hold office for life during good behavior, and in many States they sit to a fixed retirement age or for a term of from 10 to 14 years.

[10]Editorial, *Journal of the American Judicature Society*, XLVIII (1964), p. 125.

Under both of these approaches giving long tenure, generally higher judicial standards have been maintained. It is important that there be liberal provisions for the dignified retirement of judges at a fixed age. Many States and the Federal Government have authorized the continued service of vigorous retired judges, enabling the use of their experience while making room for the appointment of younger judges.[11]

DISCIPLINE AND REMOVAL

Respect for the dignity of the law and courts is increasingly important in our contemporary society. The effect of the judge on the attitudes that our citizens have toward the judiciary is in direct correlation to the attitudes they hold toward the judge. It is a truism that judges are subject to misconduct in office, just like the policeman, councilman , recorder, and so on. However, a new high standard of conduct is expected even when the conduct in which a judge engages in not clearly illegal. Fortunately, the incidence of judicial misconduct is rare. However, criminal, unethical, or indecent conduct cannot be tolerated and must be the subject of strong disciplinary action or removal.

A much more sensitive problem occurs when the judge becomes senile or, for some other health or personal reason, cannot judge cases. For example, a judge, who because of intemperance constantly errs in admitting evidence and is corrected on appeal, jeopardizes not only the party who is the subject of the error, but also public respect for a system that permits it to happen. Errors made in good faith also cause a ticklish problem. If judges were subject to removal simply for making occasional errors, their independence to act would be unduly hampered and the cure would be worse than the disease.

In the United States, the constitutions and statutes in the states generally set forth the ways by which judges may be removed and the grounds for the removal. But as a matter of public policy, the acts of a judge, even though they may be in error, are not subject to discipline unless fraud, dishonesty, or corruption are involved. Private, unofficial, and independent acts are, however, subject to disciplinary action. The disciplinary action may take the form of censure, reprimand, suspension, or, finally, removal. United States judges, including district judges, are subject to removal only by the Senate of the United States sitting as a court of impeachment.[12]

In this country, the two most common remedies are impeachment and removal by a vote of the legislature without impeachment. One must remember, however, that no matter what procedure is followed to discipline or remove, the judge's guilt must have been adjudicated in a formal proceeding at which he was offered due process of law. Also, the impeachment proceeding,

---

[11] *Task Force Report: The Courts,* pp. 67–68.
[12] *Chandler* v. *Judicial Council of Tenth Circuit,* 382 U.S. 1003 (1966).

because it is highly penal in nature although it does not extend beyond removal from office, is governed by the general rules applicable in criminal proceedings. Furthermore, a judge formally impeached and removed is still subject to criminal prosecution thereafter.

The power to suspend a judge pending the formal removal action is subject to two broad interpretations in the United States. First, some courts have held that the power to remove includes the power to suspend pending the removal hearing. It has also been held in a few states that there is no power to suspend, unless provided by statute. Ordinarily, the legislature has the power to authorize a temporary suspension during the pendency of the valid removal proceeding.[13]

The grounds for removal of a judge are usually prescribed in the statutes or constitution of the state. An example of a constitutional provision is that found in Louisiana:

> All state and district officers whether elected or appointed, shall be liable for impeachment for high crimes and misdemeanors in office, incompetency, corruption, favoritism, extortion, or oppression in office; or for gross misconduct, or habitual drunkenness.[14]

Among the more common grounds for removal of a judge from office are willful neglect of duty, corruption in office, incompetency, intemperance to such an extent that he is unfit to discharge his duties, bribing an elector to vote for him, disbarment or suspension as an attorney in the state where his office is dependent upon his status as an attorney, commission of offenses involving moral turpitude, and receiving money to which he is not entitled even though he acted in good faith that he was entitled to the money.[15] It has even been held that acts of misconduct in office that occurred in a previous term of office are sufficient for removal.

As previously mentioned, judicial incompetence, incapacity, or illegality are a matter of concern to the members of our society, but judges also care about the ethics of their colleagues. For example, in New Jersey the supervisory powers of the state supreme court are utilized to control judicial behavior.

The important part of the New Jersey procedure is the ascertainment by the supreme court that an initial complaint about a judge is true. The supreme court is charged with responsibility for overall performance of the judicial branch of government and has the implied power reasonably necessary to make appropriate rules and see to their enforcement. If, after investigation, the complaint is deemed justifiable, the chief justice as head of the court system

---

[13]California, *Government Code,* sec. 3035. "The judgement may be that the defendant be suspended or that he may be removed from office."

[14]*Stanley* v. *Jones,* 197 La. 627 (1941).

[15]*State ex rel. Power* v. *District Court,* 119 P. 1103 (1911).

may either counsel the improper judge or certify to the governor that the judge is incapable of performing his duties.[16]

Another disciplinary technique is used in New York where a court on the judiciary is convened on an ad hoc basis to try specific complaints against judges on the court of appeals and supreme court. (Contrary to the general trend, the New York Supreme Court is not the highest court in the state; rather, it is a court of general jurisdiction.) Under this procedure, there is no agency to conduct a prompt investigation that would eliminate frivolous complaints, and there is no way provided for counseling a judge on matters that are objectionable but do not warrant removal.

A third type of disciplinary device has been adopted with modifications by California and Texas. Several other states are considering its merits.[17] Under this procedure, a commission on judicial qualifications is set up. It is composed of judges, lawyers, and laymen. They receive complaints alleging unfitness. The executive secretary of the commission investigates the complaints to weed out the frivolous. If there is substance to the complaint, the matter is returned to the commission for further action. Under this procedure, the judge charged may clear up the allegation by letter or may promise to revise his conduct. If not satisfied with the judge's response, the commission may hold a hearing or request the supreme court to appoint three persons to hold a hearing. If the judge is found unqualified, the investigating body may recommend to the supreme court that he be removed or retired. Although the judge has a right of review by the supreme court, most judges resign when they are charged or retire while under investigation. The entire procedure is confidential until the judge files for a hearing with the supreme court. If he does not, the records are not revealed to the public.[18]

In 1972, the electorate of Alabama approved a constitutional procedure to remove state judges other than by impeachment. Under the amendment, if a complaint is received against a judge, the Judicial Commission of Alabama keeps the name of the judge in confidence while it investigates the charges. If found to be groundless, the charges are dismissed. If, on the other hand, the allegation appears to have substance, the commission presents it to the judge who is permitted to defend himself. Should disciplinary action be needed, a formal hearing takes place before the commission at which the judge is afforded all procedural rights. The commission can legally remove a judge from office as well as censure or suspend him. Although the commission makes its recommendations to the state supreme court which takes the final action, the commission is empowered by law to remove the judge from office temporarily and also to cut off his salary if the evidence shows wrongdoing.

---

[16]New Jersey: *Constitution,* Art. VI, section 6, paragraph 5; section 7, paragraph 1.

[17]Louis H. Burke, "Judicial Discipline and Removal—The California Story," *Journal of the American Judicature Society,* XLVIII (1965), *et passim.*

[18]*Task Force Report: The Courts,* p. 71.

This procedure provides disciplinary action if a judge is found guilty of willful misconduct in office, failure to perform his duties, habitual intemperance, or conduct prejudicial to the administration of justice.

SUMMARY

Judges operate under a highly complex system of pressures. Their decisions in complicated and emotional cases reverberate throughout the criminal justice complex. The duties and powers of the judge are contained in statutes. The moral power of his position demands an incumbent possessed of knowledge, wisdom, dignity, ethical concern, and patience. Because of his unique position, the judge is immune from suit for errors he makes in the performance of his duties. Although he is probably a lawyer, he is normally forbidden to practice while he is a judge. Being a lawyer does not qualify him to be a good judge. He should receive training in the new position he occupies, but little is given. There is a recognition in the country that the administration of criminal justice could be helped if there were educational programs to assist the judge in learning the arts of his trade. Fortunately, more of these programs are coming into being.

One of the major problems is the disciplinary removal of judges because of incapacity or misconduct. The method most frequently used, impeachment, is unsuitable in many situations and, as a consequence, states are enacting various kinds of legislation to help in removing judges. The California plan, modified somewhat by each state to fit its needs, appears to be the model for maintaining judicial standards.

QUESTIONS

1. What is a court of general jurisdiction?
2. What is the role of the judge in a criminal trial
   a. when there is a jury?
   b. when he is the trier of fact?
3. Discuss the general duties and powers of a judge.
4. What is meant by the statement that a judge may be removed only by impeachment for high crimes, misconduct, or intemperance?
5. What is the purpose of the National College of the State Judiciary?
6. What is plea bargaining?
7. How does a judge become involved in the negotiation of pleas between a defendant and the prosecutor?
8. What role does the judge have in sentencing of defendants?
9. What are the various methods of selecting judges utilized in the United States?
10. Describe the federal procedure for choosing federal judges.

11. What is the "Missouri Plan"?
12. What method of selection of judges is recommended by the President's Commission on Law Enforcement and Administration of Justice?
13. What are the two most common methods to remove judges in the United States?
14. What are the most common grounds for removal of judges in the United States?
15. Describe the method of removal of judges followed in the "Alabama Plan."

JURY
AND JURORS

HISTORY

The jury trial in criminal cases can be traced to the signing of the
English Magna Carta in 1215. This charter is regarded as the
foundation of constitutional liberties. At the time the United States
Constitution was written, the jury trial in criminal cases was part
of our judicial system. The Declaration and Bill of Rights in 1689 had as one
of its major objectives the preservation and protection of the jury as a safeguard
against arbitrary governmental rule.

12

In the eighteenth century, Blackstone, discussing the desirability and
protections of the jury, states:

> Our law has therefore wisely placed this strong and twofold barrier, of a pre-
> sentment and a trial by jury, between the liberties of the people and the prerog-
> ative of the crown. It was necessary, for preserving the admirable balance of
> our constitution, to vest the executive power of the laws in the prince; and yet
> this power might be dangerous and destructive to the very constitution if
> exerted without check or control, by justices of *oyer* and *terminer* occasionally
> named by the crown; who might then as in France or Turkey, imprison, dis-
> patch, or exile any man that was obnoxious to the government, by an instant
> declaration that such is their will and pleasure. But the founders of the English
> law have, with excellent forecast, contrived that . . . the truth of every accusa-
> tion, whether preferred in the shape of indictment, information, or appeal,
> should afterwards be confirmed by the unanimous suffrage of twelve of his
> equals and neighbors, indifferently chosen and superior to all suspicion.[1]

[1]William Blackstone, *Commentaries on the Laws of England,* Vol. IV (London: Dawsons
of Pall Mall, 1966), p. 343.

The English colonists brought the jury trial to America. It was a judicial concept that was strongly supported because of resentment over royal interference. "That trial by jury is the inherent and invaluable right of every British subject in these colonies" was a resolution adopted by the first Congress of the American colonies on October 19, 1765.[2] This resolution, among others, was considered to be one of the most fundamental and essential of the liberties and rights of the colonists.

In 1774, the First Continental Congress declared:

> That the respective colonies are entitled to the common law of England, and more especially to the great and inestimable privilege of being tried by their peers of the vicinage, according to the course of that law.

The Declaration of Independence objected to the king making "Judges dependent on his will alone, for the tenure of their duties, and the amount and payment of their salaries," which in many cases deprived the colonists "of the benefits of Trial by Jury."

Article III, section 2 of the Constitution states that: "The Trial of all crimes, except in cases of Impeachment, shall be by Jury; and such Trial shall be held in the state where the said Crimes shall have been committed."

With the addition of the Bill of Rights, the Sixth Amendment (1791) provided: "In all criminal prosecutions, the accused shall enjoy the right of a speedy trial and public trial, by an impartial jury of the State and district wherein the crime shall have been committed."

The Seventh Amendment (1791) also included the ruling that: "In suits at common law, where the value in controversy shall exceed twenty dollars the right of trial by jury shall be preserved."

Constitutions adopted by the original states also guaranteed jury trials as well as has every state entering the Union since. The variations in the present state constitutions are numerous. For example:

> The right of trial by jury shall be secured to all; and remain inviolate; but in civil actions three-fourths of the jury may render a verdict. A trial by jury may be waived in all criminal cases, by the consent of both parties, expressed in open court by the defendant and his counsel, and in civil actions by the consent of the parties, signified in such manner as may be prescribed by law. In civil actions and cases of misdemeanor, the jury may consist of twelve or of any number less than twelve upon which the parties may agree in open court. (*California Constitution,* Article I, Section 7).

> The trial by jury in all cases in which it has heretofore been guaranteed by constitutional provision shall remain inviolate forever. . . . The legislature may provide, however, by law, that a verdict may be rendered by not less than five-sixths of the jury in any civil case. (*New York Constitution,* Article I, Section 2).

---

[2] *Duncan* v. *Louisiana,* 391 U.S. 149 (1968).

That in all criminal prosecutions, the accused has a right to . . . a speedy, public trial, by an impartial jury. (*Alabama Constitution,* Article I, Section 6).

The right of trial by jury shall remain inviolate. (*Arizona Constitution,* Article II, Section 23).

The right of trial by jury as heretofore enjoyed shall remain inviolate. (*Illinois Constitution,* Article I, Section 13).

The jury trial is not based on early history alone. The United States Supreme Court only recently reiterated the fundamental character of the jury trial, ruling that: "Because we believe that trial by jury in criminal cases is fundamental to the American scheme of justice, we hold that the Fourteenth Amendment guarantees a right of jury trial in all criminal cases which—were they to be tried in a federal court—would come within the Sixth Amendment's guarantee."

In a footnote to the *Duncan* opinion, the court discussed the importance of the jury system:

A criminal process which was fair and equitable but used no juries is easy to imagine. It would make use of alternative guarantees and protections which would serve the purposes that the jury serves in the English and American systems. Yet no American State has undertaken to construct such a system. Instead every American State . . . uses the jury extensively and imposes very serious punishments only after a trial at which the defendant has a right to a jury's verdict. In every State . . . the structure and style of the criminal process —the supporting framework and the subsidiary procedures—are of the sort that naturally complement jury trial, and have developed a connection with and reliance upon jury trial.[3]

THE JURY FUNCTIONS

In practice, a jury is composed of a certain number of persons who are selected according to the law and are sworn to inquire into certain matters of fact, based on evidence presented to them, and then to declare what the truth is. The general definition of the jury and its responsibilities encompasses such bodies as petit juries, grand juries, coroner's juries, and sheriff's juries. The *trial jury* is a body of twelve impartial persons temporarily selected from the citizenry of a particular area to try or investigate a question of fact.

The right to a jury trial as guaranteed by the federal Constitution is a right that existed in civil and criminal cases at the common law and meant that the verdict of the jury was not valid unless all twelve jurors voted unanimously. Statutes may provide that the jury trial be waived with the consent of both parties. Likewise, the parties may stipulate that the jury shall consist of less

[3] *Duncan* v. *Louisiana,* p. 150.

than twelve or that a verdict of a majority of, but still less than, twelve is acceptable.

The jury is under the supervision of a judge who has the duty to instruct them on the law, advise them on factual matters, and occasionally set aside a conviction returned by the jury if the judge, for good and legal reasons, determines that this drastic step is necessary. In Maryland and Illinois, however, the trial jury determines both the law to be applied in a case and the facts.[4]

Not to be confused with the trial by jury is the *grand jury* function in our system of criminal justice. The grand jury is a jury of inquiry that is summoned by the sheriff, constable, marshal, or other proper officer to the criminal court and whose duty it is to receive complaints and accusations in criminal cases; hear the evidence that is adduced on the part of the state; and investigate, on a broad scale, corruption in government. This body is sworn and instructed by the court to which it is returned. The term *grand jury* is historical and is used because it is made up of a larger number of jurors than that found in jury trials.

At common law, a grand jury consisted of not less than twelve nor more than twenty-three men. Today, these numbers are only guidelines for the grand juries in many states, although some states vary significantly, based on statute.[5] In California, for example, every superior court (the primary felony trial court for each county), whenever in its opinion the public interest requires it, files an order with the county clerk directing a grand jury to be drawn. The order designates the number of grand jurors, which shall not be less than twenty-nine nor more than thirty-four in counties having a population of more than four million and not less than twenty-five nor more than thirty in other counties.[6]

On occasion, a *special jury* may be ordered by a court or on the motion of either party to the case to try special matters in a case that is of unusual importance or highly intricate.

TRIAL JURORS

In early Roman law, the praetor ordered jurors to be selected by lot from an official jury list to try a case. The number who were to serve varied during different periods of Roman law. Only Roman senators were qualified for jury service prior to 123 B.C. Because of a prejudice toward their own class, there

---

[4]Jay A. Sigler, *An Introduction to the Legal System* (Homewood, Ill.: Dorsey Press, 1968), p. 110.

[5]Montana: *Revised Code–1947*, Section 95–1401. Seven grand jurors comprise the grand jury. Minnesota: *Minnesota Statutes Annotated*, Section 628, 45. Twenty-three grand jurors. Hawaii: *Hawaii Revised Statutes*, Section 609–16. Thirteen to twenty-three grand jurors.

[6]California: *Penal Code*, Article 4, Section 904.

was a reluctance to convict one of senatorial rank and the people became aroused. In 123 B.C., the law was changed to secure more impartial jurors. It excluded senators but included a political group of Roman citizens who were possessed of substantial wealth (property owners). Still later, other citizen groups were added to the jury list.

From the list of qualified individuals, a jury was selected. The numbers varied but were large (from thirty to a hundred), depending on the law applied in the trial. The practice was to select the jurors by lot and permit each side to challenge or reject undesirable candidates.[7]

The procedure for selection of jurors today does not vary significantly. Both the prosecutor and defense attorney are permitted to question a larger number than twelve out of a panel chosen for jury service from a list of registered voters. Each lawyer has a number of peremptory challenges, which means that he can excuse a prospective juror arbitrarily. The number of such challenges is limited by statute. The California law, for example, states that if the offense is punishable by death or with imprisonment in the state prison for life, the defendant and the state are entitled to twenty peremptory challenges each. On a trial for any other offense, each party has ten peremptory challenges.[8] In some states, in minor criminal cases such as shoplifting, the number is five for each side.

The challenge for cause is very important in the selection of prospective jurors. This kind of challenge is an objection to a particular juror who, because of his particular background or in responding to questions from either side, reveals a bias or prejudice that prevents his being fair and impartial. In such a case, the judge may excuse the prospective juror on his own motion or at the request of either counsel. The purpose of both the challenge for cause and the peremptory challenge is to secure twelve jurors who will be fair to both sides. The desired result, however, is not always achieved.

Grounds for challenging for cause go to the essence of a fair trial. They are based, not on the general legislative qualifications for a juror, but on the crucial ability to reason fairly. To ensure this ideal, among the more common reasons that may be put forth to excuse a prospective juror are the following:

1. In the case where the prospective juror has previously served on a trial jury that has tried another person for the same offense for which the accused is about to be tried

2. Where there is a blood relationship or affinity within a specified degree to the defendant, victim, or complainant

3. In situations in which the prospective juror served as a juror in a civil action against the defendant for the act charged as a crime

[7]William L. Burdick, *The Principles of Roman Law and Their Relation to Modern Law* (Rochester: The Lawyers Cooperative Publishing Co., 1938). pp. 688–90.

[8]California: *Penal Code*, Section 1070.

4. Where there is a relationship of guardian and ward, attorney and client, master and servant, landlord and tenant, or family membership to the defendant, victim or complainant

5. In a situation where the prospective juror served on a grand jury that found an indictment, or on a coroner's jury that inquired into the victim's death

6. Where he has served on a jury trying the same charge, where the jury was discharged after submission of the case without a verdict or where the verdict was set aside

It might be pointed out that, formerly, a prospective juror could be challenged for cause if he had an objection to the imposition of the death penalty. The law now permits a juror to serve even though he is opposed to the death penalty as long as he is willing to follow the law and vote for the death penalty if appropriate in a particular case.

As the Supreme Court of the United States held, "a sentence of death cannot be carried out if the jury that imposed or recommended it was chosen by excluding veniremen for cause simply because they voiced general objections to the death penalty or expressed conscious or religious scruples against its infliction. No defendant can constitutionally be put to death at the hands of a tribunal so selected.[9]

THE JURY AS A CONSTITUTIONAL ISSUE

The integrity of the judicial process, with the inclusion of the jury trial as a fundamental right guaranteed by the federal Constitution, is basic in the U.S. scheme of government. The guarantees of a jury trial in state and the federal constitutions reflect a considered judgment about the ways laws should be enforced and justice administered. The right to jury trial is granted to defendants to prevent governmental oppression.

The authors of the various constitutions, based on their experiences and the teachings of history, were well aware of the need for this device to protect from unfounded charges, governmental harassment, and judges who were overly responsive to political winds. In creating an independent judiciary, the constitutional framers were obviously apprehensive of excessive governmental power. However, they were not satisfied and insisted on further protection against arbitrary actions. Providing an accused with the right to be tried by a jury of his peers gave him an inestimable safeguard against the corrupt or overzealous prosecutor and the compliant, biased, or eccentric judge. If the defendant preferred the common-sense judgment of a jury to the more tutored but perhaps less sympathetic reaction of a single judge, he was to have it.

[9] *Witherspoon* v. *Illinois,* 391 U.S. 510 (1968).

Beyond this, the jury trial provisions of the state and federal constitutions reflect a fundamental decision about the exercise of official power—a genuine reluctance to trust the plenary power over life and property to a single judge or group of judges. The common law recognized the expression of this fear by its insistence upon community expression in the determination of innocence or guilt. The commitment of the country to the right of a jury trial as a defense against arbitrary law enforcement found the deep-seated nature of its value in 1968 when the United States Supreme Court held that the Fourteenth Amendment guaranteed the right of a jury trial in state criminal cases that, if tried in a federal court, would be guaranteed by the Sixth Amendment.[10]

VALUE OF THE JURY[11]

The jury is not without virtues. It serves an important societal purpose by affording the ordinary citizen the valuable opportunity to act as a participant in our form of government. Hopefully, this experience will foster more healthy respect for the law. The jury also eases the burden on the trial judge by permitting responsibility to be shared. As the conscience of the community, the jury at times may afford a higher justice by refusing to enforce harsh laws or laws that are repugnant to the community. The jury may also contribute to the willingness of the general public to accept the justness of criminal judgments.

The jury system is also not without its defects that have most certainly been intensified by the ever rising demand for jury trials. It is a cumbersome process that not only imposes great costs in time and money on the state as well as on the jurors themselves, but contributes immeasurably to the delays in the courts that are so prevalent today. Untrained jurors are presumably less adept at reaching accurate conclusions of fact than are judges. This is particularly so when the legal issues are complex or large in number.

A growing number of people are now arguing that rather than enhance respect for the law, the jury trial does just the opposite by making a sham out of the truth-seeking function. The average man, it is said, does not react favorably to the notion that complex matters are to be decided by ordinary men, nor to the way that the jurors are subjected to a series of distortions presented by the counsels for the opposing parties.

Still others point out that the trial by jury is not the only fair way of adjudicating criminal guilt. England and the United States are prime examples. In England, only about 1 percent of defendants are tried by a jury. In the

---

[10] *Duncan* v. *Louisiana*, *supra*.

[11] The arguments and general discussion in this section are based on the monumental jury study by Harry Kalven, Jr. and Hans Zeisel, *The American Jury* (Boston: Little, Brown and Co., 1966), pp. 3–12. Also, see Herbert Jacob, *Justice in America* (Boston: Little, Brown, and Co., 1964), pp. 163–88.

United States, it has been estimated that of all crimes triable by a jury, 75 percent are settled by guilty plea. Forty percent of the remainder are tried by the court alone.[12]

The President's Commission on Law Enforcement and Administration of Justice identified some of the areas of its concern as they pertain to the juror and jury system. It was found that the average citizen identifies less and less with the criminal process.[13] Citizens are reluctant to come forth to serve as jurors. Although the reasons are complex, the commission was critical of the treatment accorded jurors.

The physical areas set aside for jurors, as a rule, are, at best, inadequate, and, at the worst, nonexistent. Compensation is generally so low that service as a juror imposes a heavy financial burden. Although jurors' fees are usually higher than those paid to witnesses, they still do not approach a reasonable approximation of normal daily wages. The juror knows that his duties of a citizen require some sacrifice; but repeated court appearances occasioned by trial adjournments, constant continuances granted by judges, and unavailability of witnesses interfere with the private and business lives of jurors. To the citizen, this waste of time plus the inadequate compensation, mitigate against jury duty. The juror who does come to court to hear evidence and help render a verdict and who spends most of his time being shuffled around cannot help but suffer feelings of being manipulated and being used as a pawn in the judicial game.[14]

Once the prospective juror is actually empaneled, the lack of minimally decent court facilities increases his frustration and isolation from the system.

The President's Commission on Law Enforcement and Administration of Justice recommended specifically that the following improvements be made:

1. Adequate compensation. This need not mean paying a person's full salary, but does envision more than token payment.

2. Separate and adequate lounge facilities with reading matter, telephones, and perhaps television sets.

3. More efficient calendaring and scheduling of cases and more efficient management of the courts and prosecutor's offices. By these changes, the trial times could be better related to juror needs.

4. Technology to develop new techniques for procuring the attendance of jurors. For example, those with a fixed place of work or residence might be placed on telephone alert and called shortly before their appearance was necessary. Better scheduling of cases would result in better assignment of jurors and earlier release of jurors not called upon to serve during a given day so that they might return to work. Metropolitan areas could substantially reduce the number of jurors called for service and ensure their more effective use by instituting central jury pools from which the juror needs of a number of courts could be met.

[12]Jacob, *Justice in America,* p. 190.

[13]The President's Commission on Law Enforcement and Administration of Justice, *Task Force Report: The Courts* (Washington, D.C.: Government Printing Office, 1967), p. 90.

[14]Glendon Schubert, *Judicial Policy-Making* (Chicago: Scott, Foresman and Company, 1965), p. 81.

Of course, adoption of all of these recommendations will not remove the problems of citizen apathy and hostility. They should, however, make it more convenient to become a juror and foster a greater understanding of the administration of criminal justice.[15]

THE JUROR'S SERVICE

There are over a hundred-thousand jury trials in the United States each year with more than one million persons called to report as prospective jurors. These figures alone show the importance of service as a juror. Jury service is neither a right nor a privilege that a person may claim, but an obligation imposed by law upon a designated class of people who possess certain qualifications. The state has the right to demand service of its citizens as jurors. As a general proposition, jury service cannot be shirked merely by a plea of inconvenience or loss of earning power except where it can be shown that the financial loss will impose an undue burden and hardship.[16] In a sense, jurors are officers of the court, but trial jurors in criminal cases have been held not to be judical officers within a provision of the United States Constitution, primarily because they do not take an oath to support the constitution.

Generally, a court may compel the attendance of absent jurors by arrest, attachment, or some other compulsory process. A prospective juror who refuses to serve as a juror may be cited for contempt. In order to secure unbiased service to protect accused persons, various acts and omissions by jurors have been designated criminal offenses. Such offenses include (1) soliciting or accepting a bribe; (2) responding to embracery; (3) acts or omissions relating to selecting, summoning, and empaneling jurors; (4) acts or omissions relating to influencing jurors; and (5) those acts or omissions that are directed toward those persons who must select, summon, and impanel jurors.

SPECIFIC QUALIFICATIONS

Jury service can be restricted to United States citizens according to the Constitution.[17] It is generally required that in order to be eligible a prospective juror be at least twenty-one and not more than a certain age, usually sixty-five

[15]The foregoing discussion has been adapted from: The President's Commission on Law Enforcement and Administration of Justice, *Task Force Report: The Courts* (Washington, D.C.: Government Printing Office, 1967), pp. 90–91.

[16]*Thiel* v. *Southern Pacific Company,* 328 U.S. 21 (1946).

[17]*In re Jugiro,* 140 U.S. 291 (1891).

to seventy. The latter age limits are not absolute because older persons have served competently. Another common requirement or qualification is that a juror be a qualified elector or voter in the county or district where he resides. Property owning or taxpaying qualifications can be found and formerly existed to a greater extent than at present.

The common law held that women were not eligible to serve as jurors. Now, however, women are qualified to be voters and jurors in forty-five states.[18] It has likewise been settled law, since 1880, that the states are barred from discriminating because of race by the Thirteenth, Fourteenth, and Fifteenth Amendments. The Fourteenth Amendment prohibits arbitrary exclusion by states from jury service based on race and color. The courts have constantly held that where state action permits exclusion of all persons of a particular race from jury service in a criminal prosecution, the equal protection of the laws is denied the defendant by virtue of the due process clause of the Fourteenth Amendment and by various federal statutes.[19]

Many jurisdictions by statute or state constitution require that the juror possess a good character. In most jurisdictions, statutes or constitutional provisions provide that a person convicted of a crime is disqualified from becoming a juror. Conviction of minor offenses are not often grounds for exclusion, however. Depending on the state involved, the following may be disqualifying: (1) physical and mental disabilities that preclude proper discharge of a juror's duties; (2) disloyalty to the government; (3) deafness; (4) lack of education and literacy, and; (5) lack of knowledge of the English language. Generally speaking, a person who is otherwise competent cannot be disqualified as a juror because of his religious belief. Likewise, a requirement of an oath of belief in God or a Supreme Being is a violation of the Fourteenth Amendment of the Constitution.[20]

THE JUROR AS A DECISION MAKER

The commonly held belief that the juror decides the legal issue in a case, based on the facts presented, by applying the law in a deliberate rational process of decision making, is probably not true. Jury deliberations really are of interest only in describing jury behavior. As various studies of jury behavior indicate, jury deliberations are a means of securing a concensus, once the jurors have taken an initial ballot on guilt or innocence and there is a majority one way or the other. The deliberations then are aimed at convincing the dissidents

[18]Sigler, *Introduction to the Legal System*, p. 110.

[19]*Coleman* v. *Alabama*, 377 U.S. 129 (1964); *Hollins* v. *Oklahoma* 295 U.S. 394 (1935); *Hernandez* v. *Texas* 347 U.S. 475 (1954).

[20]*Schowgurow* v. *State* 240 Md 121, 213 A 2d 475 (1965). Buddhist monk.

of the correctness of the majority. In other words, the theory of a deliberative body must be tempered with reality, because the complexities of making a decision that is based on what often are widely divergent views of the facts as presented by the evidence is at best an ideal.

Attorneys, well aware of the effect that the cultural background, value preferences, and emotional attitudes of the jurors have in a case, base their particular trial strategy on these considerations. Jurors' reactions to personalities and the ways that those reactions can be exploited by a skillful attorney are discounted only at peril. In reaching a decision, the jury is a prime example of small group dynamics as it seeks to reach a concensus. Group pressures toward conformity are prevalent. Studies of jury behavior clearly indicate that juries, with very few exceptions, decide the case in conformity with the majority vote on the first ballot. Hung juries usually occur only where there was an almost even split of opinion on the initial ballot.

The process of jury decision-making is much like the legislative function, involving compromise in some respects. Just as there are plea negotiations between the prosecutor and the defendant and arrangements between appellate court judges to reach a majority agreement, the criminal trial jury strikes compromises to reach a verdict. For example, to achieve a guilty verdict, the jury might bargain among themselves and come up with a compromise allowing the defendant to be convicted of a lesser crime or perhaps recommending a lesser sentence to the judge.

In a strikingly high percentage of cases (75 percent), Kalven and Zeisel found that the jury and judge are in agreement regarding guilt and innocence of a defendant.[21] In the remaining 25 percent, where there is disagreement, there is a serious question in the opinion of many as to the quality of justice given to these defendants. Some even say it shows that anarchy prevails in the jury row, although another group indicates that this exemplifies the eccentricity of the jurors. One reason for this division is that, although the instructions given to jurors are in lay language (this may be too oversimplified), they just do not understand them. Secondly, the jurors' reactions are different from those of professionals because of their intimate relationship to feelings of the community. However, it does appear that the jury tends to give heavy weight to the idea that there should be no conviction without evidence amounting to proof beyond a reasonable doubt in cases of fact-finding only.

In situations where the jury must find more than fact, its values are injected into its decision. A common belief is that jurors are defendant prone. Studies do not bear this belief out. The jury will move in line with the equities of the case. At a given time, a case depends partly on the state of the law and partly on public opinion on the subject. Juries do appear to be more influenced

---

[21]Kalven and Zeisel, *The American Jury,* p. 56.

in criminal cases by the type of crime and by racial and sexual factors brought out in evidence than judges would be.[22]

In reaching decisions that agree with the judge's, the jury tends to be more lenient than judges in 16 percent of the cases examined. This means that the defendant is better off to request a jury trial 16 percent of the time than he would have been had the judge alone heard the case.

Although some conclusions can be drawn regarding the decision-making function of the jurors, relatively little study can be done because of the nature of the jury's proceedings. Until much more research can be accomplished, the decision-making phenomena largely will remain a mystery. Little more than generalizations are now available and the prospects for snooping into the actual secret jury deliberations do not appear to be feasible. For example, knowledge of the effect of social background, racial, ethnic, and economic factors upon the jury's decision-making ability is badly needed to determine the behavior of individual jurors. At best, recent studies merely open the door.

SUMMARY

The trial by jury is an ancient right that has become a cornerstone protecting the public from excesses of government. It is part of the U.S. judicial system. The jury trial, although guaranteed, nevertheless may be waived by a defendant. He may also agree to be judged by fewer than twelve jurors.

The jury is not to be confused with the grand jury. The latter has a primary duty to inquire into possible criminal activities, receive and act on complaints from the prosecutor, and act as a watchdog over government.

There are over a hundred-thousand jury trials in the United States each year, and over one million prospective jurors are called. These individuals may be excused from becoming jurors for specified reasons contained in the state laws. Even when they are selected to be trial jurors, numerous grounds may exist to prevent participation in a trial, such as bias, relationship to the parties, knowledge of the case, and a fixed opinion regarding the issues in the case.

QUESTIONS

1. Trace the historical development of the jury trial beginning in 1215 A.D.
2. Under what circumstances did the jury trial develop in America?
3. What is the significance of the Supreme Court's decision in *Duncan* v. *Louisiana?*

[22]Kalven and Zeisel, *The American Jury,* pp. 78–80.

4. What is a petit jury? Distinguish it from the grand jury.

5. What article and amendments in the federal Constitution guarantee the right to a jury trial?

6. What are the functions which a jury must perform in a criminal trial?

7. What is a challenge for cause? Discuss the more common challenges for cause.

8. What is meant when it is stated that a jury trial is one of the fundamental guarantees in the federal Constitution?

9. Summarize the various arguments in favor of retaining the jury as part of the criminal trial.

10. The President's Commission on Law Enforcement and Administration of Justice recommended specific ways to improve the jury system. What are they?

11. What is a hung jury?

12. "The trier of fact must determine all factual matters in a criminal trial." What does this mean?

THE GRAND JURY

ORIGINS

The grand jury's date of origin as an agency of criminal justice is a subject of conjecture. Theodore M. Kranitz dates the grand jury from the time of Henry II (1154–1189).[1] Still another source lists the inauguration in 1164 when "the crown established the first criminal grand jury."[2] Lewis Watts states that the "grand inquest" of twenty-three men appointed by Edward III in the fourteenth century was the forerunner of the grand jury.[3] According to George Edwards:

> [there is] no obscurity surrounding the origin of the "grand jury" for it was not until the end of the 42nd year of the reign of Edward II [A.D. 1360] that the modern practice of returning a panel of twenty-three men to inquire for the county was established and this body then received the name of "le graunde inquest."[4]

[1]Theodore M. Kranitz, "The Grand Jury: Past, Present, The Future," *Missouri Law Review,* XXIV, No. 3 (1959), 318.

[2]"The Grand Jury as an Investigatory Body," *Harvard Law Review,* LXXIV, No. 3, (1961), 580.

[3]Lewis Watts, "Grand Jury: Sleeping Watchdog or Expensive Antique?," *North Carolina Law Review,* XXXVII, No. 3 (April 1959), 202.

[4]George Edwards, Jr., *The Grand Jury Considered from an Historical, Political, and Legal Standpoint, and the Law and Practice Relating Thereto* (Philadelphia: George T. Bisel, Co., 1906), p. 1.

Other researchers have indicated that its origins go back as far as the history of Athens.[5]

A primary responsibility of the grand jury at its inception was its watchdog function. The grand jury was considered to be a tool of the crown; however, in 1681, the grand jury, in spite of the insistence of Charles II, refused to indict Lord Shaftesbury on a treason charge. As a result of this boldness, the citizens gained a new respect for the grand jury system. The tradition of the grand jury as frustrating tyrannical prosecution by the crown was a primary reason why the American colonists incorporated the system into the Fifth Amendment to the United States Constitution and into the Bill of Rights of all state constitutions.[6]

The independence of the grand jury was further advanced when the body refused to explain why it *failed* to return an indictment for the crown. An English grand jury in 1689, by presentment, could bring about needed repairs to the county hall, bridges, or county gaol. More recently, the grand jury frequently has been the conscience of the county.

After the early development of the English grand jury, the concept was brought to America. By this time, the indictment had been developed theoretically to protect the citizens from government tyranny. It had acquired a tradition of exposing mismanagement of local affairs, expressing concern over public health, safety, and morality; and acting as watchdog over the spending of public funds. The procedures for accomplishing these tasks were unique and are a basic reason for the initial effectiveness of the grand jury:

1. The community, as a matter of right, was informed of grand jury activities through presentments.

2. Grand jury sessions were held in secret when the body so chose.

3. Judicial interference was not allowed because of the independent position taken by the grand jury.

The uneven, four-century history of the English grand jury faced a severe challenge when it was transported to the New World.

DEVELOPMENT IN THE UNITED STATES

The first grand jury to sit in the colonies was formed in September, 1635.[7] In 1638, a successor grand jury convened to consider a problem that seems entirely contemporary in scope.

[5]Harold Kennedy and James Briggs, "Historical and Legal Aspects of the California Grand Jury System," *California Law Review,* XLIII, No. 2, (May 1955), 251.

[6]John Oliver, "The Grand Jury: An Effort to Get a Dragon Out of His Cave," *Washington University Law Quarterly* (April 1962), p. 171.

[7]Richard D. Younger, *The People's Panel* (Providence R.I.: Brown University Press, 1963). Mr. Younger's book provides an excellent historical insight into the grand jury.

The presentments of Plymouth grand juries revealed a great interest in community problems. In 1638 a grand jury rebuked the two of Sandwich for not
having their swine ringed, complained of a lack of surveyors for repairing
highways, and questioned the right of the governor and assistants to sell land
to certain persons. . . . A subsequent jury presented various persons who failed
to serve the public . . . for neglecting a ferry at North River . . . for grinding corn
improperly . . . for giving short measure in selling beer.[8]

Historically, the grand jury has been local in nature and a tendency even
developed for grand jurors to be elected. Another early characteristic that
subsequently has become a contemporary mandate is a set of selection criteria
for those thought to be prospects for grand jury services.

Contemporaneously with the transplant of the English grand jury, the
American counterpart developed an interest in local conditions in government.
In fact, some of the historical grand jury functions are foreign to those now
performed, such as caring for public buildings, overseeing and supervising the
construction and maintenance of roads, appointing local officials, setting prices
for the sale of private property taken for public use, examining tobacco hogs-
heads to determine whether or not they were the required size, and checking
to be certain that families "planted two acres of corn for each tithable person."

In other instances in our early history, the grand jury provided assistance
in levying county taxes and auditing expenditures of county funds. In one
instance, a grand jury proposed a head tax on livestock and slaves as a means
of paying county debts. In effect, the early American grand juries provided
services that the government was not equipped to perform. In levying taxes,
managing expenditures of public funds, and proposing new taxes, the body was
performing both legislative and executive functions.

In the political upheaval of the American Revolution, the grand jury
exercised its traditional concern with political tyranny. Peter Zenger attacked
the colonial governor in newspapers and was arrested for criminal libel. Two
grand juries in 1734 refused to return indictments for criminal libel.[9] The
panel, during the Revolutionary period, actively exercised its function of protection of the individual from arbitrary political power. The grand juries took
every opportunity to thwart the crown and encourage revolutionary causes. It
was through the grand jury that declarations for freedom often were pro-
nounced.

After the revolution, the grand jury once again stepped into a void and
assisted in providing continuity of government by exercising leadership in law
enforcement, taxing, and auditing functions among others.

It was during the revolutionary turmoil and immediately afterward that
the grand jury in the United States emerged as a strong and prestigious body.
It began to function more effectively and in areas of inquiry still retained today.
As Richard Younger, who has written extensively on the history of the grand

---

[8]Younger, *The People's Panel*, p. 7.
[9]*Harvard Law Review*, "The Grand Jury as an Investigatory Body," p. 590.

jury, points out, the power and prestige of this body was a primary cause in bringing about a constitutional convention after Shays's Rebellion in 1786–87 even though no mention was made of the grand jury itself.[10]

One of the greatest political questions in our history, slavery, appears not to have been of much concern to northern grand juries. The southern grand jurors, however, took it upon themselves to ensure that there would be control over the free Negroes and those blacks who were still slaves. It is also interesting to note that the same panels took seriously the job of protecting those unfortunate persons from brutality and like offenses, occurrences to which they were particularly vulnerable because of their involuntary condition.

During the Civil War, the grand jury in both the North and South reflected the sentiments in each section. Once the war was over, the opening of the West became the prime social issue. Laissez faire was the economics of this era. The use of the grand jury closely paralleled the expanding frontier and booming economy. It was an exciting period in our history and the grand jury reflected the time. "Hanging Judge" Isaac Parker at Fort Smith, Arkansas, "dismissed all grand jurors who opposed capital punishment"; the grand jurors in Alma, Kansas, slept in a haymow; the entire court, including the suspects, slept on a mud floor in a Sheridan, Dakota Territory, courthouse.

The breadth and scope of the grand jury as a national institution is vividly summarized by Younger:

> County officials were also subject to scrutiny by the probing eye of the grand jury. In Wasco County, Oregon, jurors charged the county judge and the county clerk with receiving illegal fees. The inquest of Kimble County, Texas, sought to oust the local judge and sheriff because they failed to enforce the laws. An inquiry in Custer County, Montana Territory, resulted in indictments against three officials for continuing to defraud the county. A like investigation ... turned up corruption on the part of a county commissioner. In Phoenix, Arizona Territory, a grand jury took the initiative in uncovering graft among county officials. It not only uncovered corruption but awakened the community to the need of a thorough housecleaning. A grand jury inquest of Fremont County, Iowa, called the attention of the community to extravagance, "and in some cases something worse" in connection with expenses of the county court. It reported that the county judge had not accounted for all fees paid to him. Jurors in Gage County, Nebraska, indicted the treasurer for the embezzlement of $547, while in Ormsby County, Nevada, the inquest told the court that Robert Logan had failed to account for $1,918 received while he was a county tax collector. In Deer Lodge County, Montana, the grand jury denounced a justice of the peace for demanding fees not allowed to him by law.[11]

In the late nineteenth and early twentieth centuries, the grand jury was active on behalf of good government. In 1872, after returning indictments against Boss Tweed, the New York grand jury was commended for its industry, efficiency, and competent investigation. In the decade before the 1906

[10]Younger, *The People's Panel*, p. 44.
[11]Younger, *The People's Panel*, p. 161.

earthquake, the San Franscico grand jury played a prominent role in fighting the dual corruption of government and big business that eventually led to the grand jury's assumption of the administrative duties in the city and the naming of a new mayor.

The history of the grand jury is replete with examples of vigorous defense of the individual against corruption in government. However, the powers it has in the business world have not been exercised to the extent that they could be. In the latter part of the nineteenth century, the grand jury had concerned itself with various evil business practices such as bank failures, Wall Street speculators, security manipulations by insurance companies, usurious interest rates, illegal collusion between corrupt union leaders and employee groups, restraint of trade, and political campaign contributions by insurance companies.[12] It is safe to say that in our contemporary society, the problems of pollution, labor union strikes, and business manipulations will be within the purview of the grand jury.

FUNCTIONS, QUALIFICATIONS, STATUTORY AUTHORITY

Indictments were part of the early grand jury's business. *Indictment* is a technique used in initiating a criminal prosecution for an offense, in contrast to the now frequently utilized information and complaint. The *presentment* is an accusation or the initiation of the grand jury itself and is distinguished from the indictment which is based on a charge originating outside of the panel. The indictment originates with the prosecutor; the presentment is the document by which the grand jury notices the violation of a criminal law of its own motion without assistance of a prosecutor.

The grand jury has, throughout its history, been concerned with jails, treatment of indigents, accounting matters, public welfare, taxes, public works, and law enforcement. For example, the previously mentioned grand jury in San Francisco in the early part of the twentieth century took a deep interest in governmental corruption, civil service, misuse of public equipment, vice, election law violations, and matters that concerned the public safety, such as investigation of theaters not adequately protected against fire.

The one aspect of the grand jury best recognized by the community is its watchdog function over government activities, a function which has progressed relatively free from obstruction in this country. It is here that publicity, given to its activities in ferreting out the *crooked rascals* in positions of governmental power, often is replete with sensational news reporting that contributes to the public acceptance of the grand jury.

[12]Younger, *The People's Panel*, pp. 210–23.

Criticism often has been leveled at the grand jury. However, in many instances specific grounds for the unfavorable criticism are not given. Often, individual criticism of particular grand juries has been grafted to the entire grand jury system. The general criticisms of the grand jury can be shown to be made of two distinct types: those of a general criticism of the local grand jury system and those of the total system in the United States.

George Edwards, Jr.,[13] listed three commonly held anti-grand-jury arguments as: those who believe the grand jury is useless, the belief that it is irresponsible, and the dislike of its actions in secret meetings. Jeremy Bentham, the nineteenth century economist and jurist, condemned the grand jury for utilitarian reasons because the functions could be performed better by a competent prosecutor. He also denounced the grand jury "as an engine of corruption, systematically packed on behalf of the upper classes," and charged that juries in Britain had become assemblies composed almost exclusively of gentlemen "to the exclusion of the yeomen."[14]

Sir Robert Peel, often referred to as the founder of modern law enforcement, and a Bentham follower, advocated that the grand jury be replaced by a responsible prosecutor.

The utilitarian argument is the most widely voiced criticism today. Various U.S. legal, prosecutorial, and political groups have roundly criticized the grand jury on the traditional grounds of inefficiency, local bias, and ignorance. The most outspoken advocates for grand jury restriction are obviously public officials. One can see why officials, who are used to operating under the *spoils system,* easily find the grand jury a nuisance.

The grand jurors themselves have contributed to dissatisfaction with the panel. One Southern grand jury stated,

> it is the unanimous feeling of the members of the Grand Jury that there has occurred an unnecessary waste of time and a consequent waste of taxpayers' money in the performance of a function of questionable value or usefulness.[15]

A similar conclusion was reached by a California grand jury.

> The San Francisco Grand Jury took a wide swipe at the Board of Supervisors this week when it claimed they were ignoring the annual report submitted by the Grand Jury. Because of this, members of the Grand Jury suggested that their reports are a "complete waste of time."[16]

The complexities of government are far beyond the comprehension of the usual grand juror, states another criticism of the grand jury. If the need is for

---

[13]Edwards, *Grand Jury from an Historical, Political, and Legal Standpoint,* p. 3.

[14]Younger, *The People's Panel,* p. 56.

[15]Watts, "Grand Jury," p. 290.

[16]*Vallejo Times-Herald,* September 11, 1964.

somebody to look over county business, why should this high responsibility be given to a community-based group of laymen? The need for expertise in the fields of law enforcement, education, political science, accounting, and law are manifest in the overseeing function. It is unlikely, so goes the argument, that the ordinary grand jury possesses these needed qualifications.

Included among the frequently mentioned arguments against the grand jury are (1) legislative and executive agencies are better equipped to conduct investigations of the type attempted by the grand jury; (2) today's government is democratic and within the direct control of the people, whereas the grand jury was developed because of monarchs, tyrannical in their rule; (3) there is no evidence that the fact-finding and reporting activities of the grand jury accomplish anything; (4) not every state authorizes the grand jury to issue reports, much less set out specific findings and publicize them. One court has even questioned whether, in the absence of a specific legislative authorization, anything may be put forward beyond a statement that no misconduct was found.[17]

A summary of the various arguments favoring retention of the grand jury emphasizes its uniqueness as a fact-finding body:

1. The grand jury acts as a brake on the executive where there are few checks other than the periodic ballot box.

2. The grand jury is the only practical means to accomplish enforcement of the law, such as in election fraud and official bribery and perjury.

3. The freedom given to the grand jury function without self-serving controls has been frequently alluded to as a strength for retention of the body.

4. The study conducted by the *Harvard Law Review* in 1961 concluded that the grand jury, when properly equipped, supervised, and commissioned to investigate a specific area, "is the best adapted to carry out a dispassionate investigation (compared to the legislative committee and 'the judiciary')."[18]

5. The grand jury has been characterized as the best body to ferret out criminal activity that law enforcement chooses to ignore. Such crimes often involve governmental corruption.

6. The public is educated regarding the function of government, and, therefore, a valuable public service results from the existence of the grand jury.

7. The checks and balances in our system of government are ensured by constant oversight of the grand jury.

Other pro and con arguments may be found but, as a rule, they are refinements of those presented above.

The term *grand jury* is historical and is used because the body is composed of a larger number of jurors than that found in jury trials. At common law, a grand jury consisted of not less than twelve nor more than twenty-three

---

[17] *Wood* v. *Hughes,* 212 N.Y.S. 2d 33 (1961).

[18] *Harvard Law Review,* "The Grand Jury as an Investigatory Body," pp. 605–6.

men. Today, these figures serve only as guidelines in the various states, although some states vary greatly, based on statute.[19] In California, for example, every superior court (the felony trial court in each county) files an order with the county clerk directing that a grand jury be drawn, whenever, in its opinion, the public interest requires it. The order designates the number of grand jurors, which shall not be less than twenty-nine nor more than thirty-four in counties having a population of more than four million, and not less than twenty-five nor more than thirty in other counties.

Selection of the individual grand jurors is peculiar to the specific laws prevailing in a particular state. The names of jury prospects, generally, may be found on such official and unofficial lists as union membership rosters, telephone directories, voter's registration lists, and tax listing of primary importance; however, the names taken must be of persons who are not exempt from serving by statute. The individual juror, in general, must possess a good character, integrity, rational faculties, and be of sound judgment. To select these individuals, some jurisdictions use personal interviews, oral and written true and false examinations covering legal subjects, and, on occasion, multiple-choice questions to aid in determining competency.

In addition to the subjective criteria, the grand juror must be a citizen of the United States, twenty-one, a resident of the state and county for a specified length of time, and adequate in the English language.

Certain professional, occupational, and religious statutes may disqualify a potential grand juror; for example, employment in police work, military service law, special types of governmental service, medicine, or the ministry. The grounds for excuse of those who are otherwise qualified are normally narrow and are granted when the person would suffer irreparable harm if he served.

Once screening has taken place, a panel list is drawn up and a grand jury is selected by drawing names from a box or by some similar method. Those selected are summoned and sworn, and a foreman is chosen or appointed by the court. The court then instructs the grand jury regarding the applicable statutes, its functions, and duties. After these procedural aspects are completed, the grand jury is ready to function. Its first meeting is to organize itself into a workable group.

THE GRAND JUROR—
SOME GENERAL CHARACTERISTICS

When the court has requested that a grand jury be impaneled and has gleaned from the community those persons who meet the statutory qualifica-

---

[19]Montana: *Revised Code-1947*, Section 95–1401. Seven grand jurors comprise the body. Minnesota: *Minnesota Statutes Annotated*, Section 628–45. Twenty-three grand jurors. Hawaii: *Hawaii Revised Statutes*, Section 609–16. Thirteen to twenty-three grand jurors.

tions as well as the personal standards imposed by the court, an unorganized body of personalities remains. Even though some of the selection procedure is left to happenstance, court preferences operate to select a specific kind of person to be a grand juror.

Those finally approved by the requesting court are usually outstanding members of the community who have been chosen partly on the basis of their public-spirited activities. As a consequence, the individuals are frequently well known to the nominating judges.[20] Broad discretion is permitted in selection of grand jurors because of the kind of activities in which they become involved. A great deal of personal integrity, character, and industry are necessary, as well as a broad, general knowledge of the total community in order for the body to function adequately, efficiently, and impartially.

Many courts, in selecting prospective grand jurors, use criteria that will result in juries not susceptible of charges that they are discriminatory. Criteria commonly used in selection are occupation, sex, religion, political affiliation, and race. In one California study, it was found that no judge responding to the survey used all five of the criteria. Eighteen grounded their choice on one criterion, six on two criteria, eleven on three, and two on four. Interestingly enough, six judges did not report that they used any of the criteria or did not report what considerations were used instead.[21]

The occupation of grand jurors is difficult to ascertain, primarily because of the limited amount of research attempted on this aspect of the grand jury. However, one definitive study has found that approximately 60 percent of grand jurors found in a three-county area were employed in occupational areas (business, administrative, professional) that did not typically include hourly-paid employees.[22] An earlier study of the grand jury by Edwin Lemert confirmed these findings.[23] Lemert postulates that

> it is probably safe to conclude that at least for economic and closely related issues the tendency of grand juries has been to assume a conservatively, right of center position.[24]

However, the accuracy of this conclusion is debatable.

Olson found in his study that the selection of Democrats on the grand jury was in an inverse ratio to the numbers of registered Democrat voters: 57 percent registered Democrats (43 percent registered Republicans) versus 38

[20]"The California Grand Jury—Two Current Problems," *California Law Review*, LII, No. 1 (1964), 116.

[21]"Some Aspects of the California Grand Jury System," *Stanford Law Review*, VIII, No. 4 (1956), 638.

[22]Bruce Trevor Olson, "The California Grand Jury: An Analysis and Evaluation of Its Watchdog Function" (unpublished Master's thesis, University of California, Berkeley 1966), pp. 105–20.

[23]Edwin M. Lemert, "The Grand Jury as an Agency of Social Control," *American Sociological Review*, X (1945), 753.

[24]Lemert, "Grand Jury as Agency of Control," p. 753.

percent Democrat grand jurors (52 percent Republican grand jurors). The apparent Republican advantage on the grand jury is subject, however, to being diluted by careful committee assignments.

Olson reported that, in one instance, even with Republican dominance of the grand jury, Democrats were only slightly behind them in the number of committee assignments. Democratic grand jurors controlled several of the major grand jury committees and were equally balanced on other committees. As a consequence, it could be easily said that in spite of being in the minority, the Democrats, in fact, controlled a majority of the grand jury committees. It was also discovered that there was a tendency for Republican control of committees concerned with public works (buildings, roads, and so on), whereas the Democrats were dominant, or at least equally balanced, on those committees that had a social orientation (welfare assistance, social security).

The sex ratio of grand jurors has been established with some accuracy. Stanford University[25] found that the grand juries studied were composed of approximately one-third women. Of 1,425 jurors studied, Olson ascertained that the same male-female ratio applied.[26] One former attorney general stated that county judges tend to shy away from women unless they are prominent as civic leaders and much prefer men who are active business and professional leaders in the community.[27] The trend now is away from male dominance. However, through the years the grand juries have been found to have a high ratio of men to women.

Additional factors that are given on occasion for disqualifying or exempting individuals from grand jury duty are (1) frequent absenteeism from the county, (2) financial hardship, (3) illness, or (4) a likely claim of statutory exemption.

THE WORK OF THE GRAND JURY AND
ITS ORGANIZATION

One may ask, "How does the grand jury become advised about what it is supposed to do and how it is supposed to do it?" First, its members must consult the law. Initially, the grand jury may be explicitly required by law to perform specified tasks, such as auditing the accounts of various agencies, evaluating salaries, inquiring into willful misconduct of public officers in the county, inquiring into specified legal processes (such as the reason a person has been arrested but not charged with an offense), overseeing the management of

---

[25] *Stanford Law Review,* "Some Aspects of California Grand Jury System," p. 637.

[26] Olson, "The California Grand Jury," p. 117.

[27] Paul James, "Grand Jury System," *Journal of the State Bar of California* (March-April 1964), p. 259.

county prisons, and investigating questionable sales or transfers of land that should go to the state.

Secondly, the interest and experience of the grand jurors themselves influence to some extent the emphasis that will be given to a particular aspect of their function. Thirdly, public officials or previous juries may suggest certain problem areas to be examined. Fourthly, citizens outside of the government are also a fruitful source of information for the grand jury. In this light, the grand jurors themselves have an influence on the activities of the grand jury and may encourage investigations into troublesome areas. Finally, there are always well-known, chronic community problems that mandate grand jury attention. The grand jury is often uniquely qualified to handle these persistent sore spots because of its removal from political influence.

In order to fulfill its mandate successfully, the grand jury usually is organized into committees, each of which concerns itself with a particular aspect of the charges to the body. The trend of these committees is to multiply over the years in any county that is growing rapidly from an agricultural to an urban posture. The committee structure can be used to investigate an almost infinite number of subjects. They can be used to look into almost every facet of the political, social, legal, and economic life of the community. In approaching the issue of what to investigate, one major concern of the grand jury is to avoid spreading itself so thin that it cannot do an adequate job in any one area.

The preferences of the grand jury are reflected in the committee structure. For example, education and youth activities may be the subject areas of several committees whereas matters that are of low interest (normally nonsocial matters) will not have many committees or will be the subject areas of low membership committees. A typical committee structure would look like that in Figures 13-1 and 13-2.

In addition to the committee, subcommittees may be organized within a committee. For example, the Public Safety Committee may be organized as shown in Figure 13-3, should the workload and diversity of committee work so necessitate.

Even with a formal committee structure, the grand jury may find that a concerted effort must be made to assist in solving or investigating a newly developed area of interest. On occasion several committees combine to undertake a joint attack on the manifestations of an underlying problem.

As a general rule, all grand jury members are invited to attend all committee meetings to ensure that matters of common interest are fully and adequately aired. This approach to grand jury business has a dual benefit in that it serves as an information-imparting technique as well as a means to a more efficient operation that encourages single appearances by witnesses.

It would be fruitless to attempt to itemize the formal titles of the officers on a grand jury. However, depending on the size and complexity of the body, there may be a foreman, foreman pro tempore, secretary, assistant or coordinating secretary, treasurer, and sergeant-at-arms or doorman.

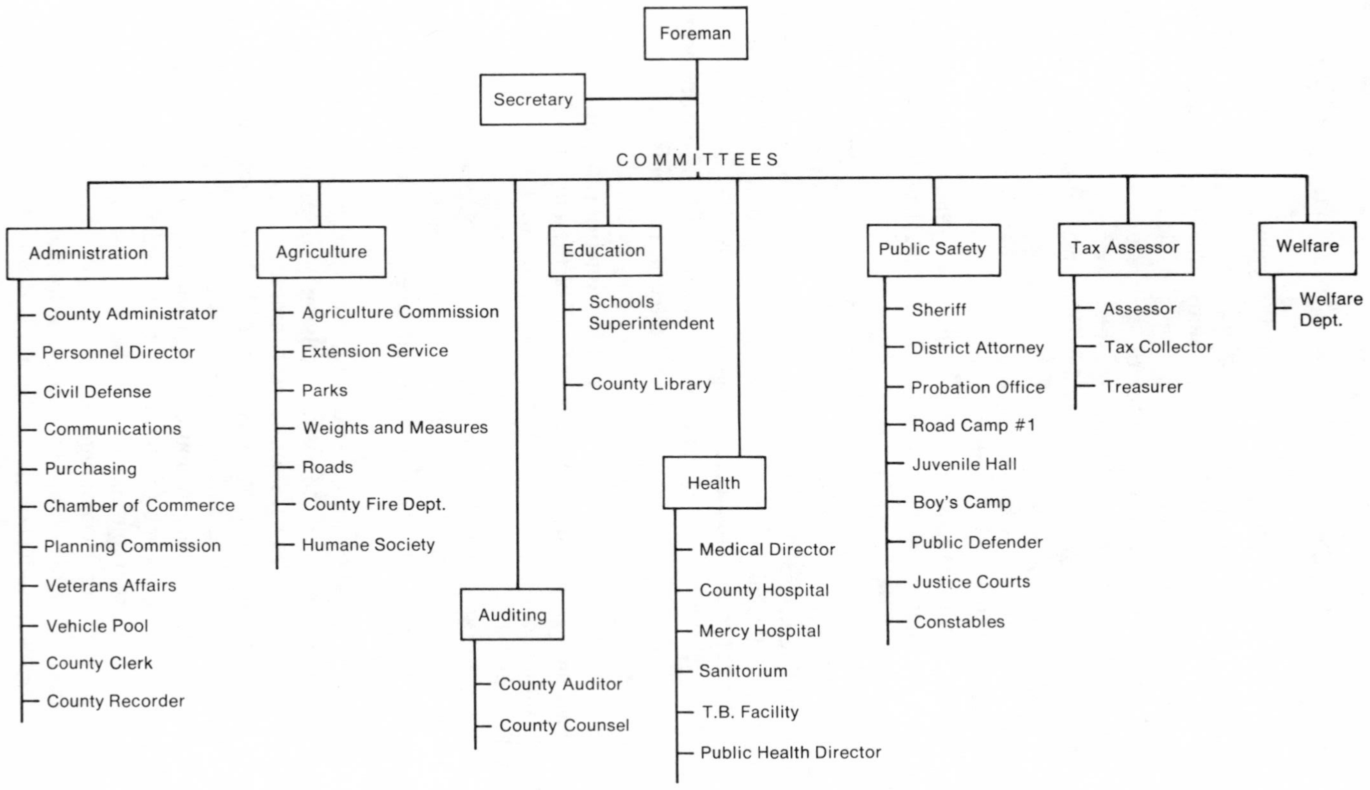

FIGURE 13–1
Organization of the Grand Jury in a Large County.

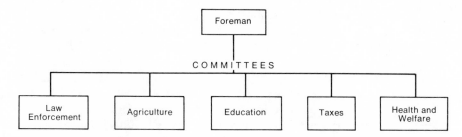

FIGURE 13-2

Organization of the Grand Jury in a Rural County.

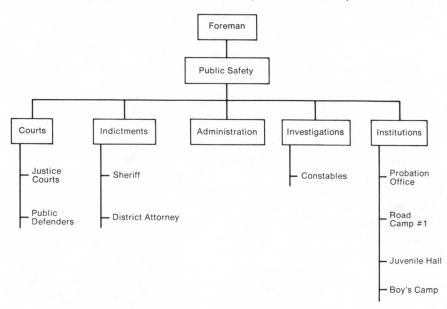

FIGURE 13-3

Organization of a Grand Jury Public Safety Committee.

SOME CURRENT OBSERVATIONS ON THE GRAND JURY

To serve on the grand jury has usually been seen as an honor. It is considered by most people to be the citizen's most powerful tool in watching government and the criminal justice system in action. As previously mentioned, in theory it has the power to carry out independent investigations, compel testimony, and take actions against the public prosecutor if necessary.

Contemporary critics of the grand jury system are aiming their attacks at the complaints portion of the grand jury work, maintaining that the jury is a *blue ribbon* panel with no balanced representation or protection for the accused. It has frequently been labeled a *rubber stamp* for the desires of the prosecution. The issue of representation on the grand jury is of nagging importance today. Civil rights groups are encouraging ethnic and societal balance to some degree. For example, on the Los Angeles County Grand Jury there were two blacks, one oriental, and one Mexican-American welfare recipient among the twenty-three members. The rest were white middle- and upper-class. The sex ratio was fourteen to nine in favor of females.[28]

One problem in the selection process stressed by former jurors in Los Angeles County is that although not discriminatory by intent, judges just do not know poor people; consequently, they recommend middle- or upper-class citizens for the grand jury, regardless of their race. Another contemporary criticism concerns the age of grand jurors. Male grand jurors are frequently in their sixties or seventies, and the women in their forties. A number of grand jurors themselves have made critical remarks about this disparity:

> The men were old enough to be our fathers. They were interested in saving taxes; we were interested in our children's future.
>
> What young man can afford to take a year off to be a grand juror? Naturally, you get older retired man.[29]

To lessen some of these complaints, many relevant suggestions have been made. Companies should subsidize their employees while they perform this most important civic duty. Judges either should know the person whom they nominate or else interview the person in depth prior to any nomination. The judge also would be wise to seek advice from such groups as the Urban League and organized labor before selecting qualified nominees. It cannot be overemphasized that the entire success of the grand jury depends upon the quality of the jurors and the diligence by which they are selected. A sincere desire to perpetuate an effective criminal justice system is a prerequisite for each juror. The court must be able to lend its full confidence, prestige, and authority to this body or else the grand jury will dissolve into an amorphous mass. Its critics will win out when they insist that a competent prosecutor should take its place.

The procedure that the grand jury follows in criminal hearings has been the target of contemporary complaints by civil libertarians and some parts of the legal profession. On occasion, the grand jury is used by the prosecution for publicity purposes or when the evidence against a person is meager. It can be used as a convenient substitution for the preliminary hearing wherein the defense is always at a disadvantage because it cannot cross-examine witnesses or ascertain weaknesses in the prosecutor's case. Nor does it learn what the real evidence is until the trial is commenced. Advocates of the grand jury explain this situation by pointing out that the jury's role is not to determine innocence or guilt, but to listen to evidence presented by the prosecutor in

---

[28]Charlot Holzkamper, "Grand Jury," *Intercom*, I, No. 4 (Summer 1970), 4.
[29]Holzkamper, "Grand Jury," p. 5.

order to determine whether or not a crime has been perpetrated and whether there is sufficient evidence to take the suspect to trial. At the preliminary hearing, the prosecutor presents evidence and the suspect, with his attorney, establishes his defense. Cross-examination is conducted, and a magistrate determines whether there is probable cause to believe the suspect committed the crime. If so, a trial will be ordered. The grand jury, however, does not hear both sides of a case; rather, it hears only the evidence presented by the prosecutor. The suspect is seldom subpoenaed but is probably notified by mail and asked if he wishes to testify on his own behalf. If he testifies on his own behalf, anything he says may be held against him. He is not permitted to be represented by an attorney and not allowed to present witnesses nor cross-examine the witnesses against him. Grand jurors submit questions in writing to the prosecutor for inclusion in the transcript of the hearing. The prosecutor can rephrase and even omit such questions if he decides that they will prejudice the previously taken testimony. Oral questions by the grand jurors are off the record. If an indictment is returned, the defendant then receives a copy of the transcript.

There is an uneasiness over this procedure. It is wondered how valid decisions can be based on hearing only one side of the evidence in a case. The opposing argument is that the grand jury does not try cases. The trial jury is charged with this ultimate decision, and it is here where the defendant is accorded full, procedural, due process.

SUMMARY

The grand jury is invested with remarkable powers. Its achievements are many, even in spite of the numerous criticisms directed at it. This is why careful selection of grand jurors is so important. In our society, this body has the potential to involve the total breadth and scope of the community in the search for good government and fair administration of the laws. It is the body which has the potential to make government more responsive to the needs of the people. Its vast powers in contemporary society must be fully and wisely exercised. Critical condemnation may eventually win out, but it must be argued that the grand jury is one of the few remaining institutions that allow direct citizen participation in government operations. In a representative system of government, this must never be screened out.

QUESTIONS

1. Historically what was the primary responsibility of the grand jury when it first came into being?
2. Describe the historical development of the grand jury in America.

3. Discuss what is meant by the statement ". . . (T)he powers it [grand jury] has in the business world have been exercised but not to the extent that they could be."

4. What are some of the more commonly found functions which are performed by the grand jury in America?

5. What are the most frequently voiced criticisms of the grand jury?

6. Who was Sir Robert Peel? What was his recommendation regarding the use of the grand jury?

7. Summarize the various arguments favoring the retention of the grand jury.

8. What are the commonly found criteria used to select grand jurors?

9. By what procedure does a grand jury become advised about what it is supposed to do?

10. Describe a typical organization of a grand jury in (a) a small county and (b) a large, complex county.

11. Critics of the grand jury contend that it is a blue ribbon panel with no balanced representation or protection for the accused. What does this mean? Is the criticism valid? Why or why not?

12. Describe the arguments of the civil libertarians as they pertain to the grand jury procedure used in criminal investigations.

MISCELLANEOUS
COURT OFFICERS

This chapter will discuss three types of staff members necessary to
the court and the functions they perform. Little can be found in
print regarding their work. However, their status in the criminal
justice system is quite important, especially for the smooth functioning of the administration of the courts.

14

BAILIFFS

Depending upon the state, the bailiff may be a police officer, the county
sheriff (California), or a civilian hired under local civil service regulations
(Alabama). Whatever the situation, the responsibility for providing security
for the court is a mandate that cannot be taken lightly. To carry out this
function, the position of bailiff is established. His primary function is to maintain law and order in the courtroom, which includes the protection of the
officers of the court and the maintenance of those procedures that add to the
dignity and decorum of the judgmental function of the courts.

The bailiff is a very real symbol of the United States system of justice.
Just as the police officer is the only contact that many of our citizens have with
the system, so the bailiff is an initial contact point of the citizen with the courts.
If the bailiff is a member of a local law enforcement agency, the contact he has
with the public lends a crucial first view of the agency and quite likely solidifies
any previously formed conclusions.

The individual bailiff administers to the needs of the court, including its convening, by following a prescribed procedure. In general, he maintains and preserves order in the courtroom to the end that decorum will be observed by the litigants, attorneys, court officers, and the spectator public. He responds promptly and properly to requests and lawful orders promulgated by the court in order to ensure its smooth operation. It is the bailiff's responsibility to anticipate trouble in the courtroom and be ready to meet and control the potential for disturbances that, with increasing frequency, arise in the courtrooms in the United States. The bailiff's duties, however, are not limited to the courtroom per se. In those states where he is a sworn officer, he must be alert to law violations outside of court.

The bailiff should always be aware of his influence in court. If a sworn police officer, he is likely to be the only uniformed officer in the courtroom. His relations with the public and the press determine to a great extent the public's opinion of the court and law enforcement.

One of the most crucial duties of the bailiff involves the procedures that are to be followed. Once he has been assigned to a particular court, the bailiff consults with the judge regarding the specific duties he is to perform. When these are determined, he has the responsibility of checking the courtroom prior to each court day to see that chairs are arranged properly, that microphones are working, and that the proper materials are available to ensure uninterrupted court sessions. Each judicial day, the bailiff contacts the court clerk to ascertain whether there are any special instructions or requests by the judge. Such instructions may concern, for example, special procedures or arrangements to be followed in regard to visiting dignitaries or possible psychiatric cases. In highly publicized cases, where there are large numbers of spectators and members of the press present, the bailiff may announce expected conduct before court begins.

Turning to actual court sessions, at the hour the court is set to convene, a signal is received from the judge that he is about to take the bench. This is the signal for the bailiff to open the court by an announcement similar to:

Everyone rise, please.

(Circuit Court, Probate Court, Superior Court) of the county of _____, state of _____, is now in session, the Honorable _____, judge, presiding.

After a recess, at the start of the afternoon session, and upon the appearance of the judge, the bailiff resumes the session by announcing: "Remain seated and come to order; court is now in session." In some instances, the judge may desire to vary the opening. The bailiff then opens court in the form desired by the judge.

The bailiff also has other significant courtroom duties. When a witness is called to testify, the bailiff directs him to come forward and to stand in a specific place. An oath then is administered by the clerk and the witness is directed to the witness stand. When exhibits are introduced, the court clerk may request assistance from the bailiff to help tag the exhibits. The bailiff also passes the exhibits to the jury for inspection and picks them up at its completion. In all situations, the bailiff has the primary responsibility for court security and stations himself in a location where he will be able to prevent the escape of prisoners. Just before the court adjourns for the day, the jury is normally instructed by the judge after which it leaves and returns to the courtroom the next day at an appointed time. The court spectators remain seated until the judge and jury have departed and the bailiff then announces, "Court is adjourned."

The bailiff's responsibilities in nonjury trials include the security of all prisoners, protection of the court, and maintenance of order both in the courtroom and adjacent areas to prevent disturbance in the court. Examples of disturbing situations include loud speaking or noise in the hallway, repair work in the building, and construction work outside the building.

Occasionally in a nonjury trial, at the request of the defendant, his attorney, or as indicated by the specific facts of the case, the court may order a closed session. The bailiff at this point clears the court promptly in an orderly and courteous manner. Normally, a sign is posted outside the door indicating that the session is closed and that there is to be no admittance. In any event, the bailiff takes a position inside the courtroom near the door to prevent spectators from entering. In most instances, members of the press and officers of the court are permitted entry to conduct business unless ordered otherwise by the judge.

When witnesses are excluded from the court by order of the judge, the bailiff dismisses them and instructs them to remain nearby so as to be available when summoned to testify. The bailiff notes any minor children present in the courtroom and guards against the possibility of their hearing obscene language. On many occasions, such situations can be anticipated from the nature of the trial and the contents of the opening remarks by the opposing attorneys. It is also important for the bailiff to familiarize himself with the case at hand and litigants involved so as to ascertain what situations may arise and what arrangements may be required in order to maintain the security of the court.

In a jury trial, the bailiff has a multiplicity of duties to perform beyond those in the nonjury trial. First of all, the bailiff must reserve sufficient seats in the courtroom to accommodate the jury panel, which is the group of potential jurors from which the final trial jury is chosen. The panel generally is composed of about twenty-five people. Twelve names are called at random, and the bailiff escorts the potential jurors to their seats in the jury box for questioning. Once the jury has been completed, they are sworn. The defendant is present during these proceedings, and the bailiff is responsible for his security. Should his attention to jury selection require too much time, the bailiff should request assistance for security of the defendant if he has such a need.

During court recesses, the bailiff announces that the spectators are to remain seated until the judge and jurors leave the courtroom. If the defendant is in custody, the bailiff returns him to the detention room first and then directs the jurors to the jury room. When court is to be reconvened, the bailiff notifies the jurors and the counsel and returns the defendant to court before the judge takes his place.

When it is necessary to view the area at which a crime took place or any material fact occurred, or if there is personal property that has been mentioned in evidence but which cannot be brought to court, the judge may order the jury to be taken to the scene by the bailiff. The bailiff is sworn to allow no person to communicate with the jury on any subject connected with the trial nor to do so himself. Usually, the bailiff also arranges for the transportation to and from the scene.

In some situations, the jurors are sequestered. The bailiff must be sworn to keep the jurors together as a body from the time the trial starts until they return a verdict. He takes an oath administered by the court clerk that he will perform this duty.

> You do solemnly swear that you will take charge of the jury and keep them together, that you will not speak to them upon any matter connected with this case, except by order of the court; and when they have agreed to the verdict, you will return them into the court, so help you God.

This same form of oath is administered to the bailiff when the case is submitted to a jury that has not been sequestered throughout the trial. In this situation, after the judge gives his instructions to the jury on the law governing the case and immediately before the jury retires to decide the case, the bailiff is sworn as above.

Once the order to deliberate the verdict is given to the jury by the judge, the bailiff picks up verdict forms, jury instructions, and any other exhibits permitted the jury, and takes them to the jury room along with such articles as pencils, paper, and water. The bailiff then instructs the jury on how to signal him or the court when a verdict is reached or if they need anything. The signal may be a simple rap on the door to alert the bailiff or a buzzer or bell system connecting the jurors and the court. When summoned to the jury room, the bailiff knocks and is given permission to enter. He then attends to any requests or instructions they may have. When the jury has agreed upon its verdict, the bailiff conducts them back to court. The verdict is read. If the defense or prosecution requests, the jury is polled. Under this procedure, each juror is asked whether it is his verdict; if anyone answers in the negative, the jury must be sent out for further deliberations. If the case is a felony, the bailiff must have the defendant who is in custody, brought to court to hear the verdict. If a misdemeanor, states vary as to the requirement of whether the defendant must be present.

When the jury has to be kept overnight, the bailiff has numerous administrative duties to perform. He must, among other things, provide for meals, hotel rooms, and special diets. Most of the details are handled by a central office in the bailiff's headquarters, but his duty is to make sure that the necessary arrangements are accomplished. The bailiff is responsible for the security of the jury and even their recreation. For instance, they may all be assembled in one room for a while to watch television. The bailiff will monitor the television shows to screen out newscasts that cover the case. He also censors newspapers, clipping out those articles concerning the case. Once the jurors retire, the bailiff assigns corridor guards to continue the security of the jury. In cases of emergency such as illness of one of the jurors, the bailiff is responsible for securing medical assistance. Finally, the bailiff must provide transportation for the jurors to and from the courtroom.

It is the bailiff's duty to have defendants who are in custody appear in court at the appointed time on the appropriate day. Each day, the bailiff prepares a list of the jail inmates who are to appear in court the next day. This list is sent to the county jail. After disposition of the case, the list is annotated to indicate the disposition of the case. If the case is continued, a new trial date is entered. If the defendant is sentenced, the bailiff indicates the kind of sentence, such as prison, county jail, fine, probation, or whatever. Usually, this list is sent back to the jail with the prisoners as they return to custody.

The security of the prisoners in the courtroom poses a problem for the bailiff. First of all, he is responsible for securing them in the local holding facilities and then bringing them into court as their cases are called. The bailiff must be particularly sure that no contraband is given to the prisoner by any attorney, relative, or friend while he is in the bailiff's custody. The bailiff sees to it that the attorney representing the prisoner is permitted to confer with his client in the courtroom, but in a manner that will not disturb the court.

A prisoner may be allowed to sit at the counsel's table with his attorney. The bailiff and any other guards station themselves in such a position in the courtroom that they may prevent the prisoner's attempting to escape or causing a disturbance in the court. During recesses, the bailiff returns the prisoner to the court's holding facilities.

Occasionally, the bailiff will be faced with a situation in which a prisoner who is considered particularly dangerous will come to trial in his courtroom. In this case, the bailiff must take adequate precautions even to the extent of requesting additional manpower. Depending on the judge, sidearms may or may not be worn in the courtroom. If the sidearm is required, the bailiff must exert extra care to see that the prisoner has no opportunity to reach the weapon. When armed, the bailiff and other guards should have little close contact with the prisoner.

Special Activities of Bailiffs

Probation and Sentence Hearings. At probation and sentence hearings, several bailiffs frequently are assigned because of the large number of hearings of this kind. Where the defendant is in custody, he is brought to the courtroom and directed to stand in a specified place facing the bench until the hearing is concluded, after which he is returned to the holding facility. Where the defendant is on bail, the bailiff summons him from the court spectators' area. In the situation where the defendant is remanded to custody, the bailiff takes him to the detention area, searches him for contraband, and has him transported to jail.

Defendants on bail and who are ordered to be released by the judge normally are not involved further with the bailiff. Where a defendant was in custody and the court orders him to be released *forthwith,* the bailiff notifies the jail of the disposition and tells the person where he can pick up his personal effects.

Juvenile Court. Bailiff duties here are a very sensitive aspect of his job. Because of the high emotional involvement of the families of the youngsters appearing before a juvenile court, and especially because of the need for extremely close supervision of the juveniles (often older juveniles require physical restraint), bailiffs assigned to these hearings are generally younger men who are in good physical condition. Juvenile court bailiffs are not armed. It is mandatory that they learn to deal tactfully with potentially explosive situations. Administratively, juveniles in custody are handled much the same as adults in such matters as ensuring their attendance and security in court. A juvenile bailiff also is involved in preliminary juvenile detention hearings and the normal adjudicative hearings in court.

Special Psychopathic Court Hearings. These present special problems for the bailiff. In those states having such courts, examinations are conducted and hearings are held concerning the mental health of persons alleged to be mentally ill. The administrative duties of the bailiff closely parallel those in other kinds of hearings except that, just as in juvenile hearings, these psychopathic court proceedings are sensitive and require the utmost tact and consideration by the bailiff.

Depending on the specific court, some of the duties and functions discussed above may be deleted; others may be added. In any case, the bailiff is a very central figure in the courtroom. His presence ensures the smooth operation of a highly complex organism.

COURT CLERKS

Another of the officials used by the court in the proper administration of its functions is the court clerk. The clerk does not perform adjudicatory functions. Insofar as the clerk is concerned, the rule is generally accepted that he is not an inherent part of the court. He is connected with it but is nevertheless different from it. The clerk's powers and duties are defined, as a normal rule, by statute.[1] Where his powers are so set out, he is restricted to them. The clerk is characterized as a ministerial officer.

> There is ample power in a court which has been regularly convened to adjourn to a future time . . .; but in the absence of a statute authorizing it, the clerk or other ministerial officer cannot act for a judge in either opening or adjourning the court. The clerk is a ministerial officer, and without statutory authority can exercise no judicial function . . . . A "court" is defined by Bacon to be "an incorporeal political being which requires for its existence the presence of its judges, . . . and a clerk . . . . There being no authority in law for the clerk to open and adjourn court, the clerk's acts were nugatory . . . . The judge had no power to authorize the ministerial officers of the court to exercise judicial powers, even in opening and adjourning the court.[2]

It should be noted, however, that by law the clerk has been given the power in some states to adjourn the court if a judge fails to appear. Such adjournment usually acts as a recess, and the judicial matters are merely carried over to the next day.[3]

The county clerk is not the same as the clerk of the court although in some states the county clerk is the ex officio clerk of courts of record in the respective county or city.[4] The clerk of the court is responsible for the performance of clerical functions necessary for the transaction of judicial business, such as checking files for information, preparing court calendars, preparing such memoranda as may be ordered or requested by the judge, attending to the matter of inquiries, filing, and examination of legal papers to ascertain if they comply with the previous orders of the court or provisions of law that may have been designated by the judge. One important note is that, as a general rule, the clerk is answerable to the judge and not the county. As a result, the torts of the clerk are not the responsibility of the county.

The clerk acts as the custodian of the records of the court. In his official capacity, subject, of course, to the orders of the court, he has complete control of the records entrusted to him. In the normal duties of the clerk also can be

---

[1] *High* v. *Pearce,* 220 N.C. 266, 17 S.E. 2d 108 (1941).

[2] *In re Terrill,* 52 Kan. 29, 34 P. 457 (1893). See also to the same effect *Cannon* v. *Briggs,* 174 N.C. 740, 94 S.E. 519 (1917).

[3] *McGarvey* v. *Southern Pacific Milling Co.,* 5 Cal. App. 2d 604 (1935).

[4] California: *Constitution,* Article VI, Section 14.

found the responsibility to maintain indexes that assure ready reference to actions and proceedings filed in the court. The usual procedure is to have separate indexes for plaintiffs and defendants in civil actions and one index for defendants in criminal cases. When maintaining the criminal calendar pending in the court, the clerk lists the cases by the date of filing the indictment or information and specifies opposite the title of the case whether it is a felony or misdemeanor. Whether the defendant is in custody or on bail is also included on the court calendar.

The clerk is responsible for issuing all required court processes and notices. He keeps the minutes and other records of the court by entering at length within the time specified by law, or immediately if not specified, orders, judgments, decrees, and similar pronouncements. Courts have the inherent power to correct their records if they are in error. This may be done on their own motions or that of one of the parties. No changes, additions, or deletions can be made on a filed document, however, except by order of the court. The changes, additions, or deletions may be made by the judge, or he may order the clerk to make them. The clerk always must be careful to enter the changes in the minutes of the court records.

The court clerk has the responsibility of ensuring that no files, papers, documents, or exhibits on file in the office of the clerk are taken from his custody unless prescribed by law. So important is the custody responsibility of the clerk that even a court cannot, without great abuse of its discretion, take away from the clerk the responsibility for custody of records.[5]

In addition to the preparation of the many and varied court documents, a very important function of the clerk is the collection of court costs from the proper litigant in civil cases. The clerk frequently prepares transcripts of trials for submission to higher courts when an appeal is taken, and it is not uncommon for the clerk to collect the costs of preparing the transcript from the appellant. With these fees, the clerk pays clerical workers for transcribing the court minutes.

The court clerk has the responsibility for supervising and assisting subordinates in checking, copying, and filing legal documents. A knowledge of the law is practically mandatory, especially because the clerk must type court orders from brief notes made by the judge. This specialized knowledge is extremely important even though the usual education requirement for the clerk's position is graduation from high school or its equivalent. Experience in some type of court work also frequently is found in the selection requirements. In many courts, the clerk issues executions for collection of delinquent judgments and court costs. In performing his work, the clerk must have clerical ability as well as the faculty to organize, communicate, and manage the general court operations in his courtroom.

[5] *Houston* v. *Williams,* 13 Cal. 24 (1859).

During the courtroom phase of the court clerk's duties, one of his functions, upon the judge's request, is to draw twelve ballots from the trial jury box, each containing the name of a potential juror. As soon as the jury has been selected, the court clerk administers an oath to the jurors that states in substance that each one of them will attempt honestly and diligently to try the matter at issue between the state and the defendant and then render a true verdict according to the evidence. The clerk also administers appropriate oaths to the bailiffs and witnesses.

At the direction of the judge, the clerk of the court prepares search and arrest warrants; subpoenas for records, persons, or physical items; and orders of the court. He also receives and tags exhibits that are presented as evidence during the trial.

Once the jury has reached a verdict, the clerk formally asks the foreman in court whether or not the members of the jury have agreed upon their verdict. If they have, the verdict is announced and the clerk records it in full in the minutes of the court.

Like the bailiff and court reporter, the court clerk handles a great administrative burden for the judge. The clerk, in maintaining the calendar of cases to be tried, hearings to be held, and administrative matters to be reviewed, ensures that the court functions properly.

COURT REPORTER

Court reporters are the means by which the court officially records the progress of a trial. These highly skilled persons can function either as free-lance or official reporters. Free-lance reporters are used, for instance, by industry and private attorneys to transcribe depositions and other legal matters before a trial commences. Our concern in this description of the court is with the official reporters who are needed in the courts; in government agencies at the local, state, and federal levels; and in the congressional and state legislative bodies.

The court reporter takes verbatim testimony at the trial. The testimony may then be compared to the statements made in previously taken depositions to show changes that have taken place. Such discrepancies may mean nothing more than innocent errors, but they may also point out false testimony. Whatever the situation, such differences in testimony can affect the final outcome of the case.

The court reporter's work is not over when the trial is completed. If an appeal is taken, the transcript must be typed and forwarded to the appellate court by the attorney of the appealing party. The exact spoken words at the first trial become the living words upon which a new decision is made in a higher court. Accuracy is therefore essential.

The work of the court reporter leaves no room for interpretation; verbatim records are required of all oral matters at a proceeding. General notes cannot be used to record the essence of a conversation as is done, for instance, in the normal work of newspaper reporters.

The court reporter is in an exciting position during a trial. During the pleas, arraignments, motions, preliminary examinations, the trial itself, closing arguments, summations, pre-sentence motions, and the various appeal arguments, the court reporter's task is exacting. Everything must be taken down by machine or manually exactly as it was said. The fury of the verbal warfare between rival attorneys is fast and ferocious, and little leeway is countenanced by either side. It is only infrequently that the confronting attorneys speak off the record and then only when permission is given to them by the judge to approach the bench for conference. The pace of the court proceedings determines the pace of the reporter. If an attorney or witness is excited and speaks in a rapid-fire manner, the court reporter has a difficult job to perform, especially during the sharp and incessant cross-examination sessions. Should the witness or lawyer speak slowly and deliberately, the court reporter's work is made easy.

A prime prerequisite for the court reporter is complete impartiality and objectivity. Because it would be possible for a court reporter to alter testimony in order to slant the court transcript toward one side or another, only persons with the highest ethical and professional values are selected. The work of the court reporter is not entirely confined to the courtroom. Upon occasion, he may have to accompany the judge, jury, or other appointed court officials to the crime scene or anywhere testimony must be transcribed.

Depending on the size of the community, actual court reporting may not be a full-time, year-round endeavor. Generally, court reporters use either of two methods for recording events at a trial: manual shorthand or machine shorthand called stenotype. Both record phonetic sounds that subsequently must be produced in typewritten form. To accomplish the latter, the reporter may type the transcript himself, turn the notes over to a typist who is a shorthand reader, or dictate the notes into a recording device to be typed.

Usually, the court reporter spends his work day in one court, but some states have judges who may hold court in two or more counties or districts. In such cases, the judges and court reporters *travel the circuit* to carry out their duties. The physical conditions under which the court reporter operates vary from the small, poorly lighted courtroom to the elaborate, electronically equipped courts in such states as Florida, California, New York, and Illinois, and in the federal government. Many are now air-conditioned; and the work area, chairs, and desks are generally comfortable, aiding the reporter in his concentration and accuracy in reporting. Recesses are provided at least once in the morning and afternoon which gives the reporter a break from the tension of the job.

Once the proceedings are under way, the court reporter must give his undivided attention to the task at hand. He knows full well that the transcript of the trial is one measure of the effectiveness and justice embodied in the system of criminal justice. Absolute concentration is difficult because, depending on the situation, a reporter may have to sit three to four hours at a time. Every word must be recorded and preserved whether it be simple English, a foreign language, slang, legal jargon, or medical phraseology.

The hours that the court reporter works frequently are long and irregular. For example, juries sometimes continue their deliberations into the evening hours and weekends. When they return a verdict, the court is reconvened and the court reporter must be present. This is not to say that the court reporter sits around doing nothing during the interval. Rather, he is probably typing, dictating, or supervising the preparation of transcripts for appeals that have been taken.

Unless prohibited by local court rules or employment regulations, many court reporters supplement their incomes by doing free-lance work. They are continually reminded, however, to avoid any situation that might involve conflicts of interest with their official court duties, such as working with a defendant or plaintiff who has a case being tried by the court for which the reporter is employed. Any conduct that may be interpreted as suspicious must be avoided.

Few occupations require such a high degree of alertness, concentration, patience, and accuracy as does court reporting. The court reporter frequently must record matters that are confidential. For example, the proceedings of grand juries are secret until the indictment is returned. The court reporter must be extremely circumspect at social gatherings or among friends. In short, the court reporter must be emotionally stable and, above all, able to remain calm and composed in the face of dramatic courtroom events.

Training for court reporting is rigorous. A professional association, the National Shorthand Reporters' Association, has set up a list of standards for reporter training at approved schools. As a general rule, court reporters must be able to take a minimum of 200 words per minute for a period of five minutes. He must have a thorough knowledge of the mechanics of English as well as an understanding of legal terminology and principles. In addition, knowledge of physiology and anatomy is highly desirable.

SUMMARY

The bailiff's status in the criminal justice system is both unique and important. He provides security for the court by maintaining order in the courtroom. He is responsible for ensuring the security and protection of jurors. The bailiff's responsibilities in criminal trials extend to the security

of prisoners, assistance to the judge as needed, and when necessary, protection of the court from disturbances.

When trials last several days and there is a need to sequester the jury,
the bailiff has the overall responsibility to arrange for accommodations,
meals, transportation, security, and various administrative details.

The court clerk is a ministerial officer who acts as the custodian of
court records; maintains index files; swears in witnesses; issues orders of
the court, processes, and notices; and directs the nonsupervisory court
personnel.

The court reporter records the official transcript of a trial in process.
He takes verbatim testimony in the heat of a trial and prepares typewritten
transcripts, if necessary, for appeals.

QUESTIONS

1. Why is the bailiff a very real symbol of American justice?
2. One of the usual duties of the bailiff is to provide security for the court. How
   is this accomplished?
3. Describe the general duties that a bailiff must perform during a nonjury trial.
4. In a jury trial the bailiff has a multiplicity of duties to perform beyond those
   in a nonjury trial. What are they?
5. What does it mean when a jury is sequestered?
6. Once a jury is sequestered, what duties must the bailiff perform?
7. What are some of the special problems which a bailiff must handle in a
   juvenile court hearing? special psychopathic court hearings?
8. What is meant by the statement that the clerk of the court does not perform
   adjudicatory functions?
9. A clerk is a ministerial officer. What does this mean?
10. Distinguish the clerk of the court from a law clerk.
11. What duties does the clerk of a court perform?
12. What is meant by the phrase "the jury is to be polled"?
13. What is the primary function of the court reporter?
14. What is the primary prerequisite for an individual to be a court reporter?
    Why is it mandatory?

V

CORRECTIONS

CUSTODIAL
AND INSTITUTIONAL
PERSONS AND PLACES

HISTORICAL SETTING

This chapter briefly will summarize the beginnings of corrections efforts in the United States. The stages that led to present-day penal and corrections systems will be reviewed. Following this overview will be a description of the nature and work of modern corrections officers.

15

From the beginning of time, society has vied with criminals in its use of inhumanity by answering offenses, in the name of social protection, with what amounted to barbaric retribution. Mutilation was a common form of punishment, dating from about 1800 B.C., that has been used practically to the present time in countries throughout the world.[1] Branding was used to supplement flogging. Included in the various *corrections* techniques were cutting off the hands of a thief or counterfeitor, slicing out the tongue of the perjurer, gouging out the eyes of the spy, and castrating the rapist. All these punishments effectively prevented recidivism on the part of the offender!

The first primitive societies simply killed a transgressor, believing that he was possessed of evil spirits. Slave kennels and galleys were common as forms of punishment in Carthage, Rome, and Greece. Early ingenuity made the life of an offender intolerable. Penal officers invented toil by treadmills and cranks with adjustable weights. Sometimes the ears of a prisoner were nailed to beams. When eligible for release, he had the choice of having a guard tear

[1]Miriam Allen de Ford, *Stone Walls* (Philadelphia: Chilton Co., 1962), p. 1.

off his ears from the nails or of doing it himself.[2] In general, jails served only for pretrial detention or as a place in which to impose a specific punishment.

The concept of punishment changed radically with the advent of the Industrial Revolution. Prior to this time, keeping a person in prison was not economically feasible. The government did not want to spend the money to house and feed prisoners. The revolution, however, created a demand for manpower and convicts became the answer. The government found that it could sentence offenders to prison and simultaneously receive a payment for lending these prisoners to industry. In effect, the government found it economically advantageous to sentence convicted prisoners to jail for a period of time as punishment. Likewise, employers found it much less expensive to hire convict labor than free men. These practices of industry also caused governments to realize that incarceration itself was punitive without the addition of special forms of punishment. Accordingly, the rise of industry and mercantilism along with its financial feasibility of utilizing convict labor spawned a proliferation of criminal laws that provided for serving different periods of time as punishment. As the laws increased, the jail system and houses of correction burgeoned.

The economic factor has been evident in the jail system from the earliest times. Early wardens bought, leased, or inherited their right to serve in that office. These officers also had *fee rights* over prisoners. They could charge entrance and discharge fees, fees for putting on and taking off leg irons, and fees for special rooms and food. Other services, from brothels to beer, also were available.[3]

The English penal system was the precursor of the U.S. system. Neither had a central authority. Jailers, through the purchase of fee rights, were free to extort, intimidate, and coerce inmates in any manner to exact fee incomes. The jails were poorly administered. There was a lack of prisoner segregation and an overabundance of constant noise, lewdness, and fights to the death. Public disinterest permitted unheated conditions in the coldest weather. Bad conditions, from general brutality by the guards to malnutrition and typhus, caused extremely high mortality rates.

By the early eleventh century, the sheriff was given the responsibility for making sure that a prisoner was present at his trial and for deputizing custodial personnel. By 1225, the sheriff had gaolers who also had assistants. In fact, being a jailer was a recognized profession by this date. These professionals had formerly been low royal officials who were looking for a better position. The

---

[2]de Ford, *Stone Walls,* pp. 2–3.

[3]Elmer Hubert Johnson, *Crime, Correction and Society* (Homewood, Ill.: Dorsey Press, 1968), p. 456.

sheriff's prison, distributed throughout England, formed the historical basis for the English prison system.[4]

Inmates in these jails were largely dependent on their own resources or on public charity for their sustenance. However, even when money was provided for payment of the jailer's fees, the funds were frequently not given to the inmates by the jailer. Duress commonly was applied to induce men already in jail to inform on those on the outside, both those suspected and those otherwise free from suspicion. This practice helped to ease the conditions of the previously incarcerated because the newly named were brought into jail, thereby increasing the fee-paying population. The early system of granting bail also was controlled by the jailer which, as one can easily infer, greatly increased his manipulating power. There was a temptation not to release profitable, fee-paying prisoners.

Lacking a stable income, the jailer was left to his own devices to further his interests, having the public's unofficial approval in this. He was not envied his job—working with violent people in atrocious conditions and with the responsibility of preventing escapes. Jailers were always faced with the threat of violent injury or death at the hands of the inmates because there were few restrictions on visiting rights, which meant less control over weapons and contraband coming into jail. Then, as now, riots were frequent and were often necessary to bring to the attention of the public the inhuman conditions that existed in the jails.

This short review of the English system is sadly similar to the birth and development of the corrections system in the United States. The American charter colonies established their own general court system and, gradually, their own rudimentary system of criminal justice. Colonial courts, like the English, prescribed payment of fines, lashing, branding, and mutilation. Hanging was the prescribed punishment for a varying number of offenses in each of the colonies. There were early movements by concerned citizens, mainly Quakers, to substitute imprisonment for the harsh corporal and capital punishments.[5]

In 1632, a small wooden structure was erected in Boston to serve as a jail for the Massachusetts Bay Colony. This building served for eighteen years until jails were built in other towns.[6] In 1655, the General Court of the Massachusetts Bay Colony ordered that "there shall be a house of correction

---

[4]R. B. Pugh, *Imprisonment in Medieval England* (Cambridge, England: University Press, 1968), p. 148.

[5]American Correctional Association, *Manual of Correctional Standards* (New York: American Correctional Association, 1962), p. 4.

[6]Robert Carter et al., *Correctional Institutions* (New York: Lippincott Company, 1972), p. 19.

provided in each county at the counties charge"[7] to house the idle drunkards and other petty offenders. The socially inept and indigent sentenced there were to be taught useful skills.

After the adoption of the Constitution, the Commonwealth's first prison was erected on Castle Island in Boston harbor. The first maximum security facility was opened in Charleston in 1805. The procedures to be followed by corrections officers were simple and direct. The Massachusetts General Court stipulated:

> That at the first coming into the house, the master of the correction house himself . . . shall whip the delinquent not exceeding ten stripes and after than he shall employ him or her by dayly stint; and. if he or shee be stubborn, disorderly or idle, and not performe their tasks, and that in good condition, it shall be in the master's power to abridg them of part of theire usuall food, or give them meete correction, as the case shall requier from time to time."[8]

The colonies began their penal system using fees and other features of the English system. Town constables early played the role of the English sheriff and coordinated their efforts with prison officials in securing guards and jailers for jail duty. The fees charged the inmates covered many services, including "turning the key" to lock up or release prisoners. Eventually, prison guards came to be known as turnkeys, a term still in use today. After functioning initially with makeshift facilities, the United States went forward to establish long-term imprisonment as a punishment in itself. Philadelphia's Walnut Street Jail was opened in 1790 as a solitary confinement facility.

Quaker reforms, first begun in England, led to abolishment of the fee system with the concomitant implementation of a system in which the state furnished the necessities of life. In 1819, the *Auburn type* of prison began at the state prison in Auburn, New York. It featured separate, inside cells with a great degree of inmate interaction in congregate labor shops. The *Pennsylvania type* was introduced in 1829 at the Eastern Penitentiary at Cherry Hill. The separate cell structure forced the inmates both to live and work in complete segregation. Most United States prisons during the nineteenth century were patterned after the Auburn type.[9] Early corrections officers were guided by specific directives expressing the penal philosophy of the day:

> A prisoner's mind ought to be reduced to a state of humiliation and discipline. . . . Communication with each other, "and more especially with the world, ought to be suppressed, except on the most urgent occasions." The officers of the prison should bear in mind that, as a body, the convicts are depraved charac-

[7]Edwin Powers, *Crime and Punishment in Early Massachusetts* (Boston: Beacon Press, 1966), p. 222.

[8]Powers, *Crime and Punishment in Early Massachusetts*, p. 257.

[9]Carter, *Correctional Institutions*, pp. 25–26.

ters, constantly plotting mischief. They should consider the prison as a volcano containing lava which if not kept in subjection, will destroy friend and foe, and therefore they should even be on their guard for corruption.[10]

U.S. JAILS TODAY

Although enforced degradation and hopelessness have proven to be a costly failure in the war against crime, implementation of enlightened methods have always lagged behind in the field of penology. The most unchanged of our social institutions is the jail, the predominant method of incarceration in the United States. The jail is a county institution which is normally used to incarcerate persons who have been sentenced to less than a year for a misdemeanor. It is also used for short-term detentions. The prison, however, is the correctional institution to which persons are sentenced for terms of longer than a year. Prisons are also state-controlled institutions whereas the jail is local in nature. City and county jails throughout the country have been serving as detention centers and houses of correction. Workhouses still remain, along with work farms and camps, but jails far outnumber all other penal or correctional institutions. There are some 4100 county and municipal jails which compares with fewer than 150 state and federal prisons and reformatories. Some have stood over 160 years; over a third are over fifty years old; and another third are between twenty-five and fifty years old.[11] Of the nearly two million commitments to all correctional facilities in 1965, over two-thirds were based on misdemeanor convictions. Of total misdemeanor arrests, almost five million annually, motor vehicle law violations and drunkenness represent a substantial percentage of jail traffic. Jails are the housing institution for minor offenders and the initial receiving center for felons who will be sent to serve sentences in state and federal prisons.[12]

In general, jails in the U.S. are poorly segregated, crowded, and lacking in safe control and supervision. The jail serves as a warehouse. A survey by the Law Enforcement Assistance Administration revealed that of 160,863 persons being held for a period of more than two days in the 4,037 locally administered jails in the country, 83,079 (52 percent) had not been convicted of a crime.[13]

Jailed inmates throughout the nation may languish in filth, suffer from poor food, receive inadequate health care, and be subject to guard and inmate brutality. All too often, low maintenance budgets, poor pay standards, nonex-

---

[10]Powers, *Crime and Punishment in Early Massachusetts*, p. 246.

[11]Johnson, *Crime, Correction and Society*, p. 457.

[12]President's Commission on Law Enforcement and Administration of Justice, *Task Force Report: Corrections* (Washington, D.C.: Government Printing Office, 1967), p. 72.

[13]*The Birmingham News*, February 24, 1971.

istent training programs, and meager efforts toward rehabilitation contribute to inmate misery. Frequently, a minimal staff-to-inmate ratio is the cause for poor custody and security practices. As noted by the President's Crime Commission in 1967, most of the jails are custody oriented and are supervised by ill trained, underpaid personnel. In some cases, the institution is not manned except when a police officer on duty stops by the jail during his normal shift. Trustees, pressured by the politically appointed and often inept custodial officers and by the inmate population, frequently are given control of undermanned jails.[14]

Jails may be used as penitentiaries (for those serving county sentences), federal prisons (if federally approved), and asylums (if space is unavailable in mental institutions for a person adjudged mentally deficient). In many jails, poor supervision encourages rape, murder, sickness, and suicide. For example, at New York's Riker's Island Remand Center the fifteenth person committed suicide in 1970 in New York City jails and police lockups.[15]

The President's Commission Task Force on Corrections found that only about 40 percent of the states set standards for the operation of local jails, and these focus almost exclusively on construction, basic health standards, guide lines for hard labor sentences, and similar matters. Personnel selection, salaries, and jail programs rarely are considered. Only six of the nineteen states that conduct inspections provide state subsidization to the jails. Thus, enforcement of any kind of state standards is remote. Low budgets and the sheriff's fee-collection system frequently cause drastic economies to be effected.[16]

Twenty-two percent of local jails are part of city government, and with rare exceptions, are operated by municipal police. The most common practice is for local jails to be part of the county government and to be operated by the sheriff. For all of the multipurpose usefulness of service facilities at the county level, there still is useless overlapping of functions and duplication of efforts within some areas. For example, in Sacramento, California, the county detention jail and the police jail are located in the same block. In San Francisco, the sheriff's jail and the city police jail are located on consecutive floors in the local hall of justice.[17]

Four levels of government in the United States—city, county, state, and federal, each with different sets of laws, facilities, and correctional processes—have their own prisoners. Corrections processes have always lagged most at city and county levels. Local political interference, inadequate budgets, lack of personnel qualifications and standards, and the desire of localities for autonomy and independence in handling their own affairs has mitigated against a

---

[14] *Task Force Report: Corrections,* p. 75.
[15] "No One Cares," *Newsweek,* March 2, 1970, p. 51.
[16] *Task Force Report: Corrections,* p. 166.
[17] Carter, *Correctional Institutions,* p. 92.

more responsive societal institution. Most jails lack skilled personnel to initiate and supervise jail programs. Salaries that are low do not attract intelligent career-minded individuals. As a result, almost all jails are inferior to state and federal facilities.

STATE CORRECTIONAL INSTITUTIONS

At the state level, more progress has been made in correctional functions than in the local jails. In early state prisons, the Auburn type, in which inmates were flogged for speaking to each other, was most common. Massachusetts tattooed the prisoner's name on his arm until 1829, to proclaim forever that the person was an ex-convict. In 1851, the state of California used a rotting Spanish galleon at San Pablo Bay near San Francisco for the state's first prison. Subsequently, the galleon was taken to San Quentin Point where the prisoners commenced construction of San Quentin Penitentiary. Prison officers enforced discipline by flogging and chaining inmates to walls indefinitely. In California's Folsom Prison, guards suspended inmates by block and tackle above a floor covered with chloride of lime. Additional conditioning of responses was achieved by using power streams of water from fire hoses to control the inmates.[18]

Poor food and medical care, filth and cruelty characterized the dealings of the correctional officer with offenders in the state prisons throughout most of the nineteenth century. Imprisonment for punishment was the correctional philosophy. Exploitation of prison labor was a factor in the economics of the state. Contracts with the prison for labor covered all kinds of jobs.[19] In observing the state prison system in the early part of the twentieth century, the American Correctional Association said in 1926 that:

> Exposures of brutality in chain-gangs at about the same time resulted gradually in almost complete abolition of the use of chains in state road camps ... although some counties still operate chain-gangs. Silence rules were rigidly enforced in some prisons in every section of the country as late as 1928, and are still enforced in modified form in many prisons. The number of states using flogging as prison punishment has been steadily decreasing during the last half century, but is still practiced in a few states, both officially and surreptitiously.[20]

The punitive philosophy that has dominated prisons in the United States well into the present century is gradually but grudgingly giving way to correctional training and treatment. Various reform movements have caused great improvements in state correctional institutions. Some institutions appear to be

[18]de Ford, *Stone Walls*, pp. 109–10.
[19]*Manual of Correctional Standards*, p. 12.
[20]*Manual of Correctional Standards*, p. 12.

giving more than lip service to rehabilitation, in contrast to jails, which have initiated little or no change.

In 1966, about two hundred one thousand persons were confined in state correctional institutions. Fifty-five of these institutions are maximum security facilities, and the rest include road camps, diagnostic reception centers, ranches, and farms. Overcrowding increases dormitory use and multiplies the difficulties of proper classification and segregation. In general, cleanliness and sanitation are stressed. Food is more palatable than in the past. Dungeon cells and filth are still to be found in state prisons, but it may be hypothesized that public concern and criticisms have helped to reduce these conditions. In recent years, prison scandals and riots have pointed out to political leaders that such demonstrations are more expensive than expenditure of monies to correct festering situations. In addition, these protests attract public attention and protest that increases pressure for improvements.

As a rule, state prisons house long-term prisoners and have available more varied training, educational, and recreational programs than are found in local jails. State institutions have better libraries and now are frequently providing work release programs. The state corrections officers thus may serve a more positive role in the criminal justice system than the jailer correctional officer. State prisons have been the first to reflect and to adopt the more progressive innovations of the federal prison system.

FEDERAL CORRECTIONAL SYSTEM

The federal prison system has been years in developing its present diverse stature. As late as 1930, when the United States Bureau of Prisons was established, there were only five federal prisons. The federal corrections officers were largely untrained and found in poor officer-inmate ratio. Until the federal prison system expanded, many offenders were housed in county jails and state prisons. This same situation still exists but on a reduced scale. Today, the federal system is comprised of six penitentiaries, five adult correctional institutions, seven short-term institutions, three juvenile and youth institutions, eight community treatment centers, one medical treatment facility, and thirty-five other insitutions of various kinds.[21]

The rapid and steady progress of the federal system has had a positive effect on state prisons, primarily in the fields of management and rehabilitation.[22] The federal prisons offer the most comprehensive care. For example, the federal penitentiary in Atlanta has become the center for prisoners in need of plastic surgery.[23]

[21]Carter, *Correctional Institutions,* pp. 107–9.
[22]*Manual of Correctional Standards,* p. 13.
[23]*U.S. Bureau of Prisons, United States Penitentiary, Atlanta, Georgia* (n.d.), p. 21.

Federal facilities offer progressive programs for work and vocational training, recreation, sports, education, and religious activity. The system has the means of providing for the confinement of professional criminals. In regard to the great numbers of other offenders, there is one disadvantage: confinement in federal prisons usually places prisoners far from their homes and communities.[24]

Because the federal system emphasizes rehabilitation rather than punishment, at least theoretically, it is better able to work toward its basic philosophical goal of "implementation of an individualized system of discipline and treatment."[25] Federal correctional officer training is superior to that of most other governmental correctional officers. The federal officers have a higher salary level and other benefits that offer security and job satisfaction. They face a variety of challenges similar to those confronting state and local corrections officers, but the federal officers more frequently face them with the facilities and resources necessary to allow them to practice their skills as corrections officers.

CORRECTIONAL OFFICERS' JOBS

Corrections officers today work within a wide variety of facilities. One Tennessee jail is a log cabin with two cots and sometimes up to forty prisoners.[26] At Joliet, Illinois, six hundred corrections officers supervise five thousand inmates in a highly structured system with expensively maintained facilities. In the main, legal commitment for offenses confines the lawbreaker within completely institutional surroundings.[27] The total institution requires that both inmates and corrections officers function according to formal rules aimed at achieving custodial security. Prisoners are regimented by schedules and various restraints imposed by administrators and enforced by custodial officers. All activities are confined to small spaces governed by strict rules, and presided over by a corrections officer who also adapts to the imposed regime.

An applicant for work in the correctional custodial officer field, once accepted, will face many responsibilities. He is expected to remember always that the primary mission of the jail or other custodial institution is to maintain custody of those persons who are legally committed to him until they are legally released.[28] The new custodial officer must be trained in the functioning of the various locking devices used by the institution. He must likewise be

[24] *Task Force Report: Corrections,* p. 107.

[25] de Ford, *Stone Walls,* p. 204.

[26] de Ford, *Stone Walls,* p. 93.

[27] Johnson, *Crime, Correction and Society,* p. 524.

[28] Myrle Alexander, *Jail Administration* (Springfield: Charles C. Thomas, 1957), p. 42.

trained in the techniques of self-defense which, in conjunction with a well-rounded training program, develops a degree of self-confidence that is invaluable for the officer in his daily interraction with the inmates. Rules, regulations, and procedures are of great importance in such a system; but in working with human beings anywhere, the most crucial factor is the influence of one disciplined, purposeful personality upon another.[29] Corrections officers are required to be exemplary in their personal conduct. They are expected to demonstrate their respect for the law and sense of justice for others. Development of a professional attitude by the custodial officer is vital in shaping him to be unemotional and impartial in his relations with inmates.

The safety, security, and welfare of the prisoners and the institution must be considered from the moment an individual is brought to the institution. Upon his arrival, the custodial officer (also sometimes called a warden) makes sure that the commitment papers are in proper order. This requires a knowledge of the charges and whether or not the escorting officers are duly authorized to commit a person. Legal knowledge is necessary to protect the institution and personnel from suits over improper commitment and release.

One of the initial steps taken by the custodial officer is to ensure that the new inmate is properly identified, fingerprinted, and photographed in addition to having the necessary personal data recorded. Careful searching for weapons and other contraband is performed. Medical examinations occur very shortly after commitment. The custodial officer helps to classify new inmates so that hardened criminals can be segregated from the younger, more helpless inmates. Screening out the homosexuals, mentally disturbed, and more violent types of prisoners must be done. Well-managed institutions frequently enforce a period of quarantine and spend several weeks classifying and assigning prisoners to housing.

During the admission process, the correctional officer may aid the inmate in developing a cooperative, accepting attitude toward his new status. The officer, by his own attitude and approach to such duties as the shakedown search and by an explanation of the rules, can reduce embarrassment, irritation, and apprehension. With a few positive steps, the officer may largely determine whether he will be confronted later with inmate disciplinary problems.[30] Once the new inmate is processed and assigned to housing, the custodial officer can escort him to his new "home." Inmates may be segregated from, or assigned to, the general prison population and may live either in cells or dormitories.

A typical day for the correction officer may include supervising the wake-up and transfer of inmates to day rooms where they eat and conduct many daily activities. Supervision is necessary throughout the day and during

[29]Alexander, *Jail Administration,* p. 79.
[30]U.S. Bureau of Prisons, *The Jail: Its Operation and Management* (1970), p. 16.

meals, whether served in the cafeteria, dormitories, or individual cells. The corrections officer ensures that proper sanitation standards are maintained in the cells, kitchen, and elsewhere. Care is necessary in selecting inmates for work details, considering the ever present potential for trouble from inmate hostility.

Quite frequently, correctional facilities are short of manpower, and inmates are used. Within the institution, such inmate labor may be utilized at outside doors, in elevators and admission areas, and in case assistance is needed to control unruly inmates. They may, of necessity, be used to type and to take fingerprints and identification photographs. Inmates supply kitchen labor and perform routine maintenance throughout the institution. In some facilities, inmates are dental technicians. In others, where an inmate becomes a trustee, he may assist visiting doctors and other health officials. However, as a general rule, a trustee should not be given supervisory powers over other inmates.

The corrections officer may be merely *on duty* in a poorly run institution or he may function as a selector, motivator, or supervisor over work crews, providing assistance, motivation, and guidance to the inmates. It is the skilled corrections officer who can motivate inmates, coming, as they generally do, from the lower socioeconomic classes. Many have few standards of cleanliness, sanitation, or self-improvement plus an inability to derive any satisfaction from performing productive, useful labor. In jails especially, where sentences are usually short-term in contrast to prisons, all those liberties that could serve as potential rewards, such as recreation, inmate store privileges, visiting rights, good-time allowances, and the like, are granted at the initial admission. Therefore, the inmate sometimes has little positive need or desire to exert himself in constructive activity geared toward his personal growth.

The correctional officer has various duties in the institution, such as censoring mail, supervising visiting hours, maintaining control over medical checkups, and presiding over any religious or recreational gatherings. Alert patrol and constant surveillance must be made by the officer over his duty area according to security needs. Any type of disturbance must be dealt with promptly. Searches and shakedowns are regular occurrences, and the corrections officer must be well-versed and practiced in the plans and procedures for dealing with any emergency such as fires or riots.

It is understood by the corrections officer, both as a written rule and as a necessary principle, that even if his life is in jeopardy, there can be no capitulation on the part of the institution to the demands of inmates trying to escape. An officer taken hostage and his life threatened knows that all efforts to rescue him will be taken except permitting the prisoner to leave the prison. The corrections officer realizes that if it were otherwise and escapes were allowed, the safety of all persons within the walls and that of the general public would be intolerably threatened. In the prison bureaucracy, the corrections officer is the cog that causes the wheels to turn between the chief administrators in the institution and the inmates. He has the potential of being a tremendous influence to both sides, depending upon his character and credibility. If the officer has been fair, diligent, and forceful in his daily interactions with the inmates, this fact alone may save his life if he is taken hostage.

In the traditional institution, systemized movement and regimentation of conduct are enforced to reduce unexpected nonconformity. As a general rule, attempts to circumvent rules only increase restrictions. However, the effects of correctional punishments and restrictions vary according to existing conditions. For instance, where unpalatable meals are served and then reduced as a means of control or where idleness is merely replaced by monotonous work, the impact on the inmate is not going to be very great. In too many institutions, officers are allowed to mete out instant punishment. Ideally, the problem of infractions should be dealt with by a reviewing board instead of an individual officer. Proper custody and control are necessary for rehabilitation and for the general welfare of officers and inmates. The conscientious corrections officer who works at controlling aggression, curbing exploitative types, and detecting deviant behavior will gain recognition as one who promotes safety. Anxious inmates, living in compressed conditions, can have their lives made bearable by a corrections officer who extends himself toward this end. However, control, to be maintained constantly and effectively, must be energized with positive correctional and training resources.[31]

Corrections officers deal with inmates who are illiterate or poorly educated, bitter and vengeful, or resigned and withdrawn. The general physical surroundings of the officer are drab and monotonous and the constant ring of metal against metal resounds throughout the institution. In short, a feeling of futility and frustration pervades the atmosphere about the usual correctional officer.

Exceptions are to be found. For example, at the state prison at Chino, California, there are no convicts, only inmates who are trained for the work for which they are best suited and who are paid for their industry. Creative work, study, good library facilities, television, the latest movies, and encouraged visiting with family and friends, are part of the Chino routine.[32] It has been postulated that California has the most progressive correctional system in the United States. The motto of the California Department of Corrections seems to set the tone of the correctional philosophy: Good Custody Is Good Treatment, and Good Treatment Is Good Custody.[33]

New methods in the corrections field are gradually beginning to take hold. In the past few decades, the collaborative institution, structured around a partnership between staff and inmates in the total process of rehabilitation,

[31] *Manual of Correctional Standards,* p. 209.
[32] de Ford, *Stone Walls,* p. 197.
[33] de Ford, *Stone Walls,* p. 197.

has been forerunner of a trend away from the quasi-military, impers treatment of inmates. This technique tries to assimilate inmates ir noncriminal ways of life, partly through close identification witl partly through increased communication with the outside communιy.

PROFILE OF CORRECTIONAL OFFICERS

As official methods of dealing with inmates are progressively upgraded, the caliber of corrections officers also must be raised. Officials still remain who fail to see the advantages of a well-trained, self-motivated cadre of professional correctional officers. Corrections personnel need thorough training and a knowledge of human behavior to deal with inmates often lacking maturity and self-control. Officers who specialize in negative types of discipline such as brute force, only reinforce the antisocial attitudes of the offenders. Lack of cooperation and maladjustment result from the undeviating enforcement of rules and regulations under the constant threat of punishment without the use of incentives and with no regard for the needs of the individual.[35] Prisons can no longer afford to have custodial personnel with less training and ability than animal keepers in a zoo. Maintaining head counts and causing bodies to move from one area to another are still the primary activities of the officer under the guard-versus-the-prisoner adversary system. Reform-minded psychologists say that when guards and inmates act out adversary roles, the tension defeats rehabilitation and tends to harden the inmates. Punishment is far down their list of effective ways of motivation and of modifying human behavior. They say it is not the responsibility of the guards to punish the inmates while they are in prison; the fact that the inmates are locked up is in itself the punishment set by the courts.

It is not surprising that conflict exists between correctional officers and the relatively new, reform-minded psychologists in today's prisons. Both have different concepts of what *correction* should mean. The correctional officer tends to believe that the inmate needs punitive restraint and discipline as the only method of rehabilitation he understands and to which he can respond. The psychologist tends to believe that most inmates are emotionally or mentally disturbed and therefore not really criminal but in need of psychiatric rehabilitation and less control. Naturally, the correctional officer also feels threatened by such an attitude that he fears might take away some of his authority and means of control over the inmates. As matters stand, today's prisons are somewhat split down the middle ideologically. Ideally, psycholo-

---

[34] *Task Force Report: Corrections,* p. 47.

[35] *Jailer's Correspondence Course,* "Supervision of Prisoners," U.S. Department of Justice, Bureau of Prisons, Washington, D.C. (n.d.), p. 13.

gists and correctional officers should be working together on this mutual problem of how best to handle the inmate.

The effective custodial officer is characterized by a stable personality and possession of a humanistic outlook. Unfortunately, many of the officers in institutions are shocked in the first year of their employment to find that their real problems are not with the inmates but rather with the emotional and personality conflicts among the employees.[36] Too many corrections officers today may be described as dead wood because they view their function as strictly custodial and control-oriented. Significant numbers of corrections officers believe that the true nature of their job is punitive, and they have little, if any, conception of the value of human understanding in dealing with the various personalities in inmate populations. Too often, corrections officers tacitly overlook and even participate in cover-up efforts to protect extreme authoritarian types among their ranks. To a startling degree, especially in bureaucracies with the vertical system of advancement, the corrections officer feels that he has an obligation to support a fellow employee.[37] Because it actually may not be only a matter of possible advancement but of being able to hold one's job, a *warden's ethic* may come to be that mode of survival similar to the *policeman's ethic:*

> The policeman's ethic—to eliminate (or impose arbitrary added punishment on) those who threaten authority and convict (due to failure to please highly authoritarian officers) the guilty any way he can—seems to him a logical compromise between due process and law enforcement because citizens (by tacit condonement or ignorance-is-bliss attitudes) and his superiors (by avoidance of their supervisoral responsibilities) tell him it is.[38]

Only in institutions with the highest caliber of leadership combined with an operation based on personal, professional integrity will a warden's ethic be absent.

TRAINING

Because corrections officers are responsible for maintaining the custodial supervision of prisoners in jails, correctional facilities, road camps, and state and federal penal institutions, their training must include all of the legal and practical aspects of correctional procedures. In many areas of the country, the corrections officers are sworn police personnel and frequently undergo the

---

[36]Richard A. McGee, *The Prison Warden and the Custodial Staff* (Springfield: Charles C. Thomas, 1965), p. 79.

[37]Paul Chevigny, *Police Power* (New York: Random House, 1969), p. 281.

[38]Chevigny, *Police Power,* pp. 27 and 271.

same selection processes the police department requires for all sworn personnel. In this situation, they receive the same training but, in addition, they receive training in the custodial aspects of their job. If they are designated solely as corrections/custodial officers or as wardens, a specific training program is laid out for them. Although not all-inclusive, the corrections officer's training program includes varied topics such as:

1. Administering inmate discipline in which methods and procedures are covered for reporting inmate infraction of rules.

2. State custody laws relating to the duties and responsibilities in handling prisoners.

3. Collection, identification and preservation of evidence wherein there is a discussion of the responsibilities of the first officer on the scene to preserve crime evidence. The officer is given the "Do's and Don'ts" of handling evidence. It is well to remember that crimes are frequently committed within the institution itself, and the officer must understand the law and procedures that relate to such matters as handling evidence. He is also familiarized with the methods of preserving and transporting evidence.

4. Custody and security of inmates. The officer is instructed on the primary objectives of the institution, storage of weapons, prisoner searches, control of keys and tools, prisoner counts, and methods of searching cells and dormitories.

5. Reception and classification of inmates. Included is instruction on creating a constructive atmosphere, legal bases for commitment, shakedown of new inmates, medical examinations, and inmate classification.

6. Supervision of inmates. Methods of controlling work groups, problem inmates, discipline crews, and handicapped inmates are explained.

7. Unusual inmates and those with special medical problems. These present some important and complex situations for the corrections officer. He is instructed in the methods of handling juvenile and youthful offenders, narcotics addicts, suicide risks, psychotics, and sex deviates.

8. Alcoholism and the officer, use of the baton, community relations, local government, courtroom demeanor and testifying, criminal law, crowd control, departmental policy and professionalization, emergency aspects of childbirth, use of firearms, fire suppression, first aid, health and welfare, internal discipline, laws of arrest, mob psychology, narcotics, officer demeanor, organization of the department, parole, behavior modification, physical training, report writing, searching, handcuffing, contraband control and handling, use of weapons, communications equipment and procedures, vehicle safety, and, finally, weaponless defense.

SUMMARY

The negative aspects of the corrections system today give a negative return on the investment of society. Recidivism rates are high, indicating that little in the way of correcting is being accomplished at our correctional institutions.[39] In addition to the recidivism rates of offenders, there are many negative aspects of employment such as low pay, inflexible rules and administrators, poor working conditions, and lack of sufficiently high personnel qualifications. These are a definite hindrance to institutional rehabilitation efforts and frequently cause competent corrections officers to seek other forms of employment. The professionals who are needed in corrections will not be likely to settle for goals and ethics other than those oriented towards humane rehabilitation of inmates. Furthermore, achieving change of any kind is notoriously difficult in these institutions that have been known to discourage men with progressive ideas and high-caliber training and to cause them to leave. The prospective applicant for the position of a corrections officer might not find the following description very encouraging:

> The responsibility of those who man the locks is as confining, in many ways, as is the imprisonment of those confined by them. The keeper of the keys is a prisoner too. By the time he retires, the custodian will have spent from eight to fifteen years totally within the prison walls. During this time he will have been personally and singly responsible for the custody and discipline of many thousands of inmates. During most of the time he has spent inside the walls, he will have been continually outnumbered and continually under the threat of being outwitted by inmates whose obedience to him is protected by his status as a symbol of power. His duties are as manifold as those of a commander ... of troops and as hazardous as those of the commander whose forces may at any time cross the brink of rebellion. One of the hazards of his situation paradoxically is the ease with which he can be lulled into forgetfulness of hazards.[40]

According to one survey, there is considerable support for subsidizing bigger police forces with higher salaries and more training.[41] Although there is a cry for better law enforcement, only 21 percent of the public would be willing to finance the additional cost for institutions to handle the additional felons that better police work would inexorably produce.[42] Approximately half of the inmates in the United States penitentiaries are likely to get into trouble once released. Our corrections efforts have failed. As Ramsey Clark has stated:

> No effort within the criminal justice system holds a fraction of the potential for reducing crime (as that) offered by a vigorous, thoughtful corrections program. Not even efforts directed at the underlying causes of crime, such as health services, education, employment, or decent housing, offer the same immediate potential at anywhere near the cost correction focuses directly on the highly distilled mainstream of criminal conduct. If all of our research and learning

[39] *Task Force Report: Corrections,* pp. 60–62.

[40] Lloyd W. McCorkle and Richard Korn, "Resocialization Within Walls," *The Annals of the American Academy of Political Science,* CCXCIII (May 1954), 88–98.

[41] "Justice on Trial," *Newsweek,* March 8, 1971, p. 43.

[42] "Justice on Trial," p. 43.

about human behavior, if all the teaching in our great universities of medical science, mental health, psychiatry, psychology, and sociology have any applicability to real life, it is in the field of corrections.[43]

For those who are considering a career as a corrections officer and for those in the field today, there is hope for tomorrow in bringing about a new public awareness of and revitalized emphasis on the crucial need for reforming the entire corrections field. The corrections officer is a key individual who must be a highly skilled, well-educated, and self-motivated individual who wants to be a part of this important component of the criminal justice system. As we shall see in Chapter 17, there is a growing emphasis on amending the corrections concept throughout the United States; and along with this concern are new programs and research that offer promise for the offender as well as rewards for the correctional officer.

QUESTIONS

1. What is meant by corrections?
2. What role did the English penal system play in the development of American correctional theory?
3. Describe the American penal theory from 1875–1925.
4. Discuss various reasons why it is commonly said that the federal penal system far overshadows state penal systems.
5. Discuss the development of probation in the United States.
6. What is meant by the frequently heard statement that American jails are largely a revolving door for many of the jail inmates?
7. What is meant by parole and how did it develop?
8. What is meant by "social control." Describe this as it pertains to corrections.
9. Discuss the pros and cons of having highly trained custodial officers, probation officers, and parole officers.
10. Discuss what the ideal qualifications are for various correctional functionaries, custodial officers, probation officers, parole officers.

[43]Ramsey Clark, "Why Punishment Is A Crime," *Playboy,* April, 1971, p. 100.

JUVENILE,
PROBATION,
AND PAROLE OFFICERS

HISTORICAL CONTEXT OF PROBATION
AND PAROLE

The penal system in the U.S. was inherited from the English with the establishment of prisons and workhouses. But because of the boldness of the New World experiment, different attitudes toward crime and the criminal have emerged, resulting in a probation and parole system that is unique because of its Yankee origin.

16

Probation is the name of an official correctional service and denotes the primary function of the system—investigation of offenders prior to sentence in order that the court may have detailed information. The definition of probation includes its function as a treatment program in which final action in an adjudicated offender's case is suspended; the offender remains at liberty, subject to conditions imposed by or for a court under the supervision and guidance of a probation worker.[1] The word *probation* is Latin in origin, its meaning being *a period of proving or trial.*[2]

The social climate was right for the birth of probation in the nineteenth century. In colonial times, the county and the municipality dealt with the offender. Police protection was entrusted to the city watchman and the county sheriff. Justices of the peace, city mayors, and county courts dispensed justice. The pillory, stocks, and whipping posts were placed near the city hall for convenience; the gallows were close to the county seat, and the hangman was

[1]David Dressler, *Practice and Theory of Probation and Parole* (New York: Columbia University Press, 1969), p. 19.

[2]Belle Boone Beard, *Juvenile Probation* (Boston: Montclair, 1969), p. 16.

always at hand. The jail was part of the courthouse, and was managed by the sheriff. The early houses of refuge for juvenile offenders and houses of correction for vagrants were also local institutions.

Gradually, corporal punishments gave way to imprisonment, which, for serious offenses, might be for a lifetime. The county jail was unsuitable for carrying out this new kind of penalty, and the state found it necessary to erect central prisons to house the convicted felons.

As time passed, the more populous states set up additional facilities, permitting a better selection of institution and treatment for offenders committed to state prisons. A system of specialized institutions developed, varying in degrees of security, such as special women's institutions, reformatories for the young male offenders, juvenile homes for delinquents, and institutions for the mentally ill.

The next great step in corrections development came in connection with parole, the treatment program in which an offender, after serving part of a term in a correctional institution, is conditionally released under supervision and treatment by a parole officer. The word *parole* is derived from the French word meaning *promise*. Like probation, parole is a treatment program in the interest of society and the individual. The difference is that the parolee has served part of his sentence in a correctional institution. His release is conditioned upon satisfactory behavior. He is under supervision and treatment by a person trained in parole work.[3]

The system of parole started in England, not because of humanitarian reasons, but because of economic pressures. In the sixteenth century, England's economy was in a decline, and unemployment was high. The county could not afford the cost of penal institutions. The British government decided to grant reprieves and stays of execution to convicted felons physically able to work so that they might be shipped abroad and impressed into service. The system of deportation is part of the history that makes up parole. Much of America was carved out of the wilderness by convicted felons who were shipped to the new land by the boatload.

One of the first documents pertaining to parole was the *ticket of leave*, a declaration signed by a colonial governor excusing a convict from further government work and permitting him to live independently but within a circumscribed district. Under this system, there was no counseling to the parolee as there is in a modern system.

Alexander Manonochie of Scotland is generally given credit for developing the ticket-of-leave system and also making a contribution to parole called the *mark system*—a device whereby convicts earned marks in lieu of wages and could earn early release by diligent work.[4]

[3]Dressler, *Practice and Theory of Probation and Parole*, p. 57.
[4]Dressler, *Practice and Theory of Probation and Parole*, p. 71.

Today's system of parole has become much more complex, organized, and efficient. Special boards have been organized to study and consider all prisoners for parole regardless of the nature of the offense committed, to establish the time when an inmate is eligible for parole, and to exercise full discretion in determining the time at which parole should be granted to those previously declared eligible.

There are primarily three kinds of parole-granting agencies. The first is the *institutional board,* composed mainly of members of the specific institution. This form of parole board may have an advantage over a centrally organized board because of the knowledge that the members have of those eligible for parole. The *central parole board* is a single body that meets to pass on candidates for parole from all institutions in a given jurisdiction. The major benefit of this form of parole decision-making body is the uniformity of standards governing parole that result. The central parole board is predominantly the releasing authority for adult offenders. The third kind of parole board is composed of *part-time public officials.* This organization is seldom used today because the selected members are usually too busy in their own work to devote the amount of study and time necessary to determining a potential parolee.

In the majority of states, parole board members are appointed by the governor, usually with the consent of one or both houses of the legislature. In some states, they are selected after a merit system examination. A question is sometimes raised whether parole board members should be career officials or appointees. It is generally agreed that frequently the chief executive in a state makes appointments to benefit his political career. This may occur, but the governing law frequently provides that, as far as practicable, members are to be selected who have a varied and sympathetic interest in correctional work, including persons widely experienced in the fields of corrections, sociology, psychology, and education. Terms of parole board members are "at the pleasure of the appointing authority." Appointments of from four to six years are most common, with provision made for reappointment.[5]

Probation today is felt to be the most practical method of treating large numbers of selected offenders. *Placing a person on probation* developed from the power of the court to suspend the sentence of a convicted individual. It became a device that the court used when it was reluctant to impose the full sentence for an offense because it felt that the person could still function in the community although under the supervision of the court. The person who performed the supervision became known as the probation officer. Under the early system, probation supervision was very difficult to carry out successfully except in the area of the particular court's jurisdiction. As a rule, probation

---

[5]Dressler, *Practice and Theory of Probation and Parole,* pp. 86–96.

officers were untrained; probation became a device whereby fines were collected on an installment basis; and the probation policies varied from county to county. Eventually, the state legislatures became aware of the poor probation practices and, despite strong opposition from individual courts, established centralized state supervision of probationers, sometimes entrusting this task to a central state body, or mandating that such supervision be conducted within broad guidelines in the various counties.

John Augustus, known as the father of probation, became interested in reforming individuals in 1841. In court one morning, he observed a man who was going to be sentenced to a house of correction for being a drunkard. Augustus found out from the man that he did not want to be sentenced and would stop drinking if not sent away. With permission of the court, Augustus bailed him out but with the stipulation that the man was to return in a few weeks for sentencing. Upon his return; the judge noted that the man was sober and reduced the sentence to a fine rather than jail.

Augustus continued his informal probation work, but he exercised keen discretion in the selection of probationers. Time proved him to be a shrewd judge of character; according to the records, most of his charges changed for the better. Even today, selection of the proper persons to place on probation is the most important part of probation work. A good and detailed investigation must be made.[6]

The legal authority of probation officers was first enacted in 1878 in Massachusetts when it was required of the city of Boston to appoint a probation officer. Then, in 1890, the Massachusetts legislature enacted a general law requiring the criminal courts in the state to appoint probation officers. By 1900, there was a general trend toward legislation dealing with probation.

In the years that the federal probation system has been in existence, it has greatly expanded the numbers of probation officers and of persons placed on probation.[7]

It should be noted that if a judge suspends a sentence it may be unconditional, in which case it has the effect of satisfying the offender's criminal liability and discharging him from the system. Normally, however, sentences are suspended on specified conditions. If the offender fails to comply with the conditions, his probation is revoked and he can be sentenced to prison or jail to serve the remainder of the suspended sentence. It is during this period of time, when the sentence is suspended and the individual is free from institutionalization, that he is on probation. Throughout this interval, he is counseled and supervised by the probation officer and should the mandates set out by the

---

[6]Dressler, *Practice and Theory of Probation and Parole,* pp. 23–25.

[7]Irving W. Halpern, *A Decade of Probation* (Montclair N.J.: Patterson-Smith, 1969), pp. 14–15.

court be breached, the *court, not the probation officer,* revokes the probationary freedom.

ORGANIZATION OF THE PROBATION AND PAROLE OFFICES

Because the general functions, supervision, training, and organization of the probation and parole offices are somewhat similar in scope and objectives, a description of the probation office will be used for both unless otherwise stated. The probation office may be organized in many ways, depending on the complexity of the agency. However, a usual organization appears in Figure 16–1.

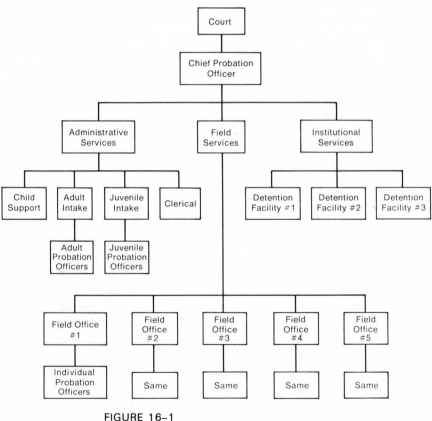

FIGURE 16–1

Organization of a Typical Probation Office.

The adult probation officer's duties vary somewhat from jurisdiction to jurisdiction but generally range over the following situations. In one type of circumstance, aid is given to the mother of a child in establishing the identity of the father. The woman signs a petition against a man she claims is the father. The probation officer then sends a notice to the man and requests that he come in for counsel. The alleged father is offered a blood test to establish whether or not he can be excluded as the father. If he refuses to take the test, a warrant for his arrest will be issued and the case will go to trial.

A second situation in which the probation officer frequently becomes involved is desertion or nonsupport cases. The probation officer has a petition signed against the offender. He then contacts the husband and counsels him as to the charges made by the wife. Should the husband refuse to cooperate, an arrest warrant will be secured and the case settled in court. The probation officer also handles cases involving assault and battery against family members, usually by other family members; violation of compulsory school attendance laws; and the delinquency or neglect of minors.

In dealing with offenders, the probation officer is involved in two types of hearings:

1. In *an informal hearing,* the probation officer counsels the offender to assist him in understanding his position in relation to the offense and what should be done to correct the situation out of court. Records are maintained of what took place at the conference.

2. *The formal hearing* takes place before the judge when the offender's case is being tried and adjudicated. Although he seldom uses his powers of arrest, the probation officer by statute is frequently given this authority.[8]

PRESENTENCE INVESTIGATIONS

This procedure applies to both probation and parole. Prior to the sentencing, the judge wants to know the individual. Here the probation officer is in a critical position in the administration of criminal justice because he furnishes this information in the form of a presentence or preparole report. The report draws a picture of the person by including information on his background, social history, present offense and behavior, his statement of how the offense occurred, evaluation by the probation officer, and his recommendations as to sentencing, including terms of probation.

The report also serves to aid the probation office in selecting the proper kind of supervision and treatment. Should an offender be incarcerated, the

---

[8]Arkansas: *Arkansas Statutes of 1947 Annotated,* Sec. 43–2805. Florida: *Florida Statutes Annotated,* Sec. 948.06. Louisiana: *Louisiana Revised Statutes,* Title 13, Sec. 1564.

presentence report may be included in the preparole report when the individual is released.

The social history of the report is crucial in determining whether or not probation will be recommended. This section presents information about the defendant's schooling, including his grades. The various types of jobs he had while growing up will be listed with his ability to accomplish various goals. This part of the investigation includes salaries, what he owns, his spouse's occupation, and references by individuals. It also contains data on family and marital relationships. Some presentence and preparole reports have a special section on usage of narcotics and intoxicants. If not, the information is included in the social history.

An evaluation of the subject is prepared by the probation officer. It consists of his beliefs about the character, background, and potential of the offender; and even about the facts in the case that resulted in conviction. The judge frequently makes use of this section when fixing the sentence, whether it be probation or incarceration.

Should he decide on granting probation, the recommendations section aids the judge or probation agency by setting forth some of the terms and conditions that should be imposed on the person. These conditions and terms theoretically should aid in the control and treatment of the offender. The offender may be directed to do any of the following:

1. Spend a suitable period of time in the county jail as part of probation.
2. Pay costs of prosecution, costs of probation, fines, and make restitution as ordered by the court.
3. Obey all orders of the probation or parole office.
4. Submit to physical and mental examinations and treatment by order of the court.
5. Refrain from associating with persons not approved by the officer and persons of bad reputation or a criminal record.
6. Report immediately to the officer any time he is arrested or questioned by the police.
7. Maintain residence as approved by the supervisor.
8. Support any dependents and assume any other moral and legal obligations due to them.
9. Make every effort to obtain and hold a legitimate job. Should the job be lost for some reason, the supervisor must be immediately notified.
10. Abstain from the consumption of alcoholic beverages and not enter places where they are sold or consumed.
11. Obtain permission of the supervisor to: leave the state or the county of supervision; change residence or employment; secure a driver's license; enter any financial or legal contractual obligation; get married, divorced, or separated.
12. Comply with all laws, ordinances, rules, regulations and orders of the court and probation office.
13. Waive extradition to the state from a foreign nation, other state, territory, or district in the union, and refrain from contesting the extradition.

14. Permit the supervisor to visit his home at any time.

15. Not possess, own, sell, distribute, or control any narcotics without a medical prescription; guns; deadly weapons; or marijuana.

16. Inform the supervisor immediately of contacts made by corrections officials or other members of the probation office.

17. Conduct himself in an honorable manner as a respectable community member and in no way jeopardize the personal property, dignity, or moral rights of others.

State statutes typically grant the court, probation office, and parole agency the authority to select and impose these and similar conditions. Generally, the statutes grant broad authority with few limitations or restrictions on the kinds of conditions. A commonly found grant of such authority is to "place the defendant on probation upon such terms and conditions as it may require." One reason for such a broad grant of power is:

> Since no specification of permissible conditions can exhaust the measures that may be appropriate in what is meant to be a flexible device for dealing with offenders, the section includes a residual clause granting broad authority. To guard against abuse that sometimes has occurred, the clause excludes conditions "unduly restrictive of the offender's liberty" or "incompatible with his freedom of conscience." We see no reason why conditions which are thus abusive should not be subject to appellate review.[9]

As a practical matter, regardless of the allowable conditions by statute, the court responsible for imposing the conditions routinely selects and imposes additional terms according to the needs of the individual offender. The court also delegates to the probation office and the individual supervisor the responsibility to impose additional conditions or, on occasion, with the court's permission, waive compliance of others. To inform the probationer fully of the conditions, he is given a written copy of routine *and* special conditions. The conditions are also explained by the probation officer at the beginning of the supervision process.

Probation and parole officers operate in much the same way. Both make investigations, submit written reports, evaluate findings, and recommend dispositions of cases. They are advisors and consultants to both the court and to the probationer and parolee. Both utilize a personal and individualistic approach in the study and treatment of offenders, although their work is conducted in an atmosphere of authority.

The probation and parole officers assist the offender on an individual basis in order to modify his behavior and attitudes so that the individual may take his rightful, productive place in society. The probation officer makes visits to his home, maintains personal contacts, and provides other kinds of assistance to encourage the individual as well as to keep informed about his conduct

---

[9] American Law Institute, *Uniform Penal Code,* Section 301.1 (Tentative Draft Number 2, 1954).

and environment. He assists in obtaining employment and even interviews prospective employers toward that end. Of course, attention must be given to any violation of the terms of probation, and if of a substantial degree it must be reported to the court or probation authority. In carrying out the supervisory function, the cooperation of the probationer must be enlisted in order to secure a friendly, helpful relationship. The authoritative and disciplinary functions of the supervisor always are present, but they must be directed in a constructive way to encourage the client to help himself rather than to be coerced into actions and activities. The coercive measures only should be used to prevent open defiance of court orders and inhibit a client from reverting to a life of crime.

In summary, it is the direct responsibility of the officer to supervise the client and ensure his compliance with the terms and conditions of the court or probation authority. He must invoke the power of the two bodies when the behavior of the charge constitutes a violation, and he has the heavy burden of evaluating the personal and social factors in each case that he is assigned.

In addition to these responsibilities, the probation and parole officers must be able to discriminate between, and utilize, the multifold community resources that have been created to help deviants and ease their return to the community. These include personal counseling services, recreation centers, churches, health agencies, employment services, and schools. The probation counselor is a link between the community, court, and probation office. He explains to the community what kind of participation will help integrate the probationer back into his social environment. The officer must convince the community that rehabilitation work can best be accomplished in a community that understands and accepts the objectives and methods of sound probation endeavors. He interprets the work of his office to the community through reports, attendance at meetings, news media, and other techniques. However, talk never substitutes for action.

The probation and parole officers use three primary techniques of supervision. The principal one is the routine office interview in which the client is required to visit the officer periodically, usually as a condition of probation or parole. Either a brief or a detailed interview is conducted, depending on the activities occurring during the interval between interviews.

A second technique is the home visit. The supervisor usually has discretion over when and whether there is to be a home visit. Most officers make home visits when assigned a new case. The visits consist of brief interviews with the probationer or parolee and any other persons who live at the address. Also, home visits frequently are made when the officer has reasons to believe there has been an infraction of the conditions of release. Quite often, the interviews are only to let the client know that the officer is interested in his welfare.

Mail supervision sometimes is used when there can be no face-to-face supervision, as would be the case when the client has been permitted to reside in another jurisdiction, usually because he has found adequate employment there. When there are large case loads, this technique also is utilized.

A repeatedly mentioned defect in the supervision of probationers or parolees is relative laxity of supervision. Primarily, the intensity depends on the case load of each supervisor and the number of presentence or preparole investigations that he must accomplish. In regard to this single element of probation and parole, the President's Crime Commission in 1967 commented:

> The statistics from the national survey of corrections make clear the vastness of the community treatment task and the inadequacy of the resources available to accomplish it. They do not convey the everyday problems and frustrations that result from that disparity. These take many forms. For example:
>
> A probation officer meets with a sixteen-year-old who two months previously was placed on probation for having stolen a car. The boy begins to talk. He explains that he began to "slip into the wrong crowd" a year or so after his stepfather died. He says that it would help him to talk about it. But there is no time; the waiting room is full, and the boy is not scheduled to come back for another 15 minute conference until next month.
>
> A parole officer feels that a twenty-nine-year-old man on parole after serving three years for burglary is heading for trouble. He frequently is absent from his job, and there is a report of his hanging around a bar with a bad reputation. The parole officer thinks that now is a critical time to straighten things out before it is too late. He tries unsuccessfully two or three times to reach his man by telephone, and considers going out to look for him. He decides against it. He is already far behind in dictating "revocations" on parolees who have failed and are being returned to prison.
>
> A young enthusiastic probation officer goes to see his supervisor and presents a plan for "something different," a group counseling session to operate three evenings a week for juvenile probationers and their parents. The supervisor tells him to forget it. "You've got more than you can handle now getting up presentence reports for the judge. Besides we don't have any extra budget for a psychiatrist to help out."
>
> In these situations the offender is denied the counseling and supervision that are the main objects of probation and parole. Because the probation or parole officer is too overworked to provide these services the offender is left on his own. If he does not succeed, he loses and the community loses.[10]

TRAINING AND EDUCATION

The educational standards for probation and parole officers are high. As a minimum, it is usually required that the applicant possess a bachelor's degree in one of the social or behavioral sciences with either (1) a year of graduate study in social work or a related field, such as counseling or guidance work;

---

[10]President's Commission on Law Enforcement and Administration of Justice, *The Challenge of Crime In A Free Society* (Washington, D.C.: Government Printing Office, 1967), p. 167.

or (2) one year of full-time casework experience under professional supervision in a social agency or a correctional program. It is preferred, however, that the officer possess a bachelor's degree in the social or behavioral sciences with emphasis on courses in crime and delinquency, *and* a master's degree in social work. An individual who has the baccalaureate degree but not the additional training or experience may be hired if the agency has a special training program for these people conducted by a fully trained social worker.

It has often been said that personality makes the probation officer. The agency, by choice, looks for a person with emotional maturity and common sense. He must also have the capacity to learn both by experience and in the classroom. A fundamental prerequisite is the capacity for and an interest in the welfare of human beings. He must be compassionate and understanding in the face of trying conditions. It also goes without saying that the officer must possess a good character and balanced personality. There is heavy emphasis on such traits as integrity, ability to work alone and with others, insight into the etiologies of behavior, and a general knowledge of the community.

A question of what the probation or parole officer needs to be taught during his professional training is answered by the setting of his work. Because he is working in a setting of the law, he needs to know criminal law: he needs to know about the courts, the machinery of law enforcement, and the penal system.

Because he is a social worker, he must know the social services and how to use them. He needs to be familiar with normal and abnormal human development. An understanding of his role is important to him if he is to be a success. The need is greater now that he is being called upon to take a more active part in assisting the court or probation agency at all stages of pre-sentence inquiries that may ultimately lead to revocation of probation. He must be knowledgeable about the law and administrative procedures affecting all aspects of his duties. He must resist the temptation to become an advocate or judge in preparing his reports, and must cope with his feelings when the court takes some action other than what he believes is best for the offender.

The probation officer must possess training in understanding the dynamics of personality. Many of the offenders coming to him are unstable in character and frequently are of borderline mentality. Because of this, the officer must be acquainted with psychological methods of understanding and classifying. As a result, he is better able to identify, refer, and cooperate in the treatment of those needing psychiatric help. Mainly, however, it helps him to exercise individual influence without weakening the personality of the one he is helping.

If an individual has a broad, liberal education, he will be well suited for the life of a probation or parole officer. However, he should be aware that the nature and quality of support given to him by his teachers will do much to set the tone of his own relationships with those he subsequently supervises or tries to influence and that his scope will be greatly restricted if he tries uncritically to impose his own pattern of life and experiences on those with greatly different backgrounds and personalities. His ability to help will be impaired if he assumes that the aspect of teaching or supervision that most helped him will necessarily be of the most value to his client.

A special area of applicable knowledge is that of institutions, especially penal institutions. The main emphasis with the probation and parole services has been to keep people out of penal institutions. The contemporary theory has enlarged on this concept to include help not only for the individual who has come out of the institution, but also for the person inside. Officers of the future may well spend part of their careers as prison welfare officers. All will need to know something of the nature of the closed institutions and their impact upon those inside, including both staff and inmate.[11]

There is a question of how much training is necessary. Some believe that one year is not long enough and recommend that from the earliest possible time, every probation and parole officer should have not less than two years of professional training before appointment. Attention is being drawn constantly to the rapid advances in the behavioral sciences, and to the increased knowledge and professional competence required, as arguments for longer training. Drawbacks to the longer training voiced by some include costs, family separation and tensions, and returning a mature applicant to immature student status.

When a new probation officer comes into the field, his training starts immediately. He is given cases of his own to help him develop his desire to learn, use his resourcefulness, and utilize his imagination. He is confronted with real problems and encouraged to present solutions.

An innovation is the employment and training of former parolees and probationers as probation and parole officers. One example is occurring in California under a program called New Career Development Project.[12] This project was originally set up to train selected inmates from various corrections institutions. They are trained for eventual work in some type of social service jobs while still in the institution and for a period after being paroled.

The training consists of lectures on current social forces, automation effects, population trends, civil rights, and various government-sponsored social programs. In the program, the inmate is trained to work as part of a team with one parolee and one professional, usually a graduate student who enters the program in partial fulfillment of work for the graduate degree. The supporters of the program point out that this type of recruitment and training helps fill manpower vacancies in probation and parole agencies.[13]

[11]Joan King, *The Probation and after-Care Service* (London: Butterworths, 1969), pp. 241–73.

[12]Paul Keve, *Imaginative Programming in Probation and Parole* (Minneapolis: University of Minnesota Press, 1967), pp. 207–8.

[13]Keve, *Imaginative Programming in Probation and Parole,* p. 217–18.

CRITICISM OF PROBATION AND PAROLE

One of the main criticisms of parole, according to the late director of the FBI, J. Edgar Hoover, is the lack of proper selection of individuals for release. He indicated that the files in police departments are filled with scores of cases where innocent members of society suffered because of inept selection of parolees by parole boards and courts. He cited one instance in which two parolees, on parole for the eighth time, murdered a Los Angeles police officer. Hoover went on to relate that twelve of fourteen FBI agents were slain by individuals previously selected for parole. Of the 202 fugitives who appeared on the Ten Most Wanted Fugitives list, 167 had previously been the recipients of some kind of parole leniency. He emphasized that the welfare of society must take precedence over release of a prisoner and demanded that there be more precise factors weighed in the probation and parole release processes.[14] Criticisms of the services have consistently been that the agencies are poorly staffed and administered. Despite these criticisms, the success of those having been placed on probation, as measured by those not having been placed on probation, is high. One survey indicated a success rate of 60–90 percent. Massachusetts and New York indicated a rate of 75 percent success.[15]

JUVENILE OFFICERS

In the general area of probation and parole, one special societal problem is becoming increasingly prominent. Juvenile delinquency is one of the fastest growing phenomena in the United States. The juvenile probation officer, as a consequence, often is faced with conflicts requiring patience and somewhat different attitudes and skills from those of the adult probation and parole officer.

"The typical juvenile officer of yesterday was easily identified. They were kindly men, but tough with it. They smoked a pipe, knew a pragmatic thing or two about half-witted magistrates, harbored a good-natured skepticism about the value of voluntary do-gooders and could call a 'screw" a 'screw' with the best."[16]

Since the beginning of the formal probation system, society has progressed as has the judicial system, and the duties of the juvenile probation officer have become more complicated. Both the unresolved juvenile delin-

---

[14]J. Edgar Hoover, "When Criminals Are Set Free Too Soon," *U.S. News and World Report,* LVIII (May 17, 1965), 21. In an earlier study, Robert Crossley arrived at many of the same conclusions: Robert Crossley, "The Killer Has Been Paroled," *Reader's Digest,* LXXXIII (April 1963), 105–8.

[15]President's Commission on Law Enforcement and Administration of Justice, *Task Force Report: Corrections* (Washington, D.C.: Government Printing Office, 1967), p. 28.

[16]D. Johnson, "Probation Officers Dilemma," *New Statesman,* LXXIII, (May 5, 1967), 614–15.

quency and overall supervision problems are serious obstacles to overcome. There must be a willingness to *inch along,* if necessary to fit the tempo of the treatment to the ability of the delinquent. A juvenile can be reached most effectively by understanding. The officer's capacity and willingness to learn are indispensable.

The rapport that the probation officer develops with the adolescent is his prime tool in helping the delinquent modify his behavior. Therefore, the better he understands his own attitudes and beliefs, the better he will be able to discipline himself and to use the developing relationship in a professional way. Furthermore, it is important that the juvenile officer understand and have a healthy relationship with society. Unless he is able to identify with community standards, he will be unable to represent them successfully to the delinquent.

The officer must not, however, overidentify with the delinquent. The juvenile may take this attitude to be sympathy for his position and, consequently, condonation of his behavior. It is likely that overidentification is due to the fact that the probation officer himself has not worked out his own conflicts with authority.[17]

Because of the sensitivity of his work, some basic guidelines are required to assist the juvenile officer in his task. Personal treatment of the delinquent is basic. He must weigh his future in terms of the past. He must not allow his attitudes to be prejudiced with popular cliches like "once a bad egg always a bad egg." Finally, he must determine the type and quality of treatment services available and select the ones that are needed.[18]

During the interval the juvenile officer is preparing the preprobation report for the use of the court, he also is preparing the delinquent and his parents for the hearing. He attempts to learn the meaning of this sometimes traumatic experience for the youth and at the same time convey to him the purpose of the court and the functions of the staff members who will deal with him. In some instances, the juvenile officer will find that the delinquent does not need the services of the court because other community agencies are available to meet the juvenile's needs. In such cases, referral by the juvenile officer will be his primary responsibility.

The juvenile probation officer must be available to help the delinquent understand and comply with the probation plan and to help him work on his problems as they relate to his delinquent behavior. The goal is to restore the person to legal freedom. Until it is safe to do this, the juvenile officer is expected to provide the necessary control and supervision.

Perhaps the most complex aspect of the juvenile officer's job is the almost endless variety of expectations that impinge on the juvenile officer and the delinquent from every side. More than once, a juvenile probation officer has asked himself, "What am I to do? The judge wants me to do one thing, the

[17]W. L. Herbert and F. V. Jarvis, *Dealing with Delinquents* (New York: Emerson Book, Inc., 1962), p. 93.

[18]Merritt Gilman, *Training for Juvenile Probation Officers,* U.S. Department of Health, Education and Welfare (Washington, D.C.: Government Printing Office, 1962), p. 73.

parents another. Still, the delinquent has his own idea of how I am supposed to act. School teachers believe something else. Even my colleagues have different ideas than I have, let alone the chief probation officer." Thus, the officer is faced with a severe role conflict that must eventually resolve itself with a satisfactory solution for everyone. Too often, however, additional control by the bureaucratic probation agency is imposed that, although intended to help, only intensifies the role conflict of the officer. In the long run, the delinquent is the one who suffers. Frequently, the juvenile officer either leaves the probation field or does not concern himself with the juvenile. He is worried only about survival.

Juvenile probation officers are in need of augmentation. It is estimated that by 1975, twenty-three thousand juvenile officers will be required to carry out the essential function of community treatment of the delinquent.[19] Juvenile probation is a complicated field that requires involved, dedicated people. In spite of the problems and occasional failure, to observe a readjusted youth on the road back to his proper place in society is all the satisfaction most juvenile officers need.

SUMMARY

The functions and personalities of the probation and parole officers are more similar than divergent. Either officer theoretically can supervise both probationers and parolees. The relationship of the probation and parole officers to the court and parole authority is that of agent. Both conduct investigations and prepare reports and both supervise offenders, although at different phases of the correction processes.

Some of the major criticisms of probation and parole derive from occasional and spectacular failures and from departments that fall short of developing a service that can be compared favorably with other social service agencies. Another factor is the large case load of probation and parole officers. They are simply unable to devote the time required for individualized treatment of each offender.

QUESTIONS

1. The juvenile court is a comparatively recent idea. What was the theory and philosophy behind its development?
2. What is meant by *parens patriea?* Has this doctrine been challenged today? Discuss this doctrine and court holdings regarding this doctrine.

[19]Gilman, *Training for Juvenile Probation Officers,* p. 73.

JUVENILE, PROBATION, AND PAROLE OFFICERS

3. Describe the historical development of probation and parole in the United States.
4. Who was Alexander Maconochie? Discuss his contribution to the "parole" concept.
5. Describe the three kinds of parole granting agencies. What are the relative merits of each?
6. Discuss the contribution of John Augustus to the development of probation.
7. Describe the general organization of a probation office. Discuss the functions performed by those in the office.
8. What is a presentence investigation? Discuss the contents of a presentence investigation report.
9. Discuss the various conditions of probation which are found frequently in the recommendations of a probation officer to a judge.
10. What are the general educational standards and training programs necessary in order to qualify as a probation or parole officer?
11. Discuss what is meant by the statement that the "main emphasis of probation and parole services is to keep people out of penal institutions."
12. Summarize some of the criticisms leveled at the concepts of probation and parole.
13. Discuss the basic guidelines which a juvenile officer should follow in his work with juveniles.
14. What is probably the most complex aspect of the juvenile officer's job? Discuss fully.

INNOVATIONS
IN
CORRECTIONS

As noted in the two preceding chapters, a dreary picture is drawn from historic practices and procedures that have not been improved upon to any significant degree. There are, however, innovations coming into the picture that, in varying degrees, promise to change the entire corrections component. There appear to be genuine efforts on the part of correctional innovators to make corrections something other than a misnomer. Treating inmates both in and outside of institutions in order to restore them to their rightful places in society emphasizes the trend away from punishment for punishment's sake and toward a more humane, pragmatic, and scientific approach to corrections.

For the student contemplating a career in the criminal justice system, there are some exciting events taking place in corrections. Few answers to correctional problem areas have been found, but attempts are being made to do so. Perhaps those students who accept the challenge of corrections will come up with some answers that today's leaders are still seeking.

This chapter will present an overview of some of the newest ideas and research being implemented in the corrections system.

TRAINING—
KEY TO CHANGE

"For a great many offenders, then, corrections does not correct. Indeed experts are increasingly coming to feel that the conditions under which many offenders are handled . . . are often a positive detriment to rehabilitation. . . . the potential for change is great."[1] The impetus for change can result from increased and more relevant training in corrections. Change, however, must not be implemented haphazardly but must be guided by the best information available in both research and experience. Positive change is not possible or probable all at once, but *it must come quickly.*

As noted by the presidential commission:

> The costs of action are substantial. But the costs of inaction are immensely greater. It could mean, in effect, that the nation would continue to avoid, rather than confront, one of its critical social problems, that it would accept for the next generation a huge if not measurable burden of wasted and destructive lives. Decisive action, on the other hand, could make a difference that would really matter within our time.[2]

Any plan of action intended to have an immediate and potentially fruitful effect will probably have to start within the correctional setting. Correctional staffs must be made to realize the necessity for change, but first there must be a definition and acknowledgment of problems.

One of the first problems for the correctional officer to face is that the traditional correctional techniques have failed to change most offenders' behavior; the recidivism rates are high. With this situation soberly confronted, correctional staffs can search for solutions. Secondly, research into the entire correctional system is an urgent need. Regardless of financial difficulties, the appropriate leaders have the obligation to demand it. Thirdly, once the problems have been isolated as a result of research, the correctional staffs would be in a proper frame of mind to study and consider new approaches to old problems.

For example, it has been shown that differential treatment of offenders, in the form of halfway houses and diagnostic centers, increased correctional success when properly implemented. Most important to a new attitude in corrections is that staffs must sense a need for change in their attempts to modify behavior patterns of offenders. Traditional corrections have not shown a commitment to change. However, an open attitude will, at the least, give those staffs one key to success in the correctional process.

It will not be a simple task to implement changes in the correctional staff. Training plays a key role here because, in many instances, whole new thought and behavior patterns must be considered and acted upon on emotional and intellectual levels.

Programs for in-service training of correctional personnel are being conducted throughout the country. Several approaches are being used, including

---

[1]The President's Commission on Law Enforcement and Administration of Justice, *The Challenge of Crime in a Free Society* (Washington, D.C.: Government Printing Office, 1967), p. 159.

[2] *The Challenge of Crime in a Free Society,* p. 185.

centralized institutes, regional short courses, circuit or itinerate programs on a regular and periodic schedule, institution or agency-based programs, and short in-house training programs.

The implications of a broad-based correctional training effort are tremendous for the corrections and criminal justice systems. In training projects now being carved out, the corrections trainee is exposed, for example, to a social work model of corrections in which the trainee undergoes a broad, abstract education program. Or he may undergo a job-analysis model of training devised through a threefold identification procedure:

Tasks to be performed
Skills required to perform the tasks
Knowledge needed to achieve the skills

The training endeavors in corrections are a relatively new and exciting area in corrections work. The career-minded student will find many innovative efforts being made in correctional instruction to provide a trained, sensitive staff for the various corrections departments and agencies intended to facilitate the rehabilitation of offenders and to improve the public image of the correctional system and its employees.

One unique research effort being attempted is the SIMBAD project. Simulation as a Basis of Social Agent's Decisions (SIMBAD) seeks to provide a practical tool for probation officers in their selection of the best treatment plan for juvenile offenders. The project involves development of operating models in the form of computer programs that predict the probation success associated with differential probation approaches as well as the probation alternatives most likely to be selected by operating agencies.

Using a predetermined mathematical basis for making classification and treatment decisions about individuals, the research was designed to aid the decision maker by reducing the uncertainty about the most appropriate course of action for a particular person.

The program had participants from probation departments of three California counties, San Diego, Santa Barbara, and Ventura. These departments had access to large-scale computer resources that provided probability estimates of success for distribution and treatment decisions at any point in the correctional process.

The SIMBAD project found primarily that the probability model was useful in assisting probation officers in counseling, decision making, and studying treatment alternatives. The SIMBAD project is only a part of the total research going on in the corrections subsystem. It is, in fact, only a single project of a comprehensive probation project in California. Its results will have widespread implications in seeking to assess the relative effectiveness of different dispositions and supervision practices in the probation system, using recidivism as a basic criterion. SIMBAD represents an attempt to bridge the gap between the results of research and the decisions of practitioners and also to introduce new knowledge and new technology into the probation aspect of the corrections system.

COMMUNITY CORRECTIONAL PROGRAMS

Correctional leaders are speaking more and more of the rehabilitative advantages of reintegrating inmates back into society. It is becoming evident that the participation of private citizens cannot be discarded in dealing with deviant members of society. However, official recognition that citizen participation is needed has not been followed by the kind of changes necessary to move the offender back into society. There has not been significant collaboration between corrections leaders and the community. Correctional administrators are inclined to conceal their difficulties from close public scrutiny while administering the monopolistic prison system with powers granted exclusively on grounds of their expertise. By preventing participation of inmates and the community, and by the frequent claim of exclusive expertise, the correctional establishment for a long time has neutralized the efforts of those seeking to change it.[3]

Correctional planning must consider the inmate, elicit his cooperation, and anticipate his problems after release. If the inmate is to learn new ways of dealing with others, he should be given the opportunity to interact with ordinary citizens in an authentic human relationship. However, some efforts along this line are being made. Instead of perpetuating the mutual isolation of inmates and the community, the correctional establishment is now seeking to provide the means by which offenders and their future fellow citizens can deal with each other under mediated conditions, such as halfway houses and work furloughs.

In the search for new and better correctional treatment, community correctional programs are being tested. These programs seek to achieve a major change in the mix of services aimed at control and treatment of offenders. Through innovative services and a greater degree of coordination of existing public and private agencies, it is hoped that existing fragmented resources will be consolidated in order to achieve rehabilitation and community reintegration of the offender.

[3]For a good discussion of inmate reintegration, see Richard R. Korn, "Correctional Innovation and the Dilemma of Change-From-Within," *Canadian Journal of Corrections,* X, No. 3 (1968), 449–57.

As a result of implementing a model community correctional program, San Joaquin County, California, has been able to inaugurate two general programs: a citation in lieu of arrest for many offenses; and a pilot release on a recognizance program operating in conjunction with the local county court. In addition, the model community correctional program prepared additional proposals to set up programs dealing with:

1. Community alcoholic rehabilitation
2. Adult felony community treatment
3. Misdemeanant probation
4. A hospital-based clinic for voluntary treatment of addicts augmented by community education programs

Community Treatment Centers (CTC)

One of the most successful new correctional treatment projects was implemented in 1961 by the Federal Bureau of Prisons—the Community Treatment Center. Such centers were initiated as demonstration programs in New York, Chicago, and Los Angeles. Centers also are now located in Atlanta, Houston, San Francisco, Kansas City, and Detroit.

The basic purpose of the CTC is to carry out a total correctional plan to reintegrate the offender into a normal community life. The centers serve as:

1. A transitional step back to the community for those completing sentence in an institution
2. A diagnostic resource to the federal courts
3. A supplemental resource for those under probation supervision

Once an inmate is within six months of release and meets the eligibility requirements, he is referred directly by the institution to a CTC in his home community. The center assumes total case management and supervision responsibility. There is emphasis on using the resources of the community in achieving correctional goals. In addition, and on a selective basis, referrals are accepted directly from the courts for diagnostic and correctional services.

Since its inauguration in 1961, 3,500 men and women have been referred to Community Treatment Centers. Approximately two-thirds have completed the program and have been released to the community. Major reasons for those failing to complete the program are disciplinary problems and escapes. In a report by the Bureau of Prisons, it was found that high-risk offenders recidivated at a lower rate than base expectancy tables would have predicted. Paradoxically, low-risk offenders may actually recidivate at a higher rate than predicted.

The Community Treatment Center concept is one of the brightest developments on the correctional scene in recent years. Its full utilization in revitalizing a correctional program not noted for its strengths has not yet fully been explored. However, the success experienced so far with the program fully justifies its expansion. The criminal justice student who wishes to see and make things happen may well find association with the CTC a challenging career.

Work Release Programs (WRP)

Work Release Programs are operated by the Federal Bureau of Prisons and by a majority of the various state correctional systems.[4] The WRP in the federal system has served as a general model for the states and will be examined in the remainder of this topic.

The Federal Bureau of Prisons operates the WRP in about twenty-two correctional facilities throughout the United States. The program was implemented in October, 1965, following the United States Prisoner Rehabilitation Act. Work release is utilized as a transitional step to better prepare inmates for their return to the community. In some local facilities such as county jails, it is also used as an alternative to imprisonment by providing an opportunity for the offender to maintain normal employment while serving a sentence.

The WRP objectives include:

1. Upgrading job skills
2. Accumulating savings for release
3. Making restitution or paying legitimate debts
4. Strengthening family ties through contributions to family support
5. Reducing the risks and fears of both the offender and the community associated with the difficult period of adjustment immediately following imprisonment

Inmates who are eligible to be released within approximately six months are considered for WRP. Within established criteria, offenders are selected for work release by the institution's classification committee. The inmate must request such a placement, and the work release program must meet specific objectives. In many cases, the work release participant is supported by casework, group counseling, and educational services.

The results of the program, according to the Federal Bureau of Prisons, are extremely encouraging. For example, from October, 1965, to June 30, 1968, 5011 offenders participated in the program. These men and women were able to assume some responsibility for the support of their families, save money

[4]Elmer H. Johnson, "Report on Innovation—State Work Release Programs," *Crime and Delinquency,* XVI, No. 4 (October 1970), 417–26; Robert Carter, Daniel Glazer, and Leslie Wilkins, eds., *Correctional Institutions* (New York: J. B. Lippincott, 1972), pp. 502–3.

for their release, pay for some everyday expenses in the community, reimburse the United States for a part of their upkeep, and still pay taxes. Further findings indicate that about two-thirds of the offenders participating in work release complete the program and return to the community. As with the CTC, escapes and disciplinary problems were the two main reasons why some did not complete the program. It also appears that the WRP is most effective for those who are considered to be most likely to recidivate. Recidivism for low-risk inmates is about that predicted from base expectancy scores, but for the higher-risk group, there was a significant reduction in recidivism.

The implications of work release are widespread. The program has gained broad acceptance as an important correctional tool in a number of state and local jurisdictions. It is still another innovation in the corrections subsystem, replacing some of the more arbitrary and punitive practices that have not corrected offender behavior.[5]

Community-Oriented Halfway Houses for Offenders

An additional attempt to integrate an offender back into the community is the use of a program that is midway between probation and confinement. A study model conducted in San Diego, California, hypothesized that inmates undergoing rehabilitation need to develop their own sense of social responsibility.[6] The inmates who live in the community-oriented halfway houses are in a home and have a schedule of daily counseling that they run themselves with help from a psychologist. Each resident/inmate is employed either in the house or in the community. Each has his own housekeeping responsibilities. The San Diego halfway house concept is unique in that the entire term of legal confinement is served within the house. The halfway house again has broad implications for the current corrections scene. In a positive effort to rehabilitate rather than incarcerate, inmates are not placed behind bars for commission of certain kinds of crimes but remain in the community, although in a controlled atmosphere.

Volunteer Community Services in Aid of Probation

Royal Oak, Michigan, is operating a project that seeks to reduce the recidivism rate of misdemeanants and their pursuit of increasingly serious criminal careers by providing adequate probation services at the lower court level. Be-

[5]For an informative article on work release legislation, see Lawrence S. Roat, "Work Release Legislation," *Federal Probation*, XXXVI, No. 1 (March 1972), 38–43.

[6]Richard L. Rachin, "So You Want To Open a Halfway House," *Federal Probation*, XXXVI, No. 1 (March 1972), 30–37.

cause of the unavailability of professional probation officers to deal with minor offenders, the project developed a method for using volunteers from the community, supervised by a professional probation officer along with psychiatrists, psychologists, and other counselors, to extend probation services to a large number of misdemeanants who, in the past, would have had to serve jail sentences. The project had the multiple objectives of reducing the minor crime rate, saving the community needless expenditures on institutional care, and developing a workable program for using volunteer manpower.

Procedurally, several hundred volunteers gave about five hours per month on a one-to-one basis with probationers. The volunteers supervise persons assigned to them, spending at least one hour per week with the probationers.

There is an orientation course for the new community volunteer. The volunteer counselors work with staff counselors, psychologists, and psychiatrists who give time voluntarily. The staff serves as a resource for the volunteer as well as for the probationer by providing therapy and counseling to the more difficult cases that a volunteer cannot handle.

Related aspects of the volunteer program include presentence investigations, work programs in lieu of fines, employment counseling, Alcoholics Anonymous, and spiritual rehabilitation.

The volunteer community services project has made a significant impact in corrections work. One of its very positive aspects is that it closely involves respected citizens with offenders. It has the potential of saving communities thousands of dollars in jail expenses while assisting offenders to remain productive members of the community. The project also has a real chance to change the behavior of offenders *before* they engage in more serious criminal conduct.

Impact of the Volunteer Approach— Hennepin County, Minnesota

Like most corrections agencies, Hennepin County Court Services has been overwhelmed by the increasing numbers of juveniles referred to the court. The high referral rate has hampered the ability of the professional staff to provide effective and meaningful treatment services. Travel time, obtaining routine data, and waiting in court for presentation reduced the overall quality of client service so that staff members were prevented, in many situations, from preparing comprehensive social investigations that would permit the judge to arrive at an appropriate disposition. Furthermore, the staff was frequently diverted from providing necessary services for delinquent youths presently on probation. In effect, the juvenile corrections system was in a precarious position as far as rehabilitation and control were concerned.

Because individual client needs far exceeded the available resources, Hennepin County decided that one viable way of increasing client service was to enlist citizen volunteers, people in the community who had the interest and talent to provide direct services to the client.

As professionals and volunteers worked together toward a common goal, a partnership between the community and juvenile corrections was formed. So, in addition to increasing client services, the use of community volunteers led to increased community sensitivity about the entire criminal justice system, in general, and to a greater understanding of the functions and needs of the correctional component, in particular.

The volunteer concept is dynamic because it makes use of those who have an interest in corrections and are willing to contribute their unique skills and talents. Most of the volunteer tasks simply require the inherent sensitivity of a concerned individual. There are no ideal volunteers except perhaps those who possess the maturity to solve personal problems and function well in society. The volunteer corrections program seeks, as one of its goals, to impress social responsibility on the client by example.

The volunteer project modifies the usual role of the probation staff. The probation officer becomes a consultant and supervisor as well as a direct clinician. This is a new role for most probation officers because they have been trained and experienced in performing direct treatment. A whole new learning experience is required to become supervisors and to understand the supervisory process.

The probation officer will be professionally evaluated, not only in terms of his direct department role but also in his new role as consultant and supervisor. The probation officer must accept the new role if the volunteer corrections concept is to succeed.

DIAGNOSTIC PAROLE

A promising corrections program currently being implemented is diagnostic parole, in which all commitments from the court are referred to a reception or diagnostic center to be screened for eligibility for parole either immediately or shortly thereafter. This program is being used increasingly in the United States.

Although most state corrections systems long have had informal arrangements for returning some cases to the community at an early date, more organized procedures are developing in this area. These quick-release programs were conceived partly in response to overcrowded institutions. The results of the programs have been successful at reintegrating offenders rapidly into the community by having a substantial increase in the volume of cases diverted from institutions to short, intensive treatment programs followed by parole treatment in the community.

For example, the California Youth Authority is making wide use of the reception center-release procedure where approximately 20 percent of the male and 35 percent of the female youths processed in juvenile facilities are released prior to regular parole or sent to foster home replacements after the reception center period which is normally a month long.

A spinoff from the above program now being utilized in California provides for the selection of cases by a clinical staff for a three-month intensive treatment program at a selected reception center. Based on the therapeutic community concept, the project involves youths in a half-day work program in institution upkeep activities, some specialized education classes, and daily group counseling sessions. Active participation is rewarded by progressively longer and more frequent home furloughs. Funds for transportation for furloughs are provided by the parents. In many cases, the furloughs are scheduled so that parents can participate in group counseling activities as they return their son or daughter to the center. Parental involvement is seen as a significant program component.

NEW VISTAS— ALTERNATIVE PROGRAMS

In recent years, the number of community-based correctional programs has grown significantly. Each differs substantially in content and structure, but all have a goal of providing greater supervision and guidance than traditional programs of probation and parole.

Among some of the more promising special community programs are guided group interaction programs that call for involving the offenders in frequent, prolonged, and intensive discussions of the behavior of individuals in the group and the motivations that underlie it. Concentrating on the participants' current experiences and problems, the group interaction approach attempts to develop a group culture that encourages those involved to assume responsibility for helping and controlling each other. The theory is that offender participants will be more responsive to the influence of fellow offenders, their peers, than to the admonitions of staff and less likely to succeed in hoodwinking and manipulating.

As the culture develops and the group begins to act responsibly, a staff member acting as the group leader seeks to encourage a broader sharing of power between the offender and the staff. Group decisions are limited initially to routine matters, such as the schedule for a particular day. Over a period of time, however, they may extend to disciplinary measures over other group members or even to decisions relating to readiness to be released from the program.

Some of the other programs now finding their way into the modern correctional setting and offering alternatives to institutionalization and traditional practices are foster homes, group homes, federal and state prerelease guidance centers, and halfway houses.

MENTAL HEALTH CARE ENTERS THE PRISONS

Never in the long, dreary history of crime and punishment have so many enlightened prison reform projects been undertaken. Never have the courts uttered so many sweeping decisions guaranteeing the rights of prisoners.

Never have prisoners themselves become so determined to win better living conditions, easier parole, and the right to a voice in their own destinies. In short, prison reform, long a staple item of cocktail party radical chic, now has become an article of faith in the ranks of the most persuaded law-and-order hardliners.

However, major problems continue to exist and vex serious reform. For example, there is an appalling famine of facts, even to the point that any determination today of the number of people who are locked up behind bars is, at best, an educated guess. The most recent, and only complete, prison census was conducted in the mid-1960s. Before that, no one even knew how many jails and reformatories there were in this country, much less how many people actually were locked up in them.

It is an irony that some of the most forward-looking innovations in corrections have won their sponsors a few unmerited lumps. In Fort Worth, a narcotics rehabilitation program has been gingerly experimenting with men and women in the same institution. Tentatively, results seem to be good. Men and women housed separately but together for meals, recreation, and therapy appear to adjust better in the relatively normal atmosphere. Nevertheless, the concept has caused controversy and criticism.

The Federal Bureau of Prisons is making a bold attempt at attacking the problem of behavior modification by commissioning the Behavioral Research Center at Butner, North Carolina. The treatment at the center will be aimed at correcting criminal behavior. When the center is operational, approximately one-third of its 340 beds will be occupied by mentally ill prisoners from other federal institutions. The inmates, however, are not mentally ill in the traditional sense. They will range from car thieves to kidnappers. The prisoners will receive therapy similar to treatment already being given in a number of other federal and state institutions. The treatment will be aimed at behavior modification through intensive psychological and psychiatric counseling.

SUMMARY

Both the federal and state governments today are devoting more of their resources than ever before to the rehabilitation of offenders. The funds are being directed toward new programs and approaches that promise the highest rate of success in restoring an offender to his rightful place in society.

In part, this has entailed an abandonment of some traditional views of punishment for crime. Alternatives to institutionalization are being sought because of the realization that incarceration is insufficient to deter an offender from further criminal acts after his release. The offender must be equipped to reenter social activities upon release. Included in this reintegration is a need for vocational and educational skills that many offenders lack.

This chapter has only skimmed some of the many innovative things happening in the field of corrections: prerelease centers, halfway houses, diagnostic centers, mental health experimentation, computerized parole decision-making, foster homes, and work furloughs. These are the kinds of rehabilitative training programs that require personnel who are highly educated and motivated to assist in bringing about change. It is in this context that the results of more effective correctional systems will come to bear on the public. The communities, private enterprise, public agencies, and local, state, and federal government agencies must be willing to devote more of their resources to correctional efforts that get the offender involved in community life rather than further estranged from it.

QUESTIONS

1. The trend in corrections is away from large, centralized institutions. Why is this occurring? Discuss.
2. The role of the correctional officer is changing to that of correctional counselor. Why is this happening? Is the change good or bad?
3. Why are the training and educational needs changing in the field of corrections?
4. Describe some of the main problems which a correctional officer must face today.
5. What kinds of training programs are being conducted throughout the country to upgrade the skills and knowledge of correctional officers?
6. What does SIMBAD stand for? What are its objectives? Discuss the program.
7. What are the reasons why community-based correctional programs are becoming more and more popular in the field of corrections?
8. What are community treatment centers? Discuss their purpose and the general concept.

9. What are the objectives of work release programs?
10. Describe the Hennepin County volunteer corrections project.
11. What is meant by diagnostic parole?
12. What are some of the future considerations for more effective corrections programs?

INDEX

Accusatory pleading, 7
Agency for International Development: criminal investigators in, 125; public safety advisors in, 124
Agriculture, Department of: criminal investigators in, 121–22; Office of the Inspector General of, 121
Air Force, Department of the, 127–28
Alcohol tax inspectors, 115
American Bar Association, 92, 148, 156, 186, 197, 209
American Correctional Association, 265
Amicus curiae, 95, 99
Apprehension, 5
Army, Department of the, 129
Arraignment, 6, 8, 187
Arrest, 5–6
Assigned-counsel system, 191–94
Attorney general, state: appointment vs. election of, 172–73; common law powers of, 170–72; impeachment of, 174; initiation of prosecutions and, 177–80; office organization of, 175–77; Omnibus Crime Control and Safe Streets Act, 181; qualifications of, 174–76; relationships with other state branches, 169–70; state police and, 180
Attorney General, United States: assistant, in charge of criminal division, 168–69; duties of, 166–67, 182; history of, 162–63, 182; and the prosecutor, 153
Attorneys. *See* Defense attorneys

Attorneys, United States, 166–68
Augustus, John, 279
Austin, Stephen, 41

Bailey, F. Lee, 10
Bailiffs: and defendants, 248–49; duties of, 245–46, 255, 256; and juries, 247–48; oath of, 248; psychopathic cases and, 250
Barristers, 184
Bentham, Jeremy, 234
Blackstone, William, 216
Booking, 6
Border Patrol Agents, 103–4
Boss, Tweed, 232

Capitol Police, United States, 131
Captain of police, 20, 22
Central Intelligence Agency, 138
Charge reduction, 154–55
Chessman, Caryl, 10
Chief of police, 20
Civilian employees, police, 21
Civil Service Commission, United States, 130–31
Clark, Ramsey, 274
Commerce, Department of, 130
Common law, 145, 145n; and jury trials, 218, 222–25; and state attorneys general, 170–72
Community Relations Service, 168

Community Treatment Centers, 296, 297
Constables, 52
Constitution, United States: on the Attorney
General, 164; and defense attorneys, 186–87;
and federal judgeships, 208, 209; and grand
juries, 230; and prosecutors, 147; on trial by
jury, 217, 218, 221–22, 224, 225
Consumer protection specialists, 135
Consumer safety officers, 126–27
Correctional officers, 106–7; conflict with
prison psychologists, 271; duties of, 268–69;
philosophies of, 272; training of, 267–68,
271, 272–73, 292–95
Correctional treatment specialists, 107–8
Corrections: *Auburn* type, 262, 265; changes
needed in, 292–93; community programs in,
295–96, 298–99, 301–2, 303; federal system
of, 266–67, 303; history of, 259–63, 276–80;
new methods of 270–71; *Pennsylvania* type
of, 262; philosophy of American, 265; in
primitive societies, 259–60; and sentencing,
206, 207; state systems of, 265–66. *See also*
Prisons; Prisons, Federal Bureau of
Court-appointed counsel. *See* Assigned-counsel system
Court clerks, 251–53
Court reporters, 253–55
Courts: federal, 133–35; prosecutors in, 150–
51; sheriffs and, 61. *See also* Judges; Juries
Criminalists: advanced, 82–83; beginning, 81–
82; definition of, 73; as expert witnesses, 83–
84; and forensic scientists, 73–74; functions
of, 73, 74; history of, 72–73, 85; laboratories
of, 73, 76, 77–81, 84–85; and science, 72, 74,
75–76; training of, 75–76, 85
Criminal Justice, Office of, 111–12
Criminal justice systems, 3, 4, 10, 11
Customs inspectors, 116
Customs patrol officers, 116
Customs security officers, 116
Customs Special Agents, Bureau of, 115–16

Defense attorneys: and the assigned-counsel
system, 191–94; history of, 183–86; and the
insanity plea, 190; and jurors, 226; and jury
selection, 188; opening statements of, 189;
public defenders as, 194–97; and trial strategy, 189–91; and *voir dire* examination, 188
Defense, Department of, 127
Deputy chiefs of police, 20, 22
Deputy marshals, United States, 109
Drug Enforcement Administration, 138–39

English law, 4; attorneys general in, 162–63;
defense attorneys in, 183–85, 186; grand juries in, 229–30; jury trials in, 216–17; parole

English law (*cont.*)
in, 277; penology in, 260–61, 262, 275; police
organization in, 16; sheriffs in, 52
Engraving and Printing, Bureau of, 119–20
Executive Protective Service, 119

Federal Bureau of Investigation: legal advisors
in, 87; positions in, 104–5
Federal Highway Administration, 120
Federal Maritime Commission, 136
Federal Trade Commission, 135
Fee rights, 260
Felony, 5, 8
Forensic scientists, 73–74, 85. *See also* Crimi-
nalists

Game management agents, 122–23
General Services Administration, 137–39
Grand juries: American development of, 230–
33; and corruption in government, 230, 231,
233; criticisms of, 234–35, 242; definition of,
219; functions of, 233, 243, 244; organization
of, 239–41, 244; origin of, 229–30; political
characteristics of, 238; presentments of, 233;
and prosecutors, 152–53, 159; qualifications
for, 236–37; and United States Attorneys,
167–68; work of, 238

Halfway houses, 298
Health, Education, and Welfare, Department
of: consumer safety officers in, 126–27; Internal Security Office of, 127
Hearings, 281
Highway patrols, state: expansion of, 39, 40;
and state police, 50

Immigration and Naturalization Service, 103,
104
Immigration inspectors, 104
Import specialists, 116
Indictment, 7, 8, 233
Industrial Revolution, 260
Information, 7
Interior, Department of, 122–24
Internal Revenue Service: agents of, 117; GS
levels in, 101; special agents of, intelligence
division, 117–18; special investigators in,
114–15
Internal security inspectors, 116–17
International Association of Chiefs of Police,
87, 90, 99
Investigations, 5–6

Jailers, 260, 261
Jails. *See* Corrections; Prisons

Judges: definition of, 201; duties of, 202; immunity of, 203; impeachment of, 211; and juries, 226, 227; removal of, 211–14; restrictions on, 203–4; roles of, 205–8; salaries of, 203; selection of, 208–11, 214; training for, 204–5
Judges Journal, 205
Juries: bailiff duties and, 247–48; and the United States Constitution, 221–22; disadvantages of, 222–24; functions of, 218–19; grand (*See* Grand juries); history of, 216–18; hung, 226; and judges, 226, 227; petit, 145, 184, 228; qualifications of jurors for, 224–25; reasons to excuse jurors from, 220–21; selection of, 220; special, 219; value of, 222–24
Justice, Department of, 98, 102–13; and the Bureau of Narcotics and Dangerous Drugs, 166–67; criminal division of, 109–11; organization of, 164–69; and organized crime, 110
Juvenile offenders, 5, 299–300, 301
Juvenile offices, 288–290. *See also* Municipal police agencies, juvenile unit of

Kennedy, John F., 203

Laboratories, criminalist, 73, 76, 84–85; elements of, 77–79; evidence storage in, 78; functions of, 79–81; model, 85
Law Enforcement Assistance Administration, 112–13, 168, 181
Lawyers. *See* Defense attorneys
Leakey, Louis, 15
Lesser offense, 151
Lieutenant of police, 20

Magistrate, 201
Mark System (of parole), 277
Marshals, United States, 108–9
"Mini-trial." *See* Preliminary examination
Misdemeanor, 5–6
Maconochie, Alexander, 277
Municipal police agencies: communications unit of, 31–32; and the community, 24, 37; data processing unit of, 31; detective unit of, 29–30; future of, 33–36, 37; history of, 16, 36; inspections unit of, 27; internal investigations unit of, 25; juvenile unit of, 30; laboratories of, 32 (*See also* Laboratories, criminalist); organization of, 19–24; patrol unit of, 28; personnel unit of, 26; planning, research, and analysis unit of, 26–27; roles of, 19–34; and state police, 40; and technology, 35–36; temporary detention in, 32

Narcotics and Dangerous Drugs, Bureau of: and the Attorney General, 166–67; compliance investigators in, 102; special agents in, 102

National College of the State Judiciary, 204–5, 214
National Crime Information Center, 31
National Highway Traffic Safety Administration, 120–21
Navy, Department of the, 130
Nolle prosequi, 145, 172

Office of the Inspector General, 121
Ordeals, 184
Organized crime: and the Department of Justice, 110; and police intelligence, 27

Pardon attorney, 168
Parker, William, 17
Park Police, United States, 123–24
Parliament, English, 16
Parole, 6, 7, 291; criticisms of, 288; definition of, 277; diagnostic, 300–301
Parole boards, 278
Parole officers, 290; presentence investigations of, 253; training for, 285–87
Patrolmen, 19, 22, 23–24
Peel, Sir Robert, 15, 16, 234
Penology. *See* Corrections
Petit jury trial, 145, 184
Plea, 6–7
Plea negotiation ("bargaining"), 8, 159–60; judicial, 207–8; and the United States Supreme Court, 208
Police. *See* Municipal police agencies; State police; Highway patrol, state
Police academies, 33
Police brutality, 10
Police legal advisors: budgets for, 89; and civil disturbances, 94; conflicts with city attorneys, 95–96; and Constitutional rights, 92; on the federal level, 97; functions of, 27, 92–95, 99; goals of, 92; history of, 87–88; and other criminal agencies, 93; and prosecutors, 93, 95; qualifications of; 92; and the Secret Service, 97–98
"Police power," 54, 71
Policewoman, 20, 22
Polling (of juries), 248
Posse comitatus, 56, 71
Postal inspectors, 132
Postal Service, United States, 132–33
Preliminary examination, 6–7
Presentment, 233
Presidential Crime Commissions, 16, 19, 23, 36; on correctional training, 293; on the future of municipal police agencies, 34, 35; on judicial power, 206, 208; on judicial selection, 210; on juries, 223; on police legal advisors, 88, 96, 99; on prison conditions, 264; on

Presidential Crime Commissions (*cont.*)
probation and parole, 285; and prosecutors, 157; on public defenders, 197
Prisons: conditions in, 263–64, 266, 270; personnel in, 264, 265. *See also* Corrections
Prisons, Federal Bureau of, 133, 266; and community treatment centers, 296, 297; model of, 105, 106; positions in, 106–8; and Work Release Program, 297–98
Probation: criticisms of, 288; definition of, 276; history of, 276–77; organization of offices of, 280–81
Probation officers: federal, 133; hearings of, 281; presentence investigations of, 281–83; training of, 285–87
Prosecution, 6–7; of felony, 8; by state attorneys general, 177–80
Prosecutors: as attorneys, 146; and attorneys general, 153; conceptions of, 149; and the United States Constitution, 147; conviction psychology of, 158–60; and courts, 150–51; and defense attorneys, 151–52; duties of, 145–48; in European systems, 156; and grand juries, 152–53, 153n; investigations by, 146; judicial restraints on, 147; localization of, 156; office of, 143–45; and police agencies, 149–50; powers of, 145, 160; qualifications of, 144; quasi-judicial role of, 154, 155, 158–59; salary of, 148, and sentencing, 153–55; terms of office of, 144, 160; training of, 157
Public defender, 151–52, 192, 193, 194–97
Public Safety Advisors, 124–25
Public Safety, Department of, 40

Recidivism, 4, 273–74, 298
Rehabilitation, 4, 9, 266, 267, 274, 293, 297
Restitution, 155–56

Scotland Yard, 16
Secondary police agencies, 38–39
Secret Service, United States, 97–98; document analysts of, 118–19; fingerprint specialists of, 119; special agents of, 118
Senate Judiciary Committee, 209
Senatorial courtesy, 209
Sentencing, 7; by judges, 206–7; and prosecutors, 153–55
Sequestering, 248
Sergeant of police, 20, 22
Shays's Rebellion, 232
Sheriffs: budgetary limits on, 65; chain of command under, 61–63; civil process duties of, 63–64; and civil unrest, 66; constraints on, 64–66; and courts, 66; deputy, 60–64; functions of, 53; grounds for removal of, 59–60; history of the office of, 52–54, 260; and individual rights, 55; and municipal police agen-

Sheriffs (*cont.*)
cies, 57; policy-making role of, 68–70; social role of, 70; state attorneys general and, 65–66, 68; suspension of, 59; terms of office of, 57–60;
SIMBAD project, 294–95, 303
Sky marshalls, 116
Socrates, 183
Solicitor general, 168
Solicitors, 184
Special officers, police, 21
Sport Fisheries and Wildlife, Bureau of, 123
State, Department of: Agency for International Development of, 124; public safety advisors in, 124–25; special agent, office of security in, 126
State Planning Agency, 181
State police: budgets of, 42–44, 50; and civilian courtesy patrols, 48; functions of, 46, 51; future of, 49–50, 51; and highway patrols, 42–44, 50; history of, 41–42; and municipal police agencies, 40; organization of; 42–45; rank system of, 44; reorganization of, 40; salary of, 43–44; training of, 46–47; units of, 49
Supreme Court, United States, 17, 36, 86; on defense attorneys, 186–87; on plea negotiations, 208; on prosecutors, 147; on trial by jury, 218, 221

Texas Rangers, 41
Ticket of leave, 277
Transportation, Department of, 120–121
Treasury, Department of the, 113–120
Treasury enforcement agent, 114
Tobacco tax inspectors, 115

Uniform Crime Reports, 16

Vacancy, 58
Voir dire examination, 188

"War against crime," 25
Wardens, 272
Warrant, 5
Warren, Earl, 203
Wilson, O. W., 88, 96
Writ of habeus corpus, 8

Youth (Aid) Bureau. *See* Municipal police agencies, juvenile unit of

Zenger, Peter, 231